The Foundations of Special Education

Selected Papers and Speeches of

Samuel A. Kirk

Gail A. Harris

Winifred D. Kirk

Editors

 Published by The Council for Exceptional Children

Library of Congress Cataloging-in-Publication Data

Kirk, Samuel A. (Samuel Alexander), 1904–
  [Selections. 1993]
  The foundations of special education : selected papers and speeches of Samuel A. Kirk / Gail A. Harris, Winifred D. Kirk, editors.
    p. cm.
  Includes bibliographical references (p.) and index.
  ISBN 0-86586-236-2
  1. Special education—United States. 2. Kirk, Samuel A. (Samuel Alexander), 1904–   3. Speeches, addresses, etc., American—United States. I. Harris, Gail A. II. Kirk, Winifred D. III. Title.
LC4031.K492 1993
371.9'0973—dc20   93-12219
                                                            CIP

ISBN 0-86586-236-2

Copyright 1993 by The Council for Exceptional Children, 1920 Association Drive, Reston, Virginia 22091-1589.
Stock No. P388

All rights reserved. No part of this publication may be reproduced, stored in a retrieval system, or transmitted, in any form or by any means, electronic, mechanical, photocopying, recording, or otherwise, without the prior written permission of the copyright owner.

Printed in the United States of America
10 9 8 7 6 5 4 3 2 1

FOREWORD

As The Council for Exceptional Children approaches its 75th anniversary, we are pleased to present *The Foundations of Special Education: Selected Papers and Speeches of Samuel A. Kirk*, edited by Gail A. Harris and Winifred D. Kirk. For over 50 years Dr. Kirk has been a major force in shaping the modern era of special education. Through his writings (selected by Dr. Kirk and the editors for inclusion in this book) and the chapter introductions written by his colleagues, readers will develop an appreciation for the connectedness of our past to the issues we wrestle with in the present. Whether the topic of concern is inclusion, definition of learning disabilities, appropriate education of students who are deaf, or early childhood education, the perspectives of the previous generations of special educators exemplified by Dr. Kirk remain relevant to today's debate. Perhaps even more important, with a greater appreciation of our history we can take comfort in knowing that the challenges we face are not new and that our wisdom is grounded in a rich tradition.

This type of publication is a first for CEC. It coincides with our establishment of the Archives of Special Education at CEC Headquarters. These archives contain the publications, papers, and memorabilia of Dr. Kirk and other special educators, as well as CEC's historical documents. The archives have two primary purposes: to preserve the history of our profession and to make that history available to future generations for study and enjoyment. We hope that you will visit CEC and the archives when you are in the Washington, DC, area. We also encourage special educators to join Dr. Kirk in donating their personal collections to CEC.

On a personal note, in reading this book I found myself impressed with Dr. Kirk as a professional. He has been advocate, researcher, teacher, and leader. His interests have crossed all areas of exceptionality and the needs of children. He has taught generations of special educators, many of whom continue to make significant contributions to our field. He has provided leadership to the field through government service and through CEC and other associations. While remaining a strong advocate for his views, he has respected the views of others. I believe that this book will offer our generation not only an understanding of our history, but also a role model whom we might all strive to emulate.

All of us at CEC wish Dr. Kirk and his wife Winifred our best and offer our appreciation for their contributions to the profession.

GEORGE E. AYERS
Executive Director

The Council for Exceptional Children

CEC: Leading the Way

The Council for Exceptional Children (CEC) is the largest professional organization internationally committed to improving educational outcomes for individuals with exceptionalities. CEC accomplished its worldwide mission on behalf of educators and others working with children with exceptionalities by advocating for appropriate government policies; setting professional standards; providing continuing professional development; and assisting professionals to obtain conditions and resources necessary for effective professional practice.

CEC: The Unifying Force of a Diverse Field

The Council for Exceptional Children, a private nonprofit membership organization, was established in 1922. CEC is an active network of 59 State/Provincial Federations, 900 Chapters, 17 Specialized Divisions, and 275 Subdivisions with reach in over 40 countries.

The CEC Information Center:
International Resource for Topics in Special and Gifted Education

The Council for Exceptional Children is a major publisher of special education literature and produces a comprehensive catalog semiannually. Journals such as *TEACHING Exceptional Children* (published quarterly) and *Exceptional Children* (published 6 times per year) reach over 100,000 readers and provide a wealth of information on the latest teaching strategies, research, resources, and special education news.

To preserve the history and traditions of special education and to celebrate the leadership of its pioneer, CEC is proud to release *The Foundations of Special Education: Selected Papers and Speeches of Samuel A. Kirk*.

The Council for Exceptional Children
1920 Association Drive • Reston, Virginia 22091
703/620-3660 (Voice/TDD)
703/264-9494 (Fax)

*This book is dedicated to Samuel A. Kirk,
a remarkable human being.
We are better for knowing him.*

This volume chronicles the development of the field of special education through the writing of Samuel A. Kirk and comments by contributing scholars in the introductions to each chapter. The selections of Samuel A. Kirk's work in areas such as mental retardation, learning disabilities, early childhood special education, deafness, remedial reading, and federal legislation evidence his contributions to the many domains of special education. The testimony and comments by contributing scholars place Dr. Kirk's work in its historical context. From this perspective, his vision and courage are most evident.

Sam insisted that his students be aware of the history of and early contributors to the development of the field of special education. He often remarked that the advances we have made to date were in large part based on the contributions of the thinkers and doers of the past: "We can see far because we stand on the shoulders of giants." Sam Kirk is indisputably a giant in the field of special education. It is important that scholars and families interested in this field have access to his writings.

It is ironic that his collaboration on this book was impeded, but not precluded, by a cerebral vascular accident. His communication skills are impaired, but his vision of what this book should be for its readers is clear.

GAIL A. HARRIS
Tucson, Arizona
January 12, 1993

ABOUT THE EDITORS

Gail A. Harris began her career in special education as a speech-language pathologist in Ohio. Her first position when she moved to Arizona in 1972 was as a speech-language specialist with the model preschool project for American Indian children designed by Samuel A. Kirk. After earning her master's degree in speech pathology, she served as designer and director of the American Indian Training Program in Speech Pathology and Audiology, Department of Speech and Hearing Sciences, University of Arizona. This was the first specialized personnel preparation program for American Indian students in the nation. She later received a grant that established the Native American Research and Training Center (NARTC) at the College of Medicine, University of Arizona, and she served as its director for the first 3 years. She received her doctorate in special education at the University of Arizona in 1989.

Dr. Harris has served as clinical instructor, Department of Speech and Hearing Sciences, and adjunct assistant professor in early childhood special education, Department of Special Education, at the University of Arizona. She currently serves as executive director of The Parent Connection, a community-based family resource center in Tucson, Arizona, and holds an adjunct faculty appointment with the Department of Special Education and Rehabilitation, where she continues her research in fetal alcohol syndrome. She is a fellow of the American Speech-Language-Hearing Association. She has lectured and written extensively regarding habilitation and rehabilitation needs of American Indian tribes.

Winifred Day Kirk received a bachelor's degree from the University of Chicago and a master's degree from the University of Michigan. She also earned a teacher's certificate and had additional training in psychology and education from the Universities of Michigan and Illinois. She has served in public schools as school psychologist and remedial teacher. Mrs. Kirk also served as research associate at the University of Illinois, where she coauthored the Illinois Test of Psycholinguistic Abilities. She served as adjunct assistant professor in the Department of Speech and Hearing Sciences at the University of Arizona. She developed a successful screening procedure and rating scale for differentiating bright children and those who have learning delays in kindergarten. Mrs. Kirk has authored and coauthored books and articles in remedial reading and learning disabilities. She has been the recipient of several international awards, including the Certificate of Merit for Distinguished Achievement from the World Who's Who of Women and the Milestone Award from the International Scientific Conference.

CONTENTS

Preface xiii
James J. Gallagher

PART I HISTORICAL PERSPECTIVES

Introduction 2
William C. Healey

Chapter 1
Autobiographical Remarks 9
Samuel A. Kirk

PART II EARLY CHILDHOOD SPECIAL EDUCATION

Introduction 42
Merle B. Karnes

Chapter 2
Preschool and Early Education Programs for Handicapped Children 49
Samuel A. Kirk

Chapter 3
The Effects of Early Intervention 57
Samuel A. Kirk

PART III MENTAL RETARDATION

Introduction 64
Herbert Goldstein

Chapter 4
Research in Education: Mental Retardation 69
Samuel A. Kirk

Chapter 5
   Special Education in the 1970s   85
   Samuel A. Kirk

PART IV   LEARNING DISABILITIES

Introduction   94
   James C. Chalfant

Chapter 6
   From Labels to Action   99
   Samuel A. Kirk

Chapter 7
   Learning Disabilities   107
   Samuel A. Kirk

Chapter 8
   Our Current Headaches in Learning Disabilities   115
   Samuel A. Kirk

Chapter 9
   Issues in Learning Disabilities   125
   Samuel A. Kirk

PART V   REMEDIAL READING

Introduction   136
   Janet W. Lerner

Chapter 10
   The Organization of Remedial Reading in the Schools   140
   Samuel A. Kirk

Chapter 11
   Characteristics of Slow Learners and Needed Adjustments in Reading   145
   Samuel A. Kirk

Chapter 12
   How Johnny Learns to Read   152
   Samuel A. Kirk and Winifred D. Kirk

PART VI HEARING IMPAIRMENTS

Introduction   158
Donald F. Moores

Chapter 13
Behavior Problem Tendencies in Deaf and
Hard-of-Hearing Children   162
Samuel A. Kirk

Chapter 14
A Comparative Study of the Ontario and
Nebraska Tests for the Deaf   168
Samuel A. Kirk and June Perry

Chapter 15
Special Education and Rehabilitation   176
Samuel A. Kirk

Chapter 16
The Federal Program for Training Teachers of the Deaf   181
Samuel A. Kirk

PART VII THE ILLINOIS TEST OF PSYCHOLINGUISTIC ABILITIES (ITPA)

Introduction   184
Jeanne McRae McCarthy

Chapter 17
Illinois Test of Psycholinguistic Abilities:
Its Origin and Implications   188
Samuel A. Kirk

Chapter 18
Uses and Abuses of the ITPA   197
Samuel A. Kirk and Winifred D. Kirk

Chapter 19
Profiles of Children with Severe Oral Language Disorders   212
*Anthony H. Luick, Samuel A. Kirk, Aleen Agranowitz,
and Robert Busby*

PART VIII CONGRESSIONAL AND GOVERNMENTAL AFFAIRS

Introduction 224
Edwin W. Martin

Chapter 20
Administration of Education Programs for Handicapped Children 230
Samuel A. Kirk

Chapter 21
Education and Training of the Handicapped 244
Samuel A. Kirk

Chapter 22
Elementary and Secondary Education Act of 1966 248
Samuel A. Kirk

PART IX SOCIAL ISSUES

Introduction 262
James J. Gallagher

Chapter 23
Education as National Defense 264
Samuel A. Kirk

Chapter 24
Education and the National Welfare 269
Samuel A. Kirk

Chapter 25
Youth Challenges Gerontocracy 274
Samuel A. Kirk

Chapter 26
The Federal Role in Special Education: Historical Perspectives 283
Samuel A. Kirk

Bibliography 293

PREFACE

It is a pleasure as well as an honor to write a preface for this volume of selected papers and speeches of Sam Kirk. Sam is one of the acknowledged early giants in special education whose foresight placed him years ahead of his colleagues. Many of the writings in this collection remain fresh and current today even though they were written 20 to 30 years ago. His foresight led him to produce many firsts in special education and developmental psychology.

- More than a decade before early intervention programs became popular, Sam Kirk conducted a carefully designed study on early intervention with children with mental retardation.
- He originated the term *learning disabilities* and became the recognized authority in that field as well as in the field of mental retardation.
- Along with his wife Winifred, he developed one of the few diagnostic tests that was theory driven, the Illinois Test of Psycholinguistic Abilities, which helped sharpen our thinking about learning disabilities.
- He organized one of the earliest multidisciplinary research centers devoted to the study of exceptional children, The Institute for Research on Exceptional Children, at the University of Illinois. Out of that center came research on the sociology of families with children with disabilities (Farber); on the learning processes of exceptional children (Stolurow and Bereiter); on evaluating the special education of children with mental retardation (Goldstein, Moss, and Jordan); and on the education of children with brain injury (Gallagher).
- Late in his career, he went to Washington, DC, for a brief time to head the Division of Special Education in the U.S. Office of Education. His work there laid the groundwork for the later establishment of the Bureau of Education for the Handicapped which has played such a central role in the last few decades of special education.

One of Sam's greatest strengths was his teaching. He demonstrated in his seminars and classrooms the ability to provoke, in graduate students and junior colleagues, both depth and breadth in thought and action. Sam was a "problem solver"—not a "problem stater"—and he encouraged his students to think constructively and independently. His respect for a good idea was notorious, and he did not care whether it came from a distinguished colleague or a first-year graduate student. He may have been at his finest in helping others to grow professionally and to think innovatively.

We should not allow the reader to believe that Sam did not have his faults and eccentricities. He smoked some of the most awful cigars this side of Cuba. At the age of 50 he took up the game of golf and wrestled it to the ground as he did his other tasks, afterwards reporting in excruciating detail his odyssey around different golf courses. His gruff manner sometimes startled new graduate students who had not yet seen the warmth beneath, nor had tasted the hospitality that he and his wife, Winnie, provided so freely.

Needless to say, Sam Kirk won almost every award and office that an admiring profession and grateful parents could provide, but possibly the one he holds dearest is the Joseph P. Kennedy International Award for Contributions to Mental Retardation. That award symbolized recognition of his work as truly international in scope. The Crystal Angel, symbol of that award, still graces his retirement apartment in Tucson.

I am grateful to The Council for Exceptional Children for.its role in publishing this set of readings as reminders of Sam Kirk's scope and incisiveness. The hundreds of students and colleagues whose lives he touched will, no doubt, join me in saying that "his like will not soon be seen again."

JAMES J. GALLAGHER
Chapel Hill, North Caorlina

Part I

Historical Perspectives

INTRODUCTION

WILLIAM C. HEALEY
Department of Special Education and Rehabilitation
University of Arizona (Tucson)

My friend and colleague, Professor Samuel Kirk, asked me to write the introduction to this book. He did not know, however, that I would take this opportunity as license to achieve two purposes. While some comments regarding the contents of the book are appropriate, I felt it important that new professionals and those who only know Dr. Kirk through his writing should learn more about him, at least from my perspective.

Sam Kirk is a scholar and, to many, this century's "father of special education." The breadth of his work in print indicates that he is, perhaps, the last of the great generalists in his profession. His scholarship is planted on a broad historic and humane foundation and has been communicated in a manner that has permitted it to be lived, expanded, perfected, and passed on. The publication of this book marks his 200th contribution to the literature of special education. It includes a collection of previously published and unpublished manuscripts. Although they were selected and organized by Sam, as he prefers to be addressed in more informal settings, he recognized the necessity for his close friend, Gail Harris, and beloved wife, Winifred Day Kirk, to edit this volume. As is often the irony of fate, this remarkable pioneer in the treatment of disability was, himself, left partially paralyzed on the right side and dysphasic by a cerebral insult in his 82nd year. Neither condition, however, could permanently stall that robust enthusiasm for which he has been known in his academic and social life. He simply expresses great frustration at the bizarre effects of stroke and the incessant slowness of the rehabilitation process, as well as the publication process.

In the field of special education, Dr. Kirk occupies the top position in the contemporary monument of fame. He has emerged as a man of supreme competence in a fledgling field, making major contributions to its development by sharing his knowledge, skills, and foresight with thousands of colleagues, students, parents of children with disabilities, legislators, and heads of governments. He has become an eminent statesman of social science and a recognized leader of thought and action worldwide. He belongs to a small company of scholars whose works have moved forward the frontiers of their discipline. In this sense, Professor Kirk is a futurist. Some would say he is a visionary, while others might tag him as a maverick. Early on, he was image-driven, with a concept of how the treatment of persons with exceptionalities ought to be and how the professions serving them could progress. From such contexts, he proceeded as a man of high initiative and balanced good judgment, with outgoing friendliness, kindness, and goodwill. His interests, writings, and activities have been so diverse that the full scope of his career and influence remains unknown to even his closest associates.

Professor Kirk prepared to be an experimental psychologist, as is exemplified by the first two papers from his dissertation research in 1935 on hemispheric cerebral dominance and hemispheric equipotentiality. Through these studies on rats, he challenged Samuel Orton's theory that conflicts in cerebral dominance caused humans to reverse words and letters when reading them. However, prior to his doctorate, he was invited to become a psychologist at the Oaks School near Chicago where, by chance, he became a teacher. He was assigned to supervise activities in a special cottage for teenage delinquent boys with mental retardation. "Mr." Kirk, at the time, recognized the need and opportunity to teach the boys how to organize their time and complete daily living tasks in exchange for free time. He demonstrated that such learning was successful. After completing his doctorate, he and his wife took positions at the Wayne County Training School in Northville, Michigan. In this institution, they conducted a series of studies that led to several publications on methods for teaching reading, especially to persons with mental retardation. These experiences and other details of his academic and administrative career are presented in his autobiographic remarks that follow this introduction and that clearly describe the roots of his philosophy and scholarship.

Punctuating his stream of books were scores of articles, many of them basic contributions to our knowledge of special education. As will be seen here in his writings and testimony before the U.S. Congress, his thoughts have a provoking habit of being enduring.

Dr. Kirk's earliest speeches and writings on remedial reading (Part V)—written from 1936 through the 1950s—described the needs of children in the schools who required special reading interventions and advocated for the preparation of specialists to assume this responsibility. Simultaneously, he was expanding his research on mental retardation (Part III), and between 1950 and 1963 made some startling but foresighted recommendations to parents about institutionalization and predictions for education from his research on how children with mental retardation and other disabilities should and would be educated in the future.

Dr. Kirk expressed an early appreciation for the diagnostic and clinical skills of speech clinicians and the instructional abilities required of teachers for the deaf. In fact, he took coursework in speech pathology and studied the influence of cerebral insult on speech, language, and hearing. This preparation broadened his interest in 1938 to include hearing impairment (Part VI). As a psychologist, he was interested especially in the social maturity of children with hearing impairments. His research showed that such children can demonstrate normal intelligence and social quotients and that children placed in residential and day schools might develop different characteristics. By 1960, he was sharing his research and observations with congressional leaders and advocating for federal assistance to prepare increased numbers of teachers in the field of hearing impairment.

All of Dr. Kirk's research and study of children with various disabilities convinced him that these children needed to be identified as early as possible and provided with appropriate developmental and educational interventions. He expressed frustration at being unable to initiate his early research on instructional methods with children under age 5. Although he spoke of the need for preschool services from the beginning of his career and published a book on the topic in 1940, his research and presentations that had the most significant impact on the development of early childhood programming (Part II) appeared from 1950 and beyond. He was a major force in the enactment of the Early Education Assistance Act in 1968, which began federal support of preschool programs for children with disabling conditions.

During his institutional work and throughout his initial research on preschool children, Dr. Kirk had become concerned about some children others had diagnosed as being feebleminded but really did not present the typical characteristics of such children. As he and his colleagues increased their studies of numerous children, he concluded that some had specific types of disabilities that were significantly different from or more subtle in their impact on learning than mental retardation or sensory disorders. In fact, he had become especially intrigued with children who displayed deviations in memory and language performance. Similarly, other researchers, educators, and some parent groups from 1947 through 1960 had begun to describe children with unique learning problems as being "brain-injured" or "perceptually handicapped." In his effort to find a generic reference to those children, he first used the term *learning disabilities* in a 1963 speech to the Conference on Exploration into Problems of the Perceptually Handicapped Child. By 1966, The Association for Children with Learning Disabilities had been formed, and an unprecedented movement that would change the face and entire character of special education had begun.

Dr. Kirk never intended for his term *learning disabilities* to be used as a diagnostic label or a separate category of disabling condition. He clearly had indicated that he was referring to a heterogeneous group of children with various types of disabilities that were not being treated properly in the schools (see Part IV). He had called for professionals to recognize these children's needs, describe their behavior, and find effective remediation methods. Instead, both parents and professionals chose to use the term as a new label that would spawn many confounding definitions. By 1977, he stated emphatically that this new specialization had grown too rapidly and had become confused. He told The Association for Children with Learning Disabilities Conference attendees in Washington, DC, that in the absence of enough qualified personnel, the field was experiencing a number of disturbing practices, including the creation of a new dumping ground for certain children, pseudo-research, territorial wars among professional groups, and quackery.

From the beginning of his career, Dr. Kirk had advocated for children with specific disabilities to be served by qualified personnel who had the understanding and skills to remediate each type of disability properly. Attempts to legislate Dr. Kirk's rather simple concept led to political and professional complicities that, unfortunately, would prevent that accomplishment of what he had envisioned. It is fitting that Part IV closes with the two presentations that he made in 1972 and 1977, respectively, on issues and "headaches" in learning disabilities that continue to distress regular and special educators even today.

Prior to his famous speech on learning disabilities in 1963, Dr. Kirk had begun to work with his students and others to develop a model that would represent, and help to explain, abilities and deficits in children that he considered important to learning. Further, he recognized the need to provide psychologists and educators with a practical but standardized set of procedures to assess specific learning abilities and disabilities in young children from approximately ages 2 through 9. Thus, the Illinois Test of Psycholinguistic Abilities (ITPA: Experimental Edition) was published in 1961, followed by the revised edition in 1968, which was designed to be used clinically (see Part VII). This test was adopted rapidly and used widely by personnel in clinics and schools throughout the United States and other English-speaking countries. Over the next 10 years, however, the test became controversial as a result of questions about its construct validity, in addition to reports of its misuse and misinterpretation of results by unqualified users. (See Kirk & Kirk, "Uses and Abuses of the ITPA" in Part VII.) Although a major research study in 1982 seemed to vindicate the efficacy of the test when used properly, Dr. Kirk no longer promoted its use because he felt the concepts and purposes had become misunderstood and misapplied.

Although Dr. Kirk's wide-ranging impact on children, parents, students, teachers, and researchers generally can only be inferred in the absence of their testimonials, several of his most significant contributions to the advancement of education for children with exceptionalities have been recorded for posterity in the *Congressional Record*. Part VIII, "Congressional and Governmental Affairs," provides readers with a front seat to an historic dialogue between Dr. Kirk (with others) and very important congressional leaders who would be persuaded during the 1960s to establish major programs and appropriations at the federal level to support research and personnel preparation. These programs continue today. They served as the single greatest impetus for the development and growth of special education and related departments in institutions of higher education, became the primary source of significant funding for research and the education of specialists, and led to a federal partnership in the finance of direct services for exceptional children. Dr. Kirk's federal administrative role is described in his autobiography. His citation from President John F. Kennedy for his work at the federal level represented one of his proudest moments of which he speaks often when visitors admire the trophy that occupies a prominent position on the wall of his living room. Ironically, he never felt equally effective in working with state legislators. He contended that, at the state level, parents were the better persons to advocate for proposed legislation because they received more respect and response than professors.

Finally, Dr. Kirk should be recognized as a social observer, historian, critic, and reformer. His views and actions, while generally emphasizing the needs of persons with exceptionalities, extended to the social injustices created from discrimination, poverty, joblessness, imperialism, and hypocrisy. Samples of his social commentary were selected for inclusion in Part IX, "Social Issues." He liked to quote Thoreau, who said, "There are thousands hacking at the branches of evil to one who is striking at the root." The speeches in Part IX show that Dr. Kirk either struck at the roots of social evils or commended others who did. While he is often dynamic, he is not an emotionalist, and he prefers to make his points with the logic and reserve expected from a competent researcher.

Despite his prolific array of roles as a scholar, administrator, lecturer, consultant, husband, and father, he regarded teaching as his most important and gratifying professional work. In fact, he frequently told young protégés that "being a professor is the best job in a university." While he was loyal to the institutions of higher learning for whom he worked, he does not regard them as being equally loyal to the professors they employ. From his experience, he contends that university administrators want to employ professors of such powerful thought and deed that they can change the world but not the universities or the minds of their administrators. Thus, his admonition to newly recruited faculty generally has been, "get the highest possible salary and rank, make significant contributions, but always take care of yourself because universities don't kiss back." As a teacher, he repeatedly urged students to use the following simple formula for clear communication with audiences: "Tell them what you are going to tell them; tell them; and, then, tell them what you have told them."

For Dr. Kirk, teaching, research, and clinical practice are never far apart. He loves to see children diagnostically and determine what method might help them in compensating for any particular disability. His remarkable clinical skills undoubtedly could be attributed to his uncanny insight, memory, and capacity for association. He became a master at using the anecdote to emphasize a clinical point or set an abstract construct into context. His seminars, where many leading scholars in special education today began their training, were demonstrations of scholarship as a creative process. Of recent note, just prior to his illness, was his use in class and in speeches of a recording, taped, he contended, with the help of a medium, on which Thomas Jefferson's voice was heard critiquing the principles of Public Law 94-142 (The Education for All Handicapped Children Act of 1975).

Whether or not Sam Kirk wished to be a "character," he became one who is admired and revered. He has a tender way of being rigorous and demanding with unformed disciples while offering the wisdom of a seasoned counselor and warmth of a friend. His great insistence with students always has been on orderly thought, and he could show infinite patience while a student under his tutelage was trying to achieve it. He still devotes time to students and continues to rejoice in their publications and other accomplishments.

As a midwesterner, he has a hearty and informal manner, an endless capacity for hard work, and a lusty humor. He delights in showmanship and is justly proud when it works to the appreciation of his audience. Observers generally perceive him to be equally comfortable with or without a prepared text. In all cases his desire was to awaken listeners to alternatives, spiced on occasion with Kirkian doctrine. He has spoken sternly against intellectual dishonesty and disdains academic intrigue. He rejects any perception of him as an administrator even though he, for many years, assumed the role and showed the organizational and problem-solving savvy required to be successful. I have never seen him flaunt his knowledge. In fact, he often deferred to the opinion of others whom he believed to be well informed. When appropriate, however, he could present a pulsating presence, be charismatic, and exert power solely on the basis of his influence and credibility, not necessarily his position.

On June 25, 1933, he married Winifred Day, whose extraordinary intellect, professional skills, and beauty illuminated all of her husband's work, some of which she coauthored. Her self-effacing comments, infectious laughter, and occasional "Now, Sam" have been effective forces in restraining his impetuosity. They have two children and one grandchild. After moving from Illinois to Tucson, Arizona, the Kirks built a southwestern ranch house, designed by Mrs. Kirk, on several acres where both could enjoy the pleasures of a pool, putting green, Koi pond, and the company of friends, colleagues, and students in a comfortable, but unassuming, lifestyle. The opening of the academic year was celebrated annually with faculty and students at the traditional pot-luck dinner in their home, until 1989 when Sam's illness necessitated their move to a retirement center. This move, however, has not convinced Sam that he should settle down and pass idle days contemplating his achievements. Instead, he pursues rehabilitation, reading, writing, telephoning, dining with friends, visiting family, and traveling, especially to his hideaway "cabin" in the mountains. There he and Winnie have all the amenities of home in addition to a pond created by Sam that is stocked with trout and other fish and shared with a host of visiting colleagues and dignitaries they have befriended worldwide. There he seems happiest and most relaxed or, perhaps, most willing to set aside scholarly pressures and complicated schedules for his unrelenting speaking engagements. Beyond these occasional escapes, he readily responds to calls from teachers, professional organizations, and heads of governments.

Sam's writing and speeches have been rational in outlook but reforming in bent. He is seldom lukewarm or neutral on any topic.

In spite of so many ominous responsibilities, he never seemed to be lacking in confidence or shaken by an unexpected turn of events. He has some sense of his eminent position in scholarship, but recently laughed aloud in disbelief at the successful sales of his books and level of recurrent income for his publisher and family. His most widely known work is *Educating Exceptional Children*, now in its sixth edition. He is a man in whose company we always felt better, became better, and spoke better for fear of disappointing him or seeming ignorant in his presence. It's hard to imagine that anyone who met him ever forgot him.

These readings are offered with the intent that no one will be deprived of his enthusiasm, munificence, and sagacity. His companionship has been a rare delight and his friendship a cherished treasure.

There may never be the likes of a Sam Kirk again.

William C. Healey began his career in 1958 as a television director and producer and assistant professor of communicative disorders at the University of Missouri. In 1962, he was appointed as the state director of special education for the Missouri State Department of Education, where he formulated state policies for education and health care of children and youth with special needs. In 1965, he became director of research and assistant superintendent of the unique experimental program for children with disabilities in the St. Louis County Special School District. In 1970, he assumed the position of school services program director for the American Speech-Language-Hearing Association.

Dr. Healey was appointed by President Carter to the President's Commission on Mental Health in 1978. He served on the U.S. Commissioner of Education's Task Force on Basic Skills in 1978–1979. He was chair of the National Advisory Committee on Learning Disabilities in 1977–1979, when he was recruited by Samuel A. Kirk and others to become a professor at the University of Arizona's Department of Special Education and Rehabilitation. He has served as assistant dean for graduate studies and research in the College of Education and a department head at the University of Arizona. He is currently a professor and directs leadership studies and the special education administrator's preparation program.

Chapter 1

Autobiographical Remarks

SAMUEL A. KIRK

Prologue

Samuel A. Kirk, born 1904 in Rugby, North Dakota, earned his B.A. in psychology (1929) and his M.A. in experimental psychology (1931) from the University of Chicago, and his Ph.D. in physiological and clinical psychology from the University of Michigan (1935).

Dr. Kirk was professor of special education at the University of Arizona (1968–85) and is also professor emeritus at the University of Illinois, where he was director of the Institute for Research on Exceptional Children and professor of special education and psychology (1952–67). In 1963–64, Dr. Kirk served as director of the Division of Handicapped Children and Youth in the United States Office of Education. He was director of the Division of Education for Exceptional Children (1935–47) and also chairman of the Graduate School at the Milwaukee State Teachers College (1946–47). He has been a consultant and advisor in Germany (1950 and 1951), a lecturer for the National Broadcasting Corporation (NHK) in Japan (1965), and a consultant to the government of Brazil (1979).

Former president of the International Council for Exceptional Children (1940–42) and vice-president of the American Association on Mental Deficiency, Dr. Kirk is a diplomate in clinical psychology and a fellow of the American Psychological Association, the American Association on Mental Deficiency, and the American Academy for the Advancement of Science.

In 1962, Dr. Kirk became honorary vice-president of the British Association of Special Education, and in the same year, received the First International Award in Mental Retardation from the Joseph P. Kennedy, Jr. Foundation. He is also the recipient of the J. E. Wallace Wallin Award from The Council for Exceptional Children (1966), the International Milestone Award from the International Federation of Learning Disabilities (1975), the Distinguished Service Award from the American Speech and Hearing Association (1976), an Award of Merit from the Division of School Psychology of the American Psychological Association (1979), the Award of Recognition from the Division of Early Childhood of The Council for Exceptional Children (1981),

---

From B. Blatt & R. Morris (Eds.), *Perspectives in Special Education, Personal Orientations.* Glenview, IL: Scott, Foresman, 1984.

and the Edgar H. Doll Award from the Division of Mental Retardation of the American Psychological Association (1981).

He received the honorary degree of Doctor of Humane Letters from Lesley College in 1969 and the honorary degree of Doctor of Letters from the University of Illinois in 1983.

Early Education

When I first enrolled at the University of Chicago in 1925, after graduating from a small-town high school, I was unaware of the international reputation of that great university. I had not anticipated how much intellectual and scientific stimulation such an institution could offer a Midwest country boy suddenly exposed to a new world of thought.

At that time the University of Chicago gave a great deal of freedom to individual initiative in course selection. They awarded a Bachelor of Philosophy degree (Ph.B.) for only three requirements: 1) nine quarter units constituting one full year of work in an academic major, 2) three quarter units in a foreign language, and 3) a total of four years of coursework. The student was then free to explore many fields of study and concentrate wherever he or she saw fit. It was also possible to shop around during the first days of each quarter. If one did not like the professor or the subject matter, it was possible to change to a different section or a different course.

It was through this course selection process that I came in contact with the great minds of the world. The internationally known physiologist Anton Carlson taught an introductory course in physiology; the outstanding anthropologist Fay Cooper Cole taught the introductory course in anthropology; and Harvey Carr, the head of the department of psychology, taught the introductory course in psychology. I mention these facts because today few internationally known professors teach undergraduate courses, since their load of graduates and Ph.D. candidates is very heavy compared to that of professors in the 1920s. Few at that time scrambled for research funds, but they still conducted profound research on their own and with their students even without large grants.

Upon graduation I enrolled for a master's degree in psychology at the University of Chicago while working in a school for subnormal delinquent boys. At that time the functional school of psychology offered courses emphasizing experimental psychology. The requirements for a master's degree consisted of two or three thoroughly experimental courses in the psychology of learning and in work and fatigue. All students were required to take at least two courses in statistics from the father of factor analysis, Leon Thurstone, and a course in neurology from Judson Herrick, a famous neurologist of his day.

It was also a tradition of the University of Chicago to invite famous professors from other universities to teach during the summer quarter. We considered it a privilege to take advantage of this tradition. The university invited one of the few psychologists in special education in the U.S. in the late 1920s, Dr. J.E. Wallace Wallin, to teach during the summer quarter. In 1924 he had published a scholarly and authoritative book, *The Education of Handicapped Children*, one of the earliest books in the field of special education. This book and Dr. Wallin's lectures were inspiring and very helpful. Actually, it was the only course in handicapped children that I had during my undergraduate or graduate work.

I also enrolled in a very inspiring course taught by Dr. Stevenson Smith, the director of the child development laboratories at the University of Washington in Seattle. He scoffed at psychoanalysis, saying that you don't psychoanalyze a child who is biting his nails; you consider nail biting a habit which needs breaking by symptomatic training. He stated in class that if you file the nails short so that they will not be rough, you will aid the child in overcoming the fingernail-biting habit. Five years later at the Wayne County Training School I did just that—filed the nails of 40 fingernail biters and assisted most of them in breaking the habit.

In addition to taking several courses relating to the nature of intelligence, I enrolled in one course offered by Visiting Professor Charles Spearman of England, the first theorist to describe intelligence as consisting of a general factor and many specific factors. He used as a text for the course his 1927 book, *The Nature of Intelligence and the Principles of Cognition*.

Early Experiences

My professional interest in the field of deviating children began when I took a course in mental testing from Andrew Brown at the Institute for Juvenile Research (IJR) in Chicago. Here I was initiated into mental testing and became acquainted with behavioral problem children by attending case conferences for mentally retarded and delinquent children at the Institute. Through this contact I applied for a position in an experimental school for delinquent, mentally retarded boys aged eight to sixteen near Chicago. The Oaks School had been designed by Dr. Paul Schroeder, a psychiatrist and director of IJR, as an experiment to determine whether freedom of choice would ameliorate behavior problems and help resolve mental retardation.

In 1929, at the beginning of the Depression, I was happy to be offered the position of "resident instructor" at the Oaks School even though at that time I had had no experience or training in education. Fortunately, they did not require teacher certificates in this area. My job was to manage 50 delinquent, mentally retarded boys, providing recreation in the late afternoons and evenings and on Saturdays and Sundays. In the evenings I helped the nurses in the dormitory put the boys to bed and see to it that they stayed in bed. In the morning I attended graduate classes at the University of Chicago working toward a master's degree and in the afternoon I drove to Oak Forest, Illinois, in a fifty-dollar Model T to work with these boys.

After several days at this residential school, two of the sixteen-year-olds came to me after a football game and wanted to wrestle. I avoided this personal contact for a day or two. On Saturday, however, it was raining, and the 50 boys were forced to retreat to the gym. The two boys again met me in a corner of the room and insisted on wrestling. By this time I knew that my predecessor had been forced to quit because these boys had wrestled and successfully fought with him. I quickly scanned my psychology courses to find a psychological technique for avoiding this confrontation, to no avail. I decided to bluff by saying to them, "I don't want to wrestle two of you; I'll wrestle the whole group." They were delighted at this offer, calling the other boys and informing them that Mr. Kirk would wrestle all of them.

I explained the rules of the game as I had previously explained other games. The rule was that when any one boy was down, he was out of the game. When I went down, the game was over. The two boys rushed at me. I tripped the first one and threw down the second. The other 48 ran to the other end of the room. I was the winner. If the reverse had happened, I might have been forced to seek another career.

In reading the clinical folders of these children, I noticed that one boy was labeled *word blind*, a term I had never heard before in my psychology courses. He was a nonreader, ten years old, and had a recorded IQ of 82. The clinical folder referred to Marion Monroe's monograph on reading disabilities, Hinshelwood's book on congenital word blindness, and Fernald's kinesthetic method. After reading these references at the university the next day, I arranged to tutor the boy at nine o'clock in the evening, after the boys were supposed to be asleep. This boy, who was eager to learn, sneaked quietly out of bed at the appointed time each night and met me in a small space between the two dormitory rooms—actually, in the doorway of the boys' toilet. We both knew we were violating a regulation by making this arrangement since the head nurse had directed me not to allow the boys out of bed after nine o'clock. When she came down from the third floor, the boy and I went into the boys' toilet so she did not catch us violating that sacred rule. I often state that my first experience in tutoring a case of reading disability was not in a school, was not in a clinic, was not in an experimental laboratory, but in a boys' lavatory.

This boy was very eager to learn to read and within a period of seven months was reading at the second- to third-grade level. An examination at the Institute for Juvenile Research indicated that he was now reading at beginning third-grade level. The Institute, following the recommendation of Dr. Marion Monroe, who examined him, obtained a parole from a juvenile court judge, returned him to his home, and had him enrolled in a fourth grade. I hypothesized at that time that remedial reading might alleviate delinquency in some children.

The Institute for Juvenile Research had been organized in Chicago as a service and research institute and housed research psychiatrists, sociologists, and psychologists. Among the early researchers were William Healey and Augusta Bronner, who made major contributions to the study of delinquency; Clifford Shaw, the sociologist who studied the delinquency areas in Chicago; L. Hewett and R. Jenkins, who made a lasting contribution in their studies of patterns of maladjustment; Carl Lashley, who in a rat and monkey laboratory conducted research on neuropsychology; Chester Darrow, one of the first psychologists to research the E.E.G; and Andrew Brown, who headed the clinical psychology section and conducted research on mental testing.

It was this research environment that Dr. Marion Monroe, a former affiliate of Dr. Samuel T. Orton, was conducting relevant research on reading-disabled children. In her office I received individual tutoring and guidance in the diagnosis and remediation of reading disabilities. Many years later, unbeknown to me, Dr. Monroe was asked to review my first book (*Teaching Reading to Slow Learning Children*, 1940) and to write a foreword to it.

It was at the Oaks School that I conducted my first published experimental project using single-subject research. The research dealt with the Fernald kinesthetic method. I used six boys at the school, teaching them to read five words one day using the look-and-say method, and five words the next day using the Fernald manual tracing method. On the third day they relearned the words to determine how many fewer trials they took (retention savings score), and then learned another five words. This experiment continued for thirty days. In contrasting the Fernald method with the look-and-say method, I found that the number of trials for learning was the same for both methods but that retention over 24 hours was greater when the manual tracing (kinesthetic) method was used (Kirk, 1933).

In 1931 the Great Depression hit the United States. The banks were closed and Cook County, Illinois, in its attempt to retrench, closed the Oaks School. I became unemployed and applied for job after job, in most instances receiving no answer. At about this time, the Wayne County Training School at Northville, Michigan, was looking for a psychologist with a master's degree who was trained and experienced in reading disabilities of the mentally retarded. Dr. Marion Monroe recommended me for the position in spite of my meager experience which consisted of tutoring approximately three children with reading disabilities. There seemed to be a shortage of people who had done research in the remediation of mentally retarded reading cases. For this reason, I was offered the position.

My work at the Wayne County Training School consisted of half-time teaching and half-time research. At this residential training school the children had many disabilities—reading, language, perceptual, and behavioral. I was fortunate to have this great opportunity to teach and conduct research on children with a variety of problems.

In the early 1930s great emphasis was placed on brain theory and its relationship to aberrations of behavior, such as mirror reading, mixed eyedness and handedness, and strephosymbolia. Brain dysfunction was proposed by Samuel T. Orton, Lee Edward Travis, and others to explain many of these aberrations. At that time cerebral dominance and the concept of strephosymbolia were the most prominent theories held to account for stuttering, disorders of reading, and language. Since the children with whom we worked had reading, language, and perceptual problems, it was necessary for us to understand the workings of the brain. I consequently enrolled in a doctorate program at the University of Michigan. The emphasis of the Department of Psychology was on physiological and experimental psychology and on neurology. Dr. Normal Maier, who did his postdoctoral work in Berlin in Gestalt psychology and studied with Carl Lashley for two years, was my advisor.

My doctoral research consisted of testing the handedness of rats and training them to discriminate between an *F* and a mirrored *F* on a Lashley jumping apparatus as described in "Cerebral Dominance and Hemispheric Equipotentiality" (Kirk, 1935). Studying physiological psychology and neurology and conducting experiments with the brains of rats bore little relationship between what I did then, and what I have done since, or to what I do now for children with learning disabilities. It did teach me, however, that the study of the brain and behavior is important and that eventually scientists may bridge the gap between neurology and psychology, and between psychology and education. When this occurs we may have an integrated discipline entitled "neuropsychological education."

At the Wayne County Training School I had the rare opportunity to spend half-time teaching mentally retarded children, supervising graduate students from the University of Michigan who were interning in the research department of the institution. I was also doing research, and taking courses at the University for a Ph.D. in psychology. This opportunity was afforded me by an unusual superintendent, Dr. Robert Haskell, a psychiatrist who had ambitions in research and science. He established a department of research in this children's institution and treated the department as a "sacred cow." He insisted that an institution was responsible for conducting research and advancing knowledge.

Dr. Haskell knew that the Vineland Training School had become famous through the research contributions of Dr. Henry Goddard and Dr. Edgar Doll. He wanted the Wayne County Training School to become as famous as Vineland through research. He appointed Dr. Thorleif Hegge as director of research and asked him to develop research related to the academic abilities of mentally retarded children. Dr. Hegge, a native of Norway, had obtained his Ph.D. in psychology from Gottingen, Germany, and had spent a year in the research department at Vineland with Dr. Edgar Doll.

The research department was manned primarily by psychologists and graduate students in psychology, speech pathology, and social work from the University of Michigan. The list of the scientists who worked in the research department at the Wayne County Training School testifies to the insight of the superintendent and Dr. Hegge. Among them are Alfred Strauss, Heinz Werner, Sidney Bijou, Newell Kephart, Boyd McCandles, William Cruickshank, Bluma Weiner, and many others. It is interesting to note that these people developed their own ideas in an institution for the mentally retarded rather than in a university. After World War II many of them accepted positions in universities when their contributions from this institution became known. Unfortunately, today few residential schools offer such outstanding opportunities. Few serve as centers of research, and few feel that among their obligations is the advancement of knowledge.

Major Influences

It is difficult to list in order the many contacts and experiences that influence one's thinking and one's career. In most instances there is a combination of influences and, sometimes, the accident of the environment. Nevertheless, I shall try to list in retrospect some of the people and conditions that may have directed my thinking.

The first influence, of course, was the contact with great thinkers at the University of Chicago. Harvey Carr's functional school of psychology had a profound impact. It was a precursor to Skinner's behaviorism, which Calfee (1982) states had its roots in American functionalism. The application of the principles of learning to education and teaching was dominant. The names of Watson, Thorndike, and Judd were in the forefront of psychology.

The second major influence (in the 1930s) was Dr. Marion Monroe and her research. Her many years of research at IJR resulted in a book entitled *Children Who Cannot Read* (1932), which was, for a while, my bible. Her work was an outgrowth of her association with Dr. Samuel T. Orton at the University of Iowa. Her system of diagnosing errors in reading (repetitions, reversals, omission of sounds and words, etc.) is still used today. Through standardization of these errors for each grade from one to four, she was able to draw a profile of the kinds of errors each child made. Her hypothesis was that if we are able to eliminate the symptoms of poor reading through the correction of reading errors, the reading level will improve. Many years later I used the same approach in profiling the abilities and disabilities revealed by the Illinois Test of Psycholinguistic Abilities (Kirk, McCarthy, & Kirk, 1968).

The remedial methods which we later developed were influenced by Marion Monroe and the Fernald kinesthetic method. Fernald and Keller had published an article which was impressive (1921). The Hegge, Kirk and Kirk Remedial Reading Drills (1936) evolved from trial-and-error teaching of children with reading disabilities. This grapho-vocal phonic system evolved independently at about the same time as the Gillingham method, both influenced by Samuel T. Orton and Marion Monroe. The Hegge, Kirk and Kirk Remedial Reading Drills were developed in 1933 and 1934. They emphasized the principles of learning from the Chicago school of functional psychology in a way similar to the emphasis in programmed instruction promoted more recently by the behavior analysts.

The third influence was my experience at the Wayne County Training School. This experience exposed me to several personalities who influenced my future. One was Dr. Thorleif G. Hegge, who took a personal interest in developing in me the same accuracy and careful interpretation of data he had acquired in his German university training. Another was my wife, Winifred Day Kirk, also a graduate of the University of Chicago functional school of psychology and a team member in the research department at the Wayne County Training School. We have been professionals as well as family partners ever since.

Dr. Robert Haskell, the forward-looking superintendent, taught me much about techniques of interviewing youngsters. As a lowly psychologist, I screened boys in the psychiatric office for his evaluation. In this position I learned a great deal about the practical application of psychoanalysis, milieu therapy, and behavior modification. I also learned from Dr. Haskell the value of holding on to the goal of research and scientific approaches even in the face of financial and political opposition. Dr. Haskell maintained our research department against much opposition throughout the Great Depression of the 1930s.

The experience at the Wayne County Training School pointed out to me that much more could be done with handicapped children than most people believed. The case histories and diagnoses by clinics and schools in the Detroit areas and by the staff of the Wayne County Training School were an education in case analysis and procedure. Case conferences added to the belief that many children considered hopeless in behavior or learning could be rehabilitated. One boy, with whom we worked for three years, had a low IQ on the Binet, was declared delinquent, could not read two words. The only thing he could write was his name, and that he wrote backwards. This boy was trained by me one hour a day, five days a week, outside of his classroom. After two years of tutoring he was reading at the beginning fourth-grade level. He could score at a seventh-grade level on the Gray's Oral Reading Test because of his decoding abilities, but his comprehension was at the beginning of the fourth grade. He was tutored for a third year in an attempt to increase his comprehension. At the end of the year he was testing at the middle fourth-grade level in comprehension. On a repeated psychometric test at the age of 15 he showed an IQ of 70 and was consequently paroled to his grandmother. In a follow-up study it was found that he not only had become a self-supporting citizen but was also supporting his grandmother and his sister while working for a fair salary at the Ford Motor Company.

The fifth major influence was my education after I acquired the Ph.D. While attending the University of Chicago we had discovered that Leon Thurstone was taking advanced courses in mathematics because he was trying to develop factor analysis. This activity demonstrated to us that the Ph.D. degree does not complete one's education and that it is necessary to continue studying. With this in mind, I registered for a two-semester laboratory course in speech pathology at the University of Michigan. In addition, I learned a great deal from working with the speech clinicians. While at the Milwaukee State Teachers College and after that, I attended courses in the education of the deaf and in cerebral palsy and took a workshop in the visually handicapped. I make these statements because I do not wish to leave the impression that one can make progress in teaching and research in special education without study or experience in the field beyond courses in experimental and physiological psychology. Special education knowledge and skills had to be acquired through experience and through related course work after the Ph.D.

College Teaching

My first appointment in college teaching was a fortunate one. In 1935, fresh out of direct work with children and with a brand new Ph.D., I was offered a position as Director of the Division of Exceptional Children at the Milwaukee State Teachers College. This was an unusually fine institution which later became the University of Wisconsin, Milwaukee branch. With Frank Baker as a socially minded, flexible president, this institution had initiated many innovative ideas. Geared primarily to kindergarten/primary, elementary, and secondary education, the college also offered degrees in special areas such as music education, art education, and the education of exceptional children.

Students in this state college were offered free tuition and free textbooks. Because of the small size of the building and faculty, the college restricted its enrollment to 1200 students. Out of several thousand applications each year, it admitted 500 freshmen who ranked at the top of their high school graduating classes. This selection process tended to elevate the caliber of instruction offered.

One outstanding feature of the program was that the students completed their liberal arts courses and studies in related areas during the first three years of college and devoted the senior year to concentrated practicums in teaching and small-group instruction. During this fourth year, students were enrolled in practice teaching for three hours each morning for nine months, with practice in several grades. Each faculty member was assigned twelve students to supervise in the morning; they taught them methods, theory, and curriculum in the afternoon.

This College served as a postdoctoral training center for me since teacher education was relatively new to me, especially at the kindergarten/primary level. It thrust upon me new responsibilities: directing the Division for Exceptional Children; training teachers of the mentally retarded; chairing the Counseling Department; chairing the freshmen selection committee; and giving preservice training to kindergarten/primary and elementary students in the management and teaching of handicapped children in the regular grades.

This intensive teacher education program was successful because it provided a low student/faculty ratio and extensive and varied practice teaching. What teacher training program today assigns students for practice teaching in different settings for a full year? What teacher training center today assigns one faculty member to twelve undergraduate students with no other course requirement except to supervise them, show them how to teach, and give them didactic experiences on what to teach, how to teach, and why.

Since few people know everything, each one of the instructors at this teachers college invited others to help with their students. My involvement was the result of a trade-off with instructors in the elementary and kindergarten/primary divisions. They supervised and instructed the students majoring in the deaf and the mentally retarded, and in elementary education, while I reciprocated by instructing their students in handling children with minor handicaps found in the regular class. This required that I visit classes for normal children, study school curricula, observe techniques of instruction, and apply what theoretical knowledge I had in learning, reading, and child development to the program for primary and elementary grade students. By combining my theoretical training in psychology and observing teaching techniques, I obtained postdoctoral training in the education of normal children from the professionals in the field. It was necessary for me to observe how elementary teachers managed a class, taught the children, and handled problems. These observations helped me diagnose children who had problems in the classroom and show the student teachers how to adapt instruction to minor handicaps in the regular grades.

This experience is related to the current trend toward mainstreaming, in which elementary teachers are asked to manage minor handicaps in children in regular classes. This was the system in the 1930s, since special classes at that time only served children who were definitely handicapped.

Interest in Preschool Education

The contact with the kindergarten/primary division at the Milwaukee State Teachers College aroused my interest in the programs for preschool children of normal intelligence. In supervising and assisting student teachers in the correction of minor problems in children in nursery school and kindergarten, I obtained some experience in teaching and in the programs for so-called average children.

In 1939 I attended a lecture at one of the social welfare meetings in which Harold Skeels told about early training of the mentally retarded. He described his experience in rehabilitating young mentally retarded children in a state institution for the mentally deficient. He described how he had placed two young mentally retarded girls from an orphanage on separate wards of an institution for mental defectives and asked the retarded women in the wards to play with them and to teach them to talk and to walk. Several years later these two girls were nearly normal and were paroled to foster homes. Skeels proceeded to take twelve other children from the orphanage who tested low in intelligence tests and left thirteen similar children in the orphanage. Two years later the IQs of the children placed in the wards of the state institution with the older mentally retarded women had increased by 27 points, while those of the thirteen children left in the orphanage dropped 27 points.

When I questioned Skeels about these results that evening, he showed me a manuscript by Alfred Binet published in 1911, *Modern Ideas About Children*. In the chapter, "The Educability of Intelligence" Binet presented a curriculum to develop memory, attention, reasoning, language, and other vectors of intelligence. In other words, Binet was not obsessed with the constancy of the IQ, but believed that it can be changed through educational intervention. (See a reprint in Kirk & Lord, 1974.)

That article and the work of Skeels had a profound effect on my future interest and activities. My experience at the Wayne County Training School also biased me toward a belief in the power of intervention.

While teaching at the teachers college and shortly after the contact with Skeels, I began an experiment with six- and seven-year-old mentally retarded children in Milwaukee in an attempt to improve their behavior and their intelligence. The public school had organized a special class of young retarded children who were causing great difficulties in the classrooms. These children were not as young as I wanted, but they had IQs in the 50s and 60s and histories of behavior problems in school in addition to the inability to learn. The curriculum was organized around Thurstone's primary mental abilities which isolated seven factors in intelligence. These seven factors would be related to ordinary readiness activities such as language training, quantitative thinking, space relations, and so forth. The teacher selected for this class had minored in arts and crafts and was interested in organizing games for the development of such functions in children (Kirk & Stevens, 1943). She devised a great number of educational games of interest for these children, all designed to develop the primary mental functions.

Formal evaluation of this class was never accomplished, since with the incursion of World War II, I was commissioned in the Army and had to drop the program. The principal of the school believed, however, that it was the best-behaved class in his school since these children were happily working whenever he came to their class.

Special Education During World War II

During World War II the Army discovered that it could not reject all the illiterates who were drafted. They decided to accept 10% of the illiterates going through the induction stations each day. As a consequence, it became necessary to organize special training units in various camps to teach these inductees how to read and write. These soldiers were required to attend special training classes for eight weeks, eight hours a day.

To organize these programs and to develop appropriate tests and training materials, the Army commissioned Dr. Paul Witty and me as the reading experts and stationed us in the Pentagon. Our duties were to (1) develop tests for screening illiterates, (2) develop training materials and books, and (3) conduct workshops for officers in charge of special training units in the various camps. These special training units enrolled 385,000 illiterate soldiers during World War II.

Later in the war, I was assigned to Walter Reed Hospital in Washington to rehabilitate wounded soldiers and to organize appropriate training programs for the disabled returnees. These two experiences served to remind me that we cannot wait for a war to recognize such problems. It is necessary to expand education for all children as an important function for national defense.

Research

Following World War II, the state of Illinois developed an extensive program in special education but was extremely short of professionally prepared personnel. Through the urging of the State Department of Public Instruction and Mr. Ray Graham, the Director of Special Education, the University of Illinois decided to employ one person to launch a program in special education. Having been asked to fill that position, I soon discovered that a large university of that type was not equipped to prepare teachers. Instead, it seemed wiser to concentrate on research and graduate programs. Therefore, we minimized undergraduate teacher training and attempted to develop a research and graduate program leading to a Ph.D. in special education.

To continue my previous research I applied for a grant from the Institute for Mental Health, in spite of the fact that at that time the institute was not allotting money for educational research. The project for which I sought funding was a study of the effects of preschool education on the social and mental development of young mentally retarded children. It was also supported partly by the Illinois State Department of Social Welfare and the State Department of Public Instruction. This experiment was conducted for approximately five years both in an institution and in the community. The results of the study were published in book form in 1958 under the title *Early Education of the Mentally Retarded* (Kirk, 1958). Together with the Skeels study, it had an effect in stimulating research on disadvantaged children, in influencing the initiation of Head Start, and in persuading Congress to enact the Early Education Assistance Act in 1968 (Kirk, 1968). By way of comment, it is interesting to note the extensive lag that exists between social science research results and the response of society. The Skeels study was reported in 1939. It was not widely accepted at that time. The Kirk study was reported in 1958. Not until 1968 did Congress enact legislation to promote preschool education for the handicapped, ten years after the Kirk study and thirty years after the Skeels study.

In addition to experimental results that have been reported for the preschool children, there are a number of observations that may be even more important. To organize a program for mentally retarded children it was necessary for us to observe their behavior and to organize programs for each child's particular needs. For each child we asked the questions: "What abilities does this child have: What deficits exist? What do we do about these particular deficits?"

The analysis of the preschool children—to find out what they could do and what they had difficulty doing—alerted us in the early 1950s, to the fallacy of classification. Their classification as mentally retarded had little relevance to the training of these children. Each child needed a diagnosis, and each child needed a different program.

One child with marked nystagmus as a result of rubella was diagnosed as legally blind and severely mentally retarded (an IQ of below 50). She was recommended for commitment to a state institution for the mentally retarded. In spite of severe nystagmus we found that she could learn to respond to and label pictures if we waited long enough for her to overcome the effects of her nystagmus. It appeared that this child's nystagmus and visual problems resulted in a deficit in speed of perception. Through the use of a tachistoscope, this central dysfunction improved over a six-month training period until she could respond to pictures at 1/25th of a second. This improvement transferred to a life situation where she was able to decode and describe pictures. At the age of ten, in a follow-up study, she was doing adequate third-grade work in the regular classes. Through intensive training, this child, diagnosed as severely mentally retarded and legally blind at the age of four to five, was at the age of ten considered within the average range educationally and intellectually.

Another child in the same school labeled "mentally retarded" had a recorded IQ of 37. She could not talk. She did not even understand language, but used gestures. With this child we organized a different remedial program, namely, auditory training, auditory discrimination, and teaching her to listen and decode auditory stimuli. Within nine months this girl was talking; at the age of eight her psychological tests ranged between 80 and 90, and her progress in the regular grades was slightly below average.

After finding a number of children with functional deficits in auditory reception, verbal expression, speed of perception, memory, and other problems, we began to look for tests to confirm our clinical diagnoses. At that time (1950) there were very few tests of specific functions. We began in 1950 to develop tests of abilities to aid us in diagnosing the specific problems of these children.

After ten years of work with these concepts we were able to organize an experimental edition of the Illinois Test of Psycholinguistic Abilities (Kirk & McCarty). After it was used for approximately six or seven years, it was revised and published in final form in 1968 (Kirk, McCarthy, & Kirk). The ITPA was popular from the beginning because it is an intraindividual test, comparing the child's own abilities and disabilities for the purpose of organizing remediation for deficits. The times were apparently right for working with individual children instead of classifying them into groups for instructional purposes. The ITPA has been translated and standardized into eight other languages. Unfortunately, this test has also spawned many illusions and false hopes. Some people have taken the ITPA as the instrument for the diagnosis of all ills and educational problems. In spite of our numerous warnings, it is being used for junior high students even though it was intended for young children. This problem, of course, is common in many areas of assessment and remediation. We misuse tests and other materials by taking remedial methods developed for one type of child and using them for children for whom they are not suitable. The ITPA, like many other instruments, is only an aid to clinical judgment for children with language and related disorders (see Kirk & Kirk, 1971, 1978).

The Responsibility of a Major University for Future Research

The experiment on preschool education at the University of Illinois was a joint venture of the university, the state Department of Public Instruction, and the state Department of Welfare, which operated the state institutions for the mentally retarded. This experiment demonstrated the advantages of research conducted as a joint venture of several state agencies. The effectiveness of this cooperation stimulated the participating agencies to establish a research institute that would utilize their resources. With the help of the forward-looking Director of Special Education in the state of Illinois, Ray Graham, and the enthusiasm of Dean Willard Spalding and President George Stoddard of the University of Illinois, an Institute for Research on Exceptional Children was organized and approved by the two operating agencies and the trustees of the University of Illinois. (For a description of the institute, see Kirk & Spalding, 1953.)

The faculty of the institute consisted of professors who held joint appointments with other university departments, plus research associates from the state Department of Public Welfare and the state Department of Public Instruction.

The initial university faculty, James A. Gallagher, Bernard Farber, Oliver Kolstoe, Lawrence D. Stolurow, Herbert Goldstein, Merle Karnes, Clifford Howe, and Samuel Kirk, served between 1952 and 1967. This small but high quality faculty produced volumes of research in many areas of exceptionality (see Kirk & Bateman, 1964).

The state departments were happy to have a research team base at the university to assist in answering some of their practical problems. One project that was dominant in the early 1950s was the problem of trainable children: are they the responsibility of the Department of Public Welfare or of the schools? This became a national problem. At a meeting of the institute, the state Department of Public Instruction, and the school boards (who were opposed to admitting trainable children to public schools) it was decided to ask the legislature for funds to conduct pilot projects and to evaluate the programs after two years. The legislature accepted the report and appropriated funds for the project. The organization of 24 classes was arranged and financed by the state Department of Public Instruction, while the institute coordinated the evaluation. This project led the way to the organization of programs for trainable mentally retarded children in many other states (Nickel, 1954).

Another practical problem at this time was how children with high IQs were adjusting or progressing in the regular grades. The problem of gifted children had been worked on sporadically in a number of places, but the state was interested in a practical answer. These problems were partially solved from the pooling of resources, physical and financial, of the university and the state Department of Public Instruction. Again the legislature accepted the reports of research and appropriated funds to extend these services in the public schools in Illinois.

The Parents' Movement

In the late 1940s and early 1950s parents of retarded children became frustrated by the schools' refusal to admit children with IQs below 50. The institutions were so overcrowded that they were unable to admit them. The parents were taxpayers like everyone else; they paid school taxes, and also paid taxes for the support of the institutions. They were being refused services from both these state agencies.

The parents consequently began to organize locally and to operate schools for their trainable children. These organizations finally founded The National Association for Retarded Children. This movement became a political force and, in the middle 1950s, obtained legal and financial support from state and federal sources.

Later, in the early 1960s, another group of parents whose children were not mentally retarded, or blind, or deaf, or crippled, became concerned for their children who were not learning for other reasons. A.A. Strauss had postulated that these children were brain-injured. They had relatively normal intelligence, often had no obvious overt difficulties, unlike children with cerebral palsy, or the deaf, blind or crippled. Following Strauss' impact and his book in 1947, parents began to organize under such names as The Society for Brain-Injured Children, or the Society for the Perceptually Handicapped. After many such state and local organizations were formed, the groups decided to hold a national conference. This Conference on Exploration into Problems of the Perceptually Handicapped Child was convened in Chicago in April, 1963. Professional people active in the field (including Myklebust, Kephart, Lehtinen, and I) were invited by this organization to present their points of view concerning children who did not fall into the traditional categories of exceptionality but who nevertheless appeared to be handicapped in learning. Since many names were used for this group, the parents were seeking an inclusive name for their national organization.

In my address to them I stated

> Recently I have used the term "learning disabilities" to describe a group of children who have disorders of development, in language, speech, reading, and associated communication skills needed for social interaction. In this group I do not include children who have sensory handicaps such as blindness or deafness, because we have methods of managing and treating the deaf and the blind. I also exclude from this group children who have generalized mental retardation. (Kirk, 1963. See Kirk & Lord, 1974. p, 78)

After much debate on terminology the groups decided that The Association for Children with Learning Disabilities (ACLD) was the appropriate designation. Since that date the term learning disabilities has become the general term for a heterogeneous group of disabilities of varying degrees of severity which are, however, similar in that they seem to stem from intrinsic cognitive or perceptual difficulties interfering with a child's learning.

This commendable initiative and activity on the part of parent groups stimulated me to give what assistance I could. I had earlier been shocked, saddened, and embarrassed by conditions I had seen in state institutions with indifferent, underpaid, untrained caretakers in understaffed, dilapidated buildings. Tearful parents had come to me time and time again seeking counsel. Often their children had been labeled feebleminded.

At that time (the 1930s), I tried to appeal to state senators for better services for these children. I tried to explain the plight of the parents. I remember the following dialogue from that period:

Senator (looking down at me over the rim of his glasses): Do you have a handicapped child?

SAK: No, I don't.

Senator: Then why are you interested?

SAK: My interest is professional, not personal.

Senator: Oh, you are trying to make your profession important.

Another traumatic experience occurred when I presented a technical report to welfare workers. I had prepared a document with slides of statistics and trends showing wherein the state was lacking in services for the handicapped. Commenting on my speech, the state director of special education said: "These statistics remind me of the statistic which showed that the male graduates of Yale and Harvard had 2.3 children and the female graduates of Vassar and Smith had 1.8 children, thus proving that men have more children than women." With that joke he wiped out my three weeks of research on the status of handicapped children in Wisconsin. I knew then and thereafter that I was completely ineffective as a political advocate for handicapped children and that the dormant political power of parents had to be aroused.

It has been a source of satisfaction to participate and help the parent movements—first, for children with cerebral palsy, then for the mentally retarded, and lastly, for the learning disabled. I found a satisfaction in associating with many intelligent and knowledgeable parents in these organizations. I found that through association with other parents they learned what the best programs were for their children. If I were to give credit to one group in this country for the advancements that have been made in the education of exceptional children, I would place the parent organizations and parent movement in the forefront as the leading force. I am happy to see that now parents, under Public Law 94-142, are partners in the educative process.

The Federal Impact

Shortly after World War II, the country found itself with understaffed and overcrowded institutions for the handicapped. Many state institutions refused to admit more children and placed them on three- and four-year waiting lists. Although some states subsidized public school programs for children with physical and sensory handicaps, it was not until the late 1940s and early 1950s that state legislatures appropriated funds for local public school programs for the mentally retarded, emotionally disturbed, and speech impaired. These subsidies were provided before there was an adequate supply of appropriately trained teachers, creating a major shortage of well-prepared teachers of special education. In addition, the financial disproportion among states resulted in a situation in which rich states were stealing experienced teachers from poorer states through higher salaries.

It has been rumored that a prominent parent of a mentally retarded child obtained an interview with President Eisenhower and informed him of the plight of the mentally retarded. The president then requested Congress through the Department of Health, Education and Welfare to do something about the problem. At that time (1954) I was invited to Washington to help the Office of Education formulate plans for programs for the mentally retarded. The same two obstacles to the development of programs for exceptional children that existed at the state level also existed at the federal level: ignorance of what should be done with these children, and a paucity of highly trained, professional personnel. In attempting to solve these problems, the U.S. Office of Education accepted my two proposals.

The first recommendation was for educational research funds. It was pointed out that little research in the education of the mentally retarded was being conducted due to a lack of research funds specifically for education. A second recommendation was for the federal government to support the preparation of professional personnel. Only a few colleges at that time were preparing teachers of the mentally retarded, and many of the classes in the public schools were being manned by partially trained teachers. Furthermore, universities were reluctant to support a training program for minorities like the mentally retarded.

These recommendations resulted in the appropriation of funds for the cooperative research bill P.L. 83-531 in 1954. The commissioner of education was interested in obtaining research funds for all of education and believed that the prevailing interest of the Congress in the mentally retarded would help support research for education in general. It did.

One million dollars for educational research was appropriated in 1955–56, but Congressman John Fogarty amended the bill to allot $675,000 of the total appropriation to research in the education of the mentally retarded. This amendment made many people unhappy since only one-third of a million dollars was left for all education including other exceptional children. This distribution of funds appeared unfair to them. Two years later the categorical funding of research for the mentally retarded was removed.

In analyzing the grants made for the mentally retarded, I found (as shown in the following figure) that when the categorical appropriations of funds were removed, the Federal grants to researchers decreased from year to year. In 1957, 61% of one million dollars appropriated went to research on the mentally retarded. In 1959, when categorical funding was removed, the grants were 36%. Funds decreased gradually until in 1963 only 5% of the appropriation was allotted to research in mental retardation and *that* 5% was for the continuation of previously granted research. Actually, *no* new grants for research were made in 1963. These results were presented to Congress in 1966 to convince them that a categorical bureau for the handicapped was needed.

Congress had enacted the cooperative research bill in 1954 and appropri-

FIGURE 1
Proportion of Appropriations Under PL-531 for Research on the Mentally Retarded

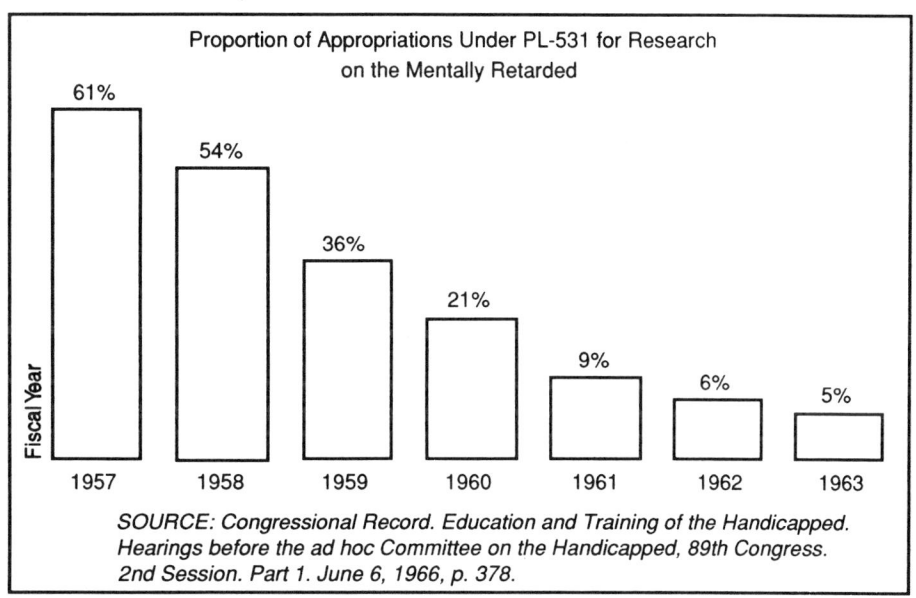

ated funds in 1956. They were reluctant, however, to accept the recommendation for the preparation of personnel. Some congressmen argued that federal aid for education would result in federal control of education. However, in 1958 Congress passed P.L. 85-296 with an appropriation of one million dollars for the preparation of personnel in the field of the mentally retarded and in 1960 provided an appropriation for the education of teachers of the deaf.

The cooperative research bill and the appropriations for the preparation of professional personnel under the Eisenhower administration was a beginning. The major impetus to the education of exceptional children, however, was launched during the short period that John Kennedy was president.

In 1962 President Kennedy sent a six-man task force to the Soviet Union to study their programs for mentally retarded children. As members of this scientific commission, Lloyd Dunn and I made a report on the status of programs for the retarded in Russia (1962). Shortly thereafter, President Kennedy presented to Congress a request for legislation providing for research and training for mentally handicapped children. In signing the ensuing bill, The Mental Retardation Facilities and Community Mental Health Centers Construction Act of 1963 (P.L. 88-164), President Kennedy stated, "I am glad to announce that we are establishing a new division in the U.S. Office of Education to administer the teaching and research programs under the act. This will be called the Division of Handicapped Children and Youth, and will be headed by Samuel A. Kirk." Previous to the announcement, the commissioner of education asked that "in the public interest" I suffer the necessary cut in salary in order to start this new division. I was informed by the president's secretaries that one does not refuse a request from the president and that if the country can draft men into the military service, they can request professionals to serve in Washington and help run the government. I was hesitant, but the president's earlier words were ringing in my ears: "Ask not what your country can do for you; ask what you can do for your country."

Three weeks after President Kennedy had signed P.L. 88-164, the world was wounded by his assassination. On my first day on the new job in Washington I attended the sorrowful funeral of President John F. Kennedy.

As indicated, the Division for Handicapped Children and Youth was organized in the U.S. Office of Education in November, 1963. The appropriation of 14 million dollars was not made until February, and the money had to be committed by the following June, the end of the fiscal year. In a short six months it was necessary to develop rules and regulations to administer the Act; distribute the rules and regulations with application forms to universities and state departments; appoint 17 committees to survey the application blanks; and have the 14 million committed by June.

This program could not have been completed in six months had it not been for a great public interest and the volunteer help I received from all parts of the United States. We received a large number of applications from state departments, school districts, and universities for research and training, and particularly for the training of professional personnel. We allowed six weeks from the deadline of the applications to the awarding of grants which were all completed by June 1, 1964. Two days after I submitted a report indicating how many grants were received for research and how much money was requested for teacher preparation, Congressman Fogarty introduced the data in the *Congressional Record* with the statement:

> At a meeting of the New England Educators held on May 22 at Rhode Island College in Providence, Samuel Kirk made a progress report on the administration of the Act by the Office of Education. In view of the great significance of the Act for education and the extent to which it will help the nation's schools fill a critical gap in teachers for handicapped children, I wish to call the report to the attention of all members of Congress.... Requests for aid that have been submitted amount to three times the funds now authorized in the Act. (*Congressional Record*, June 1964)

As a result of Congressman Fogarty's effort, Congress doubled the appropriation the following year.

Every ten years the president of the United States awards a Presidential Merit Award to the most efficient department of the U.S. government. That year, shortly after Dr. Maury Wirtz took over as Director of the Division of Handicapped Children and Youth, the Presidential Merit Award went to the Division of Handicapped Children and Youth.

It is ironic to note that, in the face of the Presidential Merit Award and other accolades, the division was abolished 18 months after its creation when the Office of Education was reorganized by the White House into four bureaus. This action caused great concern in Congress and interested groups throughout the United States. As a result, Congressman Hugh Carey, later Governor of New York, requested that Congress create a Committee for the Handicapped. My testimony at the committee hearings recommended two actions: (1) the creation of a Bureau for the Education of the Handicapped, and (2) the creation of an advisory committee of citizens to advise the bureau and to protect it against itself and against onslaughts by others (*Congressional Record* testimony, 1966).

Congress created the Bureau for the Education of Handicapped Children in 1967 with Dr. James Gallagher as director and Dr. Edward Martin as assistant director. Following this development, the work for handicapped children moved into a progressive phase. After a period of eight years the work of the bureau culminated in Public Law 94-142, the Education of All Handicapped Children act.

Reflections

For over half a century I have been privileged to study and to work in the field of special education. During this period I have seen many changes and much progress. Service programs, teacher preparation, and research have been the major areas of our professional development.

Service Programs for Handicapped Children

Residential Institutions. Our first thrust for services for handicapped children in the U.S. was the organization and development of state and private residential institutions. This was an improvement over leaving to the family all the responsibility for the care and support of these children. The enthusiasm for these residential schools between 1859 and 1900 resulted in the creation of numerous state schools for the blind, the deaf, the mentally retarded, delinquents, and orphans. After 50 years of expansion of residential schools, the enthusiasms for them began to wane. Instead of habilitation and return to the community, the children stayed in these schools, which became bigger, overcrowded, and poorly supported.

Special Classes. Not until the turn of the century were special classes for the mildly handicapped initiated in an attempt to integrate these children into the community. The special class movement progressed slowly between 1900 and 1950. A few states encouraged the expansion of special classes by providing state subsidies. However, the public school special class movement did not make marked progress until after World War II when it was found that states could not build institutions fast enough for the number of handicapped identified. Enthusiasts for this movement, including myself, alleged that segregation in institutions was not working and was inhuman and expensive. Instead these children should be integrated with the family, the neighborhood, and the public school by way of special classes.

Following World War II, state after state began to appropriate funds for the organization of local special classes for the educable mentally retarded and the emotionally disturbed, as well as continuing earlier established programs for the hearing, visually, and orthopedically impaired.

As usual in many situations, our society goes too far in one direction and then throws the baby out with the bath water. So it was with the overenthusiasm for special classes, especially classes for the mildly mentally retarded. Wisconsin, for example, in 1927 had defined the mentally retarded psychometrically as those having an IQ below 70. When funds became available for such special classes in the 1950s, school systems began to raise the IQ eligibility requirement to 75, 78, and higher.

In 1962 the American Association on Mental Deficiency defined as mildly retarded those children testing below minus one standard deviation or having an IQ of 84 or 85 and below. This eligibility criterion caused a great increase in enrollment in these classes, especially among minority groups. In addition, special education personnel readily accepted the slow and problem children referred to the special classes. They didn't exactly say, "Give me your tired, your poor,/Your huddled masses . . . . , " but they did say, "Give us your slow learners, your behavior problems, your misfits . . . ." Dr. Lloyd Dunn called this "The Sheltering Arms" philosophy. During this period, elementary teachers supported the expansion of special classes because this removed from their classes children who were causing them some problems.

The overenthusiasm for classes for the mentally retarded resulted in their becoming the dumping grounds for all unwanted children in the regular grades, including behavior problems, bilingual children, Blacks, Mexican-Americans, and Native Americans whose IQs were low, often because of language or cultural differences. Ethnic groups took special educators to court, and, fortunately, won. A reform was brewing. New ideas were needed. The concept of special classes in public schools which kept the children out of institutions, at home, and in the community was now called segregation. The new movement was mainstreaming.

Mainstreaming. The enthusiastic advocates for mainstreaming tended to disregard certain facts. (1) Mainstreaming is not new. It has been practiced since 1913 when so-called "sight-saving" classes were established in subjects requiring close eye work. "Special" students attended regular classes for other studies. (2) Speech-impaired children have always been placed in regular classrooms but given itinerant therapy. (3) Hard-of-hearing children, since the advent of the vacuum tube hearing aid, have attended regular grades but are given short periods of instruction in speech, lip reading, and the use of hearing aids. (4) Some mentally retarded and other slow-learning children have been placed in "resource rooms" with well-trained teachers. As early as 1936, Godfrey Stevens, one of my first graduates, established such a class in South Milwaukee.

Although mainstreaming is philosophically a sound idea, our enthusiasm for it is gradually waning because we have failed to train regular teachers to teach and manage these children. The grants to deans of college of education, referred to as Deans Grants, which were made by the U.S. Department of Education to educate teachers to deal with minor handicaps are, as usual, a drop in the bucket for such a task. Teachers will not be prepared for their duties by attending conferences or being harangued by their superiors or college professors about their duty to teach all the children of all the people. Taking the children out of the classes for short periods in resource rooms for tutoring in the academic subjects may not tilt the scales. Today, many regular educators are dissatisfied because they feel they have been given additional responsibilities without adequate support. Although the philosophy calls for consultation and support, adequate professional support is lacking in many school systems.

Our mistake, as usual, was to launch a program without adequate preparation and without really training the classroom teacher. I recommended to an advocate of mainstreaming many years ago that he teach a second or third grade of 30 children, accept into that class three or four mentally retarded, learning-disabled, and emotionally disturbed children, and study exactly how mainstreaming could be accomplished adequately. He did not accept my suggestion. As everyone knows, it is easy to tell someone else what to do, but it is more difficult to accomplish the task adequately and to describe exactly how it is done. We, as yet, have no detailed description of how mainstreaming is accomplished nor an exact distribution of responsibilities of both regular and resource teachers. Until and unless this is done, mainstreaming for the mentally retarded may falter or fail. Mainstreaming for other handicapped children is more readily accepted.

Community Service for the Severely Handicapped. Another major development for service has been the organization of community services for the severely retarded. Community centers for the severely retarded are now well established organizations. State institutions for the mentally retarded have been gradually replaced by community services. Although Samuel Gridley Howe, who organized the first institution, warned against their continuance saying they may be "created needlessly, sometimes even in violation of political economy . . ." (p. 4), he considered institutions as temporary and advocated boarding with families in private homes (Howe, 1957).

In 1955 Kirk, Karnes, and Kirk advocated a total community program for the retarded to be supported and managed by an intermediate governmental unit such as a county. It was proposed that this total community program include: (1) a diagnostic center, (2) a family counseling center, (3) a temporary residential unit, (4) a day care unit, and (5) a sheltered workshop (Kirk, Karnes, & Kirk, 1955, Chapter 12). Approximately 12 to 15 years later, community programs were organized in the United States after Denmark demonstrated their feasibility. This is another example that shows the lag between an idea and its implementation in social movements. How to decrease this lag is a problem for future generations.

Services for the Learning Disabled. The field of learning disabilities is experiencing the same types of expansion and difficulties encountered in programs for the educable mentally retarded. Originally we conceived of a child with a learning disability as one who has a major psychological or neurological impediment to the learning of reading, spelling, writing, or arithmetic. These are relatively rare cases, probably only 1% or 2% of school children. Today, however, the term learning disability applies to nearly every kind of learning problem a child may encounter.

That heterogeneous part of the population—now labeled learning disabled for funding purposes—appears today to consist mainly of all children not achieving up to grade level in the academic subjects, plus children with minor language problems. Whereas in 1969, 120,000 learning disabled children were reported to be enrolled in public school services, in 1982–83 over one and two-thirds million are enrolled in these services. This probably means that many slow-learning children formerly classified as mentally retarded and many children with minor reading difficulties are being assigned to learning disability services.

Before our overenthusiasm and expansion of services generates a backlash, it is necessary to find a resolution since nonlearning-disabled children with learning problems (slow learners and those with minor reading difficulties) also need services. I should like to propose two types of service delivery systems:

1. One service would include only the severely learning-disabled children who need intensive remediation, probably one hour a day, five days a week. Such children have a marked academic disability associated with a significant psychological or developmental learning disability of atten-

tion, memory, language, and so forth. The remedial program would be designed to ameliorate both the developmental learning disability and the academic disability. Such a child can attend the regular grade when not in intensive remediation. One special teacher will be able to serve only six or seven such children each day.

2. The second service would assist children who are educationally retarded as result of lack of motivation, lack of school attendance, inadequate instruction, and other environmental conditions. Such children can be educated in the regular grades supplemented by resource rooms for part of the day or through consultation and help of the regular teacher. One remedial teacher may serve 20 to 30 such children since they will learn by methods of teaching used for regular children.

Teacher Education

Having had experience in the preparation of teachers in both a teachers college and in a university, I regret that teachers colleges have tried to upgrade themselves by becoming universities instead of upgrading teacher education. By becoming universities, they have tended to minimize the importance of teacher preparation, and have begun to emphasize research and publication as their major function.

I was shocked when I went to a university from a teachers college to find that students studied theoretical courses but only had nine weeks of practice teaching in a single elementary class. The supervisor was usually a professor who had not been in a classroom for many years (if at all) and for supervision depended mainly upon the critic teacher to teach the students how to teach. At another university two professors taught the courses in mental retardation and supposedly supervised 70 students a year who had a half-day practicum throughout the semester.

Professors of education in universities and colleges of education are forced to become split personalities because their promotion in rank and pay is dependent upon their scholarly research and publications. Teacher training for those desiring quick promotion becomes a secondary duty.

It may be advisable in the future to establish centers, either as separate teacher colleges or within universities, that would require a master teacher faculty to devote 100% of their time to the preparation of teachers. Their promotion in rank and pay would be contingent upon their performance as experts in the preparation of teachers, rather than upon the length of their bibliography.

University faculties of education can then concentrate on graduate teaching and research and need not be encumbered with teacher training. Our current system of teacher training in universities with pressure on the faculty to "publish or perish" is not always accomplishing our objective of graduating master teachers or even producing many research-training and -motivated personnel. In other words, we need a two-track system for faculties, one group of faculty to devote 100% of their time to the preparation of teachers and another who would give 100% of their time to the advancement of knowledge and graduate teaching.

Graduate Programs in Special Education

In 1947, when I accepted a position at the University of Illinois, I tried desperately to find Ph.D.s who had some specialization in special education. The two or three Ph.D.s in existence at that time were directing programs and were unavailable. Since then, and with federal fellowships for graduate training, we now have a supply of individuals with doctorates in special education. The programs that have evolved have become varied, some stressing research with a heavy minor in psychology and some stressing service, teacher training, and administration. There appears to be little differentiation in course content and experience for a Ph.D. and an Ed.D.

It is my belief that there should be a difference between a Ph.D. and an Ed.D. A Ph.D. should be offered to those who desire a career in research in one or more of the areas of special education. These individuals should have had training and experience in at least one area of special education and should, at the graduate level, obtain a cognate or minor in psychology (for the areas of mental retardation, the emotionally disturbed, or learning disabilities) and in linguistics, or speech and language, or speech pathology (for the area of the hearing impaired). Such an individual will then know the major problems needing investigation and the research methodology to investigate them. The dissertation would be of an experimental nature.

An Ed.D. should require a different course of study. Since it is a professional degree, the dissertation need not be required. In its stead, the student should take an extra year to intern in supervision, administration, or teacher training. The Ph.D. degree would require a minimum of two years of course work and a substantive experimental dissertation, while the Ed.D. degree would require four years of graduate work to cover all areas of handicapped children, to intern or to conduct survey studies on problems encountered in teacher education and administration.

A two-tract system for doctoral students would allow them to concentrate either on theory and scientific methodology or on the applied and technological areas needed for quality services to handicapped children.

Research and Research Training

It was indicated that the earlier research efforts in special education were conducted in state and private residential schools; the Vineland Training School, the Wayne County Training School, and the Central Institute for the Deaf are examples. In these institutions researchers with ideas had subjects upon which research could be conducted. After World War II and with the expansion of universities, many of them moved to universities. The availability of subjects became a problem unless arrangements were made with the schools or institutions.

Currently, few residential institutions employ research personnel and few university faculties have readily available subjects for research. The problem of clearing a research project with a number of committees in a university, and then clearing it with a school board, school or institutional superintendent, and finally with parents has created a bureaucratic climate not conducive to research.

Federal funding for research has been quite useful in many instances, but the major problem here has been the short-term nature of grants. Good research is developed gradually with programmatic research. Federal grants with yearly reports and varying funding have tended to produce short-term or incomplete research projects, whose reports conclude with the traditional remark that "more research is needed." One wonders sometimes in reading some of the data-based research reports how much the results are objective and how much they are stretched to obtain further research grants.

Research production needs continuous and stable funding. It needs to be conducted in schools and other facilities which serve handicapped children. It needs a cooperative arrangement on a permanent basis between the service agencies and a university. An example is the former Institute for Research on Exceptional Children at the University of Illinois which produced a great deal of research in a 10-year period and offered a research climate for doctoral students. This organization, a cooperative effort of the Department of Welfare in charge of institutions, the state Department of Public Instruction, and the state university, has not been repeated or continued on a regular basis.

One of the difficulties encountered by this institute was that it became too large. When it operated with four and five highly dedicated research professors and a small group of selected doctoral students, research was accomplished. Generous private and federal funding increased the projects and personnel. Unfortunately, at that time there was a shortage of research personnel, and less competent individuals were employed to conduct these projects. This expansion of research with partly inadequate personnel tended to decrease the quality of research.

The lesson to be learned from the institute venture is that big is not better. If I were to do it over again, it would remain small with only four or five productive professors and a small group of highly qualified doctoral students. The desire to bring more money into the university and to expand and expand may not be in the best interests of research and development.

The Federal Roles

Education has traditionally been the responsibility of local and state governments. During the last two and one-half decades the federal government has entered the scene, first in research, second in the training of professional personnel, and last in services to equalize education for handicapped and minority children. Under the Reagan administration, an attempt is being made to decrease federal funding for all three programs—research, teacher training, and service.

It is not the purpose of this essay to discuss the pros and cons of the federal budget, but rather to present a personal opinion about our past, and possibly, our future. These opinions are naturally biased and based on my own experience. As indicated, it has been my privilege to help in forming policies, first under the Eisenhower administration when support for research for the mentally retarded was initiated and second, when funds for the preparation of professional personnel for the mentally retarded and for the deaf were appropriated. In addition, I served for a short period as a bureaucrat administering the Kennedy bill, P.L. 85-926 in 1963 and 1964. I also served as chairman of the Advisory Committee for the Handicapped for two years after the creation of the Bureau for the Education of the Handicapped and also as chairman of the Psychosocial Research Committee for Vocational Rehabilitation. Consequently, I have intimate knowledge of the role of the federal government in special education from its first intervention until now.

My comments about these developments are as follows:

First, special education would probably still be in its primitive stages if it were not for the federal leadership in research and in the preparation of professional personnel. These two support systems have made special education an important segment of education in general. Although some states, like California and Illinois, were making rapid strides for a number of years without the support of the federal government, the other states were moving very slowly.

Secondly, one concern about federal aid is that the funds allotted tend to determine the direction of the programs. When research funds became available, universities training doctoral students emphasized the training of research personnel. When teacher training subsidies were appropriated, departments of special education tended to direct their programs toward the preparation of administrators and teacher trainees. There is no question that financial support influences the direction of programs. If the federal government continues in support of research (as I think it should since research results are of national importance), some system should be developed to support the best researchers without harassment or pressure of political influence.

Thirdly, when BEH was organized, an Advisory Committee for the Handicapped was formed which was to be composed of professionals and citizens from the field. I was privileged to be chairman of this committee during the first two years. This advisory committee reviewed the work of the bureau, helped protect it from unreasonable demands of outside special interest groups, and protected it from itself. It also recommended new legislation to Congress. The advisory committee assisted the development of the bureau for the first few years but was later abolished because the appointees to the committee were selected primarily on the basis of political affiliation and their support of the administration. An advisory committee should be reinstated, but its members should be recommended for appointment by some objective group outside the federal government.

Where Do We Go from Here?

The history of special education has indicated that we tend to move enthusiastically in one direction, become disillusioned with that program, and then become enthusiastic in another direction. We first thought that residential schools would solve the problems of the care and education of the handicapped. After 50 years of building institutions, we found this procedure was not the answer. We then became enthusiastic about day schools and self-contained special classes in public schools. After 50 or more years, we decided that these classes were not the answer. We then became enthusiastic over mainstreaming. Today, some feel that mainstreaming is not the answer, especially for the mentally retarded. Many are raising questions about our future in special education.

It would be pretentious of me to predict the direction that special education will or should pursue in the next two decades. In spite of the significant progress that has been made since the end of World War II, many controversies and questionable practices still exist.

To solve many of these problems, I suggest that we create a National Center for the Study of Policies, Practices, and Issues in Special Education. This center should not be under governmental auspices, but should be privately endowed with sufficient funds to guarantee its independent existence for many years. It should be apolitical and free of pressures from private interest groups. Its function would be: (1) to study periodically practices in universities and colleges in the preparation of professional personnel and make recommendations for improvement, (2) to evaluate the practices in service delivery by local and state agencies and make recommendations for improvement, (3) to study current research productions and recommend directions for research, and (4) to investigate the current responsibilities of local, state, and federal agencies and make recommendations for the adequate division of responsibility.

This center could be staffed by a small group of the most objective and knowledgeable scholars in the field, who would be free to publish the results of their studies and deliberations and call a spade a spade without fear of political or financial recriminations. The independence of the center should be clearly delineated in the charter for its existence.

References

Binet, A. (1974). The educability of intelligence. In S.A. Kirk & F. Lord (Eds.), *Exceptional children: Educational resources and perspectives*. Boston: Houghton Mifflin Co.

Calfee, R. (1982). Cognitive psychology and education practice. In *Review of research in education* (pp. 3–74). Educational Research Association.

Fernald, G. M., & Keller, H. (1921, December). The effects of kinesthetic factors in the development of word recognition in the case of non-readers. *Journal of Educational Research, 4*, 355–377.

Hegge, T. G., Kirk, S. A., & Kirk, W. D. (1936). *Remedial reading drills*. Ann Arbor, MI: George Wahr.

Howe, S. G. (1974). Letter to the Governor of Massachusetts, 1957. In S.A. Kirk & F. Lord (Eds.), *Exceptional children: Educational resources and perspectives*. Boston: Houghton Mifflin Co.

Kirk, S. A. (1933, October). The influence of manual tracing on the learning of simple words in the case of subnormal boys. *Journal of Educational Psychology, 24*, 525–535.

Kirk, S. A. (1935). Hemispheric cerebral dominance and hemispheric equipotentiality. *Comparative Psychology Monographs, 11*. Baltimore: Johns Hopkins Press.

Kirk, S. A. (1940). *Teaching reading to slow learning children*. Boston: Houghton Mifflin Co.

Kirk, S .A. (1958). *Early education of the mentally retarded: An experimental study*. Urbana, IL: University of Illinois Press.

Kirk, S. A. (1964, June). Organization and implementation of programs for handicapped children and youth, Public Law 88-164, Title III, and Public Law 87-276. In *Administration of education programs for handicapped children*. Congressional Record. 88th Cong., 2nd sess.

Kirk, S. A. (1968, July). Statement before the Select Subcommittee on Education of the House Committee on Education and Labor on R.R. 17829. 90th Cong., 2nd sess.

Kirk, S. A. (1970). Reflections on learning disabilities. *Seventh Annual International Conference of the Association of Children with Learning Disabilities*. San Rafael, CA: Academic Therapy.

Kirk, S. A. (1978). The federal role in special education: Historical perspectives. *UCLA Educator*, Spring/Summer 20(2), 5–11.

Kirk, S. A., & Bateman, B. (1964). *Ten years of research at the Institute for Research on Exceptional Children*. Urbana, IL: University of Illinois Press.

Kirk, S A., & Gallagher, J. (1979). *Educating exceptional children* (3rd ed.). Boston: Houghton Mifflin.

Kirk, S. A., Karnes, M. B., & Kirk, W. D. (1955). *You and your retarded child: A manual for parents of retarded children*. New York: Macmillan & Co.

Kirk, S. A., & Kirk, W. D. (1971). *Psycholinguistic learning disabilities: Diagnosis and remediation*. Urbana, IL: University of Illinois Press.

Kirk, S. A., & Kirk, W. D. (1978, March). The uses and abuses of the ITPA. *American Journal of Speech and Hearing Disorders, 43*, 58–75.

Kirk, S. A., & Lord, F. (1974). *Exceptional children: Educational resources and perspectives.* Boston: Houghton Mifflin Co.

Kirk, S. A., McCarthy, J. J., & Kirk, W. D. (1968). *The Illinois Test of Psycholinguistic abilities* (rev. ed.). Urbana, IL: University of Illinois Press.

Kirk, S. A., & Spalding, W. B. (1953, May). The Institute for Research on Exceptional Children at the University of Illinois. *The Educational Forum*, pp. 413–422.

Kirk, S. A., & Stevens, I. (1943, April). A pre-academic curriculum for slow learning children. *American Journal of Mental Deficiency, 47*(4), 396–406.

Monroe, M. (1932). *Children who cannot read.* Chicago: University of Chicago Press.

National Advisory Committee on Handicapped Children. (1968). *First annual report, Subcommittee on Education of the Committee on Labor and Public Welfare, U.S. Senate.* Washington, DC: U.S. Government Printing Office.

National Advisory Committee on Handicapped Children. (1969). *Second annual report, Subcommittee on Education of the Committee on Labor and Public Welfare, U.S. Senate.* Washington, DC: U.S. Government Printing Office.

National Advisory Committee on Handicapped Children. (1970). *Third annual report, Subcommittee on Education of the Committee on Labor and Public Welfare, U.S. Senate.* Washington, DC: U.S. Government Printing Office.

Nickel, V. L. (1954). *Report on the study projects for trainable mentally handicapped children.* Springfield, IL: Department of Public Instruction.

Spearman, C. (1927). *The nature of intelligence and the principles of cognition.* London: Macmillan & Co., Ltd.

Strauss, A. A., & Lehtinen, L. (1947). *Psychopathology of the brain-injured child.* New York: Grune & Stratton.

Wallin, J. E. Wallace. (1924). *The education of handicapped children.* Boston: Houghton Mifflin Co.

Part II

Early Childhood Special Education

INTRODUCTION

MERLE B. KARNES
Colonel Wolfe School
Champaign, Illinois

I had the good fortune in 1950 to become the educational director of a pioneer program for preschool children with mental retardation with Dr. Samuel A. Kirk as the principal investigator. The project was located in a house on the campus of the University of Illinois which was owned by the university and renovated for this project. The project was a joint effort of four agencies: the Illinois State Department of Public Instruction, the Division of Special Education under Ray Graham, the outstanding Illinois state Director of Special Education; the Community Unit IV Schools located in Champaign, Illinois (Dr. E. H. Mellon, superintendent, was well known for his interest in and commitment to Special Education); the University of Illinois, the Department of Special Education, under the leadership of Dr. Samuel A. Kirk (Director of the Institute for Exceptional Children), an internationally recognized researcher and leader in special education; and the Institute of Public Health of the federal government. The financial resources to conduct the project were drawn from all four agencies.

By meshing together the expertise provided by these four institutions, the project was able to receive the kinds of support necessary to launch a research project of this magnitude. It is interesting to note that the grant from the federal government, made by the Institute of Public Health, was the first federal grant received by the College of Education at the University of Illinois. The project generated a great deal of nationwide interest. Dr. Kirk was frequently called upon at professional meetings to discuss the project and report interim results. For many years after the project was terminated and his book on the project was published, there was continued interest in his research project.

As indicated in Part I, Dr. Kirk played an important role in promoting early federal legislation for young children with disabilities. Unfortunately, it wasn't until 20 years after his research findings that the Children's Early Assistance Act was finally passed in 1968. He then served as chair of the advisory committee charged with developing plans for implementing the act.

The federal government is to be commended for its role in encouraging the identification and programming for young children with disabilities since the passage of the Children's Early Assistance Act. In the first year (1969), only $1 million was allocated, through which 24 demonstration projects were funded. These grants were funded for a 3-year period to develop, demonstrate, and disseminate viable models. In the 23 years since then, some 500 demonstration projects have been funded. Since the mid-1970s, some 200 projects with demonstrated effectiveness have been granted monies for outreach to help interested sites replicate their model. In addition, research institutes and technical assistance projects have been funded to provide the knowledge and technical assistance to move forward the field of early education for children with disabilities. Currently, federal legislation makes it mandatory to identify and program for young children with disabilities down to the age of 3.

Kirk was ahead of his time in focusing on and researching critical questions regarding early education of children with disabilities. Many of his beliefs, the issues he identified, and the solutions he proposed for dealing with these issues have been recognized and dealt with over the years. Some still remain unsolved. In the remainder of this introduction, I will compare Kirk's pioneer program with what is considered best practice today. The following represent what experts in the field feel are essential components of an exemplary program.

Identification (Screening and Diagnosis)

Kirk's procedures for identifying the children who were eligible for admission to his preschool program consisted of a house-to-house canvas of certain areas of Champaign/Urbana that seemed to produce the largest number of children with disabilities. The public schools also provided lists of younger children from families that had older children in classes for students with mental retardation. Social agencies, the university speech clinic, and pediatricians also referred some children. There was no screening instrument on the market. Data gathered from agencies, the parents, and schools were used to determine whether or not a child should be seen by a diagnostic team to determine eligibility for the program. A staffing meeting was held after the child was seen by the diagnostic team (school psychologist, pediatrician, speech therapist, social worker, and other ancillary staff such as a physical therapist or occupational therapist). At the staffing meeting, goals for the child were developed, much like the individualized education program (IEP) educators currently develop.

One major difference between the Kirk program and programs today was that parents were not involved in determining the child's eligibility and in formulating the goals for the child.

At that time, the Stanford-Binet Individual Intelligence test was administered to all of the children. Other tests were administered, contingent upon the disabilities of the child. There are tests currently available to psychologists that were not developed at the time of Kirk's project.

Ongoing Assessment and Programming

There was no commercially available, ongoing assessment instrument for teachers to use in Kirk's preschool. The teachers depended largely on the information they received at the initial staffing meeting and on their judgment based on informal observation of each child. The current practice, using ongoing assessment linked with the program, is a significant contribution the demonstration projects have made. There are a number of ongoing assessment instruments on the market, and some programs are still using project-developed instruments. Consequently, teachers are now better equipped to diagnose children's instructional needs than in the early days.

When Kirk initiated his project, there was little published curriculum for young children. Virtually no textbooks or instructional materials for young children with disabilities had been published. As I recall, teachers made their own material using pictures from mail-order catalogs and popular magazines. We now have a wealth of materials that have been generated in recent years. Some publishers offer separate catalogs for early childhood.

The emphasis in Kirk's project was largely on cognition. Language development, which is subsumed under cognition, was given considerable attention since nearly every child was lagging behind in language. The program could best be described as teacher-directed. The curriculum covered all aspects of a well-balanced curriculum (science, social studies, math, music, art, drama, and free play). Today's typical program also is characterized largely as teacher directed, concentrating primarily on accomplishing the goals delineated in the IEP.

One major difference is that Kirk's program was a full-day program. Children were provided with lunch each day and a rest period on cots each afternoon. Today, mainly because of the expense, most programs are half-day programs, with children attending preschool from 2 to 3 hours.

Staffing Patterns

The staffing pattern of Kirk's project was much like the staffing patterns of today. The ratio of adults to children was and is 1 to 4 or 1 to 5. Some children have such serious needs that one adult to an individual child is required. This was also true in Kirk's project.

One major difference is that all teachers in Kirk's program were certified teachers, usually having a background in regular preschool, kindergarten, or special education. Kirk's project did not include paraprofessionals as teachers.

Parent Involvement

The Kirk project was committed to parent involvement. In fact, we wrote a book, which we used in training parents during evening sessions and which we entitled, *You and Your Retarded Child*, by Samuel A. Kirk, Merle B. Karnes, and Winifred D. Kirk. Parent participation included conferences with the teacher, visitation in the school, and attendance at training sessions. Working in the classroom was not an option for parents. Parent involvement at this time is broader in nature. A system approach is considered best practice, and family involvement characterizes most programs.

Teaming

Kirk used much the same approach in involving staff as we use today, with the exception that parents are more involved now than they were then. The approach Kirk used could be labeled *interdisciplinary*, and, at times, there were aspects that could be regarded as *transdisciplinary*. Today the transdisciplinary approach is considered by many as the preferred approach.

Child Management

An eclectic behavior management approach was used in the Kirk project by matching each child with what seemed the most appropriate approach. At this time, such an approach is also generally favored. A few years ago, an approach adapted from Skinner's philosophy, referred to as *behavior modification*, was very popular, especially at the University of Illinois. While principles of reinforcement for desirable behavior is felt to be critical in eliciting desirable behavior, an all-out behavior modification approach is currently not as popular as it once was.

Collaboration with Agencies

Both the pioneer study and programs today advocate working closely with agencies that are working with children with disabilities and their families or that have services to offer them. At times when financial resources are limited, it is important for agencies to band together to maximize the use of the limited financial resources available.

Record Keeping

Extensive record keeping was used in Kirk's study and is felt to be of paramount importance today. A systematic approach was used to gather data. Children were periodically staffed, decisions made by the team were recorded, and files were kept. Daily anecdotal records were made on the children and on contacts with the families.

Evaluation

While the terms *formative* and *summative evaluation* were not used at the time of Kirk's study, evaluation data were collected, analyzed, and used to make decisions and to determine the effectiveness of the program. Standardized tests were used on a pre-post basis, and there was a control group. Case studies were written on children and their families, and portfolios were kept on the children. What are considered appropriate procedures for evaluation today were used in this project. In fact, the evaluation was broader than a great majority of projects today.

One major difference in evaluation is that today we do not depend heavily on IQ tests to determine the effectiveness of a program as did Kirk in the early days. In the book Kirk wrote on his research project, he pointed out that there are some children who make significant gains when provided with a certain innovation and others who do not. He advocated that we need to make a study of the "winners" and "losers" and determine why some profit and some do not. We continue to make this recommendation today.

Inservice Training

At the time Kirk conducted his study, there were no training programs for teachers of preschool children with disabilities. Teachers had to be trained on the job. Today there are numerous training programs at universities and colleges. The federal government provides monies for personnel preparation in this field. Throughout the years, the professional growth of staff has been deemed important. Kirk thought inservice training was important. Today exemplary programs recognize that to keep up to date with the latest research and best practices, inservice training is a must.

Transition

Kirk and his staff felt that procedures for helping each child make a smooth transition from the preschool to the public schools was an essential part of a program. Today transition is felt to be so critical that the federal government has financed a research institute to study the issues and problems in transition.

In the 40 years since Kirk's study, we have learned a great deal more that we have incorporated into practice. The federal government is largely responsible for the strides that have been made in identifying and programming for the young who have disabilities. The blueprint of this federal program has been so effective it should be used by the government in formulating plans for other areas of education.

Kirk was certainly a pioneer in the field of early childhood education, especially for children with disabilities. His work raised many questions. However, many continue to be unanswered today. A few of these questions follow:

- How early should intervention be initiated?
- What kinds of information or products should be included in a portfolio?
- What procedures are most effective in evaluating the contents of a portfolio?
- How can we determine the appropriate intervention for an individual child?
- What procedures best assess the impact of an intervention on the child's self-concept and self-esteem?
- What teaching strategies best facilitate social acceptance among young children with disabilities?
- Are we so preoccupied with programming for disabilities that we are neglecting the strengths?
- What are we doing about identifying and programming for the young children with disabilities who are potentially gifted?
- What are the effects of placement of a young child with disabilities in various settings to provide the least restrictive environments?

Growth of professional organizations such as the Early Childhood Division of The Council for Exceptional Children, research reports in this field appearing in the journals, the number of trained personnel in the field, and federal and state legislation are indicative of how the field is growing and becoming more sophisticated. We still have a long way to go, but it seems certain that we are going to reach greater heights. It is a fascinating and exciting time for early childhood practitioners, researchers, teacher trainers, and parents of children with disabilities.

Merle B. Karnes earned a bachelor's degree in elementary education at Southeastern Missouri State Teachers College. She began her professional career as an elementary school teacher in Missouri in 1937, and later taught regular elementary classes in Kentucky, California, and Illinois. She obtained a master's degree at the University of Missouri in 1942 and a doctorate in supervision/administration and curriculum development in 1949. Her postdoctorate work at the University of Illinois focused on special education. In the late 1940s, Dr. Karnes directed a pioneer educational program for young children with disabilities of which Samuel A. Kirk was special investigator. In 1953, she became director of special services in the Champaign, Illinois, Community IV Schools. In 1966, she accepted a faculty position at the University of Illinois in the College of Education, Department of Special Education. Currently she is professor emeritus and directs several projects focusing on children with disabilities, young gifted children from middle- and upper-socioeconomic-level homes, children with disabilities who are also gifted, and children from low income homes who are potentially gifted.

Dr. Karnes has written more than 200 books, monographs, chapters in books, and articles, as well as more than 20 instructional packages for young children. She frequently appears as a speaker at state and federal conferences and conducts workshops for Head Start and public school personnel. Among the many awards she has received over the years is the J. E. Wallace Wallin award from The Council for Exceptional Children in 1976. She has been president of CEC's Division of Early Childhood and editor of its journal for 8 years.

Chapter 2

Preschool and Early Education Programs for Handicapped Children

Mr. Kirk: Mr. Chairman, I appreciate very much the opportunity to testify in favor of H.R. 17829, the Handicapped Children's Early Education Act.

This area is not a new interest of mine. I have been for many years conducting research or directing research on the effects of early education on the development of handicapped children.

My research as well as the research of others has demonstrated quite conclusively that early education of children is beneficial, and that if we are able to initiate training at a very early age, the probability is that the child will be less handicapped in the years that follow.

Permit me to cite just a few examples from research.

In 1949 I initiated an experiment on young mentally handicapped children between the ages of 3 and 5. The purpose of this research was to determine if training begun with these children at the ages of 3 to 5 would ameliorate their handicap.

These children were mentally retarded and many of them had handicaps other than mental retardation, such as cerebral palsy, hearing handicaps, and visual handicaps.

In one experiment we organized a training program for 4-year-old children whom the courts had committed to the state institution as feebleminded on the recommendation of two physicians.

Twelve other children of the same ages and mental disabilities were selected as a contrast group or control group. The training group of 15 children remained under special training for 2 years, while the contrast group of 12 children remained on the wards of an institution, without special training. Both groups of children entered the institution's school (or if paroled, to a regular school) at age 6.

Statement of Samuel Kirk, Chairman, National Advisory Committee on Handicapped Children, to the Select Subcommittee on Education of the Committee on Education and Labor, House of Representatives. Hearings held in Washington, DC, July 16 and 17, 1968.

When the children were 7 1/2 to 8 years of age both groups were reexamined. The following graph [see Figure 1] depicts the results:

FIGURE 1
IQ and SQ Change Scores of Institutionalized Retarded Children as a Function of Preschool Experience

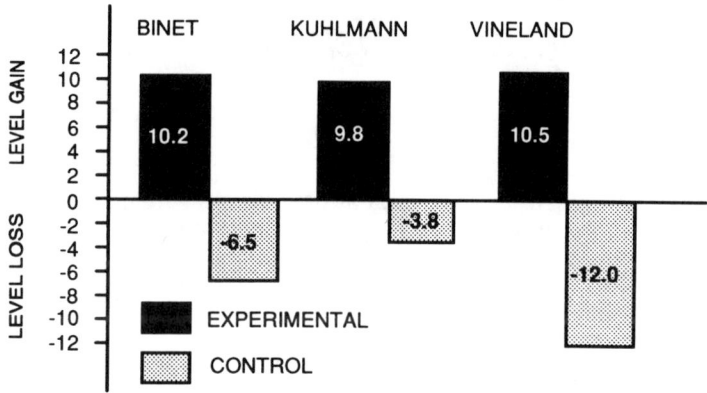

Source: Kirk, S. A. (1965). Diagnostic and remedial factors in mental retardation. In *Biosocial Basis of Mental Retardation*, The Johns Hopkins Press, p. 137.

It will be noted from this graph that the 15 experimental children increased their mental and social abilities, while the other 12 children who remained in the wards, but who later attended the institution school, dropped in rate of mental and social development over a period of 4 years.

Intelligence and social maturity quotients are only one way of demonstrating the effects of early educational experience. The main test is how these children adjust to life. Our follow-up studies revealed important results.

1. Of the 15 children who had received specialized training in the institution between the ages of 4 and 6, six of them were permanently paroled from the institution.
2. Of the 12 children who did not receive preschool training, not a single one was paroled from the institution. This is understandable since they were more mentally retarded at the age of 8 than they had been at the age of 4 as indicated on the graph, which shows a drop.

I have been interested in one of the children in the experimental group for many years. He was committed to the institution because of "convulsions and feeblemindedness."

Repeated evaluations verified the diagnosis of mental retardation, but not convulsions. Under preschool education, he made sensational improvement. He was paroled at the age of 5 1/2, placed in a foster home, and later adopted by a superior family. At the age of 22 this boy is now a junior in college and is earning above-average grades.

It has been estimated that it costs approximately $75,000 to send a child to an institution for the mentally deficient and to retain him there for his lifetime.

If we apply this type of economics to the results of this experiment, we can say that paroling six of the 15 children under training, we have saved the State $450,000.

The cost for the experiment in the institution for the 15 children and the examination of the 12 control children cost less than $45,000.

In another experiment, this one in a middle-sized community, we admitted to a special community preschool 16 mentally retarded children and compared them with their twin brothers or sisters or their siblings who did not attend preschool.

Four of the 16 children were taken out of their inadequate homes by social agencies and placed in foster homes as well as in a specialized preschool. The other 12 children remained at home but were enrolled in the specialized preschool for mentally retarded children.

The twins and siblings of these children remained at home during the preschool years without the benefit of preschool education, but were admitted to the public schools at the age of 6.

As in the institution experiment, the average age of the experimental and control children was 4 1/2 years.

As indicated the experimental children attended the preschool up to the age of 6, then were enrolled in public school classes. The twins and siblings stayed in their homes until the age of 6, and then were admitted to the public school classes.

At the age of 8, after 1 1/2 years in the public schools for both groups, all the children were reexamined.

The following graph [see Figure 2] compares the four foster home and preschool children, the 12 children who remained at home but attended the preschool to age 6, and the 15 siblings and twins who remained at home and did not enter school until they were enrolled in the public schools at age 6. Please note:

1. The four children who had the most drastic change of environment, foster home, and preschool, made the most gains.
2. The 12 children who remained at home but attended the preschool to age six, made the next greatest gains.

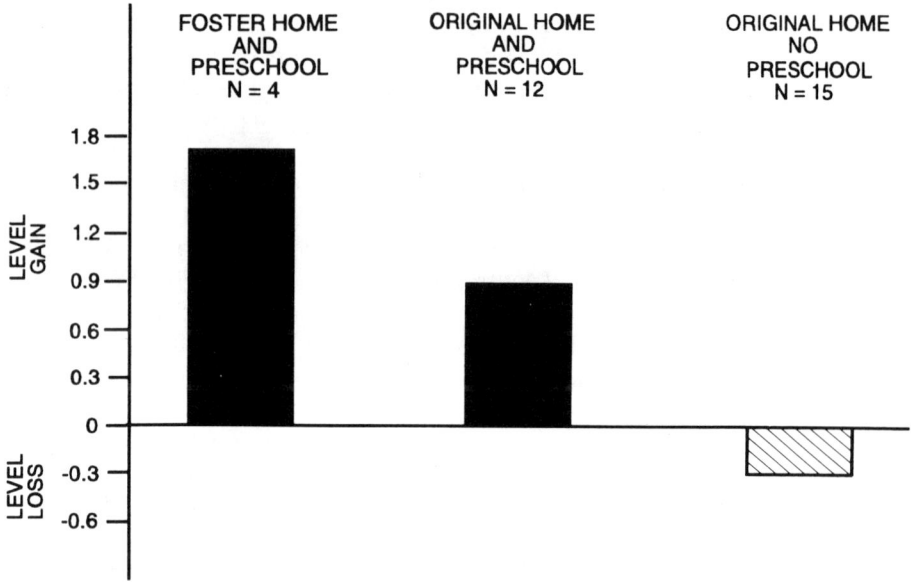

FIGURE 2

Average Change in Levels of Development as a Function of Preschool and Foster Home Experience

3. The 15 children who remained at home until the age of six (and then attended the public school) dropped in rate of mental development. In spite of two years in the public schools these 15 children were lower in rate of mental development at the age of eight than they had been at the age of four.

4. In contrast, the 16 children who had the benefits of a preschool were higher in rate of mental development at age eight, than they were at age four.

These are some of the experiments I have reported in a book entitled *Early Education of the Mentally Retarded*. It was published by the University of Illinois Press in 1958.

This report, in spite of its demonstration of the effects of specialized preschool education, made little or no impact in practice. People read it, decided it was a great report, but stated that they had no money to implement the research in practice.

I was not the first or only one to report such results. The lag between research and implementation in practice is demonstrated dramatically in the work of Dr. Harold Skeels.

As long ago as 1939, Dr. Skeels took 13 mentally retarded infants from an orphanage at ages 1 and 2, placed them in an institution for mental defectives, but provided these babies with mental stimulation in the wards of the institution by giving them 1-to-1 relationships with older girls and women.

He retained in the orphanage 11 infants who were not as markedly retarded. After 2 years he reexamined these two groups. The children who had received early education had increased their I.Q.'s by 28 points, while the 11 children who remained without early stimulation in an orphanage dropped 26 points.

Dr. Skeels' experiment was sensational—so sensational no one would believe it. As a matter of fact, he was severely criticized by his colleagues for publishing this report. They did not believe it was possible to produce such results and wrote it off as unsound research. It conflicted with the prevailing theories that I.Q.'s are fixed by heredity and unmodifiable by training and experience.

Dr. Skeels dropped the work during the war, and after the war obtained a position with the Public Health Service. He was discouraged by the negative reception of his report.

After the publication of my study on institutional and community children, and similar results by other investigators, Dr. Skeels' results a decade before did not seem fantastic.

Dr. Skeels then decided that he would make a follow-up study of his two groups after 21 years. This he did, and published the results in 1967.

The results showed that all of the 13 children who had increased their I.Q.'s as a result of early education were self-supporting as adults. He found that one-half of the 11 children who remained in the orphanage without early stimulation were now in institutions as permanent public charges.

Members of the profession and society in general, could no longer scoff at Dr. Skeels' results. Twenty-nine years after the research report, the American Psychological Association gave Dr. Skeels a merit award, and the Joseph P. Kennedy Foundation awarded Dr. Skeels the Fourth International Kennedy Award in Mental Retardation in April 1968 (approximately 30 years after his first report).

A dramatic incident occurred at the presentation of the Kennedy Award. The Kennedy Foundation had arranged to have one of Dr. Skeels' former so-called mentally retarded babies from the experiment present at the award session. This man, then a graduate student at a major university, made the presentation of the award to Dr. Skeels.

I present these cases to demonstrate the lag between research findings in the social sciences and their implementation in practice. In spite of Dr. Skeels' results in 1939, and my results between 1949 and 1958, implementation of our findings has not yet occurred.

In spite of the present acceptance by social scientists, by schools, and parents, that amelioration of mental and physical handicaps is often possible if initiated at an early age, very little has occurred in practice.

The reason for this lag is not that we do not know what to do with handicapped preschool children. It is not because of lack of finances in an already underfinanced school system. No one today except a few parent groups who have the resources are able to organize preschool education programs for their handicapped children.

In summary, permit me to repeat.

1. Research has pointed out that alleviation and amelioration of mental and physical handicaps is most effectively accomplished during the early years of life.
2. Social scientists have developed effective procedures by which these children can be educated.
3. Implementation of research findings in this area will not occur, as it has not occurred, without Federal support and stimulation.
4. Neglect of this problem further will mean an increase in prevalence of handicapped children at older ages, and greater expense in care, education, and management to local, state, and national agencies.

I, therefore, humbly urge in the national interest, that this committee give favorable consideration of H.R. 17829.

It is necessary to develop model programs in communities, if we expect to eventually prevent and decrease handicapping conditions in American society.

Mr. Daniels: Thank you. Dr. Kirk, I want to commend you for your very fine statement. Because of the lateness of the hour, the Chair is going to forego questions and call upon the gentleman from Pennsylvania to present his questions.

Mr. Dent: As usual, time runs out in these hearings, but I want to salute you for your many years of devotion in this particular field that often goes unrewarded. I know your material will be very helpful to the committee.

Of all the other handicaps we human beings are afflicted with, this is probably the worst of all as it is in the mental processes of the mentally retarded.

I applaud those like yourself who have devoted so much time and interest to trying to get the legislative branch of government to recognize this situation and have it recognized by the public. I salute you.

Mr. Daniels: Mr. Quie?

Mr. Quie: I commend you, and I note that you have mentioned Dr. Skeels' work; it is sensational. On the bottom of page 6, you mentioned the drop off of Dr. Skeels' work because he was discouraged by the negative reception given his report. Could you elaborate on that?

I would hope we don't have to wait 20 or 30 years after experimentation for implementing the programs. That would be too long.

Dr. Kirk: I think you know there were many studies in the early days on the inheritance of mental defects. It was thought that these defects were inherited, and there was nothing to do but take care of them.

I think Dr. Skeels' studies contradicted scientific findings at that time. Dr. Skeels was criticized by his associates. One critic said that Dr. Skeels' results advocated that we take our children and place them under the care of other retarded older girls in the ward instead of leaving them with their mothers.

He became discouraged and gave up doing any work with young, foster home, and mentally retarded children.

For 20 years we did not hear much about Skeels, but after I conducted an extensive study with 81 children in communities and institutions and received a favorable response from social scientists—because I think I possibly controlled some of the factors criticized in Dr. Skeels' studies—this revived the interest in Dr. Skeels' earlier experiments.

We asked Dr. Skeels to follow up these people and find out what happened. Dr. Skeels visited every one of the former babies. He went to Iowa, got addresses and followed them up to Florida, to Phoenix, and to other parts of the United States, and interviewed the 13 children in the experimental group and 11 children from the orphanage. He found out of the 13 children in the experiment, all of them were now self-supporting. Five or six of the 11 children that remained in the orphanage and that were later paroled had now been committed to some institution for the mentally retarded or emotionally disturbed.

Mr. Quie: It is my understanding that either one or two of those 13 went on to graduate degrees.

Dr. Kirk: One went for a graduate degree. He presented the award to Dr. Skeels at the Kennedy dinner. Senator Kennedy introduced this man, since he was no longer a baby. He had been removed from the institution and placed in a foster home. Before the follow-up studies, this man did not know he was part of the experiment until Dr. Skeels interviewed him and found him as a graduate student at the University of Iowa. He also was interviewed on the "Today Show" with Dr. Skeels. The case I reported as currently a junior in college was, at the age of 4, not talking. At that age, he was sitting in the wards, had an abnormal EEG, and [was] diagnosed as a child with a brain defect. At the age of 8, I had these examinations repeated, and he still had an abnormal

EEG. Since then, he has finished grade school, high school, and is now a junior in college.

The point I am trying to make is that some of these children can be rehabilitated at an early age. Others who do not obtain this help tend to remain problems and public charges.

For if they do not obtain help at an early age, the handicap increases. If we do something at an early age, we can elevate them to a point where they are able to function. I believe that if we are able to organize preschool education and develop it in this country we would be able to decrease handicapping conditions in vision, hearing, mental handicaps, emotionally disturbed, and learning disabilities by a substantial proportion of our society.

Mr. Daniels: On behalf of all the members of the committee I extend to you our thanks for your excellent testimony.

Dr. Kirk: Thank you.

Chapter 3

The Effects of Early Intervention

SAMUEL A. KIRK

It was a pleasure to review Dr. Miller's paper on theories and studies of the effects of intervention on culturally disadvantaged children. You should be complimented for bringing together many points of view from numerous publications in a field in which rigid scientific controls in such studies are very difficult.

I should like in this discussion to (a) elaborate on some of the topics he discussed, (b) focus on some recent results that appear to be consistent, and (c) indicate how far we are from definitive answers to the numerous questions raised by his paper.

The general topic under discussion relates to the old nature-nurture controversy that has plagued us for years. Can intervention at an early age accelerate intellectual development? If so, how much? And what kinds of intervention procedures produce results?

Since the results of studies thus far reported are not definitive, most of us render opinions, with supporting evidence from the literature that reinforces our own opinions. In other words, most of us have biases, and I am no exception.

In 1940, I made the following naive statement:

> Although recent evidence on the influence of environment on the IQ is taken by some to indicate intelligence is the product of training, there are others who cling to the view that intelligence is fixed by inheritance. The answer is probably somewhere between the two views. It is probable that inheritance fixes the limits of intelligence, but that there is a large range within band which the environment can raise or lower the I.Q. It is possible that a child may be born with an intelligence range of 70 to 110. A stimulating environment will probably show his I.Q. to be 110, while a routinized unstimulating environment will show his I.Q. to be 70. (Kirk, 1940, p. 45)

From H. R. Haywood (Ed.). *Social-Cultural Aspects of Mental Retardation*. New York: Appleton-Century-Crofts, 1970, pp. 490–495.

In other words, I believed at that time, 28 years ago, and I still believe today (rigidity), that environment[al] intervention accelerates social and mental development, within certain limits, based on genetic or physical limitations.

Since that time, some geneticists have postulated a concept to account for the interactionist position mentioned by Dr. Miller. Dobzhansky (1955) and Allen (1958) discussed the so-called norms of reaction or reaction range notion, which states that a genotype may determine a variety of phenotypes, each of which corresponds to the kind of environment to which it is exposed. This is reflected in the gap between the behavior of the disadvantaged child and that of children from a more stimulating environment. On the other hand, some genotypes, like those involving Down's syndrome, may have a limited range of reaction, while other children may have a wider range of reaction. This concept provides a possible explanation of why two children, under the same intervention experiment, may progress quite differently. Perhaps one child who increased 30 I.Q. points has a wider "range of reaction" than another child who, under the same stimulating environment, increases only 5 points in I.Q.

Another question raised by Dr. Miller's review is the age at which intervention is most effective. Most of the studies which have been reported intervene at age 5, some at age 4, and a limited few at age 3. After reviewing longitudinal studies on intelligence and other tests, Bloom (1964) stated that "about 50% of development takes place between conception and age 4, about 30% between ages 4 and 8, and about 20% between ages 8 and 17 (p. 88)." If this statement is correct, then intervention should begin before age 4, and preferably around ages 1 and 2. At present there are no definitive data to support this contention, except perhaps foster home studies. Another source of evidence that suggests that the earlier the intervention, the more acceleration in mental development comes from a comparison of different studies at different age levels.

In an attempt to integrate several studies on retarded children in which the intervention was introduced at different ages, I summarized (Kirk, 1965) three groups of studies suggesting that intervention at age 2 is more effective than at age 4, and that intervention at age 4 is more effective than at age 6.

The first set of data came from the classic study of Skeels and Dye (1939), which showed that when intervention began at age 2, their experimental groups increased 28 points in I.Q. while the contrast group decreased 26 points, a difference of over 50 points. In a longitudinal study of institutionalized mentally retarded children in which intervention was introduced at age 4 1/2, I reported (Kirk, 1958) an increase of 12 I.Q. points for the experimental group, and a decrease of 6 I.Q. points for the contrast group. One could conclude from these comparisons that initiating intervention at the age of 2 is more effective than intervention at the age of 4. This inference, however, may be unwarranted in view of the fact that one-half of the subjects in the experimental group in my study were organically involved, whereas Skeels' group did not have children with known organic pathologies.

Another three studies reported by me (Kirk, 1965) involved intervention in school at the age of 6. These children accelerated their I.Q. by 6 points. These groups did not have children with known organic pathologies, and no contrast group was used because all children entered school at age 6.

These three groups of studies presented only partial evidence that intervention at age 2 is more effective than at age 4, and that intervention at age 4 is more effective than at age 6.

A third major question raised in Dr. Miller's review is the effects of different kinds of intervention. Dr. Miller discusses these under the following topics: (a) cognitive variables, (b) motivational variables, (c) personal style variables, and (d) physical variables. These variables evolved from studies comparing the advantaged with the disadvantaged. The studies do not produce information on the elements in environment stimulation that would accelerate, for example, cognitive development or increase motivation or improve personal style. What is really needed are procedures to measure the elements of the environment which produce maximal growth. We have been unable to do this except in a gross way.

An attempt to compare different educational programs of intervention has been reported recently by Karnes (1968) in an unpublished report. The report was primarily a progress report and did not give final results. Karnes compared different forms of preschool education and the length of the specialized intervention for different age groups of disadvantaged children. Her preliminary and tentative conclusions were based on five different intervention studies: (a) a traditional nursery school program, (b) a Montessori program, (c) a community integrated program in which several disadvantaged children were placed in a number of middle-class nursery schools, (d) a highly structured direct verbal program conducted by Bereiter and Engelmann (1966), and (e) a program designed by Karnes to ameliorate learning deficits.

The reported increase in Stanford-Binet I.Q. for the five groups were:

Community integrated	5.1
Montessori	5.5
Traditional nursery school	8.1
Amelioration of learning deficits	14.3
Direct verbal approach	14.4

Increases on the Illinois Test of Psycholinguistic Abilities (ITPA) were:

Montessori	7.0 months
Community integrated	9.8 months
Traditional nursery school	11.2 months
Direct verbal approach	12.9 months
Amelioration of learning deficits	14.0 months

Although these results show an advantage of a specialized nursery school (the direct verbal approach and the amelioration of learning disabilities) over the more traditional approaches, the follow up reported after another year may yield the most significant data.

On the Stanford-Binet, the traditional nursery school children had an initial mean I.Q. of 94.5. After a year of nursery school, at age 5, they had a mean I.Q. of 102.6, an increase of 8 points. They were then placed in a kindergarten, and at age 6 their mean I.Q. had dropped 3 points to 99.6, a final increase of 5 points.

The group of 24 children in the program for the amelioration of learning disabilities showed initially a mean I.Q. of 96.2. After one year of specialized schooling, they had a mean I.Q. of 110, for an increase of 14.2 points. These children were also placed in the kindergarten at age 5, and at age 6, their mean Stanford-Binet I.Q. was 108.6, a slight drop in the second year but a final I.Q. increase of 12.4 points, as compared with the 5 point increase of the traditional groups.

The direct verbal approach group of 11 children had initially a mean Stanford-Binet I.Q. of 97.0. After a year with the direct verbal approach, their mean I.Q. was 111.5. This group was not placed in the public school kindergarten, but instead was retained in the direct verbal class for another year. At age 6 these children, with two years of specialized instruction, had reached a mean I.Q. of 120.4, or a total increase of 23.4 I.Q. points.

These results are indeed intriguing. They probably raise more questions than they answer. It would appear that the newer programs (amelioration of learning deficits and direct verbal approach) are superior to other more common approaches to early childhood education. It would appear also that short term training is not lasting and that a shift from a specialized program, with a ratio of 1 teacher to 5 children, to a kindergarten with 1 teacher to 30 children, will not maintain earlier gains. The children in the direct verbal group remained for two years of specialized instruction and made the most significant gains. These results suggest that it might be necessary to continue specialized training for two years instead of one, or probably for four or five years.

The crucial test of preschool programs is not whether there are increases in I.Q. scores but whether the children in the specialized programs whose

I.Q.s accelerated most will achieve a higher level educationally than will the groups in traditional programs whose I.Q.s were not significantly accelerated.

In personal conversation, Dr. Karnes informed me that the traditional nursery school groups and the two groups under special programs (the direct verbal approach and the amelioration of learning disabilities) have been followed to the end of the first grade. The results of educational testing have shown that both specialized groups have achieved higher level of reading and other educational tests than have the traditional nursery school children.

This type of longitudinal study, with ultimate criteria of social and educational achievement, is sorely needed. Dr. Miller has discussed short and long term intervention. Short term intervention varies from eight weeks to nine months. Long term intervention, as he has described, is a two or three year research project. Most of these studies consist of one year of intervention with follow up observation in the regular grades for one or two years. We do not find studies that continue specialized training over a period of three or four years. In that sense, I feel that we do not have any long term intervention programs, in the sense of long term specialized training.

As Dr. Miller says, field research in this area is "dirty research." By that he means that there are too many variables that cannot be controlled. It differs from the research of the experimentalist who is studying basic processes with animals. The laboratory scientist does not have to bother with teachers, superintendents, social welfare agencies, parent social structures, and traditions in a community. The field research has horrendous logistic problems to overcome, and these logistic problems are so great that the so called clean researcher turns away from the relevant problem which we face in studying the effects of intervention on the development of disadvantaged children.

What can we conclude from the plethora of studies on the culturally disadvantaged? If we are perfectionists and require conclusive evidence from well designed studies, we can draw very few definitive conclusions. On the other hand, if we wish to draw some tentative conclusions from the available evidence, it appears that:

1. Early educational intervention at ages 4 and 5 produces increases in test scores during the preschool period.
2. The earlier the intervention, the greater the increase.
3. Structured programs produce greater increases than do unstructured programs.
4. Increases in test scores following the period of intervention tend to be lost after the children attend the regular grades.
5. Later educational achievement may be higher for those children who received educational intervention at an earlier age, especially for those who received structured programs emphasizing cognitive development.

Where do we go from here? Do we continue short term intervention programs in many parts of the country and evaluate them for a year or two (possibly with comparison groups), or should we initiate a different approach?

What we need is not 101 short term evaluations of Head Start projects, but a monolithic center that will attempt to answer the numerous questions on a longitudinal basis for as many years [as] are necessary for more definitive results. This monolithic center would probably cost less than the 101 research projects underway, each studying a small group for a year or two. A comprehensive center would study the relevant questions such as: (a) At what age is intervention most effective? (b) How long must intervention continue in order to be effective and lasting? (c) What are the most effective intervention procedures in the home and in the school? (d) What kinds of children profit most from intervention procedures? (e) What are the predictors of later social and academic success?

All of these questions require longitudinal studies over a period of years, and also require new procedures in logistics for this type of field study.

References

Allen, G. Patterns of discovery in the genetics of mental deficiency. *American Journal of Mental Deficiency*, 1958, 62, 840–849.

Bereiter, C. & Engelmann, S. *Teaching disadvantaged children in the preschool*. Englewood Cliffs, NJ: Prentice-Hall, 1966.

Bloom, B. S. (1964). *Stability and change in human characteristics*. New York: Wiley.

Dobzhansky, T. *Evolution, genetics and man*. New York: Wiley, 1955.

Karnes, M. B. The effects of various preschool intervention programs. Paper presented at the American Educational Research Association, Chicago, February 1968.

Kirk, S. A. *Teaching reading to small children*. Boston: Houghton Mifflin, 1940.

Kirk, S. A. *Early education of the mentally retarded*. Urbana, IL: University of Illinois Press, 1958.

Kirk, S. A. Language, intelligence and the educability of the disadvantaged. In J. Squire (Ed.), *Language programs for the disadvantaged*. Urbana, IL: National Council of Teachers of English, 1965.

Skeels, H. M. & Dye, H. B. A study of the effects of differential stimulation on mentally retarded children. Proceedings and addresses of the American Association on Mental Deficiency, 1939, 44, 114–136.

Part III

Mental Retardation

INTRODUCTION

HERBERT GOLDSTEIN
Professor Emeritus
Educational Psychology and Special Education
New York University

To appreciate the importance of contributions of a bygone era, we need to take into account the state of the art and the social and technological contexts operative at the time. For example, the thinking that influenced Itard's work with Victor and the procedures he devised ultimately influenced educational programs for children with mental retardation. While the premises that supported his actions may seem naive by today's standards, in pre-mental-measurement times, they were revolutionary. Likewise, Sam Kirk and other innovators in education and psychology had to contend with advantages and limitations of the state of the art in education and the behavioral sciences, the conditions in society that had a bearing on children and youth with mental retardation, and the nature and rate of social change. What follows, then, is a brief and informal account of the conditions in society that provide a background for understanding Sam Kirk's contributions to the education and psychology of children and youth with mental retardation.

Before the turn of the century, there was a time when state residential schools for persons with mental retardation flourished. Many believed that the schools not only provided an environment superior to their homes and neighborhoods, but would also provide an education that would enable them to return to their communities as productive, contributing members. This optimism was supported by the relative technological simplicity of the times when much of the labor force was engaged in unskilled manual work. Illiteracy, while never an asset, was not the liability it became as technology proliferated. This was an interval when the circumstances and the pace of life were in harmony with the limitations of people with mild mental retardation.

However, soon after the 20th century got under way, this optimism began to fade for a number of reasons. For one, there was an inverse relationship between the high costs of building and operating the state schools and, as it turned out, the almost indiscernible rate of people with retardation returning to their communities. At the same time, reports indicated that not only was mental retardation hereditary, but that the birth rate of these people dramatically exceeded that of the population as a whole. Most critical, all aspects of society were becoming increasingly complex. Mechanization of home, farm, and factory placed a premium on performance and raised the standards for competence and the penalties for incompetence. The many housework, farming, and handwork jobs once available to men and women with retardation who emerged from the state schools all but vanished with the availability of washing machines, vacuum cleaners, tractors, automatic milkers, and assembly lines.

As state schools closed their doors to all but those persons with moderate and severe disabilities for whom placement was a pressing need, communities turned to the public schools to fill the educational gap. Administrators and teachers responded with mixed emotions. Many felt that the schools could not respond adequately to these children; that they would disrupt the education of their nondisabled counterparts. To further complicate matters, the schools were struggling with the massive influx of the children of European immigrants. Language and cultural differences created confusion in diagnosis and instruction in the schools.

In the community, mechanization spread and early efforts at automation were successful. As the labor pool mushroomed, competition for jobs became more intense. Before the problems created by accelerated technological and social change could be adequately addressed, society plunged into the Great Depression of the 1930s with its record unemployment. Unlike today, there were no federal or state support programs for the unemployed. Follow-up studies of school-leavers with mild mental retardation reported excessively high unemployment rates.

Then, when it appeared that the Depression would continue indefinitely, the United States plunged into World War II. During the war, efforts and energies were almost exclusively devoted to achieving victory; the development of public school programs for children with mild retardation, rarely a priority under the best of conditions, languished. Thus, at war's end, there was a dearth of professional personnel in these programs and a long backlog of children eligible for special class placement. It was generally accepted that the majority of eligible children with mental retardation in the schools were biding their time in regular classes. In the meantime, advocacy on behalf of individuals with moderate mental retardation began to intensify. Hardly enthusiastic about providing classes for students with mild disabilities, many administrators were even less eager to admit children with moderate mental retardation to their schools. They rejected these children, claiming that their deficits in mobility, their ability to communicate, and self-care skills rendered the schools hazardous to their well-being. Parents and other advocates insisted that the schools' curriculum should focus on the amelioration of these deficits.

The National Association for Retarded Children (NARC; later the National Association for Retarded Citizens, and, most recently, the ARC-US) encouraged parents to unite to organize and operate their own schools. Parent-supported programs for persons with moderate mental retardation opened as quickly as classrooms, teachers, and supplies could be found and transportation arranged. However, this did not divert parents from the goal of having their children educated in the public schools; litigation and legislation toward this end were in the not-too-distant future.

This was the social and technological context and the status of educational programs for these children when Sam Kirk became a member of the special education faculty at the University of Illinois. While all the problems discussed above were vital, several were critical. Among these, enhancing the collaboration between the university and local and state education and service agencies, improving professional preparation programs, conducting research on effective instruction, and the refining of diagnostic and assessment procedures became the focus of his interest.

In an important sense, Sam's establishment of the Institute for Research on Exceptional Children was a well-considered response by him, Ray Graham who was the State Director of Special Education for Illinois at the time, and the university to the continuing need for research on issues important to effective educational programs for children and youth with mental retardation and other students with disabilities. Centers such as Wayne County and Vineland Training Schools, once able to mount vital research efforts that were responsive to educational issues, were, by the late 1940s, committed to providing residential service.

In local districts, shortages of classrooms, professional staff, and funds persisted. More than a half century after the first special classes were established, a notable proportion of students with mild retardation were still languishing in regular classes, awaiting special education. At the same time, the results of studies of the postschool adjustment of adults with mild mental retardation were remarkably similar irrespective of their prior attendance in special or regular classes. However, the information that costly special class programs were not clearly superior to regular classes was almost universally ignored by local school districts and almost everyone else, for that matter.

In fact, the only developmentally organized curriculum for students with mild retardation, one that showed much promise of being able to improve the outcomes of special class placement, was developed and implemented by Richard Hungerford and his associates in New York City in the late 1940s. It was afforded little attention elsewhere in the United States and began to fade a decade or so later, even as the results of efficacy studies were being deplored. Other curriculum innovations such as Ingram's system for organizing content met a similar fate. There seemed to be tacit agreement that a watered-down version of the regular class curriculum would suffice for students with mild mental retardation. This was something any special class teacher could gobble up at little or no expense. Gradually, educational programs for children and youth with mild mental retardation began to lose their vitality and a return to pre-World War II indifference seemed inevitable. The burgeoning civil rights movement contributed to this trend.

Civil rights activists, justifiably protesting irresponsible testing procedures, encouraged parents and other advocates for children from minority groups to challenge their special class placements. Data on special class placement showed that children from minority groups were disproportionately represented in classes for children with mental retardation. Following litigation in California, a ban was placed on the use of intelligence tests to classify students from minority groups as having mental retardation. Many other state and local agencies followed suit. In short order, the number of students classified as having mild mental retardation was greatly reduced. Some school districts ignored or disallowed teacher referrals. In others, the ranks of students with emotional and learning disabilities swelled almost in direct proportion to the dwindling of educational programs for children with mild mental retardation.

Paralleling the civil rights movement, the Kennedy administration's concern with mental retardation led to legislation supporting personnel preparation and research in areas ranging from prevention to amelioration. Legislation was also enacted increasing the visibility and contribution of the U.S. Office of Education to the field of special education. This legislation proved to be a catalyst for research, personnel preparation, and administrative practices throughout special education.

In the meantime, parent groups that had formed in communities in the early 1950s had increased in number and power steadily, as did their national organizations. Local groups continued to maintain their own classes for their children. At the same time, they persisted in their demands that their school districts provide educational programs for their children. Some state education agencies responded by enacting permissive legislation, which gave local schools an option to do so. Others mandated the provision of education for these children. When it became clear that this process was slow and laborious, a series of class-action lawsuits were initiated to hasten the process. This proved to be equally time consuming, and parents, professionals, and their supporters turned to the federal government to speed things along. The result was Public Law 94-142; the rest is history.

Sam Kirk came along just as educational programs for students with mental retardation and other children with disabilities were emerging from many years of hibernation. His career spanned those years when the nature and rate of social and technological change were of such proportions as to pose challenges to every aspect of education. There was a lot of catching up to do. Sam's research and that of his colleagues in the Institute, along with his influence in policy development, vitalized these programs and, as the last of the generalists, all of special education. It will be seen in Part III of this volume that his contribution was responsive to the educational needs of persons with mental retardation, their families, and their communities. Many aspects of change not directly addressed here, including the normalization and deinstitutionalization movements, were also well served by his work.

Herbert Goldstein began his career as a teacher of children with mild mental retardation after receiving his bachelor's and master's degrees in special education from San Francisco State College. He entered the doctoral program at the University of Illinois, where he was a research assistant in the Institute for Research in Exceptional Children. While a graduate student, he developed the *Illinois Guide for Teachers of Mildly Mentally Retarded Children* for the Illinois State Department of Special Education. After receiving his doctorate in special education, he joined the faculty at the University of Illinois. With James Moss and Laura Jordan, he conducted a study of The Efficacy of Special Class Training on the Development of Mentally Retarded Children. Upon moving to New York City, he became chair of the Department of Special Education in the Graduate School of Humanities and Social Sciences at Yeshiva University. He established the Curriculum Research and Development Center in Mental Retardation and led in the development of the Social Learning Curriculum for Mentally Retarded Students. This work continued at New York University to its completion. He is presently professor emeritus.

Chapter 4

Research in Education: Mental Retardation

SAMUEL A. KIRK

Educational research is generally applied, or engineering, research. Just as medicine relies on the basic sciences for the improvement of its practice, so education likewise relies primarily on the social sciences for the improvement of its procedures. A complete review of the research that has implications for education would include many experiments in learning, the field of personality or social adjustment, measurement, sociology, and related disciplines. The present volume, however, includes chapters on the contributions of the basic sciences to the field of mental retardation. For that reason, these areas have not been included in this review. Instead, research which is related more directly to educational practice and which would not ordinarily be included in other sections has been covered here.

Special Classes Versus Regular Grades

The increases in special schools and classes have been accomplished on the basis of logic and the belief that placing retarded children in special classes is more beneficial to them than retaining them in the regular grades. We will be noted later, there is little empirical evidence to demonstrate clear-cut benefits of special-class placement. The empirical evidence is as yet inconclusive and, in a sense, contradictory. The following experiments bear on the general issue.

Bennett (1932) compared fifty retarded children in special classes with fifty retarded children in the regular grades of the same city. All children were within the twelve- to thirteen-year age group, and the two groups were matched for CA, MA, and IQ. The average IQ was about 73. Bennett reported that in educational achievement and in physical characteristics (such as vision, speech defects, and motor coordination) the special-class children were inferior to the retarded children who remained in the regular grades.

From H. Stevens and R. Heber (Eds.), *Mental Retardation.* Chicago: The University of Chicago Press, 1964, pp. 57–72.

Bennett recognized the effect of differential selection of children in the special classes, i.e., mentally retarded children who were inferior educationally and physically are the ones who are most apt to be referred to special classes, while those with similar IQs but with less severe educational retardation or fewer behavior problems are less frequently referred for special-class placement. Because this selection factor was not controlled, the Bennett study does not answer the question of whether or not special classes are beneficial. Its results indicate, rather, that retarded children referred to special classes are inferior to retarded children retained in the regular grades.

Pertsch (1936) conducted a similar study in New York City. He paired 278 children in the regular and special classes for CA, MA, IQ, sex, and racial extraction. Measures were obtained on educational achievement, mechanical aptitudes, personal adjustment, father's occupation, and personal and education data. Pertsch also concluded that those remaining in the regular grades were superior in educational achievement and personal adjustment to those placed in the special classes. In addition, Pertsch retested the children after six months to determine the relative progress of the two groups. He again found that the non-segregated group was superior in progress in reading comprehension, arithmetic computation, arithmetic reasoning, and in personality adjustment. Pertsch tended to ignore the facts that selection for special classes is often made on the basis of the failure to adjust to the regular class and that children with greater problems are probably more frequently referred for special-class placement.

Cowen (1938) re-evaluated the Pertsch study, questioning the selection factor as an error in methodology. Using Pertsch's own data, Cowen calculated the percentage of mean gain in achievement, demonstrating that this percentage was actually greater for the special-class children (except in arithmetic computation) than for the retarded children left in the regular grades. Thus Cowen reversed Pertsch's conclusions.

Blatt (1958), recognizing that the selection factor in the previous studies invalidated any definitive conclusions, attempted to control this factor by another procedure. He matched seventy-five children placed in special classes in one school system with children of similar CA, MA, and IQ in the regular grades of another school system which did not have any special classes. In this study, he found no difference between the groups in educational achievement, personality, or physical status, except that the special-class children had more uncorrected or permanent physical defects.

Although Blatt partially controlled the selection factor, he did not succeed in eliminating this very important factor, since his two groups are still not comparable. One group contained the obvious cases who were referred to special classes, and the other groups contained both the obvious cases who would have been referred had there been special classes in that community and also the less obvious cases who normally would have remained in the regular class. By thus partially controlling the selection factor, he found no difference between the groups.

Cassidy and Stanton (1959), using a design similar to that of Blatt, compared the performance of ninety-four educable mentally retarded children in regular grades in Ohio school systems which had no special classes with children in special classes in other cities. The results again indicated the superiority in academic achievement of those enrolled in the regular grades. The special-class pupils, however, were superior in some aspects of personality and in social adjustment. This superiority in social adjustment reflected the goals of the special-class teachers who, on a questionnaire, indicated they were more interested in effecting social adjustment than academic achievement.

Cassidy and Stanton noted that other selective factors besides the IQ were operating in the referral of retarded children to special classes. This study, like many others, leaves open the question of the efficacy of special classes.

Elenbogen (1957) compared the achievement of mentally retarded children in special and regular classes in the Chicago elementary schools. The mean CA of each group was 13.46, and the mean IQ was 70.5. The children in the special classes had been thus enrolled for about two years. Elenbogen's results were similar to other studies. In academic achievement, the retarded children in the regular grades were superior to those in the special class. On the other hand, the special-class teachers rated their children higher in social adjustment than did the regular-class teachers. Again, the selection factor was not controlled.

Thurstone (1959) conducted a comparative study of retarded children in special classes and similar children in regular grades in the state of North Carolina. A total of 1273 children with IQs between 50 and 79 were identified. Of these, 769 were in special classes, and 504 were in regular grades. The results of this experiment may be summarized as follows:

1. On the first evaluation with the Stanford Achievement Test, the children in the regular grades scored significantly higher than those in the special classes on all measures except arithmetic computation.

2. When the tests were repeated the second year and gain scores calculated, there was no significant difference between the gains of those in the special-class group and those in the regular grades. Neither were there any significant differences in gains between sexes or races. The only significant difference shown was for the lower IQ (50 to 59) group. For this group, the gains (except in arithmetic computation) were consistently in favor of the special-class children.

3. Sociometric and teacher ratings of the social acceptance and adjustment of the retarded children in the regular grades and in the special classes

showed a superiority of the special-class retardates. As in a study by Johnson (1950), the children in the regular grades tended to be isolated. In commenting on the teacher ratings, Thurstone (1959, p. 170) states:

> If their ratings are sound, mentally handicapped children in special classes are emotionally better adjusted, have a higher regard for their own mental ability, participate more widely in learning and social activities, and possess more traits desired by their peers than do their counterparts in regular grades.

The Thurstone study, like the others, did not control the selection factor. Its results inform us that those who are mentally retarded and also educationally retarded below their capacity are more apt to be placed in special classes. It indicates that gain scores of the two groups do not differ except for the more extreme deviates. With respect to the sociometric ratings, these and teacher ratings should be checked with the adjustment of these children at home and in the neighborhood, rather than in their own classes, where they were rated by Thurstone.

Ainsworth (1959) compared three groups of mentally retarded children under differing treatment conditions: (1) special classes, (2) regular grades, and (3) regular grades plus an itinerant teacher. The special-class group included forty-eight children with a mean CA of 126.8 months and a mean Wechsler Intelligence Scale for Children (WISC) IQ of 63.9; the seventy-eight children in the regular-grade group had a mean CA of 123.7 months and a mean IQ of 65.7; the number in the itinerant group was 48; the mean CA was 127.6 months, and the mean IQ was 62.3.

The children in the three groups were given a series of educational achievement tests in February, 1958, and again one year later. In addition, they were rated and observed on behavior and social adjustment before and after the year's interval. The results indicated that all three groups made progress in educational achievement in the one-year period but that there were no significant differences among the three groups in achievement, in social adjustment, or in behavior.

This study shows that gains made by retarded children whose training began at about the age of ten are similar under three forms of management. It should not be expected that gains would be different in a one-year period. Actually, such a study should be continued for five years before any definite results, if any, could emerge.

Wrightstone et al. (1959) compared mentally retarded children under three different types of grouping. One group was classed as high educable, with IQs roughly between 60 and 75; another group was classed as low educable, with IQs of 50 to 59; and a third group of controls contained both low and high educable children.

In academic achievement, there appeared to be no clear-cut pair-wise differences between groups. In some intangible areas, such as social adjustment and speech, the homogeneous low-educable children showed significant growth over their heterogeneous counterparts.

The Wrightstone comparison suffers from the general methodological weaknesses of *in situ* experiments of this type. First, the children in the experiment were approximately thirteen years of age; most of them had been placed in one of the special classes around the age of nine or ten, after they had failed in the regular grades. Second, the high- and low-educable categories were not discrete, since the high-educable classes contained 15% low-educable, while the low-educable classes contained 5% high-educable children. Of the 3627 pupils assigned to the experimental and control populations, two-thirds were lost to the experiment through attrition during the first year of evaluation. The pupil turnover in this year demonstrates the erratic nature of special-class enrollment. Actually, such experiments will require their initiation at the beginning of a child's school career, rather than in the middle, and more discrete and continuous education over some period of time will be required before definitive conclusions can be made.

Mullen and Itkin (1961), using a matched-pair technique, compared 140 mentally retarded children in special classes with another 140 retarded children who were in regular grades by matching them on seven variables: age, IQ, sex, socio-economic community ratings, reading achievement, school attendance in the rural south, and foreign language spoken in the home. The subjects ranged in age from seven to thirteen years, and they range in IQ from 50 to 74.

From the analysis, two significant findings resulted. The first followed an analysis of factors associated with achieving and non-achieving mentally retarded children in both groups. This part of the study showed that, although the mental ages of the two groups were the same, the achieving group (1) had in their records more questions about the validity of the IQ rating, (2) tended to come from more stable homes, (3) tended to receive higher adjustment ratings, (4) were distinguishable from the poor achievers by fewer cases of public assistance, and (5) received on the average significantly higher scores on general information and comprehension tests and on tests of ethical comprehension.

The second finding related to the comparison of the mentally retarded in the regular grades with matched controls in the special classes on pre- and post-tests after a one-year period. This comparison, as in previous studies, indicated no differences in academic achievement gains between the two groups except that the retarded children remaining in the regular grades showed superiority in arithmetic gains. In spite of the matching on relevant variables, the authors concluded that a selective factor still operated. They state:

Although bias in the comparison of the progress of special class and regular class groups was decreased in the present experiment, selective factors determining placement remained and influenced the comparisons made.

This study's major contribution, according to this reviewer, points clearly to the major methodological problems involved in *in situ* research. It points out that even when known predictive variables are carefully controlled as in this study, other variables not easily controlled can affect the comparisons. The study should end further attempts to compare children in regular grades with those in special classes in an ongoing service program.

Goldstein, Jordan, and Moss (1962) report a current research project which compares the progress and adjustment of educable mentally handicapped children in regular grades with those in special classes. This experiment, [then] still in progress, selected 120 retarded children in first grades in communities which had no special classes. They were divided into two groups by random numbers. Sixty children were placed in four special classes, while the other sixty children remained in the grade in which they were tested. The children in both groups [were] being observed and tested annually on different dimensions of development, and the study [was] to continue for at least four years. When completed, this study should answer basic questions concerning the benefits or detriments of special classes, since it is not handicapped by the selection factor which has plagued previous studies.

Adjustment in Special Classes and Regular Grades

Another type of study relating to the adjustment of mentally retarded children has been concerned with the effects of regular-class placement. Johnson (1950) studied the acceptance of mentally retarded children in the regular grades through the use of sociometric techniques. In his study, he selected communities that had no special classes. By testing six hundred children in two communities in the first through fifth grades, he found thirty-nine children who had IQs, on the Stanford-Binet Scale, of 69 and below—his definition of mental retardation. A sociometric study of these six hundred children showed that the mentally retarded children in the grades tended to be isolated and rejected by the other children in the classes.

To determine whether the results obtained by Johnson were peculiar to traditional school systems, Johnson and Kirk (1950) repeated the study in a progressive school system and found similar results. Mentally retarded children in the regular grades were isolated and rejected by their peer groups even though an attempt was made by the teachers to integrate them into the regular classroom. Johnson and Kirk concluded that the physical presence of a mentally retarded child in the regular grades does not assure social integration.

Baldwin (1958) conducted a similar experiment in a school system that had special classes. In this system, she compared those retarded who remained in the regular grades with non-retarded children in the same grades. Her results were similar to those of Johnson. In this connection, reference should be made to the Thurstone study (1950), which not only confirmed the results of other studies on academic progress but, in addition, related the sociometric data of children in the regular grades to those of children in the special class. Baldwin points out that there exist among the mentally retarded many "stars" in the special classes, but very few "stars" in the regular grades.

Jordan and deCharms (1959) conducted a different comparison of children in special classes with retarded children in the regular grades. They compared forty-two mentally retarded children in special classes with sixty mentally retarded children in the regular grades on the *n*-achievement motive (a measure of achievement motive derived from a content analysis of a modified TAT). On the *n*-achievement motive the retarded children in the special classes (although significantly lower in academic achievement) appeared to have less fear of failure than the mentally retarded children in the regular grades. In this study, as in others, Jordan and deCharms did not control for the selection factor. If their data are substantiated, it might mean that the pressure for academic achievement in the regular grades is producing fear of failure, while lack of emphasis on academic achievement in the special classes decreases the fear of failure.

Comments

Special classes for educable mentally retarded children in the United States increased in enrollment nearly tenfold between 1922 and 1958. This increase would indicate an acceptance of the advantages of special classes over the retention of mentally retarded in the regular grades. To date, however, research has not justified the faith on which this acceptance is based. Such research is surrounded by many pitfalls.

The efficacy of special-class placement has been studied in the main by comparing retarded children placed in special classes with retarded children left in the regular grades. The results of these numerous investigations have indicated that (1) the children left in the regular grades are, on the whole, superior academically to the children assigned to special classes, (2) possibly the children at the lower range of educability (low-educable) show equal or superior academic achievement in the special class, (3) children assigned to special classes appear to be superior in social adjustment to those left in the regular grades, and (4) the retarded children in the regular grades tend to be isolate[d] and rejected by their normal peers.

All the completed studies suffer from the problems of *in situ* investigation. None controlled the essential variables needed for adequate inferences. First, the selection factor in the assignment of children to special or regular grades was not controlled in any of the investigations. No investigator was able to assign children to the two treatment groups randomly.

Second, the children in the investigations attended regular grades for a number of years before they were assigned to special classes. Actually, the comparisons of the regular and special classes were made between children who remained in the regular grades and children who had failed in the regular grades from anywhere from two to five years and were then assigned to special classes. Many of the children in the experiments had been in special classes for only one year.

Third, there has not been a clear-cut delineation of a special class, the curriculum, or the qualifications of special teachers. Special classes vary widely in organization and in curriculum and teaching methods. Qualifications of teachers vary from well-trained teachers to those subjected to short-term summer courses taught largely by instructors who have had little training or experience with special classes. The administrative labeling of a group of retarded children as a special class for the purpose of receiving state subsidy does not assure its being a *special class* for experimental purposes.

Fourth, another important factor hinges on the reliability and validity of the measuring instruments used in the comparative studies. The important goals of a special class are in intangible areas, such as social adjustment, motivation, self-concepts, and so forth. Many of the studies improvised their own focus of measurement for these facets of development.

From a review of these studies, one can only concede that, until we obtain well-controlled studies of a longitudinal nature, our opinions about the benefits or detriments of special classes will remain partly in the realm of conjecture.

Modifying Intelligence Through Education

Early efforts to educate retarded children were directed primarily toward curing or alleviating the disability. The pioneers in this field—Itard, Seguin, Montessori, and Decroly (cf. Kirk & Johnson, 1951)—were interested in remedies for mental retardation. All of these physicians made their contributions, not in the field of medicine, but in the development of educational methods and systems. Their efforts were stimulated and influenced by the prevailing sensationalist philosophy that the training of the senses had a direct influence on the central nervous system and, consequently, on the development of retarded children.

Binet (1909, pp. 140–161), who is considered the inventor of the modern age-scale of intelligence, did not hold the view that the retarded child's rate of development, as measured by his tests, remained constant. On the contrary, he attempted to dispel the prejudice against the educability of intelligence. Although he furnished no empirical evidence for his training method, which he called "mental orthopedics," he stated in 1909 (p. 140): "After the evil, the remedy; after exposing mental defects of all kinds, let us pass on to their treatment."

American psychologists and educators reacted enthusiastically to the testing movement initiated by Binet. Few, however, followed Binet's ideas on the educability of intelligence. Instead, there arose a pessimistic attitude toward the training of intelligence. This pessimism arose because of three trends.

The first influence resulted from the studies of Goddard (1914) which purported to show that mental deficiency is largely inherited along recessive Mendelian lines. This research implied that a genetic component was unalterable through education. In the United States, concentration of effort was directed primarily toward eugenic lines, through the control of the mentally retarded by segregation in institutions and preventing mental retardation by sterilization.

The second influence resulted from the concept of pseudofeeblemindedness. This concept implied that the rate of mental growth is constant and that if a retarded child appeared to change his rate of growth or IQ, the original diagnosis was incorrect. This concept was introduced to explain deviations in rate of growth which is alleged to be constant. It assumes that any apparent change cannot be an actual change, since education or environment cannot produce change.

The third influence stemmed from a widely accepted definition of mental deficiency proposed by Doll (1941), who stated that mental deficiency (1) is developmental arrest, (2) of constitutional origin, (3) obtaining at maturity, and (4) essentially incurable. This is a fatalistic definition and does not encourage efforts toward educational procedures for the purpose of accelerating mental development.

Efforts to evaluate growth among the mentally retarded have been confined largely to the measurement of progress in reading, arithmetic, and other school subjects, as well as to the effects of education on social and vocational adjustment. There have been some attempts, however, to evaluate the effects of special educational procedures on the development of mental ability in retarded children. The studies reported below deal with mentally retarded populations, rather than with the wider populations of the nature-nurture studies.

Kephart (1939) organized activities to stimulate the thinking ability of sixteen adolescent mentally retarded children in a "self-determining cottage" of an institution for high-grade defectives. The IQs of this group increased from an average Stanford-Binet Scale IQ of 66.3 to an average of 76.4 in a period of three years. He compared this group with twenty-six boys living in the traditionally operated cottages and found that the IQs of the contrast group showed an average increase of only 1.9 IQ points during the same period. Kephart attributed the difference in increase to the educational program in the self-determining cottage. The selection of the cases was not randomized in this study, and the results may reflect an unknown selection factor in the self-determining cottage.

A most impressive study of young mentally defective children was reported by Skeels and Dye (1939). These investigators transferred thirteen young children under three years of age from an orphanage to an institution for retarded children. The average IQ of these children on the Kuhlmann Test of Mental Development at the time of admission to the institution for defectives was 64, and the range in IQ was 35 to 89. These babies were placed in different wards of the institution where older retarded girls were housed. The children received a great deal of attention and stimulation from the attendants and girls on the ward. After a year and a half, the IQs of these children had increased 27.5 points. Skeels and Dye compared these increases in IQs with the changes in IQs of twelve children with somewhat higher original IQs (ranging from 50 to 103) who remained in the orphanage. This group of orphanage children dropped 26.2 points during the same period. These results could not be explained on the basis of the unreliability of infant scales, since a contrast group was used.

In a follow-up study, Skeels (1942) retested the experimental and control groups two and one-half years following the experimental period. The mean IQ of the thirteen experimental children was 95.9, four IQ points higher than at the close of the experimental period. Eleven of the thirteen experimental children had been taken out of the institution and placed in adoptive homes. One stayed in the institution and one was returned to the orphanage. The mean IQ of the adoptive children was 101.4, with no child having an IQ below 90. The contrast group, which showed an initial IQ of 86.7 and an IQ of 60.3 at the end of the experimental period, now showed a mean IQ of 66.1. There had been a rise in 5.6 IQ points, but, in general, those who remained in the unstimulating environment of the orphanage continued to show retardation.

The most sensational study on the effects of education was reported by Schmidt (1946). She described an eight-year study on 245 children in special classes in Chicago. The initial average IQ was reported as being 52.1. At the completion of three years of school, it was stated that their average IQ had risen to 71.6; at the completion of five years of postschool experience, the average IQ had risen to 89.3. Twenty-seven per cent of this group graduated from high school, and 5.1% continued beyond high school training. The increases in IQ and achievement were attributed to the special-class training. These results were in such sharp contrast to professional opinion that the editors of *Psychological Monographs* felt it necessary to explain the publication of the study in a prefatory statement.

In an investigation of the Schmidt study, Kirk (1948) checked the records of the children in Schmidt's special classes in Chicago by visiting the schools where the classes were held and tabulating the test scores from the files of the Chicago Bureau of Child Study. He found the mean IQ on admission was 69. According to Kirk, 50% of the children in Schmidt's classes had IQs above 69. The lack of correspondence between the data found in the files of the Bureau of Child Study and the tabulated data reported by Schmidt tended to throw doubt on the authenticity of the report and to invalidate the study.

A longitudinal study of the effects of preschool training on the social and mental development of young retarded children in an institution and in a community was conducted by Kirk (1958). He identified 81 retarded children between the ages of three and six with IQs generally between 45 and 80. These 81 children were placed in four groups. Twenty-eight received training in a specially designed community preschool and were restudied after the preschool experience. Twenty-six children, serving as a contrast group with similar ages and level of development, were tested at the same intervals but were not given the opportunities of preschool education. Fifteen children were given preschool education in an institution, while twelve other children, serving as an institutional contrast group, remained in the wards during the preschool period and were restudied after the preschool period. This experiment was presented in the form of case studies and statistical results. The evaluation of rates of development was in terms of results of intelligence tests and other tests and observations on social development. The children were classified before, during, and at the conclusion of the experiment under six categories: average, low-average, borderline, high-educable, low-educable, questionable educability, and uneducable. Any change of one or more classification levels upward to downward was considered a significant change.

One part of the experiment dealt with a comparison of differing degrees of stimulation change. In this part of the experiment, (1) four children were taken out of inadequate homes and placed in foster homes and were also enrolled in the preschool, (2) twelve children from inadequate homes stayed in their own homes but were given preschool education, and (3) fourteen sibling and twin controls (of the twelve children) who did not receive preschool education were evaluated and compared with the twelve experimental children during and after the preschool period. The results showed:

1. The four children who were taken out of their inadequate homes by social agencies and placed in foster homes all increased their rate of development. Two increased one level in classification, one increased two levels, and one increased three levels.
2. Of the twelve children who remained in their psycho-socially deprived homes but received the benefits of preschool education, two-thirds increased their rate of development one or more classification levels, one-third retained their rate of development, and one dropped a classification level. The latter child attended the preschool only 50% of the time.

3. Of the fourteen twin and sibling controls (those who did not attend the preschool but later attended regular schools or special classes), only two children, or one-seventh, increased their rate of development; seven, or one-half, retained the same rate of growth; and five, or nearly one-third, dropped in classification as they grew older. The differences in development between the twelve experimental children and the fourteen sibling and twin controls were statistically significant at the 0.02 level.

Kirk concluded from these data that children from psycho-socially deprived homes tend to retain their rate of development or to drop in rate of development as they grow older. Preschool opportunities for these children tend to reverse this tendency by assisting more of them to increase their rate of development. When more drastic changes of environment, such as both a foster home and preschool, were introduced, more of the children increased in rate of development. These results lend support to the proposition that educational opportunities at an early age can accelerate the rate of mental growth of children reared in psycho-socially deprived homes.

Another aspect of the experiment compared fifteen institutionalized preschool children, who had intensive training at the preschool level, with twelve children who remained in the wards of the institution and did not attend school until the age of six. From age four years, four months to age seven years, four months, the fifteen children in the training group increased from an average IQ of 61 to 71 on the Stanford-Binet, from 57 to 67 on the Kuhlmann Tests of Mental Development, and from 72 to 82 on the Vineland Social Maturity Scale. In contrast, the twelve children who did not receive preschool training dropped in Stanford-Binet Scale IQs from 57 to 50, on the Kuhlmann Tests of Mental Development from 54 to 50, and on the Vineland Social Maturity Scale from 73 to 61. These differences were all statistically significant. In addition, six of the fifteen children in the training group were paroled from the institution, while none of the twelve children without training was paroled. These data are further evidence that educational treatment at an early age is effective in increasing the rate of development of institutionalized mental defectives.

Other results of the experiment showed: (1) that preschool education was less effective with children with organic involvements than with those without a definitive diagnosis or organicity, and (2) that children from relatively adequate homes tended to increase in rate of social and mental development in the first grade without preschool education. These results indicate that, for children from relatively adequate homes, the age of six is not too late to expect accelerated development as a result of schooling.

Lyle (1959, 1960) compared the performance of imbecile children in day schools and hospitals on verbal and non-verbal intelligence. He administered the verbal and non-verbal parts of the Minnesota Preschool Scale to samples of institutionalized and day-school imbeciles. Seventy-seven children were at the Fountain Hospital in London where they attended an Occupation Center. One hundred and seventeen children lived at home and attended special training schools in Middlesex. The ages of the two groups ranged from six years, six months to thirteen years, six months. All were within the range of the Minnesota Preschool Scale.

On the non-verbal tests, the 77 hospital and 117 day-school children showed grand means of 35.05 and 35.34, respectively. However, on the verbal scale "there were highly significant differences between the C-score means . . . between the Day School and Institution groups for both [children with Down syndrome and those without] in favor of the day school group." Lyle concluded that "It seems likely that long residence in the institution retards verbal intelligence much more than non-verbal intelligence."

Gallagher (1960) conducted a three-year experiment of the effects of tutoring brain-injured children on the development of intellectual functions, on social maturity, and on personality development. In this experiment, forty-two institutionalized brain-injured children, ages eight to twelve, were identified and divided into experimental and control groups of twenty-one each, matched on Stanford-Binet Scale MA scores, and placed in the experimental and control groups randomly. The experimental group received tutoring on intellectual tasks one hour a day for two years, and no tutoring for one year. The controls, who were not tutored during the first two years, received tutoring during the third year of the experiment. Comparing test-results on a variety of measures, Gallagher summarized his results as follows:

1. Improvement in the intellectual development of some brain-injured, mentally retarded children can be obtained through the tutoring methods described here.

2. The children who responded to the tutoring achieved more in the area of verbal skills than non-verbal skills, but all of the children had extreme difficulty at the higher abstract levels of conceptualization.

3. The younger children (ages 8–10) in the study showed significant improvement over the older children (ages 10–12).

4. Certain behavioral changes were noticed during tutoring; principally, an increased ability to pay attention.

5. When the tutoring procedures were removed from the life of the child, there was a tendency for his development to regress to lower levels or become arrested.

6. There was an impressive range of individual differences both in the characteristic of the children prior to tutoring and in their response to tutoring (p. 151).

Gallagher feels that the modest results which he obtained under institutional living could possibly be made more substantial under a "total push" program. He concluded by stating that:

> It is quite likely that history will also record that we have been entirely too pessimistic about the possible training potential of brain-injured children and that this pessimism has prevented us from giving them the intellectual and educational stimulation that we would wish for all our children (p. 168).

Cruickshank et al. (1961) conducted an experiment on methods of teaching brain-injured and hyperactive children. Although the children in this experiment were not designated as mentally retarded, the mean IQs for the four groups ranged from 78 to 82. In this experiment two experimental classes of children were taught by a modified Strauss-Lehtinen technique using principles of (1) reduction of environmental space, (2) reduction of visual and auditory environmental stimuli, (3) establishment of a highly structured daily program, and (4) increasing the stimulus value of instructional materials. The two matched control classes were organized according to conventional methods. The results of this experiment over a one- and two-year period indicated:

1. The children in the four experimental and control classes made significant academic progress.
2. There was no significant difference in gains in academic achievement between the experimental and control classes.
3. There were no significant increases in IQ or in other psychological factors except in the ability to differentiate figure from background. In the latter the experimental subjects exceeded the controls.

Many programs have been organized for the training of brain-injured children, but none of the programs have been subjected to more than minimal experimental evaluation. The studies of Gallagher and Cruickshank are the only ones that have subjected a training program to an experimental design.

Comments

The few studies on the effects of educational procedures on the educability of intelligence of retarded children have been sporadic and, in general, short-term studies. There are many reasons for the paucity of such studies. One reason has been the prejudice against the possibility of developing intelligence through educational procedures. Another reason is related to the length of time needed to produce reliable results. A third reason is that the factors of control, attrition, and reliability of measurement tend to discourage experimenters from launching a controlled longitudinal experiment of an educational nature.

The evidence presented indicates some positive results of educational treatment, especially with young retarded children. These results do not agree with the statement of Masland, Sarason, and Gladwin (1958, p. 158), who state: "It is our opinion . . . that educational retardation is not likely to be significantly decreased by building new and more schools and hiring more teachers." They ascribe the retardation to cultural settings and indicate that schooling per se will have little effect unless cultural changes are made. However, from a theoretical point of view, our task is to determine (1) whether environment, including schooling, can displace the rate of development of retarded children, (2) the age at which this change is most effective, and (3) the variables within a family, or the instructional program, which can determine the change in rate of growth. The problem for research on the educability of intelligence is to identify more specifically the factors in the *nature* of the child and the variables in the *nurture* provided by the environment which effect changes in rate of growth, both positively and negatively.

References

Ainsworth, S. H. (1959). *An Exploratory Study of Educational, Social and Emotional Factors in the Education of Emotionally Retarded Children in Georgia Public Schools.* (U.S. Office of Education Cooperative Research Program, Project No. 171 [6470].) Athens, Georgia: University of Georgia.

Baldwin, W. D. (1958). The social position of the educable mentally retarded in the regular grades in the public schools. *Except. Child*, 25:106–8.

Bennett, A. (1929). Reading ability in special education classes. *J. Educ. Res.*, 20:236–38.

Bennett, A. (1932). *A Comparative Study of Subnormal Children in the Elementary Grades.* New York: Teachers College, Columbia University, Bureau of Publications.

Binet, A. (1909). *Les idees modernes sur les enfants.* Paris: E. Flemmarion.

Blatt, B. (1958). The physical, personality, and academic status of children who are mentally retarded attending special classes as compared with children who are mentally retarded attending regular classes. *Amer. J. Ment. Defic.* 62:810–18.

Cassidy, V. M., and Stanton, J. E. (1959). *An Investigation of Factors Involved in the Educational Placement of Mentally Retarded Children: A Study of Differences between Children in Special and Regulatory Classes in Ohio.* (U.S. Office of Education Cooperative Research Program, Project No. 043.) Columbus: Ohio State University.

Cowen, P. A. (1938). Special class vs. grade groups for subnormal pupils. *Sch. and Soc.*, 48: 27–28.

Cruickshank, W. M. (1946). Arithmetic vocabulary of mentally retarded boys. *Except. Child.*, 13:65–69, 91.

Elenbogen, M. L. (1957). A comparative study of some aspects of academic and social adjustment of two groups of mentally retarded children in special classes and in regular grades. *Diss. Abstr., 17*:2497.

Gallagher, J. J. (1960). *Tutoring of Brain-Injured Mentally Retarded Children.* Springfield, Illinois: C. C. Thomas.

Goldstein, H., Jordan, L., and Moss, J. W. (1962). *Early School Development of Low IQ Children: A Study of Special Class Placement.* (U.S. Office of Education Cooperative Research Program, Project SAE 8204, Interim Report.) Urbana, Illinois: University of Illinois, Institute for Research of Exceptional Children.

Johnson, G. O. (1950). A study of the social position of mentally handicapped children in the regular grades. *Amer. J. Ment. Defic.* 55:60–89.

Johnson, G. O. and Kirk, S. A. (1950). Are mentally handicapped children segregated in the regular grades? *Except. Child.*, 17:65–68, 87–88.

Jordon, T. E., and deCharms, R. (1959). The achievement motive in normal and mentally retarded children. *Amer. J. Ment. Defic.*, 64:457–66.

Kephart, N. C. (1939). The effect of a highly specialized program upon the IQ in high grade mentally deficient boys. *Proc. Amer. Assoc. Ment. Defic.*, 44:216–21.

Masland, R.L., Sarason, S.B., and Gladwin, T. (1958). *Mental Subnormality.* New York: Basic Books.

Mullen, F. A., and Itkin, W. (1961). *Achievement and Adjustment of Educable Mentally Handicapped Children.* (U.S. Office of Education Cooperative Research Program, Project SAE 6529.) Chicago Board of Education, City of Chicago, Illinois.

Pertsch, C.F. (1936). *A Comparative Study of the Progress of Subnormal Pupils in the Grades and in Special Classes.* New York: Teachers College, Columbia University, Bureau of Publications.

Schmidt, B. G. (1948). Changes in personal, social, and intellectual behavior of children originally classified as feebleminded. *Psychological Bulletin,* 45(4), 321–333.

Skeels, H. M. (1942). A study of the effects of differential stimulation on mentally retarded children: A follow-up report. *Amer. Ment. Defic.,* 46:340–35.

Thurstone, T. G. (1959). *An Evaluation of Educating Mentally Handicapped Children in Special Classes and in Regular Grades.* (U.S. Office of Education Cooperative Research Program. Project No. OE SAE 6452.) Chapel Hill: University of North Carolina.

Wrightstone, J. W., Forlano, G., Lepkowski, J. R., Sontag, J., and Edelstein, J. D. (1959). *A Comparison of Educational Outcomes under Single-Track and Two-Track Plans for Educable Mentally Retarded Children.* (U.S. Office of Education Cooperative Research Program, Project No. 144.) New York: New York Board of Education.

Chapter 5

Special Education in the 1970s

SAMUEL A. KIRK

It is an honor and a privilege to give the Ray Graham lecture to the Illinois CEC. As I am sure many of you know, I left Wisconsin and came to Illinois in 1947 because Ray Graham was here; and because I knew that this man would advance, unselfishly, the program for exceptional children. I am sure many of you know the great contribution Illinois made, not only in Illinois, but throughout the nation since a large number of states copied the Illinois plan of special education. My admiration for his unselfish approach to problems and his great leadership caused me to dedicate my book on *Educating Exceptional Children* to Ray Graham, with the following quotation from Lao Tzu, a Chinese philosopher before the Christian century:

> Of a good leader
>   who talks little
> When his work is done,
>   his aim fulfilled,
> They will say:
>   We did this ourselves.

This is a profound definition of a great leader; one who stimulates others to achievement, but does not ask for any credit for himself—the highest form of maturity attained by very few.

No institution, no program, no procedure can remain static. A growing child cannot remain static. He either grows or dies. Special education in this country has been a growing child. It has not remained static. It has had, like all growing organisms, its growing pains and in the process of growth it may have developed some boils or tumors that have to be removed. It, like the larger society in which it operates, is still going through a process of change. The forces of the new are questioning the practices of the old. And, the old are annoyed at the continual cry for change.

Speech given at the Annual Convention of the Illinois Council for Exceptional Children, Chicago, April 1970.

Several years ago, Dr. Lloyd Dunn addressed this group on the problem of special classes and later revised and published the speech in the September 1968 *Journal of Exceptional Children*. This article has been misinterpreted by many as a position paper to abolish all special classes and return the children to the regular grades. I have reread the article and find that he is referring primarily to the mildly mentally retarded from low socio-economic and minority groups. He was objecting to the label "mentally retarded" and a curriculum for the mentally retarded for children whose, possibly low, IQs on middle class tests are misclassifying them and offering them a program for truly low IQ children when their needs are of a different nature. His statement that they would be better off in a regular grade with itinerant clinical teachers may be correct. But some are now placing these children in regular grades where they have failed earlier without proper special help.

In one school system the director of special education received a letter from the superintendent directing her to reduce the number of minority children in special classes. That meant closing about seven special classes, returning the children to the regular grades, and sending the special teachers to these schools to help them in the regular grades.

In the United States we tend to swing with the pendulum. It's all on one side for a while and when this one side isn't the total answer we swing all the way to the other side, which may not be the answer either. In the field of the deaf, some advocate residential schools for all deaf children and point out the advantages. Others advocate only day schools and point out their advantages. Can we have a system that will encompass the advantages of both and eliminate the disadvantages of each? This is too difficult. We would prefer propagandizing one approach or the other.

I should like to point out that for adequate progress to take place it is necessary for us to continually change and continually challenge our procedures. It is natural that as we discover facts from research or experience, we find other ways of doing things. When we find our present organization or our teaching procedures are not getting expected results we become restless. We look for other ways of doing things. But change is hard to make, and there is always resistance to change. And, sometimes the changes we make are not any better than the older methods. At that point we become restless again and either want to go back to the old method or find a new one. This phenomenon disturbs some people, but I think we should recognize that restlessness. Dissatisfaction with the old may be our salvation. But change is usually in small pieces and much of the old remains.

To understand where we are, what changes are in the wind, it is necessary for me to comment on how we got where we are. As you know, special education has existed in this country for over a century. But great emphasis and expansion occurred after World War II when states began to subsidize special classes in public schools. The laws and financial support in Illinois did not occur until 1943 and 1945. It was after this period that numerous self-contained classes for exceptional children were organized. Regular education was happy with this development since it took problem children away from the regular classroom teacher. In 1946 Ray Graham wrote to me in Wisconsin saying that the classes for the mentally retarded in Illinois were becoming dumping grounds for all types of problem children. It was at this time that qualified psychological examinations were introduced to keep out of the classes for the educable mentally retarded those who did not belong.

The number of special education classes in a city, town, or country became the measuring stick for progress. Any director who was able to multiply the number of classes under his direction was acclaimed as a progressive director. Quality of education was not the major consideration, but the number of children supposedly served was the criterion of progress. Some 10 years ago one of our faculty members made a study of directors in this state. He asked them three questions: What is the status of special education in your city? The answer was usually, "We have five classes for the mentally retarded, three speech correctionists, one class for the partially sighted, and so forth." The next question was: What was the status five years ago? The answer: "Oh, just one class for the mentally retarded and one speech correctionist." Then: What do you think will be the status five years from now? "Oh, ten classes for the mentally retarded, six speech correctionists," etc.

Their measure of special education was the number of classes in the city. Only two of the fifteen directors interviewed did not talk about numbers of classes but about curricular programs and quality.

It seems to be a tradition in this country to measure status and programs by size. The bigger, the better. Like the chambers of commerce in most cities spending their time bringing more industry into Podunk. The more, the better. The more pollution we have, the more money we make. This appears to be the current measure of progress.

I should like, at this point, to list some of the controversies that are current in special education and, hopefully, suggest some solutions.

First, many have stated that we now have "hardening of the categories." By this they mean that the categories of deafness, blindness, mental retardation, etc. are not that clear-cut, and that we should not organize special classes for these children on the basis of their major handicap. Keep them in the regular grades, they say, and give them itinerant help based on a diagnosis of their needs. Most people who make these statements have not demonstrated to us how you educate a trainable mentally retarded, or a totally deaf child in a regular grade. When we ask about these concerns we find that they are talking about the borderline child. This is not a new problem, since many years ago we took minor handicaps like the hard of hearing and organized programs of hearing aids, lip reading, etc. while they attended the regular grades. Partially sighted children have been integrated with the help of resource rooms for many years. The only one I know dealing with this problem seriously is Dr. Frank Hewitt at UCLA, who has enrolled in the same class children with different handicaps under individualized instruction in an engineered classroom. Even Dr. Hewitt does not include the severe types of handicaps like deafness or blindness or trainable mentally retarded.

A more serious criticism of special classes has been launched against those organized for the educable mentally retarded and the emotionally disturbed. These are the classes that have come under attack and these are the classes that are being closed in some parts of the country.

To understand the criticism and to ferret out the truth for decision making we must look into what we have learned over the years from research and experience. We must not arrive at conclusions from isolated facts or emotionally-toned arguments, otherwise we will be operating like the three blind men who felt different parts of the elephant and arrived at three different conclusions. Should we take the word of the blind man who felt the leg and decided it was a tree, or the word of the blind man who felt the tail and decided it was a rope? What does research tell us?

In 1951 Johnson studie[d] for his doctorate thesis the social position of the mentally retarded in the regular grades. He found that the mentally retarded were generally rejected and isolated in the regular grades. Although they were physically integrated with normal children they were socially rejected and isolated. Many quoted this study as evidence that these children would be better off in self-contained special classes. Actually, the study did not make this implication.

In the 1950s and early part of the 1960s, many studies were made on the efficacy of special classes. These studies compared the progress of mentally retarded children in special classes with those in regular grades. What did these studies find?

    a. In general, the social adjustment of educable mentally retarded in special classes was slightly superior to that of those in regular grades.

    b. But in academic learning, educable mentally retarded in the regular grades are equal to or superior to similar children placed in special classes.

    c. And, in the Goldstein, Moss, and Jordan study children with IQs of 80 and above tend to achieve at a higher rate in regular grades than similar children in special classes.

    d. But, the reverse is true for children with lower than 80 IQs. Special class children achieve a little higher than similar children placed in the regular grades.

From these isolated facts, what decisions can we make? Should we have special classes or shouldn't we? Personally, I cannot arrive at a sensible conclusion from these facts alone. But I can arrive at a conclusion if I include other factors.

Not too long ago psychologists found that when you give a group of fast learning rats to an experimenter and tell him that they are fast learning rats they excel. If he is told that the fast learning rats are slow learners, they do not learn as fast. Rosenthal and Jacobson conducted similar experiments with children. Again, they found the achievement of the children correlate with the perception of the teacher concerning their abilities. With children of the same ability, when the teacher was told that they were bright children, they achieved more than when the teacher was told they had low abilities. This raises the question of the effects of labeling children as mentally retarded when, like many of the culturally disadvantaged who test low, they are not mentally retarded!

Another factor is that we must consider whether children we label as mentally retarded are so-called "familial retarded" or culturally retarded. Jensen has tried to differentiate familial from culturally retarded children who test low on conventional intelligence tests. He found that in spite of the low IQs, the culturally disadvantaged retarded tested normal on paired associates and learning and memory, while the familial retarded with the same IQs tested low on the tests. We have found similar results on the ITPA. For example, blacks from low socio-economic areas are normal on auditory sequential memory, while Indians and Mexican-Americans are normal on visual sequential memory. Thus the label "mentally retarded" as determined by intelligence tests may be mislabeling many children from minority groups.

In many low socio-economic areas, especially among minority groups, the percentage of children labeled mentally retarded and placed in special classes is 2 to 5 times the number of whites from higher socio-economic areas that are so labeled and placed in special classes. The minority groups are objecting quite militantly to this procedure. If Rosenthal and Jacobson are right, then it would follow that if we place a child who is not actually mentally retarded in classes for the mentally retarded, he may become mentally retarded.

Another development has been the recent emphasis on learning disabilities. The learning disability approach emphasizes the analysis of the child and the correction of his disabilities. Some children earlier diagnosed as mentally retarded on intelligence tests and some emotionally disturbed have been found to have remediable disabilities and should be remediated as learning disabled instead of offering them a curriculum for the mentally retarded or the emotionally disturbed.

Taking into consideration the results of studies on the efficacy of special classes, the fact that higher children in class with lower children may regress to the mean of the group and the recent emphasis on the remediation of disabilities. What decisions should we make concerning special classes and the course of special education?

In the future, I think the percentage of such children in special classes will be less than at present, since we will have better diagnostic techniques for differentiation of those who need relatively self-contained classes.

There will be a greater emphasis on keeping emotionally disturbed, socially maladjusted, and some higher mentally retarded in the regular grades. But keeping them in the regular grade will require a new type of service that will offer either itinerant teacher or a resource room for them. This will require a new kind of special teacher, probably classed a diagnostic remedial specialist, who is skilled both in diagnosis and remediation. This kind of clinical teacher will be trained to do the whole job with ancillary help from other disciplines. She or he will be the one through whom all information from social workers, doctors, psychologists will be funnelled. She will interpret the data, discover through her own procedures the remedial method needed for each child. She will offer the remedial training for the children and also help the classroom teacher integrate the information with classroom work. At present, some schools close the classes for the mentally retarded, then ask the special teacher to be the diagnostic remedial specialist for the children in the regular grades, even though she has had no training or experience in this area. If my guess is correct, the schools of the future will be manned with those well trained clinical teachers who will help keep the children in the regular grades.

There will be an expansion of preschools for handicapped children in the United States. Today we have a few million for experimental preschools. But there are bills in Congress that eventually will pass and expand day schools, day care centers, and preschools in disadvantaged areas—not just Head Start.

One of the things that has concerned me is the lack of preschools in the U.S. for all children. The reason is the lack of money. In Paris 90% of the children between the ages of three to six go to public-supported "maternal schools," from 9:00 to 4:00—not just half days! I cannot accept the excuse of no money for children in the richest country of the world, when poorer countries support such programs. I cannot accept President Nixon's veto of the one-half billion dollar increase in the education budget on the excuse that it is inflationary, especially when the President recommends billions for ABM and other armaments as "not inflationary." I facetiously recommended at one time that maybe we should declare the United States an underdeveloped country in preschool education and ask France, England, Sweden, Germany, and the Soviet Union to appropriate some of their funds for underdeveloped countries in preschool education. We are doing that much for underdeveloped countries as far as guns are concerned. Two years ago the Federal Congress appropriated one million dollars to initiate preschools for handicapped children. I personally think that preschools for handicapped children alone is not sufficient.

We need preschools for all children from 3 to 6 and especially in low socioeconomic areas. When we have these it would then prevent some children from becoming retarded and also aid us in identifying the handicapped children as we now do for school-aged children.

I think, however, that when we come to our senses and quit thinking we must supply the world with guns and bombs to fight each other and put our money where it belongs for our own people, we will have universal preschools and national health for all our kids. You will note from my remarks that I like the younger generation who are revolting against our perverted values. I have become impatient with our government, republicans and democrats, who are allowing the military-industrial complex to run my country at the expense of our children. We must change our national priorities and emphasize the welfare, education, and health of our own people instead of expending half our Federal budget for planes, guns, and bombs, or even going to the moon.

In conclusion, I should like to say that the 1970s will see:

1. An expansion, particularly in quality, of education for the more severe types of handicapped children.
2. There will be an expansion of preschool education for all children and particularly for the disadvantaged and the handicapped.
3. An expansion of itinerant teachers and resource rooms for children who could remain in the regular grades with specialized help. This is not a new concept since speech correctionists and remedial teachers have done this for years.
4. The newer programs for learning disabilities will be our wedge between special education and regular education.
5. From the field of learning disabilities will evolve a new kind of diagnostic remedial specialist who will serve many as itinerant and resource teachers.
6. The citizens of this country are now opposing the national priorities established by our government in ways of spending our tax dollar. They will soon demand to return to the humanism that was the foundation of this country.
7. We will evolve alternative solutions to our problems—not special class or nothing, not teacher or nothing, but several ways of doing the job.

Part IV

Learning Disabilities

INTRODUCTION

JAMES C. CHALFANT
Department of Special Education and Rehabilitation
The University of Arizona, Tucson

I first met Sam Kirk in September 1959. I drove to the University of Illinois to inquire about entering the doctoral program in special education. When I was told to see Sam Kirk, I said, "Who's he?" I was directed to 1003 West Nevada Street, where I found a professor writing at his desk and smoking a big cigar. I knocked on the door and said, "Dr. Kirk? My name is Jim Chalfant, and I want to work with handicapped children. Should I get a doctorate?" He looked me over and said "If you're smart enough. Sit down." Since that day, my life has never been the same.

Nothing could give me greater pleasure than to be invited to comment on Sam Kirk's romance with children who have specific learning disabilities, particularly since I was around when much of it occurred. The four excellent papers selected for inclusion in Part IV cover a 22-year time period from 1966 to 1984, when Sam and I completed our book *Developmental and Academic Learning Disabilities*. To set the stage properly, let's go back to when it all began.

The Clinical Era

During the 1930s, Sam became interested in why children had difficulty reading, so he began teaching reading to slow-learning children. He began to link specific kinds of reading difficulty to specific kinds of learning problems. He first mentioned the term *learning disabilities* in his book *Teaching Reading to Slow Learning Children* (1940). There were very few—or no—special education services in most of our public schools prior to the late 1950s. The few programs that did exist were in a few wealthy, progressive school districts. Much of the work done between the 1930s and 1960 took place in university and private clinics by the early pioneers such as Cruickshank, Kephart, Kirk, Orton, Monroe, Myklebust, Strauss, and Lehtinen, and so on. Clinical teachers such as Marianne Frostig, Elizabeth Freidus, and others organized private remedial schools to serve these children. Parent groups had become active and organized an association called the Association for Children with Learning Disabilities (ACLD).

By 1966, the National Institute of Neurological Diseases and Blindness had established three national task forces to collate the existing status of knowledge about "learning disabilities." These task forces were directed toward (1) terminology and identification; (2) educational, medical and health-related services; and (3) a review of the research.

INTRODUCTION

Sam's paper "From Labels to Action" (Chapter 6) was presented at the first ACLD conference in 1966 at a small hotel in Tulsa, Oklahoma. Although attendance was small, nearly every contributor to the field was at this first convention. The dining room was so small that conference participants were seated whenever a chair became available at a table. After 3 days, most participants had met and dined with nearly every authority in the field. What made "From Labels to Action" a landmark presentation for that time period is how clearly Sam saw the conceptual confusion of parents and teachers about "learning disabilities." One of Sam's many abilities is his talent for cutting through to the heart of complex issues and problems. His presentation helped parents and teachers (a) clarify terminology and definitions used to describe the learning disabled population; (b) move attention from labels to the unique behaviors that characterized these students; and (c) make the link between behavioral analysis and treatment to achieve desired student outcomes. Twenty-six years later, these same issues are still being rediscovered, discussed, and debated. One of the reasons Sam's presentations were so effective is that he always illustrated each of his points through fascinating case studies and examples. This paper is a good example of his ability to make issues real and understandable through examples.

The Public School Era Arrives

By 1972, public schools had begun establishing services for children with learning disabilities, and the prevalence of these students identified as "L.D." rose every year. In Dallas, Sam spoke directly about the problems that he saw beginning to emerge from public school programs for these students. His presentation "Learning Disabilities" (1972) (Chapter 7) began with a historical perspective for the field. He pointed out how physicians were the first to describe how individuals lost their abilities to read, write, spell, compute arithmetic, understand, and speak due to brain injury. He explained the contributions of psychologists who developed assessment instruments to measure abilities and disabilities, and emphasized that the teachers, who were attempting to teach these children to learn, were now carrying the field forward.

This presentation was one of the first to point out that the increased prevalence of learning disabilities was due to the misunderstanding of what constitutes a learning disability. The lack of alternative services to help underachievers in general education also was contributing to many underachievers being classified learning disabled in order to provide help. The students with learning disabilities and those who were underachieving were being perceived as synonymous. At that time, classes for students with mental retardation were being terminated, and many of those children also were classified as learning disabled to provide needed services.

Sam described the role confusion that was beginning to appear between general education teachers and special educators. Special educators were beginning to teach every problem that existed, and general education was not meeting the needs of underachieving students. Sam believed special education was beginning to assume the responsibilities of general education. He also raised the issue that teachers could not provide differential treatment to differential problems if they were expected to serve large numbers of children in a minimal amount of time. All of these problems remain major unresolved issues in our schools today.

The Age of Controversy

For those of us who were there, the decade of the 1970s was an age of professional controversy, debate, argument, and wheel spinning. Professional journals featured articles that attacked theories, attacked tests, attacked teaching methods, attacked personnel preparation, and attacked service delivery systems, all of which were countered with resounding rebuttals. Journal reading was interesting and national conferences were verbal free-for-alls. It was a very "stimulating" time. In 1975, the *Education for All Handicapped Children Act* (Public Law 94-142) was passed and special education services were mandated. This created even more pressures on schools to provide special education services.

In his 1977 paper presented at ACLD in Washington, DC, Sam outlined "Our Current Headaches in Learning Disabilities" (Chapter 8). The title was appropriate, because most of us did have headaches during that age of controversy. The first headache Sam mentioned was the popularity of learning disabilities, which " . . . had experts coming out of the walls by the hundreds." He pointed out that many of them were confused about definition and classification, so Sam outlined three clear criteria that should be used for identification. He discussed four problems that he believed were causing great confusion.

First, the services for students with learning disabilities were being used as a "dumping ground" for a great number of children who were being inappropriately classified as learning disabled. He emphasized that these underachieving children needed the normal developmental methods, while children with learning disabilities needed specialized methods of instruction.

Second, he discussed the flaws of "pseudo-researchers" who asked the wrong questions about the wrong children and derived inaccurate results. He pointed out that the subjects of many of these studies did not truly have learning disabilities and that the use of group statistics with this low-prevalence population yielded invalid results, which only added to the confusion.

Third, the territorial wars between speech/language pathologists, remedial reading teachers, teachers specializing in learning disabilities, and so on added to the confusion.

Fourth, there was a controversy over the most effective teaching methods and materials. Sam went on to enumerate possible solutions for each of these four problem areas, which he believed would improve services to children with learning disabilities.

The Future

By 1980, Sam had been speaking, teaching, and writing for nearly a half century, and special education was being taken for granted by parents. Sam's fourth paper, "Issues in Learning Disabilities" (Chapter 9), was delivered at Flagstaff, Arizona, in 1984. This paper was written at a time when Sam was looking to the past regarding the development of the field of learning disabilities and was looking toward the future for a better way to serve these children. One evening, we were discussing the changing role of special education and how our schools might better meet the needs of children who have learning disabilities. Sam said, "Let's write a book." We completed it—*Developmental and Academic Learning Disabilities*—in 1983. It was an opportunity for both of us to pull together all we believed about learning disabilities in a single publication. It was one of the most interesting professional experiences I've ever had. During our writing, we co-taught a class and had students read and react to our chapters. It was a happy time for both of us. "Issues in Learning Disabilities" was written shortly after we had finished our book, and this paper presents the past, the present, and the future, and outlines many key issues from our book.

The first section of the paper provides a fascinating review of little-known events that were the driving force behind the federal role in special education. These firsthand observations are delivered in a storylike style that summarizes 30 years of change and make great reading. The second section of the paper reviews problems such as the increased prevalence of learning disabilities and the need to differentiate between children with learning disabilities and underachievers, and comments about the regular education initiative. The third part of the paper addresses the need to modify programs for students with learning disabilities and presents specific suggestions for the future, such as services for the preschool children with learning disabilities, the education of general education teachers to deal with minor disabilities in their classrooms, the establishment of teacher assistance teams, the availability and provision of one-to-one remediation when required, and the abolishment of self-contained classes. Many of these recommendations have been or are being implemented.

Sam Kirk is one of the most interesting men I have ever met. Among the characteristics that have made him so effective in influencing education in the United States are his ability to see needs and problems begin to emerge, his ability to conceptualize practical approaches to meet those problems, his sensitivity to people's concerns, his political savvy and ability to influence others to act, and his speaking and writing skills that enable him to communicate with and teach others.

Sam always has had one foot in the future. He has influenced not only my life, but the lives of thousands of children with disabilities as well. Their parents have also been affected by what he did.

His clarity of thought and practical recommendations have as much relevance today as they did when they were written. So, go back in time to different eras and take pleasure in reading about the way things were and what Sam Kirk thought should be done for children.

James C. Chalfant is currently a professor at the University of Arizona. He has worked as a public school teacher and for the U.S. Office of Education as Research Coordinator and Chief of Personnel Preparation Programs and State Plans for the Handicapped. He was an associate professor at the University of Illinois and director of the Special Education Laboratory. At the University of Arizona, he directed the Learning Disability Clinic and served as department head. On a year's leave, he served as coordinator of the Comprehensive Services for Personnel Development for the United States.

Dr. Chalfant's degrees are from the University of Illinois, where he was trained in all areas of special education and administration. His research and publications have been concentrated in the areas of school-based teams, service delivery, and learning disabilities. He has written 18 books and monographs and over 50 articles and chapters. He is an internationally known consultant and has worked with 41 states, all Canadian provinces, the Philippines, and South Africa.

Dr. Chalfant has led three major task forces for the U.S. government. His most recent task force and publication was the Regular Education Initiative, *Educating Children with Learning Problems: A Shared Responsibility*.

Chapter 6

From Labels to Action

SAMUEL A. KIRK

In the United States, we have given a great deal of lip service to the education of "all the children of all the people." . . . But all the children of all the people did not learn in the same way or at the same rate. It soon dawned upon authorities that children of the same age differed markedly in many respects. Some were slow learners, others very fast learners; some could not hear, and were either deaf or markedly hard of hearing; some were blind or very defective in vision; some were crippled; some were defective in speech; and some were emotionally disturbed. . . .

But there is one group of children who were not deaf but could not hear, or who were not blind but could not see, or who had difficulty in learning but were not mentally retarded. It was obvious that these children had difficulties—but their difficulties were hard to label, as they were not deaf, or blind, or mentally retarded. As a matter of fact, some of these children differed from each other so markedly that they could not be categorized. This situation became very frustrating to doctors, psychologists, social workers, teachers, and parents. We had no name that would encompass them all. But soon names were invented in order to decrease the frustration of professionals and parents. "Johnny is brain injured—that is why he does not learn." "But how do you know he is brain injured?" "Because he does not learn, although he is not deaf, blind, or mentally retarded." Few such children could be diagnosed neurologically as brain damaged; but nevertheless it was a satisfying label. People believed that the term *brain injured*, even though not neurologically verified, actually explained the functional deficit. . . .

But attaching the term *brain injury* did not solve the problem. Some children so labeled were hopelessly mentally retarded. Some with a label of brain-injury (cerebral palsy) were able to obtain M.D. or Ph.D. degrees. Thus the term *brain injury* came to have little meaning since it applied to children with very different abilities. So we used other labels—*brain injury, brain crippled, minimal brain damage, minimal cerebral dysfunction, cerebral palsy,* just plain *cerebral dysfunction, organic driveness, organic behavior disorders, psychoneurological*

Adapted from a paper presented at the Annual International Conference of The Association for Children with Learning Disabilities, Inc. Tulsa, Oklahoma, March 1966.

disorders, and a host of others. These terms, regardless of which ones were used, attempted to establish a neurological basis for the behavior deviation of the child. It was a label that implied a biological cause.

Another group of labels dealt not with etiology but with behavior. I shall enumerate a few of them:

Perceptual disorder, meaning that the child can hear and see, but does not see and hear like others. His perceptual processes, presumably due to a brain dysfunction, do not serve him effectively.

Hyperkinetic behavior, which describes the child who is always in motion.

Conceptual disorder, a disturbance of thinking, reasoning, generalizing, memory or other cognitive functions.

Catastrophic behavior.

Impulsive behavior.

Disinhibited behavior.

Another group of labels deals primarily with communication disorders. And here we have evolved an extensive vocabulary of labels—*aphasia, apraxia, agnosia, dyslexia, agraphia, acalculia,* and many other terms. These are primarily neurological terms. *Dyslexia* could mean that the child has a problem in learning to read, but the term implies that the difficulty in learning to read is related to some brain dysfunction. I should like to read to you a hypothetical conversation between a psychologist and a sophisticated 10-year-old child who was having difficulty in learning to read.

Psychologist: You took a great number of tests yesterday. Did you like them?

Boy: No, because I couldn't read them so good.

Psychologist: Yes, that is why we have the tests—to find out why you haven't learned to read.

Boy: What did you find? What is wrong with me?

Psychologist: We have found that you have a severe problem in learning to read.

Boy: Where did I pick that up?

Psychologist: You didn't pick it up. You've probably had it all along.

Boy: Is it catching?

Psychologist: No, it's not a disease—it's a condition—a condition in the brain.

Boy: A condition in the brain? Am I nuts?

Psychologist: No. You're not sick.

Boy: Will it get worse? Will I die?

Psychologist: No. It's just a condition that makes it hard for you to learn to read.

Boy: Oh, I see! That's what my teacher said—I can't read so good, huh?

The point I am trying to make is that labeling or classification of children into separate categories may be satisfying to us but not very helpful to the child. The Binet and Wechsler tests have been used primarily to determine whether a child is mentally retarded, dull, average, or superior, and have been used to place him into one or another program. Many psychologists have been concerned with the limited use of these instruments. There is criticism of an indiscriminate use of the IQ or MA, and attempts to seek a more differential diagnosis. Many diagnosticians have consequently fallen into the trap of differentiating some types of children and labeling them as brain damaged even when there is no neurological evidence supporting the diagnosis—and even though the term includes children with widely different problems. In a small proportion of these cases, the diagnosis may lead to medication, but unless it does the diagnosis is of little value. From an etiological point of view it does not disclose any cause that can be removed; and from the point of view of treatment or management or training it gives no direction or purpose. Treatment advisable for one may be contraindicated for the next.

What we really want is not labels, but analysis of behavior. Such steps may be found to reeducate or reorient or supply needed experiences on which improved functioning may be developed. At this meeting, you will hear, or have heard, of the different approaches to diagnosing and treating learning disabilities. Most of the speakers are interested in diagnosis for treatment purposes, not just for classification.

Fortunately teachers and diagnosticians are now becoming interested in organizing programs for those children—programs based on a behavioral and psychological assessment. These methods take many forms and deal with different problems. Diagnosis and treatment can work hand in hand to utilize our knowledge, understanding, and creative approaches in order to alleviate conditions and remedy behavior. Let me cite a few examples of how this approach has been successfully used.

One 5-year-old child, for example, spent a great deal of time with her thumb in her mouth. We could label the child as neurotic, or we could say the child has a tic. We could tell the mother she is rejecting the child, or that the child did not have the right sucking experiences, or that she is brain damaged. But a more effective approach was found by observing the behavior and applying well-known psychological principles. It was noticed, for example, that when the child was playing, she did not suck her thumb. But when she was watching television, her thumb was always in her mouth. The question here was what to do about it. One method was to remove the television, but this would not stop the thumb sucking, since it would occur in other situations. A simple procedure was devised whereby the mother pressed a button to turn off the television when the child's thumb went into her mouth, and then pressed the button to turn on the television when the thumb was out of the mouth. It did not take the child long to learn that if she wanted the television on, this would occur only when she was not sucking her thumb. This simple device was enough to break the habit of thumb sucking. This is what I mean by moving on from labels to action.

I think the best way to illustrate the variety of individuals who have different kinds of disabilities is to cite several case studies. Some years ago a high school graduate applied for admission to a college in which I was serving as selection officer. I refused admission because his grades in high school English had been very low and his scores on a reading intelligence test were below the lowest 25% of high school graduates. He then took courses in a junior college, repeated his English course three times before passing it with a grade of D, but obtained fairly good grades in mathematics and drafting. After 2 years at the junior college, he again applied to the college in which I was the selection officer, and again I rejected his application because of low scores on intelligence tests and his poor showing in rhetoric. But this time he was persistent. He appealed to the president for admission. I was required to give adequate reasons for rejection, or at least look into his case further. Upon analysis of this individual based on a number of tests, I found that he was quite superior in spatial ability and in quantitative ability, but very inferior in verbal fluency. I admitted him into the college with the recommendation to the English department that he be given special tutoring in diction and in English usage.

Four years later, this individual had completed not only his bachelor's degree in art, but also his master's degree. He was now art director in a very large city. He still had difficulty in English and diction, but the supervision of art programs in schools did not require great verbal fluency. Here was an individual who had a learning disability in one area. He could have been denied an education had we not been forced to look into his situation a little more closely. His case made me wonder how many others were denied further education because of a learning disability in one area.

Some years ago, a boy 10 years of age was brought to me by a school principal because of the child's inability to learn to read. On an individual intelligence test, his IQ was 140. He was now in the fifth grade, but was practically a nonreader. I found that he had two disabilities, one in auditorizing and one in visualizing. I recommended to the father that he have his son's eyes checked and that he obtain a good remedial teacher. I did not see this boy again until he was 22. He had graduated from high school and had served in the Army for 2 years. He was also enrolled in a junior college. But his basic problem remained—he could not read well. On tests, he now scored at the fifth- and sixth-grade levels in reading and spelling. He had completed high school work because his mother read his lessons to him. He was admitted to a junior college and again succeeded partially with the aid of his mother. He now requested admission to a large university, but was not accepted. After 6 months of special tutoring by a tutor in his disability areas, he now scored at the ninth- and tenth-grade levels. We asked that he be admitted to the university as an experimental case. Tutoring for 1 year in the university resulted in his achieving passing grades. Five years later, this individual had passed all the examinations and courses in animal sciences but had still failed his rhetoric exam because of a disability in spelling. It was necessary to waive the rhetoric examination that he had failed twice in order to award him a bachelor's degree in animal science.

Another interesting child was one who had been committed to an institution for mental defectives at 2 1/2 years of age because of convulsions and severe mental retardation. At the age of 4 1/2, he was given a series of examinations and scored around 50 and 60 IQ, but at that time he did not have any further convulsions. An EEG at this time, however, showed an abnormality. Here, according to our knowledge, was a child who was and could be labeled *feebleminded*. He was thus certified and labeled as such by physicians and psychologists. At this time we initiated an experiment on early training of mental defectives in the institution. Fifteen children, ages 4 to 5, were taken out of the wards daily and offered intensive preschool education, while another group remained in the wards. This boy was one of the 15 experimental children. At this time, his IQ was 50 to 60. His convulsions did not continue, although he still had an abnormal EEG. He made rapid progress in mental and social development in the preschool and was paroled from the institution to a foster home in the community. He was later adopted by a highly educated family. An EEG was repeated at the age of 7, and again it showed an abnormality. Much tutoring and care was given this boy in school, by his mother, and others. Today, at the age of 19, he is a freshman in college, with an average grade of B. Where would this boy be today had he remained in the wards? How many more of these children have we labeled, without taking the time to do what should be done with children with such problems?

I should like to present a slide of a child who was diagnosed a number of times as mentally retarded, but who was probably a severe case of learning disabilities.

Here is a child who, at the age of 4 1/2, tested below 50 IQ except for tests that required no language, and, on these, she was low average. On certain tests, she showed that she was able to understand and receive visual and auditory meanings and was able to discriminate shapes visually at an average level. She was, however, very defective in all other areas.

Intensive training with this child over a period of 4 years showed the following development:

FIGURE 1
Results of Remediation

A = Pretest – Age 4-1
B = Posttest IV – Age 6-9
C = Posttest VI – Age 8-8

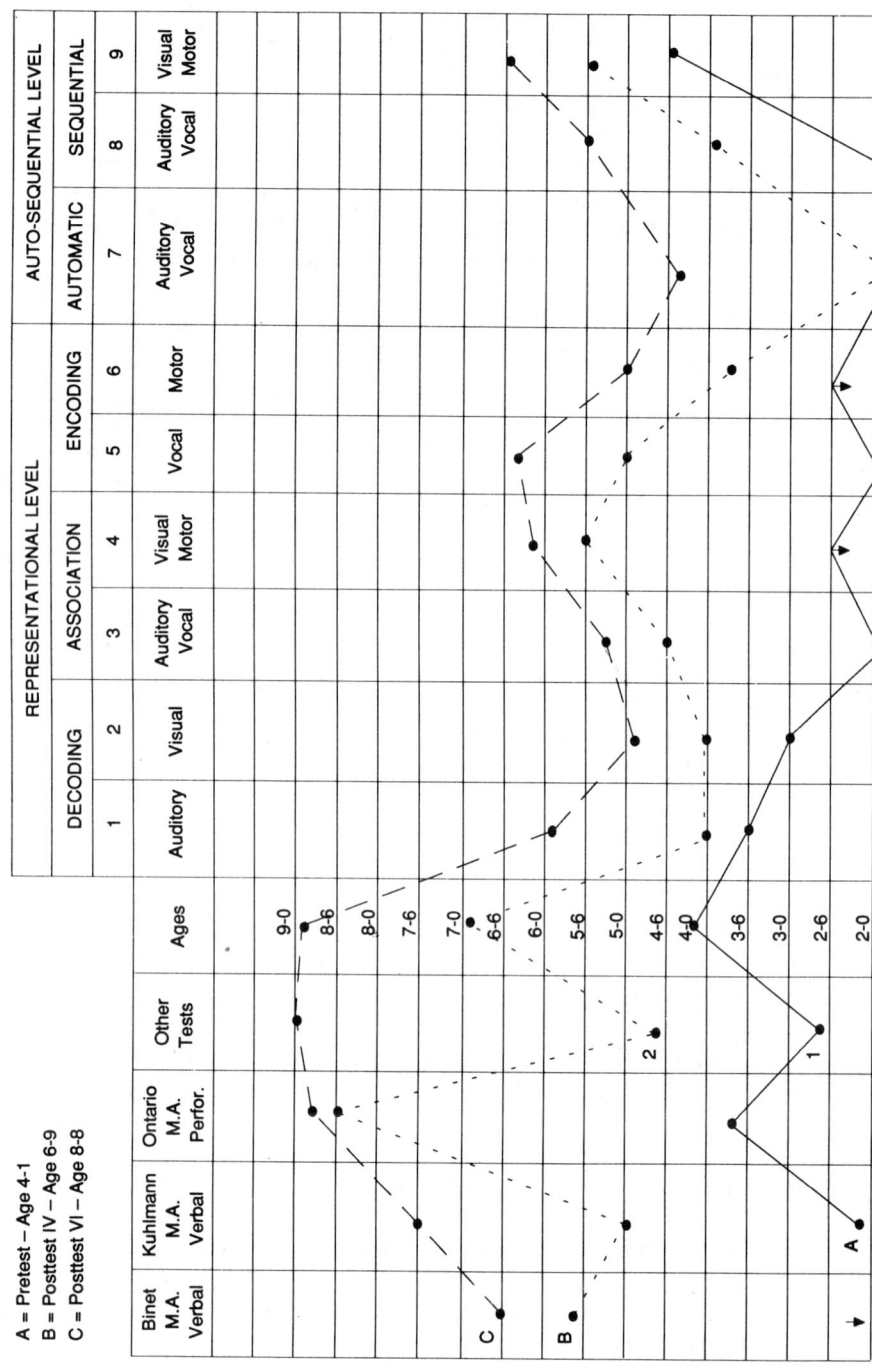

She progressed mentally a year per year under remediation and on psychological tests, whether they were performance or verbal intelligence tests. Although she was mentally about 2 years old at the age of 4, she now, at the age of 8, is mentally age 6. She is still 2 years retarded, but since the beginning of remediation she has progressed 1 year per year. The profile shows a more even development. In addition to this psychological profile, the child is doing second-grade reading and arithmetic and is only slightly retarded in academic work.

The next child is one who is 8 or 9 years of age and who appears to be average in intelligence and average in all abilities except the ability to express himself. The accompanying profile indicates that this is a child who cannot express himself vocally or gesturally. Speech correction and counseling seemed not to help him. The treatment for this boy was by the use of programmed instruction in which the child filled in what he did not know on a typewriter and a tape recorder. It will be noticed from this profile that the boy made rapid progress in 7 months of remedial instruction.

The reports of various types of disability at this conference show a major change in the approach to children with learning disabilities. Instead of classifying children into categories and instead of worrying about the etiological classifications, names, labels, and categories, the concentration of most workers at this conference—Kephart, Myklebust, Frostig, and many others—is an attempt to analyze the child's ability in such a way that remediation and training can follow.

The philosophy of remediation does not deny a basic cerebral dysfunction. It implies that children withdraw from areas that make them uncomfortable, or unsuccessful, and exaggerate the areas of response on which they are successful. If a biological defect causes a child to be unsuccessful in one area, that child will tend to avoid that area and function in a field where he is successful. At a later age when we test the child and find a marked behavioral deficit, that deficit may be only partly the result of the biological defect and partly the result of lack of development due to avoidance experience. An analogy can be made between the use of hands. If a cerebral dysfunction in the motor area makes the child's left hand uncoordinated, the child will avoid using the left hand, and overuse the right hand. As a result, the growth of the use of the right hand is average or above, while the left hand grows in coordination more slowly. Remediation in this case would be special exercise of the left hand. Thus the philosophy of remediation of deficits asserts that the deficits are totally or partially environmentally caused, generally through avoidance of essential experience. Remediation then tends to reinstate this experience, even at a later date.

FIGURE 2
Comparison of Pre- and Post Remediation Language Profiles

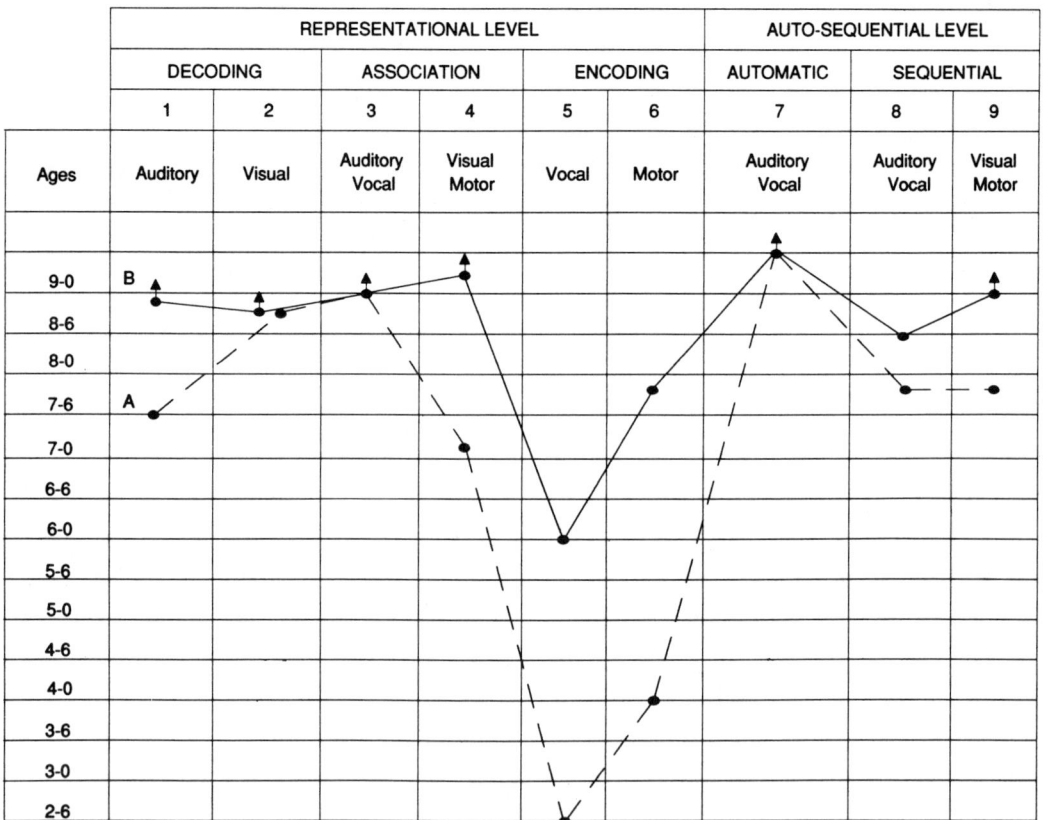

NOTE: A = Pre-remediation CA 9-11
B = Post-remediation CA 10-10

Chapter 7

Learning Disabilities

SAMUEL A. KIRK

Learning disabilities, the topic of this conference, although not a new disability to professionals, is really one of the newest categories of disabilities that is being subsidized by states and by the federal government as one of the programs of special education. It is the only category that has been defined in federal legislation and is also the most vague and illusive. It has the widest range of estimates of prevalence. Some authorities estimate that 1% of school children have a learning disability, while others estimate 50%. For some reason, the term has caught public attention. Parents like the concept, perhaps because it explains why a child is not learning in school when he is so bright in some ways and so unable to learn in other ways.

The effects of learning disabilities cut across those of other kinds of disabilities—the deaf, blind, mentally retarded—and are therefore the most misunderstood concept of any kind of handicapping condition in children.

Our concept of learning disabilities is varied and confused. Dr. Birch remembers that I gave a speech at a luncheon meeting in New York several years ago and entitled my speech, "Are We Confused?" In his speech, Dr. Birch said he was not confused, it was just Kirk who was confused. I would like to tell you this evening, I'm still confused because I'm not quite sure what learning disabilities are all about. I'm confused because everybody seems to have a different concept of what learning disabilities are. I'd like to discuss this evening how we got here, how we arrived at this concept of learning disability, what we are doing with it, and where we are going.

Historical Development

One of the things that has interested me a great deal is the evolution of many of our programs with handicapped children. In the earlier centuries—the 18th and 19th centuries and part of the 20th century—the responsibility for handi-

---

Speech given to The University of Texas Health Center, Dallas, Texas, February 1972.

capped children was the responsibility of the physician—not the psychologist nor the educator. As we look into the field of mental retardation, for example, what do we find? We find the names of Jean Marc Itard, Edward Seguin, Maria Montessori, and Decroly. These were the educators of the mentally retarded. These people—Itard, Seguin, Montessori, and Decroly—were all trained as physicians, and the most interesting thing about it was that their contributions were not in medicine, but in education.

When we look at the history of learning disabilities (it wasn't called that at first), we find the same story. The early contributors to this field were physicians—usually neurologists or ophthalmologists. Historically, we find that in the 18th century, the first man who comes to mind is a fellow by the name of Franz Joseph Gall, a Viennese physician—the father of phrenology—who recorded some cases of loss of linguistic ability as a result of head injuries. In the 19th century, the name that is best known to neurologists is John Hughlings Jackson, who formulated many of our modern theories of cerebral functions, particularly functions that explain epilepsy and language disorders. The other man who stands out historically is Henry Head, who wrote two volumes on aphasia. This morning, Dr. Schain mentioned the name of James Hinshelwood, an English ophthalmologist, who wrote a classic book in 1917 called *Congenital Word Blindness*. It is rather interesting that these people were all physicians and yet their contributions were not only in etiology or the relationship of the brain to function, but also in their contributions to training and education.

Dr. Hinshelwood made an interesting contribution (if I recall correctly). He described in his book that many children were referred to him by school teachers in England because they were not learning to read. The teachers assumed that you read with your eyes and, if you can't read, there must be something wrong with the eyes; so they sent their reading failures to Dr. Hinshelwood for an eye examination. He examined these children and could not find anything wrong with the eyes of most of them.

Hinshelwood described a case of a patient who had a brain concussion as a result of an accident and who had lost the ability to read. Dr. Hinshelwood found nothing wrong with the man's eyes, but the patient had definitely lost the ability to read. He tried to train him by the alphabet method because he could not read or learn words as wholes. Hinshelwood, furthermore, made a contract with this patient that when he died he would let Hinshelwood have his brain. Shortly thereafter the patient contracted pneumonia and died. After an autopsy, Hinshelwood concluded that the center for reading was in the left angular gyrus. When children cannot learn to read, Hinshelwood postulated that the child had an underdevelopment of the left angular gyrus.

One of the points I am trying to make is that many of the earlier authorities in the fields of language and reading were physicians whose contributions were primarily in education. Apparently, the training of physicians in the earlier days in Europe was less specialized and extended into many fields. In the United States, the training of physicians has recently become more specialized. But historically, we have had major educational contributions from some individuals trained in medicine. A noteworthy authority is Samuel Gridley Howe. He was a physician who, with Horace Mann, contributed major educational innovations. He is the man who stimulated work with the handicapped in the early 19th century and who was the forerunner of the work with Helen Keller. In 1857 he asked the legislature of Massachusetts for $2,500 to organize a program for mentally retarded children. The legislature passed the appropriation in Massachusetts, but the governor vetoed the appropriation; whereupon, Dr. Howe wrote an open letter to the governor of Massachusetts. It is a fascinating document. In this letter in the 1850s, he enunciated the rights of the mentally retarded in a democracy. The legislature of Massachusetts was so impressed with this letter that it overrode the veto of the governor, and Howe obtained his $2,500.

An early contributor to learning disabilities in the United States was Samuel T. Orton. Dr. Orton disagreed with Hinshelwood. He did not accept the contention that alexia, dyslexia, or congenital word blindness [are] the result of an underdevelopment of the left angular gyrus, but rather the result of a lack of cerebral dominance. He called the condition strephosymbolia, or twisted symbols. Lack of cerebral dominance, according to Orton, caused reversed errors in reading.

A major contributor was Alfred Strauss. He worked in Germany after World War I as a neurologist. When Hitler came to power, Strauss escaped from Germany and went to Barcelona, Spain. Here he opened a child guidance clinic. When Franco took over, Strauss went to England and then to the United States. He did not take out a medical license in this country since he desired to contribute to the *education* of brain-injured children.

What I am trying to emphasize here is that the early work in learning disabilities—reading disabilities, thinking disorders, behavior disorders, and language disorders—was originally the responsibility of physicians. Later, psychologists took over the field of mental retardation and learning disabilities. The names of Travis in speech and language disorders, [and] Marion Monroe, Gillingham, Fernald and others in reading disabilities, are a few psychologists who became prominent in the field. Here we find a shift from medicine to psychology. The shift then went to the psychologist educator. However, in the last 10 to 15 years, the bulk of the work that is being done in these disabilities is being done by a new kind of educator who is, to some extent, interdisciplinary, trained in psychology, biology, and special education.

The major impetus to learning disabilities in children in the last three decades, I think, should be attributed to Orton, Marion Monroe, Fernald, Strauss, and a few others. The modern reference to brain-injured children was popularized primarily by Alfred Strauss. As I indicated earlier, Alfred Strauss came to this country in the late 1930s. He came with Hans Werner, a Gestalt child psychologist from the University of Berlin.

Dr. Strauss, Hans Werner, and Laura Lehtinen worked at the Wayne County Training School (where I was at one time). They worked with brain-injured, mentally retarded children. Here Strauss, Werner, and others conducted research on hyperactivity, thinking disorders, and perceptual disorders of brain-injured children. You may disagree with his neurology, but I think we can say that Strauss's book *Psychotherapy of Brain-Injured Children* at least said to parents: "We can do something for your children; they are not all mentally retarded. Some of them have disabilities in perception, behavior, and thinking that can be ameliorated through special education."

Parents are a very important group for the development of programs, for their effect on legislators, and for the motivation of professionals. I recall with interest the development of the national program of ACLD. In 1966 the Chairman of the program committee telephoned me and requested that I give her the names of the 10 most prominent individuals in learning disabilities in the world. I informed this parent that most world authorities are busy and that most of them did not have funds to travel to deliver addresses. Since the organization did not have funds, it would be an imposition to ask them to come at their own expense, especially from a foreign country. The response over the phone was, "I asked for the names of the 10 greatest authorities; I did not ask you about our business operations." I then gave her the names of one person in London, one in Brisbane, Australia, and others in the United States. Within two weeks she called me to inform me that she had phoned and obtained 7 of the 10 as speakers for the ACLD Conference, including the one from London and the one from Brisbane. The meeting was held in Tulsa, Oklahoma. The hotels could not accommodate the large crowd enrolled at the conference. So the next year the meeting was held in the Waldorf Astoria Hotel in New York. These incidents demonstrated to me the interest in the field and also the power of the parents' groups to affect the interest of both parents and professionals.

Prevalence

Why the sudden interest in learning disabilities? Apparently, the reason [there were] 6,000 people at the meeting in New York was because every parent with a problem child (mentally retarded, emotionally disturbed, hyperactive, inability to read, educationally retarded, etc.) came to find the solution in the new movement. That is probably the reason why prevalence figures range from 1% to 30%. A recent questionnaire sent to 50 so-called experts in learning disabilities gave the percentage of learning disabilities as 1% to 5%. Some gave the prevalence as 10%, and one indicated it could be 90%.

I am getting a little concerned about the expansion of the field to include very minor problems that really do not need specialized remediation. That is what happened in the field of mental retardation. In 1920, we passed state laws about mental retardation indicating that the mentally retarded were those who had IQs of 69 and below. Then we extended it up to 72, then to 75, and to 80 and even 85. This resulted in the organization of many special classes. In the larger cities we found the greatest enrollment [in special classes] to be among Blacks and Chicanos. Apparently, minority children could not pass the tests standardized on middle-class whites. As the classes became predominantly minority-group children, their parents objected to having their children in special classes, so they took their case to court and won. Now we have discredited the IQ, not because the IQ isn't all right, but because we have misused it.

In this respect, we seem to be following the same history as that of the Soviet Union. In 1936, the *Communist Manifesto* abolished what they called pedalogists (psychologists) from the schools in Russia. They claimed that the Binet test discriminates against the children of the working class, and that this school procedure is just a capitalist method of discriminating against the working class. In the U.S., we are now saying the same thing. We are discriminating against minority groups by giving tests that have been standardized on middle-class whites and classifying the children as mentally retarded.

Prevalence figures depend on the definition and the cut-off point. In a normal distribution, one standard deviation below the mean gives 17%. Seventeen percent of children have IQs below 84. If we give a reading test, 17% of the children are going to be one standard deviation below the mean. I am afraid that our prevalence figures are the results of the administration of a test and then taking the lower one-sixth of the curve as [the population with] learning disabilities.

In many places, underachievement is becoming synonymous with learning disabilities. A child who is [behind] (a year or two) in reading or arithmetic in school is called learning disabled. But there are many reasons for underachievement. One could be mentally retarded and be underachieving. One can be disadvantaged or lack educational opportunity and be underachieving. The child can have no motivation for school and be underachieving. He can have visual or auditory problems and be underachieving. In other words, there are a great number of reasons for underachievement in school.

We also seem to forget normal variation in every group. Some people are short; some people are tall. That does not mean that they are abnormal or that they require special remediation. Every fourth-grade teacher has children reading at the third-grade, the fifth-grade, and the sixth-grade level. Every class has a certain range within it. We should expect this variability. This should be the responsibility of the regular grade teacher. We should not take away this responsibility by offering remediation to the one-sixth of the children [who are] at the lower end of the normal curve.

The National Advisory Committee for Handicapped Children, of which I was privileged to be chairman for a while, tried to define learning disabilities. It was necessary for us to not only define learning disabilities, but also to "guesstimate" a prevalence figure. Earlier in 1963, Congress passed the Mental Retardation Construction Act (Public Law 88-164). It provided research facilities, affiliated centers, and training of personnel in special education. It included [funds for] the mentally retarded, the deaf, the blind, etcetera. It did not include [funding for children with] learning disabilities. However, the training of personnel was accomplished under the provisions for "crippled and other health handicaps that require special education."

In 1967 The National Advisory Committee defined learning disabilities as disorders of language, thinking, reading, writing, and arithmetic, and included the conditions we formerly called aphasia, brain-injury, [and] dyslexia. The definition excluded primary mental retardation, sensory handicaps, emotional disturbances, and disadvantaged children. In other words, it did not include all the handicapping conditions [for a handicap] for which we already have legislation.

How do we determine prevalence? The National Advisory Committee decided to give the prevalence for the more severe cases, and indicated that the prevalence was 1% to 3% of a school population. If we have 3%, we would have 1 1/2 million school children; 10% would be 5 million school children. Therefore, if we think of one teacher for every 10 learning disabled children, we would need 50,000 new teachers.

These figures are really big orders, but we have had some people testify before Congress and state that 20% to 30% of school children are learning disabled. Many of us wonder about what groups they are talking.

As a result of the clarification of the definition and prevalence rates, a bill was passed by Congress in 1969 entitled the Learning Disabilities Act of 1969. The bill made provisions for research, training, and service. Please note that it took six years between 1963, when P.L. 88-164 was passed, and 1969, to obtain a bill for learning disabilities. However, the passage of a congressional bill with a definition did not solve the practical problems.

Terms and Labels May Not Be Helpful

Learning disabilities encompass all kinds of disabilities not [classified] under mental retardation, deaf, blind, and crippled, and the traditional categories of handicapped children. There are many disabilities under the general categories. A few years ago, the Secretary of Health, Education and Welfare, at the request of President Johnson, organized a President's Committee on Dyslexia. As soon as people heard that there was a Dyslexia Commission in Washington, the chairman got something like 10,000 letters from parents asking him to solve the problem for their dyslexic child.

Sometimes it is an evasion of responsibility when a psychologist or a neurologist writes "dyslexia" on the chart; and when the parents ask "What's that?" he says, "Go and read Critchley's book on dyslexia." The use of a label such as *dyslexia* may be a block to progress, since it may give the impression that a scientific solution has been found. Marion Monroe wrote a book on reading disabilities after 20 years of research and entitled it *Children Who Cannot Read*. To me, that title is most parsimonious and consequently most scientific. If a parent describes a child with the descriptive terms "cannot write," "read," "spell," or "talk," I consider these more understandable and more useful than terms such as aphasia, dyslexia, and apraxia.

I am happy to see that the medical school here has an interdisciplinary team working on learning disabilities. They will tend to keep each other honest. Under this kind of organization, the pediatrician, psychologist, or educator won't get too cocky because none of them really knows the answers to all our problems. Our diagnostic and remedial practices in this field are based on about 20% or 30% knowledge and 70% or 80% guesswork. We are dealing with a very complex problem and we have to make the best guess we can for each child.

I was in France 2 or 3 years ago, and I noticed that in one of their clinics they had special teachers for special subjects. If the child did not read at a particular level, he went to Teacher A for remedial reading instruction. If he could not do arithmetic, he went to Teacher B for remedial arithmetic instruction. If he could not talk, he went to another special teacher. In other words, each remedial teacher specialized and worked with one particular disability.

In this country, we are so imbued with mass education that every time we start something we have to play the numbers game. We employ a teacher of learning disabilities and tell her to take as many kinds of children as she can. I am not sure that a teacher of remedial reading is a specialist in training a child with delayed speech. Yet we employ a learning disability teacher and ask her to treat "anything that comes around." A child with a visual channel disability is going to require a very different kind of treatment than the child with an auditory channel disability. [This concept] is similar to the [idea of] training the deaf through the sense of touch and vision and training the blind through the sense of hearing and touch.

I believe that in the future we will probably employ specialists for certain kinds of severe disabilities. In many of the public schools today we have to account for so many children that we tend to serve the mild cases and neglect the more severe ones. We followed that procedure in the field of speech correction when the state declared that "every speech correctionist had to have a caseload of at least one hundred." Under that sort of a caseload, the speech correctionist could not deal with severe language disorders, since this kind of a child required 5 hours a week of her time. She devoted her time to [children with] mild articulatory disabilities. As a result, the severe language-handicapped child was neglected. Today I notice that in some school systems [children with] severe learning disabilities are being neglected in favor of [children with] milder handicaps who can be remediated in groups.

I have taken up a lot of your time, so let me state in summary that:

1. Learning disabilities has now become a confused concept including a heterogeneity of disabilities, and with some including all underachieving children, regardless of origin.
2. Historically, physicians dealt with brain-injured adults, but also contributed to educational procedures. Later, psychologists became prominent, and today psychoeducators have taken over most of the responsibility for behavioral diagnosis and remediation.
3. The prevalence of the condition has ranged from 1% to 20%, depending on whether one is dealing with the severe disabilities or the very mild.
4. The medical terms used for the different disabilities—dyslexia, aphasia, echolalia, agraphia, etcetera—are being replaced by behavioral and descriptive terms such as, "the child can't read, or talk, or write."
5. It is likely that in the future we will categorize children according to the remediation they need, rather than by labels. Specialists in reading, language, writing, arithmetic, etcetera might be employed for remediation, rather than expecting one person to be an expert in remediation for all disabilities.

Chapter 8

Our Current Headaches in Learning Disabilities

SAMUEL A. KIRK

The topic assigned to me is quite complex—"Our Current Problems in Learning Disabilities"—but I will make use of the speaker's prerogative and change the title to "Our Current Headaches in Learning Disabilities." I should like this morning to discuss a few problems that are current.

First, a persistent problem has been the clarification of the definition and the concept of learning disabilities. We have not been required by legislation to provide operational definitions for mental retardation, or emotional disturbance, or speech defects, or other handicaps, but we are now requested to define learning disabilities operationally. Perhaps this request has been necessitated for a good reason. It may be that our parent and professional groups, as well as our journalists, have differing concepts of the learning disabilities and have consequently confused the public and our legislators. I must admit, too, that this has confused me.

For many years some of us have used a three-pronged criterion to identify a child with a learning disability. This morning I should like to start by repeating these three criteria; namely, (a) a discrepancy criterion, (b) an exclusion criterion, and (c) a special education criterion. Let me explain:

A Discrepancy Criterion

Children with learning disabilities have significant discrepancies in the development of their psychological processes (perception, seeing relationships, motor ability, attention, memory) or unexplained disparity between their potential judged by some abilities and their academic achievement. Developmental imbalances in psychological, social, or motor abilities are generally noted at the preschool level, while discrepancies between general or specialized intellectual development and academic achievement are observable factors at the school-age level. A child, for example, who does not talk at the age of four

---

Paper presented at the Association for Children with Learning Disabilities Conference, Washington, DC, March 1977.

but who has other perceptual, cognitive, and motor abilities that appear normal, would be considered a child with a learning disability at the preschool level. The school-age child who is relatively average in mental ability, who has made normal progress in arithmetic computation but who has not learned to read after 3 years of adequate schooling, would indicate a learning disability at the school-age level.

An Exclusion Criterion

Most definitions exclude from the learning disability designation those difficulties in learning that can be explained by general mental retardation, auditory or visual impairment, emotional disturbance, or lack of opportunity to learn. This exclusion factor does not mean that children with hearing and vision impairments or children who are diagnosed as mentally retarded cannot also have learning disabilities. These children require multiple services.

Need for Special Education

Children with learning disabilities are those children who require special education for their development. A child who has not had an opportunity to learn and is retarded educationally will learn by ordinary methods of instruction at his level of achievement. For example, if a child comes out of the woods and has not been in school up to the age of 9 or 10, but upon examination is found to have normal cognitive and perceptual abilities but has not learned to read or achieve in arithmetic, this child could not be considered to have a learning disability even though he has a discrepancy between ability and achievement. Such a child will learn by ordinary methods of instruction and does not need special education. In other words, the addition of the criterion of the need for a special method because of some psychological disorder that has inhibited his ability to read is an important criterion.

Any program of identification of learning disabilities should use these three criteria: a significant discrepancy between development and achievement; a discrepancy that cannot be explained by other handicapping conditions such as deafness, blindness, [or] mental retardation; and the need for a special remedial instruction program because of a process disability.

In many discussions of the meaning of learning disabilities, these three criteria are forgotten. Instead we may hear disturbing remarks, even from some professionals, such as:

1. "There is no such thing as a learning disability."

or

2. "Children with learning disabilities are the same as the mentally retarded and the emotionally disturbed."

or

3. "Every child who has a school problem [has] a learning disability."

or

4. "It is a 'kitchen sink' term; a 'garbage can' concept."

or

5. "It is a political creation that is attached to children in numbers that maximize local school subsidies for special education programs."

or

6. "All you need for your learning disabled child is to buy 'my method' or maybe 'my vitamin.' "

With such statements—coming from not lay people, but professional people—no wonder some journalists are having a field day denying the needs of learning disabled children.

One possible reason for these controversies and confusions is that we have grown too fast. A few years ago we had difficulty interesting professionals in the field of learning disabilities. But since the movement became popular we have so-called learning disability experts coming out of the walls by the hundreds, writing books and articles and making speeches on the state of the art. We have, in a sense, opened up a Pandora's box—giving forth a great number of programs and including conditions not included in the original concept of learning disabilities.

I should like to discuss four of our problems and practices that may be causing difficulty, namely; (a) the "dumping-ground" practice, (b) pseudo-research, (c) the territorial war, and (d) the panacea of methods and materials.

1. The Dumping-Ground Practice

Learning disabilities programs in public schools are now including a great number of children who should not be classified as learning disabled. Among the LD population are included *minor reading problems, behavior problems*, and *slow-learning children*. Often included are many children whose aspiring parents feel they are not obtaining good enough grades in schools.

This phenomenon of elaboration, extrapolation, and exaggeration is not new to the field of special education. Hard-of-hearing children have been classified as deaf. Visually impaired children with some sight have been taught Braille when they could read print.

We have gone through the same problem with the mentally retarded. When I started in special education in the early 1930s, special classes for the mentally retarded included children whose IQs were between 50 and 70. This was the psychometric definition of mental retardation in Wisconsin in 1927. Following World War II, many states passed laws appropriating funds for special classes for the mentally retarded in the public schools. As more funds became available, the acceptable upper limit of the IQ for admission went up and up and up, and the enrollment in special classes increased from 113,565 in 1952 to 703,800 children in 1969.

The American Association on Mental Deficiency (AAMD) defined mental retardation psychometrically as one standard deviation below normal, or IQs below 85. The special classes then enrolled behavior problems and many minority group children (Blacks, Mexican-Americans, Puerto Ricans, and American Indians) who were tested with intelligence tests standardized on Caucasians. Special classes for the mentally retarded became the "dumping grounds" for children the teachers didn't want in their classes. But the minority groups caught up with us. They challenged our concepts of mental retardation and methods of dealing with their children. They even took their case to court and won.

So what was our reaction? The AAMD redefined mental retardation as minus two standard deviations, or IQs below 70. And now we are back to our earlier concepts of mental retardation during the 1920s and 1930s. But what do we now do with the 10% or 15% of the children [who have IQs] between 70 and 84? Now they are called "learning disabled" and mainstreamed. In other words, we have a new name—learning disabilities; we have a new organization—mainstreaming—for children who should not have been in special classes in the first place.

We originally thought that children who are severely retarded in reading and who are found to have a psychological disability that has inhibited their learning to read under ordinary instruction have a learning disability. The differentiation between a child who is merely retarded in reading and a child who is learning disabled in reading is based on a diagnosed psychological disability associated with the reading retardation. But in our schools we find many children who have minor reading retardation due to lack of opportunity, lack of motivation, poor home backgrounds, and other *extrinsic* factors not related to the child's *intrinsic ability* to learn to read. These children need help, but not in the remediation of a learning disability. The lack of opportunity to learn to read required giving adequate opportunity with developmental reading materials—not the remediation of special disabilities. Such children need opportunities with developmental methods, not specialized methods of instruction.

2. Pseudo-research

Another phenomenon that emanated from Pandora's box is pseudo-research that is creeping into the literature. Although one can find some modest research reports, many of the reports are not leading to any constructive solutions. Why? Probably because many of the studies are asking the wrong questions [as a basis for their research or] are dealing with the wrong subjects.

We have study after study that compares, for example, poor readers with good readers on certain psychological functions such as visual discrimination, visual memory, auditory memory, sound blending, etcetera. Many of the studies are conducted at the third- or fourth-grade level with children whose psychological functions score at the top of the norms used. [Not finding] any difference between good readers and poor readers in sound blending, auditory discrimination, etcetera, they erroneously conclude or imply that these psychological processes or psychological functions or abilities have nothing to do with learning to read.

I think the major difficulty with most of these studies is the fact that when they study visual discrimination, for instance, they are not really dealing with children who have *major visual discrimination problems*. For example, you and I know that [a] child who cannot visually discriminate between 'a' and 'b' or 'was' and 'saw' or 'man' and 'dog' [cannot] learn to read. The reason why negative results are found in such studies is because 99.9% of school-age children have enough visual discrimination to learn to read at the age of 6.

A typical example of research now found in the literature is [a study] testing the visual discrimination or sound blending or visual memory or whatnot of 30 third- or fourth-grade children who are reading a year or more below grade [level] and comparing them with those reading at grade level. The lack of significant difference between the groups' results leads to the conclusion that visual discrimination, sound blending, or visual memory has no relation to reading. One of my colleagues, Dr. Jerry Senf, has maintained that this is the wrong question for research in this area. If we test 30 mentally retarded children and compare them with 30 average children on tests for cretinism or hydrocephaly we will likely find no significant difference. We might run the data through computers using analysis of variance or discriminant analysis or what have you, then erroneously conclude that cretinism or hydrocephaly is not a correlate or cause of mental retardation.

If, on the other hand, we ask the question, "What is the probability of cretinism or hydrocephaly causing mental retardation?" we will obtain a different answer. This research will require that we find untreated cretins or hydrocephalics. When we find that mental retardation exists in the group, the probability is very high that a disability will result from cretinism or hydrocephaly.

The same experimental logic applies to learning disabilities. If we test 30 poor readers in the third grade with a visual discrimination or an auditory discrimination test and compare them to 30 children who have learned to read, we may not find any significant difference between the good and poor readers in visual discrimination, probably because all of them have sufficient discrimination to learn to read. It is absurd to conclude from the results of this research that visual discrimination is not necessary for reading. The right question for research is "What is the probability of a child with very inadequate discrimination, or visual or auditory memory, having difficulty learning to read?" This will mean finding (out of 10,000–20,000 children) some 15 or 20 children with very poor visual discrimination or poor sound blending or visual or auditory memory (probably 3 standard deviations below normal). It will require this kind of an experiment to answer the question of whether very inadequate visual discrimination ability contributes to reading retardation.

What I am trying to say is that Pandora's box has been opened and [has] cluttered up the journals with articles that are asking the wrong questions and that are probably producing the wrong answers. It has given a forum for iconoclastic critics who are on an ego trip with negative rather than positive approaches.

3. The Territorial War

A third wave from Pandora's box has resulted in a war between professional workers in learning disabilities, speech pathologists specializing in language disorders, and specialists in remedial reading. The International Reading Association has passed a resolution requesting legislatures to certify graduates of reading-language programs as learning disabilities specialists. The August issue of the *Journal of Learning Disabilities* asks: "Does this mean that IRA wants LD jobs?" And so it goes. The American Speech and Hearing Association is also active in this field, asking for a limiting license to diagnose and remediate learning disabilities.

The major issue at stake, as far as I can determine, is that special education funds have been appropriated for the support of learning disability specialists and not for specialists in communication disorders or remedial reading. Each area feels their territory has been invaded by the learning disability specialists, often after taking only a few summer school courses in learning disabilities.

4. Remedial Panaceas

A fourth, and most important, area of woes released by Pandora's box is the battle over methods and materials for learning disabilities. I have tried to analyze the different approaches used and have concluded that we have three major approaches to remediation that guide methods and materials. I label these (a) task or skill training, (b) process training, and (c) process-task training or aptitude instructional interaction. I should like to discuss these three basic methods.

Skill or Task Training

Classroom teachers have always had the responsibility of finding out what a child can do and what he cannot do in content subject. Procedures have been developed to assist the teacher in informally making an inventory of what a child can do in reading, writing, spelling, and arithmetic. In reading, the teacher determines at what level the child is reading—that is, the independent, instructional, and frustration levels. After inventorying the child's level and reading skills, she organizes a remedial or corrective or developmental program. Good teachers diagnose children in the manner described, defining daily objectives to be attained, and start the child at a comfortable but challenging level. They break down the lessons into subskills that would aid the child in progressing in that skill or content area.

The applied behavioral analysis approach is a refinement and a more adequate system of what a good teacher normally does. This approach advocates: (a) finding out what the child can and cannot do in a particular skill, (b) analyzing the behaviors needed to succeed in the task, (c) defining the behavioral objectives, and (d) organizing a systematic remedial program using reinforcement techniques. The applied behavior analyses do not infer processes that underlie difficulties but rely solely on behavioral events and environmental conditions. [Advocates of this approach] feel that their approach, which is task-oriented and observable, is the most parsimonious approach, and, to some, the only approach needed.

Process Training

Another remedial method that is common may be labeled *process training*. Process training assumes that what the child produces (that is, the products) are dependent upon intrinsic psychological processes and that for these skills to develop, it is necessary to train the underlying process. If a child is expected to learn to read, for example, it will be necessary for him to have visual discrimination, sound-blending ability, and a host of other cognitive and perceptual skills. If the child is to learn to talk, it will be necessary for him to decode verbal language and to encode his concepts into verbal expressive language. Some try to train a process in isolation, hoping that the ability will facilitate or automatically transfer to the learning of a skill at a later date. For example, if a child has poor visual discrimination, he is given visual discrimination exercises, discriminating between circles and squares, etcetera, hoping that this training will develop an ability that will facilitate learning to read later. The opponents of process training state that research has not demonstrated that visual discrimination training or the training of other processes facilitates learning to read. Materials and methods that are currently used to train psychological processes in children have been challenged as worthless.

As I indicated earlier, the research in this area has been difficult to control and most studies have dealt with children who already have sufficient visual discrimination ability or visual memory ability to learn to read.

The other approach to training processes is to train [in] a process for its own sake, without reference to transfer or how it facilitates learning at a later date. Sometimes the process itself is the skill to be developed. If a child does not decode language, has not learned to listen, we train the process of listening for its own sake. If the child does not discriminate objects in his environment, we train him to discriminate objects in his immediate environment. If he does not discriminate between touching a hot stove and a picture of a fire, nature teaches him to visually discriminate for its own sake.

In other words, there is a question about the practice of [teaching] processes in isolation, hoping that they will transfer to a skill at a later date. Few, however, question [teaching] a process for its own sake. The whole program, and curriculum, and [set of] activities found in kindergarten and nursery school deal with [teaching] processes for their own sake as well as for later development.

The Process-Task Approach (Aptitude Instructional Interaction)

Some specialists feel that for the ordinary child with problems evolving from poor teaching or lack of opportunity, the skill or task training approach is adequate and effective. Children with severe disabilities, however, require "child analysis" as well as "task analysis." The resultant remediation will involve process and task training in the same remedial procedure; that is, teaching the child to utilize a particular process in accomplishing the desired task. We can label this approach as *process-task training* or as *aptitude instructional interaction*. This means that we match the instruction to the aptitude or lack of aptitude in order to produce the best interaction. It means that we integrate the process and task in remediation. Instead of teaching visual discrimination in isolation, we will train visual discrimination of letters and words. The process-task approach integrates the process deficit with the task development as analyzed. This approach is the one generally used by those who analyze the abilities and disabilities of the child and who make a task analysis of the sequence of skills required by the task itself. Those who practice the process-task or aptitude-instructional-interaction approach are considered diagnostic prescriptive teachers, since they do both child analysis and task analysis.

An example in reading may be given to illustrate the process-task approach to remediation. A child who had attended school regularly up to the age of 9 was referred because he was unable to learn to read in spite of his tested IQ of 120 on the WISC. The analysis of the child's information processing abilities showed a process deficit in visual memory. He was unable to reproduce, in writing and from memory, words presented to him visually. He demonstrated the deficit in visual memory both on norm-referenced tests and on criterion-referenced tests. The process-task remediation procedure in this case called for a program that would develop visual memory with the words and phrases to be taught. This procedure of training the process of visual memory on the task itself is process-task training. Actually, the Fernald Kinesthetic Method is a system of training memory for words—*not* in the abstract, as is done in process training alone—but directly with the words and phrases needed by the child in learning to read. The Fernald method is a process-task approach, since it trains visual memory with words and phrases.

I have tried to present briefly three schools of remediation as I see them. I am sure you will note overlaps in concept and you will note in some instances that the line between process and product is not clear-cut.

What I have tried to point out is that all three remedial approaches are adequate in different situations or with different children. Each is valuable when used in the appropriate setting. Task training is sufficient for minor problems in children and for the majority of corrective academic problems. The process training approach is suitable for training the process for its own sake and especially at the preschool level. Most curricula for nursery schools and kindergarten train processes for their own sake, and sometimes for possible transfer to later tasks. The process-task approach or the aptitude-instructive-interaction approach may be necessary for the more severe problems who have a double disability of task and process. The diagnostic prescriptive approach relies heavily on process-task training. Dogmatism for one approach over another is not warranted.

Possible Solutions

If you recall Pandora's box, you will remember it released evils, but it also contained in the bottom of the box something called *hope*. So I shall reopen the box and release the following hopes:

First, it is hoped that regular elementary education will assume the full responsibility for the minor problems of educational underachievement and for the minor behavior problems and the slow-learning child. It is hoped that the present practice of mainstreaming children who should never have been in special classes will educate the elementary teacher to her responsibility. There is no reason why elementary education cannot try to deal with children who are underachieving due to lack of motivation, poor instruction, or inadequate backgrounds. There is no reason why we cannot reinstate reading teachers and reading supervisors to assist the regular teacher in assuming her responsibility. In other words, it is hoped that elementary education will assume the responsibility for children who *do not* have basic psychological impediments to learning that require remediation. Then the learning disability specialists can devote their time to the training of the hard-core or severe cases of learning disability who require intensive instruction and who cannot be trained by the regular teacher. But we must remember that the minor reading problem, the minor behavior problem, and the slow learner should not be neglected. They need maximum services also for their maximum development.

Second, it is hoped that we will begin to develop sound research that will answer many of our questions. During the past 20 years, we have had a shortage of teachers and teacher-trainers. Colleges of education in universities that were at one time research institutions have often been converted primarily to teacher training or to the preparation of teacher-training personnel. We must begin to train research personnel for this field, personnel who can ask the right questions and give us sound answers. This will require humility and scholarship, the essentials of a scientist not now obvious in many so-called researchers.

Third, it is hoped that the territorial wars now rampant among professionals in remedial reading, communication disorders, and learning disabilities will result in a cross-fertilization encompassing all three disciplines. At present, specialists in learning disabilities are being prepared by eclectic courses only partly covering the skills and knowledge of the professionals in language disorders and remedial reading. Because of the shortages of personnel in this expanding area, learning disability teachers are being prepared in short summer-school courses with minimal clinical experience. It is hoped that in the future, these teachers will be prepared by professionals from remedial reading, speech communication, and learning disabilities. The preparation of personnel from one discipline alone is not sufficient.

Fourth, it is hoped that the air will soon be cleared with respect to methods of remediation. Instead of being an evangelist for one method or approach for all children, we can delineate the specific approach for the specific child and his specific problem. Phonics may be valuable for one child and of little use to another. The Fernald method may be useful to one child and not to another. Each of the procedures—the task-training approach, the process training approach, or the process-task training approach—may be of value, each in its own place for a particular group of children.

In conclusion, I should like to say that when these hopes are realized, we will be of more service to more children, even though we may be stepping on the toes of some professionals.

Chapter 9

Issues in Learning Disabilities

SAMUEL A. KIRK

Many people today believe that what we are doing currently in special education has always existed. As an introduction, I should like to give you a little background of where we came from, when things happened, and where we stand today in special education, and particularly in the field of learning disabilities.

As you probably know, most of our special education after 1900 and before 1950 was conducted in residential institutions for the deaf, the blind, the mentally retarded, the emotionally disturbed, and the delinquent. During World War II, states did not have the funds to build buildings. Consequently they could not keep up with the increased enrollment in institutions.

Parents became extremely frustrated during this period because they did not receive the services for their children either in residential schools or in public schools. As a result they organized, established their own schools, and then pressured their legislators to provide services for them. Their argument was that they were taxpayers like everyone else and that the denial of services to their children in public schools and overcrowding in institutions was not an American procedure.

As a result of parent political action, especially for the mentally retarded, states began to subsidize special classes in public schools. Illinois started [schools for the mentally handicapped] in 1946, and California, I believe, started to subsidize classes in 1947 or 1948. Other states followed. Arizona established its institution at Coolidge and later subsidized public school classes for the mentally retarded after 1960. Since that time Arizona has moved forward rather rapidly.

Adapted from a speech given at Northern Arizona University, Flagstaff, Arizona, 1984.

The Federal Role

The federal government did not support special education before 1955 or 1956. Their argument was that education was a state and local affair and that if the federal government entered the scene we would have federal control of education.

In about 1954, the well-known author Pearl Buck, a parent of a retarded child, was urged by parents to help organize aid at the federal level. Pearl Buck obtained an audience with President Eisenhower and discussed with him the plight of the mentally retarded. She informed him that there was a severe shortage of professional personnel to provide services for these children and that the richer states were stealing good teachers from the poorer states for their expanding special education classes.

In 1955, I was Director of an Institute for Research on Exceptional Children at the University of Illinois, one of the few organizations in the United States doing work in this area at the university level. I was asked to go to Washington to help the U.S. Office [of Education] organize a federal program. After I arrived, I found that the [staff in the] Office of Education was quite disturbed that the Secretary of Health, Education, and Welfare had assigned a young psychiatrist from the Institute of Mental Health to organize programs for education. The [staff] said that they had already made proposals that were not accepted and resented the fact that the medical profession was going to organize education for them.

That afternoon we had a meeting with people from the Children's Bureau, the Institute of Mental Health, Vocational Rehabilitation, and a few other constituents of Health, Education, and Welfare. The meeting was getting nowhere. The psychiatrist who [had been] assigned by the Secretary to organize an education program passed me a note saying, "We are not going to get any place at this meeting; come to my house for dinner tonight and we will discuss the issues over dinner."

That evening I met with this young psychiatrist and several other friends from the Institute of Mental Health. I had become acquainted with the Institute of Mental Health earlier because it had given me grants for a study I made on the effects of preschool education on the social and mental development of mentally retarded children.

At this dinner, I was informed that the Office of Education had proposed a budget of [only] $60,000 to organize several classes for the mentally retarded in Arlington, Virginia to be supervised by the Office of Education. They told me that the Secretary became quite disturbed that the Office of Education did not understand that Congress was interested in a national program, not a state program operated by the Office of Education. It was for this reason that the Secretary assigned the psychiatrist from the Institute of Mental Health to organize education, because he felt that the Office of Education did not understand what Congress wanted.

The next day I did not go to the Office of Education but stayed in my hotel room and wrote a plan consisting of a program of research on a national basis, and a plan to subsidize the training of professional personnel, particularly teachers. These two recommendations—(a) research, and (b) the preparation of professional personnel—were presented to the Office of Education the next day, and later to the Secretary and then to the U.S. Congress.

In 1957, Congress appropriated $1 million for cooperative research, not only for exceptional children but for all areas of education. One year later, in 1958, it appropriated $1 million for the training of professional personnel in mental retardation [alone].

I was on the committee to help organize this program. We decided at that time that $1 million would not train very many teachers, and the best thing we could do with $1 million was to provide funds to universities and state departments for the training of leadership personnel. . . . This was a fortunate decision since it resulted in organizing departments of special education in universities and preparing Ph.D.s to head these departments.

Three years later in 1961, $1.5 million was appropriated for the training of teachers of the deaf.

The Kennedy Era

The next step was what I call the Kennedy Era. President Kennedy, as you know, had a sister who was mentally retarded. The Kennedys had established the Joseph P. Kennedy Foundation to help advance work in the area of mental retardation. Shortly after President Kennedy was elected, he established a committee on mental retardation. This committee sent teams to England, Denmark, Sweden, and Norway, and one team to the Soviet Union in 1962. I was fortunate enough to be on the team to the Soviet Union, where we spent three weeks studying the research and services the Soviets were conducting. At that time we were very impressed with the work the Soviets were doing.

After we returned, the chairman of our committee met with President Kennedy. He reported to the President the extensive research establishment the Russian government had developed under the Academy of Pedagogical Science. He described the Institutes of Defectology in Moscow, Leningrad, and Kiev. In addition, the Ministry of Education had established well-manned schools for the blind, the deaf, and the mentally retarded. Their teacher-training colleges required 5 years of training for a teacher in the defectology program.

About halfway through his report, President Kennedy appeared angry. He turned and said, "Doctor, do you mean to tell me that the Communists are doing a better job for their handicapped children than the greatest and richest country in the world?" The chairman responded, "That's what I'm trying to tell you, Mr. President."

I understand that President Kennedy then left the meeting without hearing the rest of the report and ordered that an extensive bill be prepared to conduct research in medicine, psychology, and education, and to prepare personnel to work with all handicapped children. The bill [was] passed in the fall of 1963 and President Kennedy signed it in October, [just prior to his assassination]. [Kennedy] had asked me to come to Washington and head the Division for Handicapped Children and Youth, which had [been] created in the Office of Education....

After launching the program that entailed spending [a] $14 million appropriation, I made a report describing the program of teacher education and research. I had tabulated the thousands of dollars requested by the states and by universities that could not be supported. We had a budget of $14 million but received requests for something like $60 to $80 million. The late Congressman Fogarty published [my] speech in the *Congressional Record* the next day with a statement to Congress. "I want to bring to your attention a highly successful program that we passed last year. It is necessary for us to give this matter serious attention." The next year Congress appropriated $24 million for research and training. This is the story of the beginning of federal support, which now is not $14 million or $24 million, but is in the billions [of dollars].

The Influence of Parents' Groups

The term *learning disabilities* did not exist in the definition of handicapped children in 1964 when I took over the Division of Handicapped Children in Washington. Earlier, however, groups of parents of learning disabled children, like the parents of mentally retarded children, began to organize....

In 1963, the various associations of so-called brain-injured, or perceptually handicapped, children met in Chicago. Their purpose was to discuss the problem and to organize a national association. They also wanted to develop an appropriate name, since many felt the term *brain-injured* was not the most appropriate.

At that time, I agreed with them that the term *brain-injured* did not have any educational relevance, and that for a service organization they should use a term related to teaching or learning. I mentioned to them that I had used the term *learning disability* as an umbrella term for many of these learning problems.

At their business meeting that evening, they considered a number of names and finally decided on the name: Association for Children with Learning Disabilities (ACLD).

State legislators accepted the name learning disabilities and introduced it as one of the handicaps to be supported under the caption "crippled and other health impaired [children] requiring special education." In 1969, Congress passed the Learning Disabilities Act.

The Growth in Enrollment in Classes for Learning Disabled

I should like to discuss the growth of enrollment in classes for the learning disabled as compared to the growth in classes for the mentally retarded. The enrollment in classes for the mentally retarded had started out at 125,000 and, after the 1962 definition of minus one standard deviation, began skyrocketing, reaching a maximum of 1,350,000 children enrolled in programs for the mentally retarded in 1975.

I should like to comment that the increase in enrollment in classes for the mentally retarded was somewhat deceptive. These classes included bilingual children, children with learning disabilities, behavior problems, and slow learners. These were all labeled mentally retarded because they tested below 85 on the Binet and Wechsler tests, especially if they came from disadvantaged homes.

[In 1975], the definition was changed to minus two standard deviations. The enrollment then began to drop. In 1984, enrollment was 750,000, one half of what it had been in 1975. In contrast [in 1984], there was an increase in enrollment for classes for learning disabled.

In the field of learning disabilities we are seeing similar trends. There were no children enrolled in classes for the learning disabled in public schools in 1965. There were, however, many in parent-sponsored schools. In 1969, when the Learning Disabilities Act was passed, we had approximately 120,000 children enrolled in programs for the learning disabled. By 1978, 10 years later, enrollment was over one million. By 1984, it had reached over 1,800,000. The increase in enrollment has not stopped; it is still going up.

Shepard and Smith (1983) in Colorado studied 1,000 children assigned to programs for the learning disabled. They found that only 43% of the children enrolled in classes for the learning disabled were truly learning disabled according to the state department criteria. Of those not considered learning disabled, 7% were bilingual, 11% were slow learners, 4% had minor behavior problems, and 10% had other handicaps, including mental retardation and emotional disturbance. The rest were either not below grade in achievement or difficult to classify.

These results would indicate that we are now placing in classes for the learning disabled some children we formerly placed in classes for the mentally retarded. It should be pointed out that some children who are emotionally disturbed or who are slow learners or mentally retarded could also be learning disabled.

Classifications of Learning Disabled

One of the problems [in] the [field of] learning [disabilities] is our lack of agreement on what constitutes a learning disability. I have recently divided learning disabilities into two types, and I should like to present this to you because I think it helps clarify the definition and education a little bit.

Learning disabilities include two types of problems: (a) developmental learning disabilities, and (b) academic learning disabilities. Developmental learning disabilities occur primarily at the preschool level and persist into the school-age level. The developmental disabilities are listed as attention, memory, perceptual-motor disorders, including thinking disorders and language disorders. If we were to look for preschool learning-disabled children, we would examine their language disorder, their thinking disorder, hyperactivity, [and] perceptual-motor deficits of memory and attention.

Learning disabilities, however, [are commonly] thought to be a school-age problem manifesting itself as disabilities in reading, writing, spelling and written expression, and arithmetic. The academic disabilities may be related to developmental learning disabilities [and school problems].

Academic Underachievement

The major criticism of the programs for the learning disabled is that we are unable to differentiate learning disabled children from children who are underachieving for reasons other than the child's idiosyncratic characteristics. In a number of studies it was found that there were not reliable psychometric differences between children assigned to learning disability programs and those labeled *low achievers* in the regular grades.

Theoretically, learning disabled children have an intrinsic disability such as in memory, attention, perception, thinking, and language. These developmental disabilities manifest themselves in academic underachievement at the school-age level. These children require special methods of instruction that will ameliorate or accommodate to the developmental deficit and the academic disability.

A non-learning-disabled, underachieving child is one whose developmental learning abilities are intact but whose underachievement is due to environmental or extrinsic factors. Underachievement in children can result from many extrinsic factors. The presence of learning disabilities is only one reason for underachievement.

One current practice, however, is to lump all underachieving children under the caption *learning disabled*. A child who is underachieving and whose developmental abilities are intact may not require special methods of instruction. Such children will learn by methods used for regular children when given an opportunity. If we define a learning disability as an underachievement related to a developmental disability, we can then differentiate an underachieving child from a child with a learning disability. The treatment of a learning disability may require a change in the developmental [sequences]. One example of [such] remediation that I can give is the kinesthetic method. Some children have a marked visual memory disability [and] are unable to remember; they are labeled dyslexic. We need a method to train their visualization ability as well as their ability to remember the words. The Fernald kinesthetic method and other related methods are such methods. The kinesthetic method tries to have the child reproduce words and sentences from memory. [Hirsh has reported that] the kinesthetic method trains visual memory in the recall of words and sentences. In other words, it treats the developmental disability and the academic disability by the same strategy.

Regular Education Initiative

I am sure you have all heard that some specialists in the Office of Education and others in the field have been developing what is known as the *Regular Education Initiative*. This [recommends] the education of handicapped children by regular classroom teachers in regular classrooms and implies that we do not need [specific] special education [programs] for them. Margaret Wang in Pittsburgh and Maynard Reynolds at the University of Minnesota have been advocating that we cut out much of special education and train elementary teachers to handle these children in the regular grades. They want to integrate special education under one system. You will hear more about that in the near future, since the position paper is just being prepared and will be published soon. This point of view maintains that:

1. The special education system is flawed.
2. A coordinated system of service delivery is preferable to the present array of service programs.
3. We need supportive services for children who are not learning, but this should not be offered through special education.
4. Only one system is needed, not the dual system of special education and regular education.

I think most of us agree that for the minor problems of learning, we do not need special programs, and that many of these children can be aided in the regular grades. I wrote about this in 1941 in the President's Page of *Exceptional Children*, as follows:

> There appears to be some confusion in the minds of certain educators of who should care for or educate exceptional children. One group alleges that exceptional children should be educated in special classes, while the other group maintains that exceptional children should be educated by the regular teacher in the regular grades.

Actually the education of exceptional children is not wholly the responsibility of any one group of teachers. All educators and teachers have exceptional children under their care. The special class teacher usually has the extreme types of exceptional children—those that because of their handicaps or special abilities cannot be educated properly in the regular grade. The lack of special equipment, the lack of special skill on the part of the teacher, and the large classes found in many schools make it difficult to adapt instruction to the wide differences among individuals. The regular class teacher, on the other hand, has many children that are not mentally defective but are dull; children that are not markedly visually handicapped but have some visual defect; children that are not completely deaf but have some degree of impairment of hearing; children that are not delinquent but have minor behavior difficulties; children that are not gifted, but still are quite bright; and children that are not so crippled that they need special equipment, yet have minor physical handicaps. In other words the regular classroom teacher has in her class not only so-called average children, but many that possess minor handicaps or special abilities. Every teacher, therefore, is to some extent a teacher of exceptional children, and should utilize with some modifications the techniques employed to educate the more extreme forms of handicapped or gifted children. It is encouraging to note that many educators in the field of exceptional children are conscious of the problems of handicapped and gifted children in the regular grades. For example, the Michigan Conference on the Education of Exceptional Children, in cooperation with the Michigan Society for Crippled Children, and the State Department of Public Instruction, has just published a pamphlet entitled *Helping the Exceptional Child in the Regular Classroom*. This is a noteworthy attempt on the part of special class teachers and educators to help the regular teacher care for exceptional children in her classroom. It is hoped that in the future all special class teachers will not only be responsible for the education of children in their classroom, but will take on the added responsibility of contributing their knowledge and special skill to the regular classroom teacher who has always had, and probably will always have, many minor forms of exceptional children in her classroom. (Kirk, 1941, p. 35)

Suggestions for Modification of LD Programs

To adapt programs to a wide variety of handicapped children, school systems have organized various delivery systems. These include (a) self-contained classes that teach 12 to 15 children for most of the day, (b) resource rooms that teach one or more (usually two or three children) at a time, thus serving 20 to 25 children a day, (c) consulting teachers who advise and assist the regular teacher in organizing remedial instruction for the minor handicaps in his or her class, and (d) variations of these delivery systems. I would like to suggest that the following changes be considered.

Abolish self-contained classes. Teachers of self-contained classes for children with learning disabilities find it difficult to provide remediation for specific learning disabilities of 12 to 15 children with different disabilities in the same class. This alternative was used because it is administratively feasible and supposedly inexpensive. Most teachers of these self-contained classes would inform you that they do not have adequate time to give each child differentiated remediation for his or her idiosyncratic disability.

Organize one-to-one remediation for the severe learning disabled. Many children with severe learning disabilities require one-to-one remediation, probably 1 hour per day five times a week. In this situation remedial instruction can be adapted to the idiosyncracies of an individual child in an effort to ameliorate the deficit or deficits. Such a program may not be more expensive than the self-contained class when we consider the progress such a child can make under one-to-one remediation. It is believed that a child can learn as much in one semester of one-to-one remediation as that child could learn in at least two semesters in a self-contained class.

Organize teacher assistance teams. Chalfant, Pysh, and Moultrie (1979) reported a system that helped regular teachers cope with the problem of underachieving children in the regular grades. Within a building, three teachers are elected to help other teachers cope with their problem children. The team and the teacher who referred the child conduct a problem-solving session. Procedures of group dynamics are applied by the team members to specify objectives, give alternate suggestions for intervention, and plan follow-up activities. The teacher leaves the meeting with a carbon-copy of the recommendations. In one study of the effects of a teacher assistance team, teachers referred 200 children for diagnosis. The team was able to help teachers cope with 88.7% of the children who were educationally underachieving. This procedure demonstrates that not all children referred for special education need a thorough examination, but that with a little peer help, teachers can cope with most of the underachieving children in their classrooms. The learning disabled children, however, require special education to ameliorate the developmental and academic disabilities.

Identify and remediate learning disabilities at the preschool level. The typical learning disabled child at the preschool age has intrinsic developmental disabilities that vitiate learning. Hyperactivity, memory deficits, attention, perceptual motor disabilities, and/or thinking and language disorders are disabilities sometimes found in preschool children. The amelioration of these disabilities or disorders at an early age may tend to prevent or reduce academic disabilities at the school-age level.

Educate teachers to deal with minor handicaps in the regular grades. Colleges of education preparing elementary and secondary teachers have neglected to educate student teachers in the skills necessary to teach [children with] minor handicaps in the regular grades. Much has been written advocating mainstreaming, but little has been done to educate regular teachers in the skills necessary to teach handicapped children once they are mainstreamed. What is needed is the employment of specialists on the faculties of elementary and secondary education. This faculty member will be responsible for giving didactic instruction on the use of the many methods and materials that have been developed to teach learning disabled students. In addition, this faculty member can supervise practice teachers and demonstrate how to use the special methods that are applicable to children with learning problems, slow-learning children, and other underachieving children who are not truly learning disabled.

References

Chalfant, J. C., Psych, M. V., & Moultrie, R. (1979). Teacher assistance teams: A model for within building problem solving. *Learning Disability Quarterly, 2*(3), 85–96.

Fernald, G.M. (1943). *Remedial techniques in basic school subjects.* New York: McGraw-Hill.

Hirsch, E. D. (1963). *Training of visualizing ability by the kinaesthetic method of teaching reading.* Unpublished master's thesis, University of Illinois.

Kirk, S. A. (1941, November). President's page. *Exceptional Children*, p. 35.

Shepard, L. A., & Smith, M. L. (1983). An evaluation of the identification of learning disabled students in Colorado. *Learning Disability Quarterly, 6*(2), 115–127.

Ysseldyke, J. E., Algozzine, B., Shinn, M., & McGue, M. (1982). Similarities and differences between underachievers and students classified learning disabled. *Journal of Special Education, 16*, 73–85.

Part V

Remedial Reading

INTRODUCTION

JANET W. LERNER
Professor of Special Education
Northeastern Illinois University, Chicago

It is an honor to have the opportunity to write the introduction to Part V, "Remedial Reading." The timeliness of the discussions is remarkable; so many of the "new ideas" of today have their roots in Sam's incredible vision.

My relationship with Sam Kirk covers a period of 40 years. His ideas have profoundly affected my views on education, the teaching of reading, and the field of learning disabilities.

My first encounter with Sam Kirk occurred when I was an undergraduate student at Milwaukee State Teachers College (which subsequently became the University of Wisconsin in Milwaukee). I was one of seven students majoring in the mental retardation program. (The only other program in special education was in deaf education.) In addition to being head of the program, Sam Kirk was also my student teacher supervisor. His observation of my student teaching was an unforgettable experience and demonstrated his perceptive abilities. Knowing I was to be observed, I had carefully prepared my teaching lesson for the class of students identified as having moderate to severe mental retardation. During the lesson I frequently called on Mike because he always knew the answers. Sensing the lesson went very well and expecting high praise for my teaching, I was surprised when Dr. Kirk asked, "That red-headed kid Mike. When was he last diagnosed?" I had no idea. Dr. Kirk "diagnosed" Mike on the spot, and reported that his IQ score was 95. Dr. Kirk's comment on my lesson was, "Miss Weiss (my maiden name), the reason Mike was able to answer all of your questions was not due to the quality of your lesson, but that Mike was misdiagnosed. He should never have been placed in this class." Another incident that affected my life during my undergraduate days was that in our senior year, Sam Kirk informed us that we could not graduate unless we attended the weekly seminar he was planning. We all grumbled about commuting from home to the college on the cold winter evenings in Milwaukee. The seminar we were forced to attend was called *Psychopathology and Education of the Brain-Injured Child*, and the instructors were Alfred Strauss and Laura Lehtinen. Of course, it turned out that this valuable seminar set the stage for my professional life.

In my later encounters with Sam, he continued to reveal his wisdom and profound understanding of children with disabilities. In his duties as special education editor for Houghton Mifflin, he was asked to read a draft manuscript of a book on learning disabilities. He did not recognize my married name, Janet Lerner, but he readily identified many of the ideas that he had taught me. He immediately phoned me to find out who I *really* was. When

Sam discovered that I was the Janet Weiss who had been in his class at Milwaukee State Teachers College, it all made sense. His advice and consulting were invaluable in the publication of that book.

I also had the privilege of collaborating with Sam Kirk and Sister Joanne Kliebhan on the book, *Teaching Reading to Slow and Disabled Learners*, published in 1978. This was a revision of Sam Kirk's first book, published in 1940, *Teaching Reading to Slow Learning Children*. (Sam recalled the price of the 1940 book was $1.50.) While writing this book, Sam, Sister Joanne, and I met many times during CEC and LDA conferences. From these meetings, I learned more about Sam's philosophy about how people learn and his psychological theories of teaching.

Part V contains three of Sam Kirk's publications. My comments on each publication are intended to place these publications in historical perspective and to show how they apply to the problems we face today. The three publications are:

1. "The Organization of Remedial Reading in the Schools," presented in 1936.
2. "Characteristics of Slow Learners and Needed Adjustments in Reading," published in 1949.
3. "How Johnny Learns to Read," published in 1956.

The Organization of Remedial Reading in the Schools, was written in 1936, long before the field of remedial reading came into being. In this paper, delivered at the Midwestern Psychological Association in a symposium on reading and speech disabilities, Sam foresaw the critical need for remedial reading programs in the schools. He also forecast the need to train educators who could both diagnose and treat reading problems. His report on a survey of schools in Wisconsin shows that in virtually all of the schools at that time, the classroom teacher was responsible for students with severe reading disabilities. (It seems that the policy of mainstreaming, REI, and inclusion was in full force some 56 years ago.) Sam urged that schools develop remedial reading programs to help students with reading disorders who were not being served. He also suggested a way of organizing the remedial reading programs according to the severity of the problem. Since there were no college programs to train remedial reading teachers at that time, he also urged colleges to establish courses to train remedial reading educators.

In addition, he discussed the remedial reading drills that he had developed and reported on the positive results of using these materials with students identified as having mental retardation. In a period of 5 months, these students progressed 1 1/4 years in reading level. The *Remedial Reading Drills*, which were written by T. Hegge, S. Kirk, and W. Kirk, were published in 1936.

In 1985, Sam Kirk, Winifred Kirk, and Esther Minskoff revised them as the *Phonic Remedial Reading Skills*, and they were published by Academic Press. Built into these remedial reading materials were many of today's linguistic theories of phonics generalizations and minimal contrasts, as well as contemporary cognitive theories of the need to develop atomization and fluency in reading.

Characteristics of Slow Learners and Needed Adjustments in Reading was published by the University of Chicago Press in 1949 as a Supplementary Monograph. As is typical in special education, the field was trying to find appropriate labels for children who were having difficulty. The nomenclature in vogue at this time was *slow learner*, a euphemism that was being used for children with a wide range of problems. Kirk argued that the term *slow learner* should be restricted to the child who does not have the capacity or potential to learn academic skills at the same rate as average children. He described the characteristics of slow learners, including their high drop-out rate. Kirk admonished the schools, especially the high schools, to adapt instruction for students who are slow learners. He emphasized that slow learners can profit from good programs of instruction and proceeded to outline the qualities of a good remedial reading program:

1. Consider the child's maturation level before beginning formal reading.
2. Select reading materials at the appropriate difficulty level for these students.
3. Provide direct and systematic instruction.
4. Provide many opportunities for the children to read enjoyable and easy materials.
5. Provide guidance to develop independence in word attack skills.
6. Motivate students with easy, interesting reading material.
7. Make the education practical and purposeful for life after school.
8. Introduce reading activities of daily life: newspapers, magazines, directions, application forms, income-tax forms, and so on.

These principles for teaching reading to students with reading disabilities are just as timely today as when they were written, some 44 years ago.

"How Johnny Learns to Read," by Sam Kirk and Winnie Kirk, was published in *Exceptional Children* in 1956. The poignancy of this article can only be appreciated in terms of the considerable splash and far-reaching impact of Rudolph Flesch's "angry" book *Why Johnny Can't Read*, published in 1955. Flesch was critical and hostile to the schools' method of teaching reading, and he especially blasted the popular basal readers for teaching children to recognize sight words. ("Basal bashing" has been going on for a long time; it did not start with proponents of "whole language" instruction.) In his book, Flesch maintained that children only needed to learn the sounds of the letters in order to learn to read. There was only one reading instructional material that Flesch praised: the Hegge, Kirk, and Kirk *Remedial Reading Drills*.

Sam and Winifred Kirk wrote this article to respond to the Flesch accolades of their *Remedial Reading Drills*. The Kirks pointed out that these materials were not intended to teach reading to all children in the schools; most children actually did not need them. They were intended for children who were having difficulty in learning to read, and then only for a small portion of the reading instruction.

The Kirks also asserted that Rudolph Flesch had no understanding of the psychology of learning, and even less of how children learn to read. Their explanation of learning in general and learning to read specifically is both sensible and contemporary. They outlined three stages: first, the child perceives a gestalt (or wholeness) of words; in the second stage, children pay attention to the details (word recognition and phonics skills are useful at this stage); and, in the third stage, children look at the whole again, but now adding meaning and comprehension. Flesch mistakenly advised teaching only the second stage, learning phonics skills.

Flesch also argued that reading problems occur only in the United States—not in other languages and countries. The Kirks pointed out that this was misinformation. The problem of reading disabilities is cross cultural, occurring in every nation, culture, and language. Today, there is growing evidence of this observation.

In summary, the three publications in Part V present Sam Kirk's views about reading problems. From today's perspective, the ideas are visionary and wondrously contemporary. These publications are classics; they are as valuable today as at the time they were written.

Janet W. Lerner earned her bachelor's degree in special education at the University of Wisconsin in Milwaukee, where Samuel Kirk was chair of the Department of Exceptional Education. She earned her master's degree from National-Louis University and her doctorate at New York University. She was a classroom teacher and a special education and remedial reading teacher at public schools in several states. She also taught at the college level at the City College of the City University of New York, National-Louis University, Northwestern University, and Northeastern Illinois University. She is currently a professor of special education at Northeastern Illinois University.

Dr. Lerner is the author of *Learning Disabilities: Theories, Diagnosis, and Teaching Strategies*, currently in its sixth edition. She is coauthor of *Reading Problems: Assessment and Teaching Strategies, Special Education for the Early Childhood Years*, several other books, and numerous articles. Her current research interests are special education technology and attention deficit disorders.

Chapter 10

The Organization of Remedial Reading in the Schools

SAMUEL A. KIRK

The earliest interest in reading disabilities was shown, not by psychologists or educators, but by members of the medical profession. It is well known that during the earlier part of this century, Hinshelwood stimulated interest in reading disabilities under the concept of word-blindness. Other medical men, mainly neurologists and psychiatrists, took up the problem of reading disability, labeling it variously as *word-blindness, alexia, dyslexia, visual-aphasia,* or *strephosymbolia.*

During the past 10 or 15 years, psychologists have become interested in the problem and have done considerable research on diagnosis, etiology, treatment, and prevention. Educators are now coming into the picture and are recognizing that reading disabilities are not usually medical, but mainly a psychoeducational problem. They cannot evade the fact that children suffering from reading disabilities are in the public schools; and the public schools must provide adequate training for them. Some schools are taking the results of psychological research and are putting them to practical use. Eventually, the public schools will be forced to provide for the training of the reading disability cases.

As yet, however, the schools have not fully recognized their responsibility, and the problem is rarely being handled in the schools. A survey ... attempted to discover to what extent reading disabilities are being handled by the school systems in the state of Wisconsin. The response to a questionnaire gave the following results:

1. Three systems reported that remedial reading is handled by the classroom teachers without guidance from a clinic or from the administration.
2. Seven systems reported that their remedial reading classes are conducted by the classroom teachers under the direction of a principal or supervisor.

Paper presented before the Symposium on Reading and Speech Disabilities at the Midwestern Psychological Association, Northwestern University, April 24, 1936.

3. Only *one* system reported that it provided a remedial reading teacher to handle the most difficult cases and asked the classroom teachers to handle the cases which had minor reading deficiencies.

Thus only eleven systems in the state of Wisconsin reported that they were doing something about the problem of reading disabilities. But educators in Wisconsin are beginning to recognize their responsibility, for the Wisconsin Conference of State Supervisors has recently organized a five-year plan of study of reading and reading disabilities.

When the educators assume this responsibility, they will ask how the psychologists' methods of diagnosis and treatment can be applied to mass education. And, it will be up to the psychologist to offer some form of organization so that his methods may be introduced into the schools.

Our problem is, then, how we are going to aid the educator in the organization of remedial reading in the schools? Psychologists have been employing clinical or individual methods in the treatment of reading disabilities. The schools, imbued with the philosophy of mass education, want a method by which they can help 30 or 40 children at one time. They insist that the individual method is too expensive. Our problem is, then, to find an efficient and effective method [that] will appeal to school administrators.

Several years ago, working with Dr. Thorlief Hegge, I attempted to develop a remedial reading program by which the clinical method could be made more efficient and more appealing to school people.[1] We trained 10 retarded readers, with IQs ranging from 65 to 86. Although these cases were 11 to 17 years old and had attended school a number of years, they tested [at the] first- or second-grade [level] on standardized reading tests. These children were trained individually or in groups of two for one-half hour a day over a period of 5 months. At the completion of the 5-month period of training, they were retested. It was found that, on average, they had progressed 1 1/4 grades in reading during this period. They had also progressed substantially in other school subjects. We then discontinued remedial training and after another 5 months retested them again. They had continued to show substantial progress.

To determine the significance of this progress, we tested a group of 100 children with similar mental retardation and similar mental ages, but who did not show a reading disability. The comparison showed:

1. That the reading cases progressed five times as much as other children in the regular special classes at the Wayne County Training School during the same length of time.
2. That following the initial period of training, or in the posttreatment period, the reading cases continued to progress. The rate of progress in the classroom was twice that of the rate of other children.

3. That on the Stanford Achievement Test, which tests other subjects besides reading, the rate of progress was twice the rate of other children during both the period of training and the posttreatment period.
4. And, most important of all, those children who were trained in a group of two made the same progress as those children trained individually.

At that time, I wrote

> On the basis of these results the following question may be raised: Why were these children not treated and corrected at an earlier age and thus aided in adjustment? Some of them might even have been saved from contact with the Juvenile Court and from institutionalization. The answer given by educators is usually that the treatment of reading cases, individually or in small groups is too expensive, and, especially in the case of mentally deficient children, futile.
>
> We are in disagreement with these viewpoints and propose to discuss the problem as follows: It has been shown that the cases were given 68 standard lessons of thirty minutes duration. This is, of course, and average of THIRTY FOUR HOURS of one remedial teacher's time for each child. Let us now compare these thirty-four hours of remedial teaching (which have resulted in significant improvement) with the time involved in teaching such a child for many years WITHOUT RESULTS; the time spent by truant officers, and various clinical, social, and judicial agencies and the cost of penal and custodial institutions and training schools. Such comparisons and the results reported in this paper even suggest that in the LONG RUN A SIGNIFICANT SAVING would probably result from a comprehensive program of remedial reading in schools, special classes, and institutions. (*Journal of Juvenile Research*, July 1934)

I should like to emphasize that these results and these remarks were based on work with mentally handicapped problem children. I am inclined to think that the 34 hours' work with each child was probably not as much time as was put in by the truant officer trying to keep that child in school. From that point of view, it was an economical method.

Before the meeting is opened for discussion, I should like to outline how a remedial reading program might be organized in a public school system.

A remedial reading program should consist of two services: (1) diagnosis, and (2) treatment.

The diagnosis of reading cases should result in findings giving the degree of reading retardation as well as the symptoms and etiology. At the completion of an adequate diagnosis, the reading disability cases in a school system will fall roughly into the following five treatment groups:

1. A group of reading cases with special idiosyncracies who can be aided only by individual treatment and individual drill to overcome their particular reading difficulty. This group will probably consist of some men-

tal retardates, speech defectives, nonreaders, and personality cases who could not be trained in a group.
2. A group of reading cases similar in many respects to the deficient readers mentioned above but whose difficulties can be removed more readily and who can be trained individually for a short period and then placed in a remedial reading group.
3. A group of reading cases who can cooperate with other children and whose difficulties can be removed in a group. These cases are usually ones who require drill on some particular aspect of reading, such as increasing the rate of silent reading.
4. A group of minor reading cases who do not require a remedial teacher but who can be trained in the classroom with proper supervision. For this group, the diagnostician could recommend to the regular classroom teacher the type of treatment necessary.
5. A group of young school entrants who are beginning to exhibit signs of potential reading retardation and who possibly require a preventative program so that they will not develop into reading disability cases. Possibly, when our reading aptitude tests have been sufficiently validated, we will know when these children should start learning to read, and what methods are best applicable to their "mental make-up."

With this grouping of reading cases, one remedial teacher can train a large number of cases a year. She can train some individually two or three periods per week, and can train groups two or three or four periods per week. Some reading disability cases can probably be corrected in a 6-week period of training, while others will require 3, 5, 7, or 9 months of training. The remedial teacher should know how often she should give remedial treatment to a child as well as when the child has profited sufficiently to be returned to the classroom. Considering all of these factors, one remedial teacher should be able to train 40 or 60 reading cases during the course of 1 year.

I should like to mention a word about personnel. Who is going to do the diagnosing and who is going to give the remedial treatment? I think this is one of our most serious problems. We do not often find in the catalogs of universities and teachers colleges courses in diagnostic and remedial reading. People who are doing remedial reading are often not trained in diagnosis and treatment. Ordinarily, the clinical psychologist has not had training in the problems of reading, and the teacher has not had training in psychological diagnosis and remedial methods. Consequently, much of the remedial reading work is being done by people untrained in one phase or the other.

To aid this situation, we are introducing a summer course in diagnostic and remedial reading at the Milwaukee State Teachers College. This will be the first attempt in the state of Wisconsin to offer opportunities for the training of such teachers. I hope that this procedure will be a stimulus to remedial reading elsewhere, as well as a method of training a few interested teachers to carry on the work.

To summarize, a remedial reading program in a school system will require an expert diagnostician who can also do the remedial work; or, if the system is large enough, employ trained remedial reading teachers. The diagnosis should result in a grouping of reading cases into a number of remedial reading groups according to degree of retardation and type of treatment necessary. Factors such as distributed practice and length of training period should be adapted to the individual needs of the children. And, to insure adequate remedial training, universities and teachers colleges should introduce courses in diagnostic and remedial training.

NOTE

[1] The program mentioned here refers to the Hegge-Kirk-Kirk *Remedial Reading Drills*, 1936, George Wahr Publishers, Ann Arbor, MI.

Chapter 11

Characteristics of Slow Learners and Needed Adjustments in Reading

SAMUEL A. KIRK

The term "slow learner" has been applied to children with greatly different characteristics. Today the term has become ambiguous. It has been used by different authors to refer to all children who are not making adequate educational progress regardless of the cause. It has been variously used to denote the following kinds of children.

The feeble-minded or mentally deficient child. The term "slow learner" has sometimes been used here because of its ambiguity, rather than because of its clarity. Parents accept this term more readily than the term "feeble-mindedness"—hence its rather free usage by many workers in the field.

The educable mentally handicapped child. The term "slow learner" applies more adequately to this category of intelligence classification than to the feeble-minded. This group, however, should be called mentally handicapped since they require a different curriculum rather than a curriculum which has been merely reduced.

The border-line or dull-normal child. To most individuals this group of children is properly termed "slow learners," since they are neither feeble-minded nor normal. Their school achievement shows slow-learning ability as compared to the general learning ability of the normal children with whom they are grouped in school.

The child educationally retarded due to emotional instability. These children are not retarded educationally because of an intellectual defect but because of emotional factors retarding school progress. Since their educational progress is retarded, they are sometimes considered "slow learners."

Reprinted from *Supplementary Educational Monograph 69* (October 1949), University of Chicago Press, pp. 172–176.

The child educationally retarded due to an educational disability. Such children are of average or superior intelligence but are retarded because of such factors as a reading disability. They are likewise considered by some to be "slow-learners" because they are slow learners in reading.

The child educationally retarded due to other factors. Such children may be retarded because of lack of school attendance, interfering home factors, inadequate educational opportunities, or other environmental conditions. The term "slow learners" has been applied to them because they are sometimes grouped with some of the other children mentioned above.

It should be noted that the term "slow learner" has been applied to children (1) who are low in intelligence or (2) who are average in intelligence but who are retarded educationally because of emotional or other causes. Actually, children with severe sensory handicaps, such as deafness or blindness, are slow learners in some areas but because of the obvious cause of their slowness are not considered "slow learners."

The term "slow learner" should be restricted to the child who does not have the capacity or potentiality to learn intellectual things, such as reading, at the same rate as average children. It should not be used to refer to educational retardation regardless of the cause.

Strictly speaking, the term should refer to children of relatively low intelligence whose learning in school subjects is significantly slower than that of children of average or superior intelligence. Feeble-minded or mentally deficient children who cannot learn the intellectual materials of the school should not come under this category. The slow learner is the child whose intellectual level on verbal intelligence tests indicates a retardation in intellectual development which will affect the child's rate of learning intellectual materials. At most, "slow learner" should include the dull and border-line children, with intelligence quotients of approximately 75–90, and, if we stretch the term, the mentally handicapped, with intelligence quotients from 60 to 70 or 80. The discussions in these proceedings include these two groups of children, who, because of low intellectual ability, are unable to cope with the curriculum of the regular school and require adaptations of instruction and materials for their maximum growth and development.

General Characteristics of Slow Learners

Slow-learning and mentally handicapped children do not differ markedly from other children in most characteristics except those involving intellectual materials.

In physical characteristics slow-learning children show as much variation as average children. There is some evidence, however, that slow learners as a group show slight inferiority in physique and health as compared to average or superior children. Cyril Burt (1937, p. 206) states that these children suffer more from general debility, possibly innate or due to environmental factors of poor feeding and poor medical care in early childhood. They do not have more major serious physical disabilities than average children but a plurality of minor troubles. Baker (1945) states that in the case of the "mentally retarded there are likely to be two or more of these abnormalities per child whereas the normal seldom have more than one" (p. 261). In general, and from statistical studies of a large number of children, the slow learners and the mentally retarded are slightly inferior physically to children of average intelligence. Generalizations concerning a particular child are difficult to make since many of the slow learners are superior to many average children in physique and health.

In emotional and social behavior it is difficult to distinguish the slow learner from the average child except in specific situations. Featherstone (1941) observes:

> Slow-learning children are very often alleged to be uncommonly lazy, and with good reason, but one should be careful not to assume that laziness is constitutional. Laziness is frequently due to ill health, and even more frequently to educational maladjustment. (p. 5)

In general, the behavior characteristics of slow-learning children are adjustment processes to continual retardation and failure in school, such as lack of motivation, dislike for school, compensating traits in other than intellectual areas, truancy, and dropping out of school at the end of the compulsory age limit of school attendance. Their behavior traits show the deviations found in children who are forced into a position where there is a discrepancy between their capacity to perform and the requirements of the school environment.

In a comparative study of children of superior and inferior intelligence in junior and senior high school, Blair (1938) found significant differences in interests and activities. The inferior children assumed few or no positions of leadership, participated in fewer school activities, read less, and read primarily detective and pulp magazines. Their school interests were not in the academic subjects but in such offerings as shop and home economics. In general, the children with inferior intelligence came from lower socioeconomic levels.

In summarizing the characteristics of the slow-learning child, it can be said that because of their slower progress in school, possibly due to poorer health and home conditions, as well as low intelligence, these children are usually at the lower end of achievement in academic subjects in both the elementary school and the high school. Many times they are older than the children in their grade because they have been held back a grade or two. In high schools they are placed in the lower sections of English, mathematics, and so forth. They tend to drop out of high school before completion and at the end of the compulsory school age. They are slow learners until the age of sixteen when we expect them to become fast learners in life, since they leave school at a younger age than their superior classmates. The high schools, not adapted to their learning rate, have tended to have a low holding-power for the slow learner. Schools must adapt instruction to the slow learners as they are attempting to do for the average child.

Differences Between Slow and Fast Learners

In adapting instruction to slow-learning children in school, it is necessary, first, to determine the major differences which contribute to learning to read between the slow-learning and the average child. Some of these differences are:

1. It should not be expected that the slow learner should learn to read at the [chronological] age of six when he enters the first grade. Most of them make inferior progress in reading at that age level.
2. Their rate of learning to read is slower than that of other children. It takes longer to cover the reading required in primers or first-grade books than it does in the case of the average child.
3. Throughout his school career the slow learner has not been able to succeed in reading like other children. Reading has been laborious, due to the pace he has been required to keep with other children. Failure and insecurity rather than success and security and reward have been his lot in school.
4. Possible health and poorer environmental handicaps have been found more frequently in the slow learner, thus contributing to his reading retardation.
5. Other school subjects, like history, geography, and even arithmetic computation, have been difficult since they require efficient reading habits.
6. Due to difficulties in reading, lack of interest in recreational reading, and avoidance of an unpleasant task, reading does not become a part of the life of a slow learner.

Some Basic Principles for Promoting Growth In and Through Reading

A program of reading for the slow learner in school as reported by Center (Center & Persons, 1937) showed that significant improvement in reading could be effected by remedial instruction and that this increased ability tended to lower failures in other subjects.

The literature shows that the slow learner can profit from good programs of instruction and that it is necessary that a good program be provided for the slow learner. A description of a thorough program of reading for slow learners is beyond the scope of this paper. It will suffice to list a few of the major principles for promoting growth in and through reading.

1. For a number of years educators have advocated delaying reading instruction until children are seven or eight years of age. There have been some experiments which demonstrated that postponing formal instruction in reading until the second year of school produced accelerated reading in the children a number of years later (Morphett & Washburne, 1940, pp. 21–25). Although these studies have been made with children of average and superior intelligence, it is more important that formal instruction in reading be delayed a year or more for slow-learning children. In relatively few cases do slow learners learn to read in the first grade before the age of seven or eight. It is necessary that they not face this failure during their initial school career and that schools be so organized as to enable slow learners to begin reading at the maturation level at which they can succeed and derive pleasure from reading.

2. Slow learners should be advanced to more difficult reading materials only as fast as they can read adequately and with pleasure. This suggestion is easier to accomplish today than it was twenty years ago, owing to the existence of many supplementary reading books for each grade level. When teachers had only one first-grade book and one second-grade book, they were forced to advance slow learners beyond their ability rather than repeat the first book. Today there are many first-grade books with the same vocabularies and a series of supplementary books which repeat the vocabulary in a different context and with different stories. Slow learners, in particular, need much repetition of words before they are mastered and before they really become part of the children's vocabulary. The supplementary readers and many other books now available provide this repetition in a variety of settings and situations. For the slow learner, supplementary materials are absolutely necessary.

3. Slow learners need systematic instruction in reading at all age levels. Superior children may learn to read incidentally and naturally. Even they might learn to read better if systematic instruction were introduced. Slow learners are not going to pick up reading incidentally through other activities. They require systematic and planned instruction both for developing the perceptual process of reading and for developing understanding and interest in reading. Dice (1943) had shown that the direct method of teaching reading was more beneficial for the dull children but made little difference to the average or superior group. The latter learned equally well by either approach. In Gates' and Pritchard's (1942) study of slow learners, the activity method was used, but in addition, certain pe-

riods of the day were devoted to planned and systematic instruction. Gates demonstrated that the slow learners (average intelligence quotient of 85) were able to read up to their mental level when such procedures were used.

4. Slow learners in school have usually been given reading materials a little above their reading ability. This is due to the practice of attempting to keep them at the same level as average or superior children. It is important for growth in reading that the slow learner read with ease and with pleasure. Consequently reading materials should be, as with all children, a little below their reading level. With the many easy books on the market for each grade level, it is more feasible now to provide reading materials within the slow learner's reading ability.

5. Independence in word attack should not be left to chance. The slow learner, because of his lower abilities, needs guidance and instruction in developing independent word attack. Instructional procedures should include activities that will develop independence in word recognition through sight vocabularies, context clues, word forms, structural and phonetic analysis, adequately described by Gray (1948).

6. Slow learners can enjoy reading and participate in recreational and leisure time reading when their interest in reading has not been thwarted by excessive and difficult demands in school. It is important in developing growth in and through reading that emphasis be given to developing interest and pleasure in reading. This can be accomplished when the children's interests are taken into consideration, when proper motivation for reading has been achieved, and when appropriate easy reading materials along their lines of interest have been provided.

7. Slow learners are not going to attend the traditional college or university. Their education must be practical and focused on social adjustment and occupational competency. The curriculum of the secondary school must be made more practical for them, to assist them in adjusting to life. Their reading, therefore, must be integrated with their school activities for two reasons: (a) to give reading a purpose, to relate it to other school activities, and to motivate reading in the areas in which they are active and interested, and (b) to promote growth in other activities through the information derived from reading.

8. Before the slow learner leaves school, he must be introduced to the reading activities of daily life. Critical reading of the common newspapers and magazines, the importance of reading directions in filling out application blanks, insurance blanks, and income-tax blanks must be emphasized. They should know where to go for information from reading, what the public libraries furnish, and the sources of information about occupations and jobs.

References

Baker, H. (1945). *Introduction to exceptional children*. New York: Macmillan Co.

Blair, G. M. (1938). Mentally superior and inferior children in the junior and senior high school. *Teachers College Contributions to Education*, No. 766. New York: Bureau of Publications, Teachers College, Columbia University.

Burt, C. (1937). *The backward child*. New York: D. Appleton-Century Co.

Center, S. S., & Persons, G. L. (1937). *Teaching high school students to read*. New York: D. Appleton-Century Co.

Dice, L. K. (1943, March). An experimental study of two methods of teaching beginning reading: The direct versus the preparatory approach. *Journal of Educational Research, XXXVI*, 535–45.

Featherstone, W. B. (1941). *Teaching the slow learner*. New York: Bureau of Publications, Teachers College, Columbia University.

Gates, A. I., & Pritchard, M. C. (1942). *Teaching reading to slow-learning pupils*. New York: Bureau of Publications, Teachers College, Columbia University.

Gray, W. S. (1948). *On their own in reading*. Chicago: Scott, Foresman & Co.

Morphett, M. V., & Washburne, C. (1940). Postponing formal instruction: A seven year case study. In *The effect of administrative practices on the character of the education program* (pp. 21–25). Washington, DC: American Educational Research Association.

Chapter 12

How Johnny Learns to Read

SAMUEL A. KIRK
WINIFRED D. KIRK

Both parents and educators have had a lot to say about the place of phonics in the teaching of reading. It is probably not a question of "phonics versus no phonics," as Rudolf Flesch (1955, p. 222) indicated in a recent book—a book described by its publishers as "an angry book by an aroused parent." Few educators advocate no phonics, and few parents or educators advocate teaching reading entirely and completely by the use of phonics. This "angry book" has, however, brought the issue into clear focus by advocating an extreme use of phonics and exaggerating the opposing point of view.

But the problem is really not so difficult when we analyze the process of learning to read (Kirk, 1940). How *does* Johnny learn to read?

In the first place, he probably learns to read just as we learn many other things such as certain physical tasks. In trying to swim for the first time, for instance, one moves about in a generalized fashion, making many random and unselective movements. In this first stage of learning the whole body is acting as a unit. Later, in the second stage, the swimmer learns or is taught to differentiate certain muscles and select certain movements, perhaps developing each movement separately. He may practice proper breathing; he may practice his kicking; he may practice arm movements or trunk movements. In this second stage of the learning process he has to differentiate one part of the activity from other parts. But he must go on from there to the third stage. He never becomes a good swimmer until he can coordinate these different movements into one smooth operation. The various parts must work together and become automatic. All parts of the activity must become integrated into a smoothly operating total activity.

Reprinted from *Exceptional Children*, 22(4), 1956, 158–160.

Reading Processes

Similarly, in learning to read, Johnny seems to respond first to the whole word or group of words. In this first stage he seems to get an impression of the total structure of the word or group of words—a vague impression of the shapes of words, of blocks of letters with gaps between them. One little Johnny, for instance, at the age of three was able to distinguish some two dozen phonograph records by the general configurations of the labels. No adult was able to discover what clues he was using, but apparently he had some method of distinguishing one record from another without knowing a single letter or a single word. In this first stage he may not have known what the method was any more than the person trying to swim for the first time knew what he was doing when he paddled about trying to keep his head above water.

During the second stage of learning to read, Johnny begins to notice details of words. When he reaches this stage, he is ready for some form of word attack, the most systematic of which is phonics. If he confuses *sat* and *not*, or *man* and *ten*, or *boy* and *dog*, or *car* and *cart*, he may need some help in learning to recognize differences between words, of systematically analyzing the word from its parts and seeing how it is made up of smaller parts. Just as in learning to swim one has to pay attention to some of the details that make up the total activity, so in learning to read Johnny has to go through a stage of paying attention to the structure of the words. *It is in this second stage in the reading process that phonics can help.*

But if he is going to progress in reading, Johnny must get into the third stage of the learning process. He must go beyond the detailed analysis of words (whatever methods have been used in analyzing details). In learning to swim, one is not a good swimmer until the breathing and kicking and arm movements and body movements are integrated and coordinated into one smooth operation. By that time the movements have become automatic and the swimmer does not think much about them. He just swims. In this stage of reading, Johnny "just reads." He has learned to short-circuit many of the perceptions and associations which he had laboriously gone through earlier. The use of phonics in the second stage enabled Johnny to see the word *map*, to associate the *m* with its sound, the *a* with its sound, the *p* with its sound, then to blend the sounds into the auditory word *map*, and finally to associate that sound with the meaning of the word. In the third and final stage, these steps follow automatically in a split second, or the in-between steps drop out and the total appearance of the word again determines the meaning just as it did in the first stage. At this point Johnny can understand the thought from a printed page without being aware of each word or the parts of each word. But until then he is not an efficient reader.

Misuse and Oversimplification

Now it so happens that the first stage and the third stage in learning to read have something in common. In both stages the individual is paying attention to larger units and does not break up the words into little parts. For this reason, some people who say Johnny should learn to read by the word method (or the sight method, or the look-and-say method, or the whole method) have neglected the second stage in the learning process. On the other hand, people, like Mr. Flesch, who believe that all you have to do is "teach the child what each letter stands for and he can read" are completely eliminating the first step and wholly ignoring the third step of the learning process. This would make Johnny begin and end in the second stage of the process, unless the child himself devises a means of going beyond it.

This is where Mr. Flesch has failed to understand the way children learn to read. As in other instances, he does not seem to comprehend some of the psychological bases for learning. In so doing, he has misapplied a technique which is very helpful to *some* children under *some* circumstances. He believes that *all* children should learn to read "by memorizing the sound of each letter in the alphabet." What is more, he believes that children should be taught these sounds at the age of five by their parents. How simple learning to read would be if this were all! This oversimplified and inappropriate method has had disastrous effects in many cases when used as he recommends. Hundreds of children have developed an antagonism to reading because they have become so hopelessly discouraged during the bewildering period of learning a bunch of sounds that they could not yet appreciate. Others have become befuddled because no one has ever taught them to blend a series of sounds into a word. This is an ability which many children and some adults have considerable difficulty in acquiring. Usually it can be taught, but without this sound-blending ability phonics is more confusing than other methods. However, the reader of Mr. Flesch's book is given no hint of this possible pitfall.

As one argument for the use of phonics in the initial stages of teaching reading, Mr. Flesch has stated that "there are no remedial reading cases in Germany, in France, in Italy, in Norway, in Spain—practically anywhere in the world except in the United States," because every other country teaches children to read by teaching them the sound of each letter. It is unfortunate that the public should be exposed to such misinformation. We have visited some of these countries and made a study of the German schools in an official capacity. We were particularly interested in the *hilfschulle* (help school) classes which correspond roughly to our classes for the mentally retarded. In Germany the majority of the children in these classes are not mentally retarded, but are children who have not made progress in reading. No remedial reading cases in Germany? Perhaps they are not sitting in the regular classes. No, they have been shunted off to the classes for the mentally retarded! But they are there just the same, and we dare say every country has its share and has always had its share.

The German language is much more phonetic than English. Mr. Flesch recognizes but makes light of the fact that at least 13% (more than one out of every eight) words in the English language are non-phonetic, that is, are not sounded according to a consistent rule. And many of the essential common words are included in this 13% (was, one, put, done, the, come, are, and so on), so that Johnny is going to meet far more than 13% of words which are non-phonetic. He will probably meet one or two in nearly every sentence. How much better it would be to be honest with him and say that some words just cannot be sounded out and that these words will have to be learned as wholes.

Touché!

Although the Hegge, Kirk, and Kirk, *Remedial Reading Drills* (1936) are one of the few sets of materials for which Mr. Flesch has a kind word, the authors of this article would like to go on record as disapproving the use for which Mr. Flesch has recommended them. These *Remedial Reading Drills* as well as their counterpart in the form of Mr. Flesch's *Exercises* are not applicable as a sole method for teaching beginning reading. The *Remedial Reading Drills* were designed to help that limited group of children who have difficulty in the second stage of the reading process, that is, the stage where they need some help in recognizing details in the words. Most children acquire this ability independently. (It must be remembered that Mr. Flesch's Johnny is not representative of average children. He represents only one child out of 10 or 20.) When and if a child has needed such help, the *Remedial Reading Drills* have proven most successful. But to say that all the children in all the schools of all the land should use them at the age of five reduces them to an absurdity.

This is likewise true of Mr. Flesch's *Exercises*, most of which are condensations, modifications, or combinations of the Hegge, Kirk, and Kirk *Remedial Reading Drills*. Although Mr. Flesch states that he "knew of a way to teach reading that was altogether different from what they do in schools or in remedial reading classes or anywhere else," he has promoted a series of exercises for which he has leaned heavily on the *Remedial Reading Drills*. The basic system is the same and the resemblance between the two is obvious at a glance. Unfortunately, Mr. Flesch has disregarded many of the basic psychological principles upon which the *Remedial Reading Drills* were developed.

Regardless of the propriety or the adequacy of Mr. Flesch's *Exercises*, it seems to the authors of this article that he has misused and oversimplified a technique which, if properly used, can be very beneficial to certain children.

And it may well be that with a still greater number of children phonics should play a more important role and that it should be taught in a more systematic manner. But this does not mean that all children should begin reading by drilling on the sounds of the letters.

References

Flesch, R. (1955). *Why Johnny can't read*. New York: Harper.

Hegge, T. G., Kirk, S. A., & Kirk, W. D. (1936). *Remedial Reading Drills*. Ann Arbor, MI: George Wahr.

Kirk, S. A. (1940). *Teaching reading to slow learning children*. Boston: Houghton Mifflin.

Part VI

Hearing Impairments

INTRODUCTION

DONALD F. MOORES
Gallaudet Research Institute
Gallaudet University, Washington, DC

The opportunity to write an introduction to Part VI, "Hearing Impairments," has provided a new perspective on the contributions of Dr. Kirk to the welfare of exceptional children and adults. As a graduate student in the Department of Special Education and a research associate in the Institute for Research on Exceptional Children from 1964 to 1967, I was able to observe first hand how a consummate professional and academician functioned. Dr. Kirk provided an ideal model as he moved with apparent ease across his various roles of teacher, advisor, administrator, researcher, and advocate at the state, national, and international level. At this point in time, the extent of his impact on theory and practice, legislation, and teacher training is difficult to comprehend. It was a mystery to his students how one man could be a driving force behind federal legislation and the creation of federal agencies and at the same time sit in on classes to increase his knowledge, go over a dissertation draft line by line with a frustrated graduate student, and lead the development of the Illinois Test of Psycholinguistic Abilities.

Dr. Kirk instilled a striving for excellence and a commitment to children that will long survive any particular piece of work. His openness to new ideas and commitment were balanced by a healthy skepticism and a belief that everything should be subject to verification. For my own part, when I had the opportunity to head a federally funded research center on the education of children with disabilities at the University of Minnesota and later, when I was able to participate in the establishment of the Center for Studies in Education and Human Development at Gallaudet University, I consciously tried to follow the basic principles established by Dr. Kirk at the Institute for Research on Exceptional Children. The fundamental requirements are a multidisciplinary core of highly skilled professionals, with adequate support, working cooperatively on well-defined programs of inquiry. In other words, find the very best people you possibly can and turn them loose.

Turning to his work on children who were deaf and hard of hearing, which is exemplified in this chapter, one can see the research and practical concerns that are the hallmark of his work. The first paper (Chapter 13), "Behavior Problem Tendencies in Deaf and Hard-of-Hearing Children" (1938) concerned the applicability of the Haggerty-Olson-Wickman Behavior Rating Scale to elementary-school-age children who were deaf and hard of hearing. Following an item analysis, he quickly concluded that Schedule A of the Scale was invalid for use with this population due to the contaminating effects of spoken language on scores. Following the same procedures, he ascertained that items on Schedule B were valid, and he analyzed the results in four categories: (1) intellectual traits, (2) physical traits, (3) social traits, and (4) emotional traits. He reported essentially normal ratings in the first three categories, but found that children who were deaf and hard of hearing were rated as having more emotional problems than hearing children. This study represents one of the first attempts to take into consideration item-appropriateness in assessment of children who were deaf and hard of hearing. Although the discussion did not highlight it, the study was one of the first to report findings supporting the essential intellectual normalcy of these children.

The second paper (Chapter 14), "A Comparative Study of the Ontario and Nebraska Tests for the Deaf" (1948), was, to the best of my knowledge, the first investigation of two performance tests constructed specifically for and standardized on children who were deaf. The development of these tests themselves represented the first attempts to move away from complete reliance on measures standardized on hearing children in the assessment of children who were deaf. Kirk implicitly and explicitly investigated several questions in this study. First was a comparison between the Ontario School Ability Examination and the Nebraska Test of Learning Aptitude. Both of these were administered to sample populations of deaf and hearing children. Second was a comparison of each of these two tests with the Stanford Binet. Since this test was heavily reliant on oral English skills, it was administered only to hearing subjects. The results were clear cut. For both hearing subjects and those who were deaf, scores on the Ontario were significantly higher than on the Nebraska. For the hearing children, scores on the Binet were significantly higher than on the Nebraska, but they did not differ significantly from scores on the Ontario. For deaf and hearing subjects, mean scores were identical on both the Ontario (103) and Nebraska (96) tests. From a practical point of view, extrapolating from results with deaf and hearing subjects, Kirk concluded that the Ontario appeared to be superior to the Nebraska, with the qualification that this would hold only if the Binet has any relation to learning ability.

Of immediate interest for our purposes is the finding that deaf and hearing subjects performed in a similar manner on both the Nebraska and Ontario tests. Kirk published his findings at a time when persons who were deaf were generally viewed as cognitively and intellectually inferior to the hearing population, with the average retardation set at 10 IQ points by Pintner (Moores, 1987). Kirk's work in this area presaged research in the 1970s that established the cognitive and intellectual capacity of persons who are deaf as normal.

The next section in Part VI, Chapter 15, is devoted to more practical—and political—considerations—that is, the relative roles of institutions of higher education and residential schools for students who were deaf, as represented by the Conference of Executives of American Schools for the Deaf (CEASD), now the Conference of Educational Administrators Serving the

Deaf, in the preparation of teachers of the deaf. Until that time, with a few notable exceptions, preparation of teachers of students who were deaf had been under the aegis of residential schools. Although the programs frequently were affiliated with colleges, instructors typically were members of residential school staffs, and trainees often were housed at the schools, working as dormitory supervisors in exchange for room and board.

At the time of Dr. Kirk's testimony, I was a teacher at a residential school for students who were deaf, and I can attest to the fact that his position was strongly opposed by CEASD. It was felt that education of these students was so specialized and unique that movement of teacher training responsibility to colleges and universities, where there were few or no professors with practical experience in teaching such children, would be a disaster. At that time, education of students who were deaf was thought to be restricted to residential schools and to a small number of segregated day schools in large cities. Educators were not aware that a shift had begun to take place shortly after the end of World War II toward public school education of children who were deaf. By 1971, half of all such children attended public schools, and more than three-fourths attend public schools today.

After his testimony, Dr. Kirk was questioned by Congressman Al Quie of Minnesota, who expressed the opinion that Congress would have to make a compromise between the two sides. Since his congressional district included the state residential school for deaf children in Faribault and he had a record of involvement and concern for special education throughout his congressional tenure, Congressman Quie had great insight into the issues in question.

The final paper in Part VI (Chapter 16), is a report to a conference on the preparation of teachers of the deaf students held in 1964. As Dr. Kirk stated, the conference included not only educators, supervisors, and administrators of programs for students who were deaf, but also people in general education, psychology, and speech and hearing. It was a time of optimism, as legislation originally addressing mental retardation was being amended to include all children with disabilities, including those who were deaf. With new legislation, colleges and universities would receive support for training teachers of students who were deaf at undergraduate and graduate levels, as well as supervisors, administrators, college instructors, and researchers. Students themselves would receive tax-free stipends, with additional dependency allowances.

At this point, Dr. Kirk saw education of students who were deaf to be at the threshold of major breakthroughs involving the interaction of highly trained educators of these students with colleagues in related disciplines. He envisioned the development of new methods of teaching, innovative demonstration projects, and major research efforts. To some extent, his hopes for the education of students who are deaf have been realized, although revolutionary changes have not occurred. Since the late 1960s, there has been a steady improvement in academic achievement of these students, although results still remain far below norms for hearing students. Partially based on research results, there has been a general acceptance of the use of manual communication in educational settings. As early as 1960, Dr. Kirk was encouraging research into this area. Moreover, the efficacy of preschool programs has been documented by research. Finally, there is a small, but steadily growing, core of professionals who are deaf assuming leadership roles, not only in education but in other fields. Gallaudet University, which did not accept students who were deaf into its graduate teacher training programs before 1960, now has a president who is deaf. Of perhaps most satisfaction to Dr. Kirk is the fact that the Assistant Secretary of the U.S. Office of Special Education and Rehabilitation Services, arguably the most important position in special education in the world, is Dr. Robert Davila, who is deaf.

For the most part, educators of students who are deaf are not aware of the debt that we owe to the leadership of Dr. Kirk. I hope that the chapters in Part VI will help to eliminate this ignorance.

Reference

Moores, D. F. (1987). *Educating the deaf: Psychology, principles, and practices*. Boston: Houghton Mifflin.

Donald F. Moores is director of the Center for Studies in Education and Human Development and professor of educational foundations and research at Gallaudet University, Washington, DC. He is editor of the *American Annals of the Deaf*. He received a master's degree in education of the deaf from Gallaudet, a master's degree in special education administration from the Leadership Training Program in Deafness at California State University, Northridge, and a doctorate in special education from the University of Illinois, where he also worked as a research associate at the Institute for Research on Exceptional Children on the standardization of the Illinois Test of Psycholinguistic Abilities. He was professor of special education at the University of Minnesota from 1967 to 1977 and was director of the Research and Development Center in Education of Handicapped Children there for 6 years. He was head of the Department of Special Education and Communication Disorders at Pennsylvania State University from 1977 to 1980. Dr. Moores received an honorary appointment as professor at Huazhong University in Wuhan, China, and was selected for the USA/USSR research exchange of scholars program. In 1980, he was awarded the E. A. Fay award for outstanding scholarly achievement.

Chapter 13

Behavior Problem Tendencies in Deaf and Hard-of-Hearing Children

SAMUEL A. KIRK, Ph.D[1]
Director, Division of Education of Exceptional Children
Milwaukee, Wisconsin

The behavior, personality adjustment, and emotional thwarting of deaf and hard-of-hearing children have not been extensively studied. It has been suggested, however, that the disability of defective-hearing serves to thwart many children and results in emotional disturbances. Menninger (1930) feels that deafness is a permanent handicap to adjustment, and the few experiments in the field tend to confirm his observation. Lyons (1934) gave the Thurstone Personality Schedule to older deaf children and concluded that they have more emotional problems than do normals. Pintner (1937) gave the Bernreuter Personality Inventory to deaf adults at Gallaudet College and to 126 other deaf adults, and concluded that the deaf are slightly less dominant than normals. There was no difference between the deaf and hard-of-hearing. Madden (1931) using a short rating scale found that the hard of hearing are not rated as leaders, and are often more shy and solitary than normal children.

Problem

The purpose of this study is to compare the behavior problem tendencies of deaf and hard-of-hearing children in an elementary day-school for the deaf with those of normal-hearing children on the Haggerty-Olson-Wickman Behavior Rating Schedule (Haggerty, Olson, & Wickman, 1930).

Reprinted from *American Annals of the Deaf*, (March 1938), 83, 131–137.

Procedure

Trained teachers of the deaf at the Paul Binner School, Milwaukee, Wis., rated 112 deaf and hard-of-hearing children on the Haggerty-Olson-Wickman Behavior Rating Schedule. The children rated were from seven to sixteen years of age and were in the first to the eighth grade.

The Haggerty-Olson-Wickman Behavior Rating Schedule (Haggerty, Olson, & Wickman, 1930; Olson, 1930) has two parts: Schedule A and Schedule B. Schedule A, the Behavior Problem Record, consists of 15 items that indicate undesirable behavior, such as: Disinterest in school work, lying, speech difficulties, etc. The rater is asked to check each of these as: (a) has never occurred, (b) has occurred once or twice, (c) occasional occurrence, and (d) frequent occurrence.

Schedule B consists of four divisions: Division I, intellectual traits; Division II, physical traits; Division III, social traits; and Division IV, emotional traits. An example of one item under intellectual traits is (Haggerty, Olson, & Wickman, 1930):
"4. Is he slow or quick in thinking?

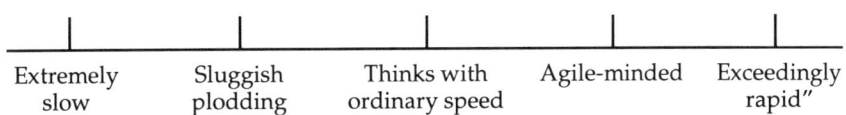

| Extremely slow | Sluggish plodding | Thinks with ordinary speed | Agile-minded | Exceedingly rapid" |

The rater is asked to observe the child and to check the phrase or expression that best describes the reactions of the child.

Results on Schedule A

Table 1 compares the medians of deaf and hard-of-hearing children with those of normal-hearing children on Schedule A. For 61 deaf and hard-of-hearing boys the median score was 30.6, as compared to a median score of 13.2 for Olson's normal-hearing boys. For girls and for the total of boys and girls a similar large difference is noted. The high scores on these scales indicate undesirable behavior.

An analysis of the items in Schedule A showed that the deaf and hard-of-hearing children were given the highest possible scores on Item 10, "speech difficulties." Obviously deaf children are defective in speech and the rating for problem tendencies becomes exaggerated because of this item.

To determine what the results would be if the item of speech difficulties were excluded, a recalculation was made. Each deaf child was given an average speech difficulty score similar to that obtained by normal children as described by Haggerty (1925). Medians were then calculated and are shown in the last column of Table 1. The medians for the 61 boys and the 51 girls were

TABLE 1
A Comparison of Deaf and Hard-of-Hearing with Normal-Hearing Children on Schedule A

	Deaf and hard-of-hearing		Normal-hearing children[2]		Deaf and hard-of-hearing corrected for speech	
	N	Median	N	Median	N	Median
Boys	61	30.6	1098	13.2	61	18.7
Girls	51	24.7	1065	6.1	51	11.5
Total	112	28.75	2163	8.6	112	15.5

18.7 and 11.5 respectively, again showing a higher behavior problem score than that found with normal-hearing children. We could have made similar corrections for unnecessary tardiness (which does not occur because the children are all brought to school by busses) and for imaginative lying (which is difficult for teacher to detect because of the language handicap). However, correction for these two items would, if anything, only further exaggerate the differences between the group with defective hearing and normal-hearing children.

It is the writer's opinion that Schedule A is not a valid rating scale for deaf children because of the factors mentioned above. If any conclusion can be drawn from the data, however, it is that the deaf and hard-of-hearing group show greater behavior problem tendencies than do normal-hearing children on this rating scale. Furthermore, deaf and hard-of-hearing boys appear to be greater problems than deaf and hard-of-hearing girls, in the same way as normal-hearing boys exceed normal-hearing girls on this scale.

Results on Schedule B

Schedule B does not offer the same difficulties as Schedule A. An analysis of the items shows that deaf children can be rated on them without difficulty. No item such as "speech difficulties" occurs in Schedule B to make interpretation difficult.

Table 2 gives the number of cases, the means, and the probable errors of the means for boys and for girls in each of the four divisions of Schedule B. It includes the scores of the deaf and hard-of-hearing children and of normal-hearing children as given by Haggerty et al. (1930). Critical ratios for the differences between the deaf and normal-hearing averages are shown in the last column.

It should be noted from Table 2 that in the results for boys on Division I—intellectual traits—there is a difference of 1.10, indicating a greater degree

TABLE 2
A Comparison of Deaf and Hard-of-Hearing Children with Normal-Hearing Children on the H-O-W Behavior Rating Scale—Schedule B

	Deaf and Hard-of-Hearing Children		Normal-Hearing Children (H-O-W,2)		Difference between Deaf and Normals	Critical Ratio
	No.	Mean and PEm	No.	Mean and PEm		
Boys Division I Intellectual Traits	61	19.30 ± .65	300	18.2 ± .23	+ 1.10	1.6
Division II Physical Traits	61	13.56 ± .28	300	14.1 ± .15	− .54	1.73
Division III Social Traits	61	22.98 ± .58	300	22.4 ± .25	+ .58	.91
Division IV Emotional Traits	61	25.52 ± .82	300	20.4 ± .27	+ 5.12	5.92
Total Boys	61	18.16 ± 1.81	1473	72.4 ± .32	+ 8.76	4.77
Girls Division I Intellectual Traits	51	18.37 ± .53	326	17.1 ± .21	+ 1.27	2.23
Division II Physical Traits	51	14.94 ± .58	326	13.5 ± .18	+ 1.44	2.38
Division III Social Traits	51	21.61 ± .58	326	18.2 ± .18	+ 3.41	5.6
Division IV Emotional Traits	51	21.90 ± .71	326	18.1 ± .22	+ 3.80	5.1
Total Girls	51	76.11 ± 1.85	1394	65.9 ± .29	+ 10.21	5.5
Total Boys and Girls	112	78.88 ± 1.31	2867	69.2 ± .22	+ 9.68	7.3

of problem tendencies in the group with defective hearing. However, this difference is not at all significant since the critical ratio is only 1.6. On Division II—physical traits—the normal exceed the deaf and hard-of-hearing by a score of .54, which again is not significant as judged by the critical ratio of 1.73. Similarly, Division III—social traits—shows no significant difference between the defective-hearing group and normals. But on Division IV—emotional traits—there is a difference of 5.12, pointing to excessive problem tendencies in the group with defective hearing. The critical ratio of 5.92 indicates that the difference here is statistically significant. For the total score for boys the critical ratio of 4.77 is again statistically significant. From these results we may conclude that in emotional traits specifically, and for Schedule B as a whole, deaf and hard-of-hearing boys exceed normal-hearing boys in problem tendencies.

The results for the girls are very similar to those for the boys. On all traits—intellectual, physical, social, and emotional—the deaf and hard-of-hearing girls show higher scores than the normal-hearing girls in problem tendencies. For intellectual and physical traits the critical ratios of 2.23 and 2.38 cannot be considered significant.[3] For social and emotional traits, on the other hand, the critical ratios of 5.6 and 5.1 are significant. From these results it may be concluded that our group of deaf and hard-of-hearing girls exceed normal-hearing girls in problem tendencies in social and emotional traits. Again, for Schedule B as a whole applied to the girls, the critical ratio of 5.5 indicates that the defective-hearing girls have significantly greater problem tendency scores than normal-hearing girls.

The results on the combined scores of the boys and girls show a critical ratio of 7.3, indicating greater problem tendencies in the group with defective hearing. It should be noted also that deaf and hard-of-hearing boys exceed the deaf and hard-of-hearing girls in problem tendency scores. This difference represents the same tendency that is found in normal-hearing boys and girls.

A separate analysis was made of the behavior rating scores of the deaf and those of the hard-of-hearing children to determine whether or not there was a difference in problem tendencies between these two groups. The results of the analysis showed no difference between the children considered deaf by their teachers, and those considered hard-of-hearing.[4] For the deaf group the mean score was 78.5 ± 1.9, while for the hard-of-hearing group the mean score was 79.5 ± 1.8. The difference of the means divided by the probable error of the difference of the means showed a critical ratio of .38, indicating that the slight difference is not significant.

Summary and Conclusions

One hundred and twelve deaf and hard-of-hearing children in grades 1 to 8 were rated on the Haggerty-Olson-Wickman Behavior Rating Schedule. From the data we may conclude that:

1. Deaf and hard-of-hearing children as a group present significantly greater problem tendencies than normal-hearing children.
2. The greatest difference was found in emotional traits, while the least difference was found in intellectual and physical traits.
3. As with normal children, defective-hearing boys exceed defective-hearing girls in behavior problems.
4. There was no difference between the deaf group and the hard-of-hearing group in problem tendencies.
5. This study confirms the observations of others that children with defective hearing have more emotional problems than do normal hearing children.

References

Haggerty, M. E. (1925). The incidence of undesirable behavior in public school children. *Journal of Educational Research, 12*, 102–122.
Haggerty, M. E., Olson, W. C., & Wickman, S. E. (1930). *Haggerty-Olson-Wickman Behavior Rating Schedules: and Manual of Directions*. New York: World Book Co.
Lyons, V. W. (1934). Personality tests with the deaf. *American Annals of the Deaf, 79*, 1–4.
Madden, R. (1931). The social status of the hard-of-hearing child. *Contribs. to Educ.*, No. 449, Teachers College.
Menninger, K. A. (1930). *The human mind*. Alfred A. Knopf Inc.
Olson, W. C. (1930). *Problem tendencies in children*. University of Minnesota Press.
Pintner, R. (1937). Latest phases of psychological testing with the deaf. *American of the Deaf, 82*, 327–337.

NOTES

[1] The author wishes to acknowledge his indebtedness to Dr. Milton C. Potter, superintendent of the Milwaukee Public School, for his kind permission to carry on the investigation; and to Miss Sadie Owens, principal of the Paul Binner School for the Deaf, for her generous aid and cooperation in this study. The assistance of Miss Hazel Zanzig in the tabulation and calculation of the data is greatly appreciated.

[2] Haggerty-Olson-Wickman norms—see Haggerty, Olson, & Wickman, 1930.

[3] Eighty-nine of the 112 children of this study were given Grace Arthur Performance tests. The average IQ for this group was 99.4. The fact that the group showed average intelligence on this objective intelligence test confirms the rating of the teacher that the group studied did not differ from normals in intellectual traits. Similar independent checks are not so easily found for the ratings in emotional traits, where we found a significant difference between the defective-hearing group and normal-hearing children.

[4] The deaf group had an average hearing loss on the 2-A audiometer of 72. The hard-of-hearing group had a hearing loss of 50.

Chapter 14

A Comparative Study of the Ontario and Nebraska Tests for the Deaf

SAMUEL A. KIRK
University of Illinois

JUNE PERRY
Milwaukee State Teachers College

Introduction

In the past deaf children have been tested with non-language performance tests such as the Grace Arthur Point Scale, Cornell Coxe Performance Tests, and the Pintner Patterson Scale. These tests have all been standardized on hearing children. Although these tests are non-language in so far as the child's response is concerned they still involve the use of language in giving and understanding the oral directions. Of necessity pantomime is often substituted for, or added to, the oral directions. This may or may not affect the test results. In addition many of these tests are heavily weighed with form boards, thus giving an uneven sampling of abilities.

Recently two tests have been constructed specifically for deaf children. The first test, the Ontario School Ability Examination, was published in Canada in 1936 (Amos, 1936). This examination was standardized by selecting performance items used with hearing children, adding some tests, such as the Knox Cube, the Healy Fernald Puzzle, etc., and administering the battery to deaf children; and also to hearing children who had been given the Stanford-Binet examination. It was found that there was a close correlation between this test and the 1916 Revision of the Binet Scale. It was then standardized on 288 deaf pupils at the Ontario School for the Deaf.

The Nebraska Test of Learning Aptitude (Hiskey & Marshall, 1941) was standardized on 466 institutionalized deaf pupils in Nebraska, Kansas, Mis-

Reprinted from *American Annals of the Deaf*, (September 1948), 93, 315–323.

souri, Illinois, Indiana and Ohio as well as some pupils enrolled in day schools for the deaf in Lincoln, Nebraska. The author did not use a mental age concept because he did not wish to confuse it with tests given to hearing children such as the Stanford-Binet. He preferred using learning age or Learning Quotient (LQ) to using mental age of IQ.

The major difference in standardization between the two tests is that the Ontario Test was calibrated with the old Binet examination for hearing children, whereas the Nebraska Test used an age scale based on other estimates of learning ability. The Nebraska Test was standardized on children from three years six months to nine years nine months; the Ontario Tests included children between the ages of five and twenty-two years. Both tests were standardized primarily on children in residential schools for the deaf. There are no coefficients of reliability for the Ontario Test. The Nebraska Test lists a coefficient of reliability of .963.

The Problem

Since psychologists who are charged with the examination of deaf children are interested in knowing the significance of their results, it is important that a comparison of the results of these two tests be made. The problem, then, is to determine the relative ratings which deaf children receive when both tests are administered to the same individual. Also, in order to determine how these tests compare with the Binet, it is important that some comparison be made between these two tests and the Stanford-Binet examination.

Procedure

To compare the results of the Ontario School Ability Examination with those of the Nebraska Test of Learning Aptitude the following procedures were established:

1. Subjects: Forty-nine children from the Paul Binner Day School for the Deaf, (Milwaukee, Wisconsin) were selected for this experiment. The 49 deaf and hard-of-hearing children were given the Ontario and Nebraska Tests for the Deaf, each child being given both of these tests within a period of not less than three days and not more than one week. One-half of the children had the Nebraska Test first; and the other half had the Ontario first.

2. For the second part of the experiment 49 hearing children of varying ages from the public schools were selected. These children had been given the Terman Merril Stanford-Binet. As with the deaf children, one-half of the group was given the Ontario first; the other half the Nebraska first.

3. Ages: In both groups children of varying ages were selected so as to include children from five to eleven years. There were from six to eight subjects at each age level.
4. Selection of Cases: Since the experiment involved the administration of all tests to the same child, the selection factor was unimportant. Availability of children for the examination was the major consideration.

Results

Analyzing the data from the three tests, results were studied by (1) comparing the Ontario IQs with the Nebraska LQs obtained from the administration of the tests to deaf children, (2) comparing with each other the Binet IQs, Ontario IQs and Nebraska LQs obtained from the administration of the tests to hearing children, and (3) comparing the Ontario IQs with the Nebraska LQs obtained from the combined groups of deaf and hearing children.

1. Results with Deaf Children.

For the 49 deaf children examined the mean IQ for the Ontario Test was found to be 102.9. The mean LQ for the Nebraska Test on the same group of children was 95.8. It can be seen that there is a difference of seven points in IQ between the mean on the Ontario Test and the mean LQ on the Nebraska Test.

Table 1 shows the means, difference between the means, the standard error of the difference, and the critical ratio for the Ontario and Nebraska Tests when administered to the same group of deaf children. It will be seen from this table that the seven point difference in IQ between the two tests is statistically significant since the critical ratio is 4.4.

Figure 1 shows the mean IQs and LQs for the 49 deaf children at each chronological age level. It will be seen from this figure that the mean IQ at each age level is higher for the Ontario Test than the mean LQ obtained from

TABLE 1

The Means, Difference Between the Means, the Standard Error of the Difference, and the Critical Ratio for the Ontario and Nebraska Tests When Administered to a Group of 49 Deaf Children

	Ontario	Nebraska	Difference between Means	S.E. of Difference	Critical Ratio
Means	102.857	95.816	7.041	1.6	4.4
S.D. of Dis.	16.296	15.037			
S.E. of Mean	2.33	2.15			

FIGURE 1

The Mean I.Q. and L.Q. At Each C.A. Interval for the Deaf Children

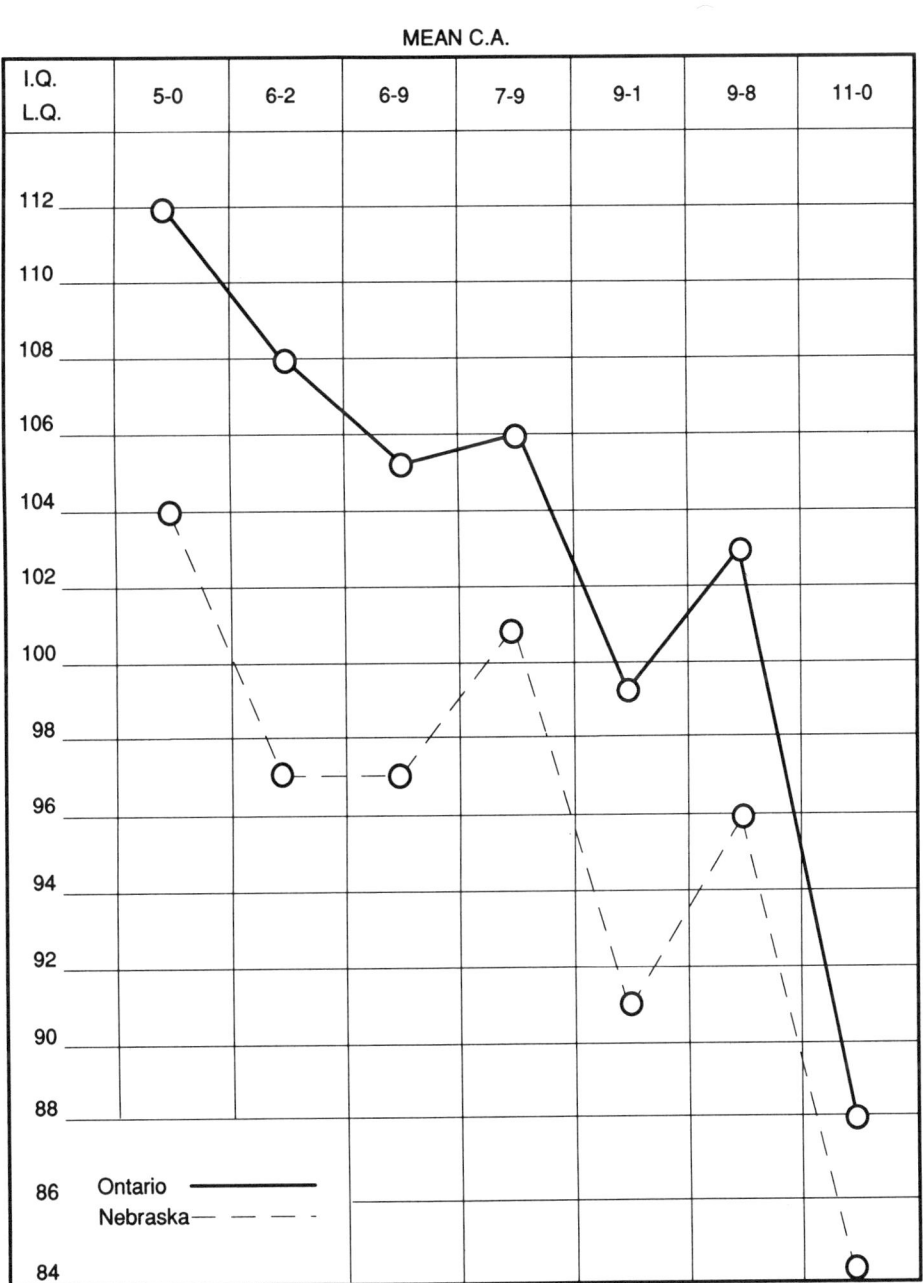

the Nebraska Test on the same children. It appears then that the Ontario School Ability Examination not only shows a significantly higher IQ score at each age level than does the Nebraska Test of Learning Aptitude. The apparently higher IQ and LQs for the younger children in Figure I probably have no significance but may be due to a selection factor.

2. Results for Children with Normal Hearing.

Table II shows the results of three tests administered to hearing children in terms of the means, difference between means, standard error of difference, and critical ratio for the Ontario, Binet, and Nebraska Tests. It will be seen from this table that the children obtained a mean IQ of 107.3 on the Binet Test, 102.9 on the Ontario Test, and a mean LQ of 95.7 on the Nebraska Test. This table also shows that there is a significant difference between the Nebraska and Binet Tests, and between the Ontario and Nebraska Tests on hearing children, whereas the difference between the Binet and the Ontario does not show high statistical significance.

An analysis of the results for each age level as presented in Figure 2 shows, as it did with deaf children, that the Ontario Test gave a higher score than the Nebraska Test at each age level. The Binet Test showed a slightly higher score than the Ontario Test for all age levels except age eight. It is concluded therefore that the Ontario Test gives a rating on hearing children more similar to the Binet Test, than does the Nebraska Test of Learning Aptitude.

From Table 2 and Figure 2 it may be concluded that when all three tests were given to the same hearing children, the Binet showed the highest IQ, the

TABLE 2
The Means, Differences Between Means, Standard Error of Difference, and the Critical Ratio for the Ontario, Binet, and Nebraska Tests on a Group of 49 Hearing Children

Tests	Means	S.D.	S.E.	Difference between Means	S.E. of Difference	Critical Ratio
Ontario	102.9	21.24	3.04	4.39	2.00	2.19
Binet	107.3	21.81	3.12			
Ontario	102.9	21.24	3.04	7.16	1.35	5.32
Nebraska	95.7	17.47	2.50			
Nebraska	95.7	17.47	2.50	11.55	1.70	6.79
Binet	107.3	21.81	3.12			

FIGURE 2

The Mean I.Q. and L.Q. At Each C.A. Interval for the 49 Hearing Children

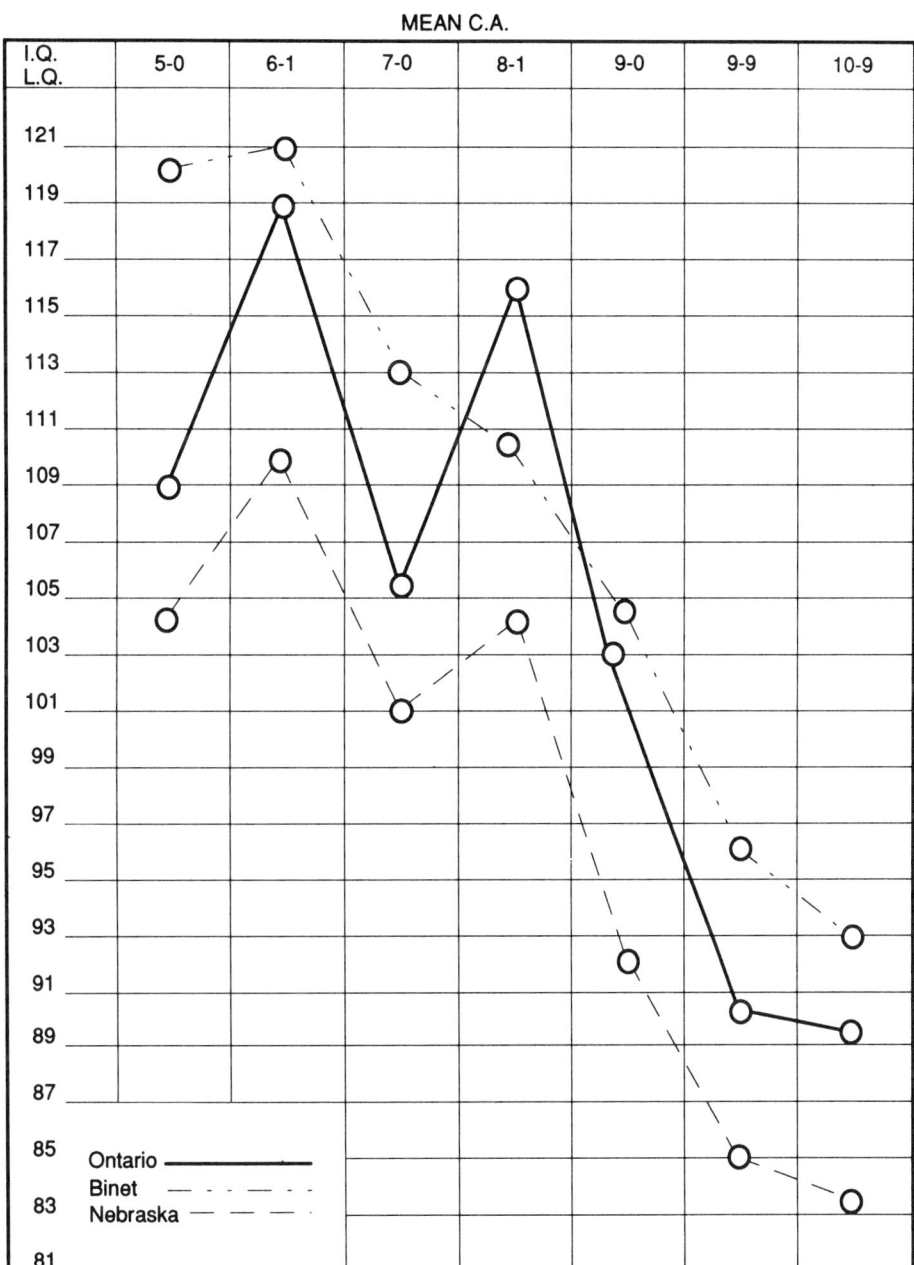

Nebraska the lowest LQ, and the Ontario was found to give an IQ that was closer to the Binet than was the Nebraska Test. It was found also that the Binet and Ontario tested consistently higher than the Nebraska at all age levels.

3. Comparison of the Combined Group of Hearing and Deaf Children.

When the data from deaf and hearing children were combined, the following results were obtained. On the Ontario Test the mean IQ was 102.9. The mean for the Nebraska Test was 95.8. It is apparent that the mean IQ obtained from the Ontario Test is over seven points higher than the mean LQ obtained from the Nebraska Test. The critical ratio for these two groups was 6.8 showing a significant difference between results obtained on the Ontario and Nebraska Tests on deaf and hearing children taken as a group.

Summary and Conclusions

The purpose of this study was to compare ratings from the Ontario School Ability Examination with those from the Nebraska Test of Learning Aptitude. An attempt was made (1) to compare the Ontario IQs with the Nebraska LQs when both tests were administered to a group of deaf children, and (2) to compare the Ontario IQs and Nebraska LQs with the Stanford-Binet IQs when all three tests were administered to a group of hearing children.

From an analysis of the data it appears that:

1. The Ontario School Ability Examination tested consistently higher than the Nebraska Test both when administered to deaf and when administered to hearing children. This difference was shown to exist between the means for both groups and also at the various age levels tested. The difference between the mean IQ and LQ was found to be of statistical significance.
2. When the Ontario, Binet, and Nebraska Tests were administered to a group of hearing children, it was found that the results obtained from the Ontario examination were closer to the results obtained from the Binet test, than were those obtained from the Nebraska Test.
3. The results of this experiment should not be interpreted as a real measure of validity of either the Nebraska or the Ontario tests, unless one considers the Binet test as the criterion upon which other tests must be based. A real measure of the validity of these two instruments will depend on a study of the correlation of either of these tests to the deaf child's ability to learn speech reading, language, speech, and school subjects. Until such an experiment has been conducted, we must evaluate the tests on another basis.

4. From a practicable point of view it would appear that the Ontario School Ability Examination is superior to the Nebraska Test if the Binet examination has any relation to learning ability. In addition, the Ontario Examination takes less time to administer, is simpler to handle and carry, is easy to score and administer, and costs considerably less than does the Nebraska Test Learning Aptitude.

References

Amos, H. (1936). *Ontario School Ability Examination Manual of Directions.* Toronto, Canada: The Ryerson Press.

Hiskey, M. (1941). *Nebraska Test of Learning Aptitude, Manual of Directions.* Lincoln: University of Nebraska.

Chapter 15

Special Education and Rehabilitation

SAMUEL A. KIRK
University of Illinois

Dr. Kirk: Mr. Chairman and members of the subcommittee, my name is Samuel A. Kirk. I am director of the Institute for Research on Exceptional Children and professor of education at the University of Illinois. Our purpose is to train teachers, to train leadership personnel at the doctoral level, and also to advance knowledge in the field of exceptional children through research. Our present staff at the university consists of 11 professors with doctor's degrees and approximately 12 other professional workers on full or part time.

I appreciate the opportunity to appear here and express my views. However, because of the time element, I would like to confine my remarks to House Joint Resolution 494, Title 1, pertaining to training of teachers of the deaf.

As indicated to you by many individuals, there is a marked shortage of qualified teachers of the deaf. I believe that deaf children today are obtaining poorer education than ever before due to the shortage of qualified teachers. There is, however, a still greater shortage of professionally trained leaders in the education of the deaf, since it is practically impossible to find a professional educator of the deaf with advanced training at the doctoral level to train teachers of the deaf. I have had a vacant position at the university for approximately 8 years and only last year was able to find a qualified university professor for this work.

The bill as it stands has two major items which I should like to see amended.

First, the bill should be broadened to include not only the training of teachers of the deaf at the undergraduate level, but also the training of college teachers who, because of advanced graduate training, would qualify to prepare teachers of the deaf. We cannot train teachers unless we have highly

---

Testimony before the Subcommittee on Special Education of the Committee on Education and Labor, House of Representatives, 86th Congress, Second Session. Hearing held in Chicago, Illinois, May 13 and 14, 1960.

qualified college personnel to prepare such teachers. Therefore, I would like to suggest that Section 101 of Title 1, read: "for teachers of the deaf and college personnel for the preparation of teachers of the deaf."

Second, Section 105(a) deals with the composition of the advisory committee. It provides that the advisory committee consist primarily of members from residential institutions for the deaf. There is a danger [in] a small group consisting of people in administrative positions dictating the nature of the program of deaf education in the United States. This may result in the exclusion of the thinking of qualified university personnel.

I believe that you should know that a difference of opinion has arisen between college training centers preparing teachers of the deaf and the superintendents of institutions now members of the Conference of Executives of American Schools for the Deaf. Recently, the Conference of Executives, consisting primarily of superintendents of residential institutions—who, according to the [American] *Annals of the Deaf* of November, 1959, sponsored this bill—has taken it upon itself to accredit colleges and to certify teachers. They charge teachers $5 for a certificate which has no legal basis since certification of teachers of the deaf and all teachers is the responsibility of state departments of public instruction. This certificate does not legally qualify a teacher of the deaf for employment, since such teachers must obtain a legal certification from their state department of public instruction. The Conference of Executives is the only association which has requested that universities and colleges apply to them for approval. No other association in education (in the mentally retarded, or blind, or the crippled, or in elementary or secondary education) attempts to approve colleges and universities or solicits their applications. No other professional group attempts to assume the role of state departments of public instruction by issuing their own certificate to teachers for a fee.

This group of superintendents of residential institutions for the deaf, through their organization, is now requesting Congress to put into a law a bill which would require the Commissioner of Education to appoint an advisory committee consisting of a majority of their own members.

If this section were to remain as is, it will tie the hands of the Commissioner of Education in his appointments, and will tend to give a legal basis of control (of the field) to the Conference of Executives. In a sense, their attempt to control the field has held back progress in the education of the deaf—as represented by their neglect in this bill for requesting the higher professional training for leadership positions such as the training of college personnel for preparing teachers of the deaf. In addition, this bill concentrates on the status quo for institutions and is very careful to exclude the cooperation of universities that are engaged in research and training of personnel.

I recommend that this committee consider amending Section 105(a) by substituting the following:

The Commissioner of Education will appoint an advisory committee of 12 individuals, 6 of whom are selected from among professional educators engaged in the preparation of teachers of the deaf, 3 from among professional educators and 3 from among lay personnel interested in the education of the deaf.

This amendment will give the Commissioner of Education freedom to select a broad representation from among teacher-training institutions, including those residential institutions affiliated with colleges and universities.

My plea to this committee is to develop sound legislation for the education of teachers and leaders in the education of the deaf so that it will be consistent with the training of personnel in other areas of education, science, medicine, and other professions. Only by placing support and responsibility for professional preparation of personnel on the institutions of higher learning will the desired goal be achieved.

It is dangerous to assume that educational procedures for the deaf have reached heights of efficiency and effectiveness. Will progress come from service-oriented groups whose major endeavor is the management of installations and personnel, or will the new developments come from the agencies and personnel who are employed by our society for research, development, and the training of personnel—the faculties of the institutions of higher learning?

It is obvious to me that the present bill fixes the status quo. It may increase the number of teachers of the deaf, but will not develop the quality desired. Placing the responsibility on the great institutions of higher learning as suggested by the amendments would not only increase the quality of professional personnel but would provide for qualitative development of the field.

The point of view presented here is not a lone and individual one. This problem was discussed in Los Angeles in April at the recent meeting of The Council for Exceptional Children, an organization of over 13,000 educators of exceptional children. At this meeting, resolutions were passed, and Dr. Maurice Fouracre was sent from Los Angeles to Washington on April 22 to testify at the Senate hearing on Senate Joint Resolution 127. Among other things Dr. Fouracre, in behalf of The Council, stated:

> We urge objection to the statutory description of the detailed composition of the advisory committee. We believe the members of the advisory committee should be selected on the basis of individual professional competency and at the discretion of the U.S. Commissioner of Education or his administrative superior.

The above quotation was the intent of a series of resolutions by The Council of Exceptional Children, the Division of Teacher Education, the Council of Administrators of Special Education in Local School Systems, and the National Association of State Directors of Special Education.

I appreciate the opportunity to present these points of view and trust that Congress will pass sound legislation for the benefit of deaf children in this country.

Mr. Giaimo: Thank you, Dr. Kirk.

I recognize the gentleman from Minnesota.

Mr. Quie: Dr. Kirk, I want to commend you for your good statement here.

[First], I think so often we have neglected this concept in the past, that when you are going to educate teachers of some special educational group you forget about the instructors or professors needed to educate them and many times they are not available, and I surely think this is a good suggestion that you have.

And, secondly, I want to commend you on bringing out into the open this schism between [higher education] groups and the special education groups. Most people come before us and do not say anything about it. Well, I am fully aware that this is in the background at all times.

So I think that those of us on the committee can better understand the problems that you have in this field by bringing out into the open these problems, as you have done.

Now, in the bill, where it states that six of such appointed members shall be individuals identified with institutions engaged in the training of teachers of the deaf—are the residential schools considered as institutions for training teachers of the deaf?

Dr. Kirk: Yes.

Mr. Quie: And this would not in any way mean colleges?

Dr. Kirk: No; not from the group.

Mr. Quie: As you understand the definition?

Dr. Kirk: They provide there in the bill, sir, that three can come from institutions of higher learning, provided they are affiliated with institutions for the deaf. I would, therefore, interpret that to mean . . . .

Mr. Quie: Of course, you go to the other extreme, and recommend that they be professional educators engaged in the preparation of teachers for the deaf, and also three professional educators, which really means nine, doesn't it?

Dr. Kirk: Yes. Well, three that are engaged in the preparation of teachers of the deaf, because we would like the opinion of other educators, deans of graduate schools and deans of colleges, and professors in other areas, medicine or . . . .

Mr. Quie: So this would prevent any of the so-called six from being appointed unless they fit into this group of three who would be called lay personnel interested in the education of the deaf.

Would the teachers and administrators of the residential schools—could that be construed as being lay personnel?

Dr. Kirk: No. Some of the people in the residential schools are high-level professionals. They have appointments in universities. They would qualify, even though they are appointed by the institution, and a joint appointment with the university with which they are affiliated.

Mr. Quie: But unless they were professional educators, or completely separate from the educational staff, except as they are interested as lay people, they couldn't be appointed. This means that six of them have to be people from these institutions.

On the other side, you precluded any of them from being appointed unless they happen to be professional educators?

Dr. Kirk: I am not sure I understand; and I wouldn't press for the division. I was trying to harmonize it more with the original bill.

However, what I said was six individuals identified with training teachers of the deaf, because we would expect them to know what the field would be.

The bill says "identified," and there's a difference there, because that might mean a superintendent, or it may be someone else [who] is not necessarily a professional educator of the deaf.

Mr. Quie: Well, it seems to me, and I surely agree with you, that one way appears to be rigged for the benefit of people on one side, and the other way is rigged for the benefit of people on the other side, and we will have to make a compromise.

But again I want to say that I am impressed by your willingness to express this frankly—and just one more question:

I imagine you must be knowledgeable on the subject of speech pathologists and audiologists as well, and in that Section 205 of the bill they set up again the criteria of who should be appointed.

Do you feel that this is restrictive in any way?

Dr. Kirk: Yes, sir; I do. I think that the Commissioner of Education's hands should not be tied, and that he should seek adequate advice and appoint an advisory committee that would be able to do the best job for the country without attempting to introduce in the bill a control by any one group or another, because there are many people working in speech correction and audiology in many different organizations.

Mr. Quie: I surely want to thank you for that.

Mr. Elliott: Thank you very much, Dr. Kirk.

Chapter 16

The Federal Program for Training Teachers of the Deaf

SAMUEL A. KIRK

I am not only pleased but actually enthusiastic about the conference and the people participating in it. For many years, I have been considered a critic of teacher training programs, not only in the deaf, but in other areas of special education. I have felt that we have not placed sufficient efforts on improvement of teacher education but that we continue to do what we have done for many years.

My general impression now is that the special education of the deaf is moving at a more rapid pace than other areas of special education. Public Law 87-276 has injected not only a ray of hope, but also a great deal of enthusiasm within and outside of the profession. This conference is unique and I will predict that the deliberations of the group and the results will accelerate the education of the deaf by 5 years.

As I am sure all of you know, Congress amended Public Law 85-926, which dealt with the training of professional personnel in the mentally retarded, to include all handicapped children. This bill, Public Law 88-164, is a very broad bill. Title III includes training of professional personnel in all areas of the crippled and other health-impaired, the emotionally disturbed, the deaf, and other specialized personnel required in the program for the education of handicapped children. Under this bill, we are now authorized to train (a) teachers at the senior undergraduate level, (b) teachers at the master's degree level, (c) supervisors and administrators of teachers, (d) college instructors, and (e) research personnel.

For 1964, training teachers of the deaf was not included in the general bill since up to June 30, 1964, Public Law 87-276 is in force and the $1.5 million appropriated will, under forward financing, include teachers of the deaf for

---

Reprinted from Stephen P. Quigley (Ed.). (1966). *Preparation of Teachers of the Deaf*. (OE-35059, Bulletin 1966, No. 8). A Report of a National Conference, Virginia Beach, Virginia, March 15–19, 1964. Washington, DC: U.S. Government Printing Office.

1964–65. Next year teacher training for the deaf will be under Public Law 88-164. This means that:

1. We will be able to train teachers of the deaf at the senior level and at the first-year graduate level similar to the present program under Public Law 87-276.
2. In addition, next year we will be able to (a) train supervisors and administrators of programs for the deaf at the graduate level, (b) train college instructors to train teachers of the deaf, and (c) train research personnel.
3. There will be a change in stipends for students in the education of the deaf under Public Law 88-164 next year. Undergraduate students at the senior level will receive $1,600 stipend as before. At the first-year graduate level, they will receive a $2,000 stipend. At the second-year graduate level, they will receive a $2,400 stipend, and at the third-year graduate level, they will receive a $2,800 stipend. In addition to this, a dependency allowance of $400 for each dependent will be given to all fellows at the graduate level.
4. At the present time, colleges at the graduate level receive $2,000 support grant. Under the new program next year, colleges and universities will receive $2,500 support grant for each graduate fellow.
5. In addition to training programs, we also have under Section 302 of Title III a research and demonstration program. Actually, research and demonstration applies to the 1964 budget in the field of the deaf as it does in all other areas. Consequently, we will now have an opportunity to develop new methods of teaching, to conduct research on major problems for the deaf, and to conduct demonstration programs on new developments.

The results of this conference give you the deliberations of the group of specialists in the deaf and specialists in the related areas. I stated earlier that this was a unique conference since it included not only educators, supervisors, and administrators of programs for the deaf, but it also included many people in the general field of education, psychology, speech and hearing, and other areas related to the programs of deaf education. This is a significant forward step since any field can learn from related disciplines and related disciplines always contribute to any field of education.

… Part VII

The Illinois Test of Psycholinguistic Abilities (ITPA)

INTRODUCTION

JEANNE McRAE McCARTHY
University of Arizona

It has been a rare privilege to have been associated with Samuel A. Kirk in a variety of roles over the last 35 years and to be asked to trace the elements in his background that coalesced in the development of the Illinois Test of Psycholinguistic Abilities (ITPA). In an effort to provide a historical perspective of the field and of Kirk, the man, I shall trace my contacts with him over the period from 1958 to the present.

My first contact with Dr. Kirk was as a member of the audiences who flocked to hear his unique view of children in the late 1950s and as an observer of his efforts to address the needs of those whose learning and behavior problems did not fit into the neat, well-defined categories in existence at that time.

My next interaction with Dr. Kirk was as a doctoral student returning to academia under a Public Law 85-926 federally funded fellowship, with Dr. Kirk as my advisor, a role in which he played the benevolent despot, always setting higher goals for his students than seemed possible to achieve. In this capacity, as his graduate associate, I gained firsthand knowledge of the concepts underlying the ITPA. I brought to this role my experience as a clinical psychologist and a school psychologist, plus my personal experience of mothering two little girls. Both Dr. Kirk and Winifred Day Kirk, herself a school psychologist, made use of this experience and that of all the other doctoral students involved in the project in developing tests to be administered experimentally to children before they were modified, improved, included, or rejected for use in the experimental edition of the ITPA. This involvement in the standardization of a new approach to the assessment of young children was an important part of the training of most of Kirk's doctoral students, including Barbara Bateman, Corinne Kass, Dorothy Sievers, Douglas Wiseman, James Chalfant, and hosts of others.

During that time, he shared the knowledge he had acquired since he completed his bachelor's and master's degrees in psychology, which was heavily influenced by Marion Monroe in remedial reading, J. E. Wallace Wallin in children with disabilities, and Harvey Carr in the functional school of psychology. His doctorate in physiological and experimental psychology and neurology underlined his interests in brain theory and relationships to aberrations in learning and behavior and in Orton's work on strephosymbolia. As he has stated in an account of his own personal perspectives, "It became obvious to me that to understand all those language, perceptual and reading disability problems, it was necessary to understand the workings of the brain" (Kauffman & Hallahan, 1976). Because of his extensive work in these areas, Dr. Kirk was able to urge his students and the field of special education to reject an emphasis on the "medical model" and to develop a model that more directly assessed the learning and behavior problems of children for whom no services were available under existing categorical labels.

Dr. Kirk's growing interest in the "psycholinguistic" approach to assessment and remediation was supported by a growing interest in the field in brain-behavior relationships evident in the work of D. O. Hebb, Penfield and Rasmussen, and Smith and Carrigan, and Lashley's early work on localization of brain function. As students, we were asked to compare and contrast such concepts as "cell assemblies," "phase sequences," and the functions of acetylcholine and cholinesterase in facilitating or inhibiting neural transmissions. And yet, we were encouraged to concentrate on behavioral symptoms of learning problems, and not get "bogged down" in the unknowns of cerebral dysfunctions, as the first article in Part VI makes clear can occur.

In addition, Dr. Kirk had been heavily influenced by Alfred Binet, who, in 1909, wrote persuasively on the education of intelligence and said,

> Now if we consider that intelligence is not a single function, individual and of a particular essence, but that it is formed by the union of all the little functions of discrimination, observation, retention, etc., whose plasticity and extensibility have been determined, it will appear undeniable that the same law governs the ensemble and its elements, and that consequently anyone's intelligence is susceptible of being developed; with augmenting attention, memory, and judgment, and in becoming literally more intelligent than before; that improvement will continue until one reaches one's limit. (Binet, 1909)

At about this same time, Guilford's work on the structure of intellect, which was being used in research on the gifted by Gallagher and Aschner at the Institute for Research on Exceptional Children (IREC), lent another dimension to Dr. Kirk's thinking about a test that would measure such constructs in young children as described by Binet and by Guilford. This line of thinking was supported by J. McV. Hunt's work on Piaget's research on the development of intelligence, which supported the notion that intelligence developed sequentially in young children and might then be responsive to environmental manipulation. Since Hunt worked next door to the IREC, his influence was in proportion to his proximity. These strands of Kirk's thinking on the educability of intelligence are evident in the first article in Part VII (Chapter 17, "Illinois Test of Psycholinguistic Abilities: Its Origin and Implications"), written after more than 10 years of developing and implementing the experimental edition of the ITPA.

Later, as a professional, I continued to be involved in his thinking, applying what had been learned at the university to the development of programs and services for children with disabilities in the public schools. As a public school person, I found myself involved in testifying in support of the

Learning Disabilities Act of 1969, turning to Dr. Kirk's original definition of learning disabilities, which had first appeared in his book *Educating Exceptional Children* in 1962 (p. 263). This same definition had been accepted by the Association for Children with Learning Disabilities (ACLD) in 1963, was expanded by the National Advisory Committee for the Handicapped (which he chaired) in 1968, and appeared in federal legislation, with minor modifications, in 1969. It was then folded into Public Law 94-142 in 1975 and has served the field, albeit not without some difficulty, since that time.

As his career shifted to Washington in the early 1960s and he tackled the job of building what was to become the Bureau of Education for the Handicapped, now the Office of Special Education and Rehabilitative Services, he continued to influence my professional life with new research and model demonstration grants funded under Public Law 88-164 by the Bureau of Education for the Handicapped to public school programs serving students with specific learning disabilities. As recipients of one of these grants in 1965, my colleagues and I were able to develop a model demonstration project in Schaumburg, Illinois, that implemented the psycholinguistic approach to assessment in the "real world" of the schools and relied heavily on the ITPA, with Dr. Kirk available to help solve the problems that inevitably arise in such a project.

This ongoing association with Dr. Kirk was further expanded when I was offered a position at the University of Arizona in 1972 as the Director of the Leadership Training Institute in Learning Disabilities (LTI-LD). Our primary objective was to provide technical assistance to the states who had applied for grants to develop programs of service to children with specific learning disabilities. Dr. Kirk had retired from the University of Illinois and moved to the University of Arizona, where he was able to develop a personnel preparation program for teachers of students with learning disabilities and to attract Corinne Kass and James Chalfant to his staff. He agreed to help to develop the technical assistance function and the research function of the LTI-LD. Working as his colleague at the University of Arizona, it was possible to follow the development of his thinking prior to the advent of the ITPA and after watching for 10 years the use and misuse of the instrument and the concept of specific learning disabilities. It was during this period that he wrote the second article in Part VII (Chapter 18, "Uses and Abuses of the ITPA"), after assisting in the development of learning disability programs across the country and completing research on the characteristics of children being served in each state in their model centers for students with learning disabilities.

Readers of Part VII will be able to follow Kirk's thinking prior to his search for a theoretical model upon which to build an instrument that would lead directly to remediation, his awareness of the appropriateness of the Osgood psycholinguistic model, and his efforts to develop an instrument that would measure components of central processing in young children.

It is my conviction that the ITPA filled a void in the field of psychometrics as no other instrument had been able to do. It moved the field away from its fascination with the IQ as a measure of children's learning abilities and focused on the diversity of learning abilities and central processing functions that influence school learning and behavior. We were provided with a measure that could dissect the more generalized IQ and look at aspects of the learning process that would lend themselves to remedial efforts. The ITPA moved the work of Strauss forward by focusing not on "brain damage," which was generally considered to be structural and difficult to document, but on the central processes of learning, which were generally considered to be functional, observable in behavior, and more amenable to remediation. The psycholinguistic model of the ITPA, focusing as it did on the perceptual, linguistic, and memory abilities and disabilities of young children, provided a bridge to the later development of human information processing models and the recent current fascination with strategies of learning.

References

Binet, A. (1911). L'education de l'intelligence. In Ernest Flammarion (Ed. and Trans.), *Les idees modernes sur les enfants* (pp. 141–161). Paris: 26 Rue Racine.

Guilford, J. P. (1967). *The nature of human intelligence.* New York: McGraw-Hill.

Hebb, D. O. (1949). *The organization of behavior.* New York: Wiley.

Hunt, J. McV. (1961). *Intelligence and experience.* New York: Ronald Press.

Kauffman, J. M., & Hallahan, D. P. (1976). *Teaching children with learning disabilities.* Columbus, OH: Merrill.

Kirk, S. A. (1963). *Educating Exceptional Children.* Boston: Houghton Mifflin.

Lashley, K. S. (1951) *Cerebral mechanism in behavior.* New York: Wiley.

Penfield, W., & Rasmussen, T. (1952). *The cerebral cortex of man.* New York: Macmillan.

Piaget, J. (1936). *The origins of intelligence in children.* New York: International Universities Press.

Strauss, A. A., & Lehtinen, L. (1947). *Psychopathology of the brain-injured child.* New York: Grune & Stratton.

Jeanne McRae McCarthy received her doctorate from the University of Illinois, majoring in special education and minoring in psychology. Heavily influenced by the creative thinking of Samuel A. Kirk, J. McV. Hunt, Hobart Mowrer, and their predecessors, she set out to translate such principles into programs in the public schools. Since 1976, her primary interests have centered on services to young children with disabilities or those who are delayed or at risk, with special emphasis on early identification of and intervention with preschoolers with specific learning disabilities. She has functioned as a consultant to the U.S. Department of Education, Office of Special Education Programs, for the past several decades. Because of her public school orientation, she has been able to bridge the gap between research and service during a time when knowledge in the field of special education, especially early childhood education, has been exploding.

Chapter 17

Illinois Test of Psycholinguistic Abilities: Its Origin and Implications

SAMUEL A. KIRK

The Concept of Learning Disability

The concept of learning disability has recently evolved to designate the heterogeneous group of children not fitting neatly into the traditional categories of handicapped children. There is a substantial number of children who show retardation in learning to talk, who do not develop language facility, who do not develop normal visual or auditory perception, or who have great difficulty in learning to read, to spell, to write, or to calculate arithmetic problems. These children are not deaf or blind or mentally defective. Some of them are not receptive to language but are not deaf, some are not able to perceive visually but are not blind, and some cannot learn by ordinary methods of instruction but are not mentally retarded. Although these children form a heterogeneous group and fail to learn for diverse reasons, they have one thing in common, namely, developmental discrepancies in abilities. The term *learning disability* can therefore be defined as . . . a specific retardation or disorder in one or more of the processes of speech, language, perception, behavior, reading, spelling, writing, or arithmetic. . . . The definition implies that the retardation . . . exists in spite of the fact that the child has certain abilities in other areas. . . . [It] does not imply that a mentally retarded child, diagnosed as such by ordinary mental tests, cannot also have a learning disability. . . . A learning disability implies certain assets in addition to specific disabilities or wide discrepancies [among] abilities. . . .

Adapted from *Learning Disorders*, 3 (July 1968), pp. 397–427. Special Child Publications, 4545 Union Bay Place, Seattle, Washington 98105.

The Educational Emphasis on Remediation

While the medical specialist is concerned primarily with etiology and with the relationship between communication disorders and the location of a possible cerebral dysfunction in children, the special educator is concerned primarily with the assessment of the behavioral symptoms and with special methods of ameliorating the disability. In education, a child who has the basic potential to learn, but does not learn after adequate instruction, [may be] a child with a learning disability. The [medical] etiology of the disability, in most instances, is not helpful to the organization of remedial procedures. Whether a child is labeled as brain-injured or not (usually inferred from behavior) does not [necessarily] alter the remedial procedure.

With school-age children, the diagnosis of learning disability is generally preceded by failure in academic subjects. In preschool children, the disabilities are primarily in the behavioral and the communication processes. Such problems with young children presented themselves to the writer and his associates when they were conducting an experiment in the early education of the mentally retarded as far back as 1949. During this period it was apparent that many young children needed evaluation and diagnosis so that a specific educational program could be provided. Among the group were children who were classified as mentally retarded but who had specific disabilities, such as language disorders, perceptual disorders, and behavior disorders.

Like that of many clinicians, the diagnosis was informal since no adequate tests, apart from general intelligence tests, were available for the evaluation of the language ability of these children. Adopting customary clinical procedure, data from tests such as the [Stanford]-Binet, [the] Kuhlmann, and the Vineland Social Maturity Scale were analyzed. Observations were also made [of] the children's behavior and their responses to intellectual tasks. The diagnostic tools were clearly inadequate. . . .

Early Development of the ITPA

It was at this time (1950) that the origins of what ultimately became the Illinois Test of Psycholinguistic Abilities took form. Several attempts were made to develop language and perceptual tests for these children. The original attempt consisted of a method of evaluating receptive language in which the child was required to point at objects and pictures after verbal directions. Attempts were also made to measure vocal expressive ability, primarily through time sampling. These efforts to develop a clinical diagnostic test did not come to fruition, partly because we did not have a theoretical model upon which to construct a comprehensive language test.

Several years later, Professor Charles Osgood at the Institute of Communication of the University of Illinois organized a course on "Experimental

Communication Processes." The writer audited this course in order to obtain ideas for a language model upon which a test could be constructed. In this course, Professor Osgood was developing his generalized behavioral model which (in oversimplified terms) cross-classified behavior according to:

1. The processes of decoding, association, and encoding.
2. The organizational levels—the integrative (perceptual and motor integration) and representational (symbolic processes).
3. The channels—namely, visual and auditory sense modalities and vocal and motor expression.

The following year, Dorothy Sievers, then a graduate assistant in the preschool [for mentally retarded children] enrolled in this course for the purpose of studying the model and organizing research [that] would lead to a diagnostic examination. After considerable study and many trials, Sievers developed a number of tests following the Osgood model. Several hundred children below the age of six were examined with these tests, resulting in a doctoral dissertation entitled "A Language Facility Test" (Sievers, 1955).

To assess the clinical value of this test, James McCarthy (1957) used the battery of tests developed by Sievers to examine athetoid and spastic cerebral palsied children at Dr. Perlstein's Clinic in Chicago. McCarthy found that the general rationale of this test was useful, but that each test in the battery was contaminated by other factors and could not therefore pinpoint discrete abilities and disabilities as was desired. For example, the labeling test in Sievers' original battery required both visual reception and vocal response.

From these two doctoral dissertations, the writer decided that a new test should be devised [that] would try to isolate specific skills uncontaminated by other channels, processes, or levels, and also to include certain kinds of functions such as visual sequential memory and auditory sequential memory, which clinical experience suggested were of value in relation to reading ability. It was felt that a combination of the theoretical model and empirical evidence should be used to evolve a **clinical** model from which tests could be generated.

For three years, one test after another was tried and evaluated until the material could be narrowed to a workable battery. One of the major difficulties encountered was in developing tests that could be used with two- and three-year-old children. The customary digit repetition test as administered in the Revised Binet and WISC, for example, could not be used successfully with very young children, nor did it discriminate adequately among children at different chronological age levels. In order to overcome these difficulties, several modifications were made. One modification in procedure was to give the child a second chance with each sequence of digits if he failed on the first attempt.

This introduced an element of learning. Also, the time interval between digits was reduced. Instead of using one second between each digit as on the Stanford-Binet, we found that younger children could repeat the digits more readily if we presented them at half-second intervals. By using these two variations in technique, we were able to develop an auditory sequential test [that] discriminated between children at different age levels and measured the ability of younger children.

At this stage of the development of the ITPA, it was decided that rather than undertake another five years of developmental research on the tests so as to refine them still further, they should standardize and publish an experimental edition so that the general usefulness and validity of the tests could be evaluated. The most successful tests were therefore standardized for children between the ages of two and a half and nine. Thus the experimental edition of the Illinois Test of Psycholinguistic Abilities was published in the summer of 1961 (McCarthy & Kirk, 1961).[1]

The Clinical Model of the ITPA

The ITPA and the clinical model from which it was generated have been described in numerous publications (Kirk, 1966; Kirk & McCarthy, 1961; McCarthy & Kirk, 1961; Bateman, 1965). Only a brief description of the clinical model and the subtests of the ITPA are included below.

The clinical model of the ITPA is diagrammed in Figure 1. This diagram presents the three dimensions of the model: (a) the channels of communication, (b) the psycholinguistic processes, and (c) the levels of organization. The numbers in the boxes refer to the numbers of the subtests of the battery and are placed within the model at the appropriate intersections of channel, process, and level. For example, Test Number 1 (Auditory Decoding) measures the process of auditory reception at the representational (meaningful) level, while Test Number 2 (Visual Decoding) measures the process of visual reception at the representational level. In the model, S represents either an auditory or visual stimulus, while R represents the response, either vocal or motor.

Channels of Communication

The channels or routes through which the functions of communication flow include the sense modalities by which linguistic symbols are received and the forms of expression by which a response is made. Since the most common stimuli used in communication and teaching are what you hear and see and the common forms of expression are vocal and gestural, we have labeled these the auditory-vocal channel and the visual-motor channel. Theoretically, other channels are possible. Helen Keller received communication through a tactile

FIGURE 1
Clinical Model of the ITPA

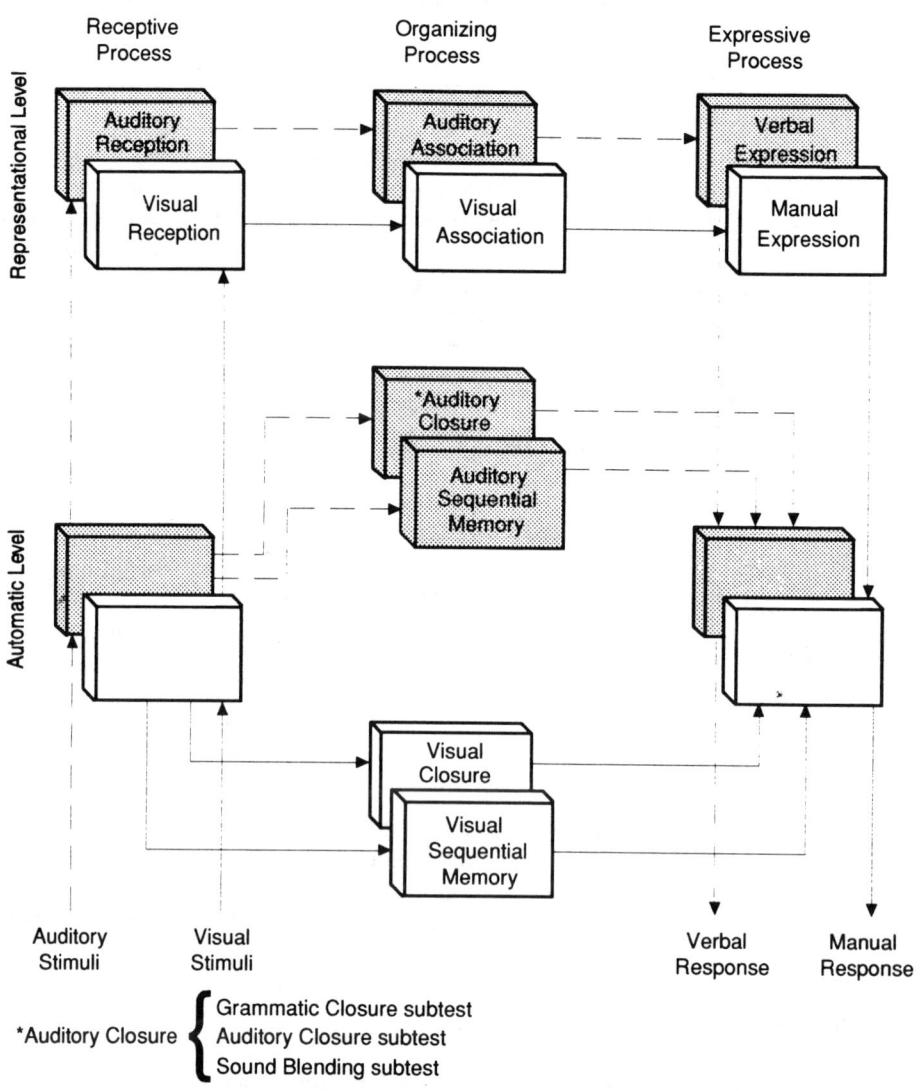

modality. Cross channel communication is also possible whereby the receptive process could involve auditory stimuli while the ensuing expressive process could be motor instead of vocal. Similarly the receptive process could be through the sense modality of vision and its response or expression could be verbal instead of motor. However, in testing a child's ability in various channels, time and feasibility limit these tests to the two most common channels of auditory input with vocal output and visual input with motor output.

Psycholinguistic Processes

In dissecting the habits necessary for language usage, three main operations are considered: (a) decoding or reception, (b) association, a mediating process, and (c) encoding or expressing. *Decoding* is the act of obtaining meaning from sensory stimuli, that is, receptive understanding of words, gestures, pictures, and occurrences which are seen or heard. *Association* includes the manipulation of concepts and linguistic symbols internally. It is a central mediating process which is elicited by decoding and which in turn elicits expressive processes. *Encoding* is the function of expressing ideas in words or gestures. All of these processes are interdependent, both in their operation and in their development.

Levels of Organization

In the act of communication, the necessary degree of language organization within the individual is described by the *levels* of the organization. The two levels identified as being modifiable by learning and of interest to the language clinician and the teacher are (a) the automatic/sequential or nonsymbolic level, and (b) the representational or symbolic level. Nonsymbolic and symbolic, these terms were discarded earlier.

Abilities of the *automatic/sequential* level include such acquired psychological functions as auditory and visual discrimination, auditory and visual closure, auditory and visual sequential (short-term) memory, and, at the response end, verbal and motor mimicry or imitation. Activities requiring the retention of visual or auditory sequences and automatic habit chains regardless of their meaning or content are mediated at this level. Vocal and motor imitation such as doing "pat-a-cake" or repeating "da da da" without having established meaning fall at this linguistic level. Thus this level includes less voluntary, more automatic processes than those at the representational level. Defects at this level interfere with sequential imitation and the ability to retain sequences of visual and/or auditory stimuli.

The *representational*, or meaningful, level encompasses activities using the meaning or significance of auditory or verbal symbols. When a child learns to say "da da" and attaches it to the appropriate father object, he is operating at the representational level. Meaningful auditory and visual decoding and association and verbal and motor encoding function at this level.

The model of the ITPA has been used to generate discrete tests for the purpose of assessing special abilities of children. Wide discrepancies between abilities and disabilities identify a child with a learning disability.

Summary Statement

Learning disability has been presented as a behavioral and educational concept, referring to developmental discrepancies in the communication processes of children. These include disorders or delay in development in one or more of the processes of speech, language, perception, reading, writing, spelling, and arithmetic, sometimes with associated behavioral disorders.

The ITPA was developed in an attempt to analyze children's psycholinguistic functioning in the three dimensions of (a) the processes of communication, (b) the channels of communication, and (c) the levels of organization. Its nine subtests evaluate three processes (decoding, association, and encoding) in each of two channels (auditory-vocal and visual-motor) occurring at two levels of organization (symbolic and nonsymbolic). The clinical model on which the ITPA was based serves the two related functions of (a) generating discrete tests for diagnostic purposes, and (b) organizing educational and remedial programs for children. Its major use is with preschool and primary-aged children, and its end goal is the prevention and amelioration of psycholinguistic learning disabilities.

Research on the psycholinguistic characteristics of different groups of children lead to the following generalizations:

1. Reading disability cases (dyslexics) tend to have superior abilities at the conceptual or representational level as compared to their abilities at the automatic/sequential level, including grammatic closure and auditory and visual short-term memory. This raises the question of the trainability of these psychological functions, and the effect of early training in perceptual speed, closure, and visual and auditory sequential memory in preventing reading disabilities.
2. Mentally retarded children appear to be superior in representational functions as compared to those at the nonsymbolic (or automatic/sequential) level, that is, grammatic closure and visual and auditory sequential memory. The studies with the ITPA confirm other experimental studies on the deficiency in short-term memory of the mentally retarded. These findings apply equally to educable mentally retarded, mongoloid, and nonmongoloid trainable mentally retarded children.
3. Mongoloid children[2] show a superiority in motor encoding as compared to vocal encoding as well as to other psycholinguistic abilities. The mon-

goloids are also superior in motor encoding when compared with non-mongoloids of the same age and mental age. In this connection, it should be recalled that Luria, of the Soviet Union, has stated that mental defect represents a dissociation of the two aspects of the second signal system, the vocal and the motor. Since in our studies only the mongoloids appear to show a significant discrepancy between the vocal and motor expressive abilities, it is possible to conjecture that Luria's hypothesis applies only to the mongoloids.

4. Normal children with articulatory speech defects appear to have the same disabilities on the ITPA as dyslexics and the mentally retarded; namely, a deficiency in the automatic/sequential level—grammatic closure and auditory and visual sequential memory. They also show a deficiency in vocal encoding on the ITPA.

5. Spastic cerebral palsied children tend to be inferior to athetoid cerebral palsied children in psycholinguistic functions at the representational level. The status is reversed at the automatic/sequential level, where the spastics are superior to the athetoids. The latter show a marked deficiency, like the mentally retarded and dyslexics, in grammatic closure and auditory and visual short-term memory.

6. Young middle-class Negro children show a normal profile on all psycholinguistic abilities except the auditory-vocal automatic ability (auditory short-term memory). In the latter, these Negro children are superior to their other abilities and also superior to the standardization population. Lower-class Negro children show deficiencies on psycholinguistic functions as compared to both the standardization population and the middle-class Negro children. The one exception is again in auditory short-term memory, in which the lower-class Negro children are superior to their other abilities but still inferior to the short-term memory ability of young middle-class Negro children.

7. As would be expected, legally blind children show inferiority in visual-motor channel as compared to their auditory-vocal channel functioning. On the other hand, partially seeing children not diagnosed as legally blind do not show this inferiority. These findings lead to the conclusion that with children having visual acuity better than 20/200, the ITPA is testing central rather than peripheral processes.

8. Studies on hearing-defective and sensory-aphasic children indicate that the deaf and hard-of-hearing perform at a higher level on tests utilizing the auditory channel than do sensory aphasics. This again suggests that the ITPA is measuring central rather than peripheral abilities.

Remediation of children's disabilities found by the ITPA presents encouraging results. Idiographic as well as nomothetic research in this area point to the conclusion that different disabilities identified by the ITPA can be ameliorated through systematic remedial programs.

The ITPA, along with other diagnostic tests that have been or are being developed, represents a new approach to the management of children with learning disabilities; namely, diagnosis of children for the purpose of remediation, in contrast to assessment for the purpose of classification or categorization.

References

Bateman, B. (1965). *The Illinois Test of Psycholinguistic Abilities in current research: Summaries of studies.* Urbana, IL: University of Illinois Press.

Kirk, S. A. (1966). *The diagnosis and remediation of psycholinguistic disabilities.* Urbana, IL: University of Illinois Press.

Kirk, S. A., & McCarthy, J. J. (1961). The Illinois Test of Psycholinguistic Abilities—an approach to differential diagnosis. *American Journal of Mental Deficiency, 66*(93), 399–412.

McCarthy, J. J. (1957). *Qualitative and quantitative differences in the language abilities of young cerebral palsied.* Unpublished doctoral dissertation. University of Illinois.

McCarthy, J. J., & Kirk, S. A. (1961). *The Illinois Test of Psycholinguistic Abilities.* Urbana, IL: University of Illinois Press.

Osgood, E. E., & Sebech, T. A. (Eds.). (1965). *Psycholinguistics.* Bloomington, IN: Indiana University Press.

Sievers, D. J. (1955). *Development and standardization of a test of psycholinguistic growth in preschool children.* Unpublished doctoral dissertation. University of Illinois.

NOTES

[1] The ITPA [was] being revised. The revised test [was] available in the summer of 1968, [and included] a visual closure test and two supplementary auditory closure tests. The other tests are essentially similar to [previous] tests, with minor revisions in content.

[2] This older terminology refers to children who manifest Down syndrome.

Chapter 18

Uses and Abuses of the ITPA

SAMUEL A. KIRK
WINIFRED D. KIRK

Before we discuss the uses and abuses of the ITPA, we will summarize the original major purposes of the ITPA:

1. The ITPA was designed as a diagnostic test to delineate intraindividual variations in functioning in those areas involved in language and other forms of communication. We called it a psycholinguistic test because it was concerned with psychological functions of information processing, perception, and memory as well as the use of linguistic codes. The term may not now [in 1978] be an adequate designation of the test, but it was suitable in 1961 before linguists developed their own use of the term.

2. The test is designed to measure some areas in which a child succeeds or fails, not to obtain an IQ or its equivalent for classification purposes (Kirk & McCarthy, 1961).

3. It is a test for young children. The norms range from two and one-half to 10 years, but its greatest usefulness is between four and eight, since the norms at both extremes were obtained to increase the ceiling for eight-year-olds, or to show a deficit for three- and four-year-olds.

4. The functions it tests are designed to denote deficits that require remediation. If the child has difficulty in communication because he cannot translate the code used in spoken language, that is, if he does not understand auditory language (receptive aphasia), then a remedial program should be organized to teach him to understand language. If he is delayed in talking (expressive aphasia), he should be taught techniques for expressing himself verbally. If he has a deficiency on a number of auditory vocal tests and is average or above on visual motor tests, remediation should be organized to improve the whole range of auditory

Reprinted from *Journal of Speech and Hearing Disorders*, 43 (February 1978), pp. 58–75.

vocal abilities. Furthermore, if the child has superior abilities in some functions, they should be used to develop parallel abilities in the deficient areas.

Evaluation of Practices

After describing the purpose of the ITPA and its possible uses as a diagnostic and research instrument, we want to discuss its misuse and some pitfalls in administration, scoring, and interpretation. It should be emphasized that the ITPA is not all things to all children. It is not the solution to all children's problems. It is one step beyond global tests that may lead to a program of remediation. One of its greatest abuses is to consider it a solution to all problems and to use scores as a final diagnosis instead of another possible aid to clinical judgment.

Five specific problems should be noted:

1. The ITPA is not an easy test to learn, although conscientious professionals can learn to administer it efficiently if they are willing to put in the time and practice. It does require careful study, but the material for such study is available in the *Examiner's Manual of the ITPA* (Kirk, McCarthy, & Kirk, 1968) and in the later booklet *Aids and Precautions in Administering the ITPA* (Kirk, 1974).

2. Many individuals are misusing the test by not following directions in the manual. We have found many using the test inappropriately. In one workshop designed for so-called experienced examiners, we found only three out of the 17 enrolled who could adequately administer the test. One was a school psychologist, one a speech-language pathologist, and one a learning-disabilities teacher. In another workshop we found that the college instructor teaching the ITPA had not taken the time to learn the test.

3. Many universities are now offering courses on the administration and interpretation of the ITPA. Unfortunately, however, many of these courses are being taught by people who do not know how to administer and interpret the test adequately. Hopefully, as more and more people are adequately trained to use and understand the test, this situation will improve.

4. Lack of understanding of the basic concepts that underlie the test often creates misinterpretation of the test results. Even if the test has been well administered, the test results are of little value if the scores are not adequately interpreted. Using the overall score to evaluate a child or to compare him with other children rather than to compare his own subtest scores with each other are common misconceptions of the use of the test.

Mechanical use of scores and labels without their relationship to other information is also a common mistake. The concept of intraindividual differences is difficult to understand since we have for many years dealt only with interindividual differences. Kirk and Kirk (1971) have published a text on interpretation and remediation.

5. Another error that is made is the use of the test with the wrong subjects. A differentiation must be made between the clinical use of the test and its use for research purposes. Some clinical use of the test can be made even at the top and bottom range of the norms, which extend from two and one-half to 10 years. Scores above and below these ages of course do not define the child's abilities; and, as with any test, scores at the upper and lower limits of the norms are somewhat tenuous. Clinical prudence is necessary in interpretation of such scores. Some clinical use can also be made with atypical subjects outside the normative ages, for example, with aphasic adults. Such use, however, is usually made to supplement other clinical evidence.

    For research purposes the test is practical only for children of about four to eight years of age, since many four-year-olds score lower and many eight-year-olds score higher than the test limits. A buffer zone above and below these limits is essential for reputable research. It is most disconcerting to peruse research reports where the ITPA has been used with third- and fourth-grade children, many of whom undoubtedly score at or above the normative limits.

Criteria in Evaluation of Research

In discussing some of the research presented herein, we may appear to be somewhat critical. For that reason, we are presenting some criteria we use in evaluating research projects.

1. First, research using experimental and control groups is very difficult and, in many cases, impossible to conduct because of the difficulty in finding comparable cases. Populations of children with learning disabilities are so heterogeneous that it is practically impossible to form experimental and control groups of children with the same problems. Some of the children's cases are so rare that their prevalence is probably one in 5,000 children, and such cases cannot be used in nomothetic research.

2. A second criterion for research is that of using appropriately aged children for the study. It must be remembered that research in contrast to clinical work with the ITPA is applicable only to young children between the ages of four and eight. When research conclusions are based on data from nine- and 10-year-old average children, the results are of dubious

import. Some of the children in such groups reach the ceiling on most of the subtests and many reach the ceiling on one or more of the subtests, thus invalidating the research results. Such instances will be pointed out in the review of research studies.
3. A third criterion is the qualification of those who administer the tests for the research project. Many studies are made, and many children are tested by people inadequately trained and prepared in the administration of the ITPA.

These criteria should be borne in mind in evaluating the voluminous research using the ITPA. Much solid information on the meaning and interpretation of the ITPA and its concepts can be derived from the research, although some research conclusions are contradictory because of variations in methods, subjects, designs, and administration. Several excellent reviews of research using the ITPA have been made by Bateman (1965), Sedlack and Weener (1973), Proger, Cross, and Burger (1973), and Buros (1972).

We would like to make note, however, of the following topics of research: (1) the equivalence of the experimental and revised editions of the ITPA, (2) factor analysis on the ITPA, (3) relationship of the ITPA to other tests.

Equivalence of Experimental and Revised ITPA Editions

One question asked frequently relates to the equivalence of the experimental and the revised edition of the ITPA. Can results from the two be safely compared? Two studies have been conducted to answer this question. One study (Hubschman, Polizzotto, [&] Kaliski, 1970) found a correlation of 0.95 between two administrations of the experimental edition and 0.93 between the second administration of the experimental edition [and] the 1968 revised edition. These correlations are much higher than those found in the test-retest stability measures conducted by the authors. In examining these studies we found that the researchers did not partial out age or IQ, thus producing spuriously high correlations. Another study by Waugh (1975) that controlled for age obtain correlations of 0.65. The latter is probably a more accurate correlation.

Relationship of the ITPA to Other Tests

There have been many studies relating the ITPA to other psychometric tests. Most of the studies compare the global scores of the ITPA to IQs or mental ages.

By administering the Stanford-Binet, WISC, and ITPA to 100 first-grade children, Huizinga (1971) found that the ITPA correlated 0.90 with the Binet and 0.80 with the WISC full scale. The WISC correlated 0.84 with the Binet.

The auditory-vocal scaled scores correlated 0.84 with the Binet and 0.75 with the verbal scale of the WISC. The visual-motor subtests correlated 0.68 with the Binet and 0.58 with the Performance WISC. Other correlational studies relating the ITPA to the full scale WISC were Polley's (1971) showing a correlation of 0.49, Guest's (1970) with a correlation of 0.67, Humphrey and Rice's (1973) with a correlation of 0.88, and Bartin's (1971) with a correlation of 0.61.

The conclusion from these studies is that the ITPA correlates quite highly with the Binet, less with the WISC, and still less with the Performance scale of the WISC.

Factor Analysis of the ITPA

In the book on the *Development and Psychometric Characteristics of the Revised ITPA*, Paraskevopoulos and Kirk (1969) stated:

> The intercorrelations among ITPA subtests are too complex to achieve simple structures. . . . Attempts to factor analyze ITPA data would probably generate results yielding only confusion, rather than simplicity and parsimony. (p. 184)

In spite of our warning, many factor-analytic studies have been made. The availability of computer programs for factor analysis has resulted in report after report of factor analysis of ITPA data. After reviewing the results of 20 factor-analytic studies on the ITPA, Sedlack and Weener (1973) concluded that the factor-analytic studies yielded "confusing and contradictory results" as we had predicated. They stated:

> It is safe to say that no more factor analyses with small Ns using only ITPA subtests are needed. The availability of computer routines for factor-analytic procedures has resulted in a tendency for researchers to factor-analyze whenever they have more than five variables available on a set of subjects. This tendency has risen to promiscuous levels in the case of the ITPA. Future factor-analytic work should proceed from a careful a priori theoretical framework, should use a large number of subjects from different age and ability subpopulations, and should be done by those with a thorough grasp of factor-analytic procedures. (pp. 123–125)

Taken all together, we feel that the numerous factor-analytic studies of the ITPA have neither proven nor disproven the construct validity of the ITPA.

A different technique of studying the construct validity of the ITPA has been postulated by both Cohen (1973) and Elkins (1973).[1] They used a Guttman-Lingoes nonmetric space-analysis technique. Both found that the process and channel dimensions were supported, but the levels (representational and automatic) were not clear. Apparently, the Grammatic Closure Test factors out as a representational rather than an automatic level test. Aside from this, the levels appear to have some validity.

Even after Sedlack and Weener's review, Hare, Hammill, and Bartel (1973) conducted a further analytic study using 126 third-grade children. They included a very important technique of factor-analyzing ITPA data along with other reference tests. Seven factors emerged and accounted for 66% of the variance. They concluded that the ITPA does have construct validity. Unfortunately, the authors of this study used eight- and nine-year-old children—children at the upper levels of the norms. The study, however, using reference tests, is in the right direction.

In an attempt to determine the psycholinguistic correlates of academic achievement, Hammill, Parker, and Newcomer (1975) tested 137 children in the fourth grade with an average age of nine years and four months. A short form of the ITPA was given, using alternate items from eight of the subtests—basically the even-numbered items, although some arbitrary selection was used. They then gave the California Achievement Test (CAT) and calculated correlations between the subtests of the shortened form of the ITPA and the CAT subtests of reading, language, spelling, and arithmetic. They found (1) 45 out of the 60 correlations were significant, (2) Using a correlation of 0.35 and above (since they were concerned only with the predictive indicators), grammatic closure was the only subtest to show a satisfactory correlation, [and] (3) There was little difference between the correlations of the low, high, and average performers on the CAT except in grammatic closure. They concluded that the ITPA does not predict academic achievement.

In evaluating this study as an example of other similar studies, a number of questions can be asked.

1. *Who administered the tests?* One prerequisite of a reported study is that a clear statement be made of the qualifications of the examiners. No mention is made in this article concerning the qualifications of the examiner or examiners, but in another article by the same authors the testing was done by 67 students (Newcomer and Hammill, 1974). Were these student-practice tests? With so many examiners of questionable experience, and with the well-known factor of examiner variability, how valid are such results?
2. *How valid are the results of any correlational study using subjects at the upper limits of the norms of the tests used?* In several of the studies the subjects were nine-year-old children in the fourth grade, some of whom inevitably reached the top of the norms, thus depressing the measure of the ability of some. If fourth-grade children are tested on a reading test with a ceiling at fourth grade, of course you would narrow the range of scores since many fourth-grade children can read above that level.

Hammill et al. (1975) recognized the problem of a ceiling, since they state that "it is necessary to demonstrate that ceiling effects are not present" with fourth-grade children. But they brush aside this caution by saying, ". . . no more than the expected number of children reached the test's ceiling." If the expected number of children reached the test's ceiling, that in itself should invalidate the correlations.

3. *How valid are assumptions that correlations based on the short form of the ITPA apply also to the long form?* By using a very questionable short form of the test, Hammill et al. concluded that there is no relationship between academic achievement and most of the subtests of the Illinois Test of Psycholinguistic Abilities. Newcomer and Hammill (1974) published a study in which they tried to correlate the full form of the ITPA with a short form that they had devised. The correlations were surprisingly high, but it was pointed out by Kirk (1975) in the *Journal of Learning Disabilities* that the correlations were spurious since Newcomer and Hammill had not partialled out chronological age. This was an obvious flaw in the study and a criticism with which the authors agreed. It is a little difficult to understand how the authors drew conclusions about the ITPA when the ITPA as standardized was not administered.

4. *Why are these correlations labelled "predictive" instead of "concurrent"?* Both the CAT and the ITPA were given in the fourth grade. Even if they had correlated highly, they would not have been "predictive." This is a concurrent correlation, not a predictive correlation. Such a study would require testing the children in kindergarten, finding the children who show discrepancies in development, and then testing them in the second grade to see if the children with deviations failed in academic subjects. Even this approach would not completely answer the question since intervention could change the picture.

Newcomer and Hammill recognized that few decisive predictive studies have been conducted. They state, "It is particularly unfortunate that we could locate no studies which evaluated the psycholinguistic competencies of preschool children and followed them up through the second or third grade" (Newcomer & Hammill, 1975, p. 736). On the same page, despite their own statement, they mention the Hirshoren (1969) study, which did exactly what they said they could not find. In Hirshoren's study, 41 white children were tested in kindergarten with the Stanford-Binet and the experimental edition of the ITPA. These children were then followed up two years later in the second grade with the CAT. Hirshoren reported (1) The median correlation between the composite scores of the ITPA given in kindergarten and the achievement variables of the CAT given in the second grade was 0.60. The median correlation between Binet IQ's similarly administered was 0.56. (2) Among the correlations of the subtests of the ITPA, the visual sequential memory test was 0.61 for reading vocabulary and 0.51 for reading comprehension. (3) Auditory association correlated 0.53 with vocabulary, and 0.41 with comprehension.

5. *Why shoot down a straw man?* The authors of the ITPA have never claimed that the test has predictive value for reading. The test was devised to analyze various aspects of the children's communicative abilities. It was an effort to diagnose children's behavior by assessing variations in abilities within the child. It was not organized to predict academic achievement in the three Rs in third and fourth grades. Hammill, Parker, and Newcomer (1975), as well as other researchers, have set up a straw man in order to shoot it down.

In addition to the above comments on research with third- and fourth-grade children, other speculations can be made to explain the different results correlating reading ability to the ITPA subtests. Few if any of the studies took into consideration the Aptitude Treatment Interaction Factor. In England this is called the Aptitude X Instruction Interaction Factor. This means that the results that we obtain are dependent, not only on the characteristics of the child, but also on the instruction he receives. The teaching of phonics is a point in question. The earlier studies that showed a strong relationship between poor reading ability and visual sequential memory ability were all done in the sixties when less emphasis was placed on the formal use of phonics in teaching reading. Toward the end of that decade, much greater emphasis began to be placed on phonics until today the State Board of Education in Arizona, for example, has prescribed that all schools must use readers that emphasize phonics. The teaching of phonics emphasizes the sequence of letters and their sounds in a word and in so doing teaches the child to use visual sequential memory in learning to read and spell. The more recent studies have been conducted with children who are more sophisticated in this process. As a result of this, children who would have had weak visual sequential memory may have overcome their potential deficit through the training in phonics by the time they reach third or fourth grade. Cronbach and Snow (1969) report that auditory sequencing correlated positively with "look-say" methods of teaching reading, and negatively with phonic methods.

Another explanation of the differences between the earlier studies and the later ones is that the earlier ones used first- and second-grade children whereas the later ones used third- and fourth-grade children. Sound blending is important at the early stages of learning to read (Grades 1 and 3) but of much less importance in the later stages as in Grades 3 and 4.

In brief, it is illogical for us to study the relationship between certain characteristics or aptitudes of children and their school achievement without also evaluating and defining the environment and teaching methods used.

The child's experience and environment may also be significant in determining his psycholinguistic abilities.

The Uses of the ITPA

The ITPA, as described earlier, was developed to assist clinicians and teachers diagnose visual-motor and auditory-vocal abilities and disabilities in linguistic, cognitive, perceptual, and memory functions of young children. It assesses deviations in functioning within a single child so that remedial programs for the use of these functions can be formulated.

As indicated earlier, the ITPA has been used in situations and under conditions that were not intended by the developers of the test. The test was not designed to solve all problems of all children as some users imply. It was not designed to be used as a classification instrument or as a predictor of academic achievement in the third and fourth grades as a number of studies have attempted to assay. It has repeatedly been emphasized that it is not to be administered by untrained examiners—a procedure that is detrimental to clinical practice and to research results.

The test was designed to be used primarily with young children to obtain clinical insights into those who have communicative problems. Its main function is to help assess discrepancies in cognitive and perceptual functioning, and in some aspects of language and memory performance. Since the latter is the main purpose of the test, a report on one child will be made.

A four-year-old child was diagnosed as having Down syndrome since a chromosomal translocation of the type found in children with Down syndrome was present. The child's features did not have the usual appearance of mongolism. He did not talk, and on the Stanford-Binet he was said to be untestable, with an IQ below 50. He was considered to be functioning at the trainable retarded level and was assigned to a preschool class for trainable mentally retarded children.

Figure 1, Profile A, shows the profile of this four-year-old on the ITPA. It will be noted that this child scored at or near the five- and six-year levels on some of the visual motor tests (visual reception, visual association, manual expression, and visual closure) but was unable to score on the auditory and verbal tests. He was obviously not mentally retarded, but he was unable to use the auditory-vocal code that others used. His basic need was to learn to talk and to understand speech. It should be noted that this boy's visual-motor channel was superior to his chronological age, whereas his auditory-vocal channel was inferior.

Profile B on the same profile shows a child of five whose IQ was similar to that of the child with a chromosome aberration. This child's abilities were depressed below his chronological age on all linguistic, perceptual, and memory tests. While the child who was purported to have Down syndrome shows

FIGURE 1
ITPA Profiles for Two Children

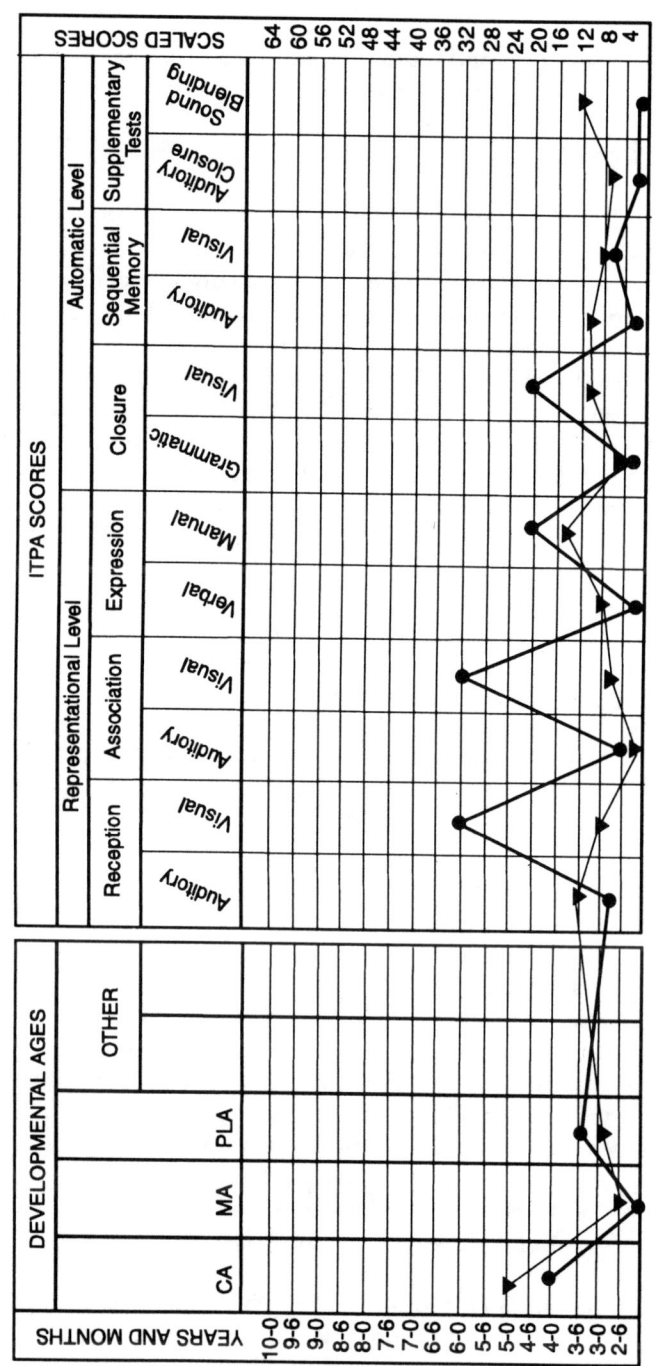

significant discrepancies in abilities, the second child is more evenly retarded and requires a more general curriculum rather than a program of remediation of specific deficits.

What does Profile A tell us? We knew beforehand that the child did not talk. What did the ITPA profile contribute to our knowledge of this child?

1. First, this four-year-old child was not simply mentally retarded as diagnosed by physicians and psychologists on the basis of the chromosomal translocation and the lack of verbal communication. He scored significantly above his chronological age on the visual tests and on manual expression, in spite of low scores on the auditory-vocal subtests and on the intelligence tests. This is one major use of the ITPA, to differentiate between mental retardation, where all the abilities are deficient, and a language-disordered child (learning disability) where some of the abilities are average or superior while the others are depressed.
2. Second, the ITPA profile tells us what strengths can be used to overcome the deficits. The visual ability may be used as a bridge to understanding the verbal code, just as motor ability may serve to spark the use of words. We can use the abilities to train the disabilities by organizing a program that will associate doing with saying, and seeing with understanding the words.

Conclusion

In conclusion, a few generalizations can be made.

1. The ITPA, with all its limitations (and it has many) has become popular nationally and internationally. Why? Because it is a diagnostic rather than a classification test. If properly administered, it helps pinpoint some abilities and disabilities in children between the ages of two and 10 (or four and eight). This kind of assessment gives badly needed cues to a remedial teacher or clinician in designing a program to help the child develop more effective use of his abilities. The test profile approach helps the teacher in organizing a remedial program by understanding why the child has difficulty in some accomplishments.
2. Children with developmental disabilities of one kind or another show certain kinds of deficits on the ITPA that can be of value in organizing programs for some groups. From the research that has been reported, we can generalize the following:
    (a) Many minority children, Mexican Americans, [Native Americans], some blacks, and others who are bilingual are relatively normal on

visual-motor psychological functions but deficient in the auditory-vocal functions. Educationally, this means that they need a curriculum that develops success in auditory-vocal interaction between the teacher and the children. Contrary to this need, we find many such children working on visual-motor workbooks in classes because such tasks require less teacher-pupil interaction and it is something the child can do by himself. The auditory-vocal curriculum requires more work on the part of the teacher and a higher ratio of teachers to children.

(b) The mentally retarded, children with articulatory disorders, athetoid cerebral-palsied children, and some other types are more deficient at the automatic level than at the representational level.

(c) Children with severe reading disabilities show varying deficits, probably related to the reading level studied and the teaching method used. Studies show that in the first or second grade, visual sequential memory and sound blending are correlates of reading difficulty. In the third and fourth grades grammatic closure and auditory association are correlated with reading ability. During the early part of the century when phonics was emphasized in teaching reading, the reading clinics were full of children who were word callers and did not derive meaning from reading. Later, when phonics fell into disuse and sight reading was emphasized, the reading clinics were full of children who needed phonics to learn to read. Have we come full circle in our schools? As with many social and educational issues, we allow the pendulum to swing from one extreme to the other.

3. There is no psychometric instrument that is highly reliable and valid. Mechanical use of psychometric tests sometimes tends to lead to misdiagnosis. Tests cannot substitute for good observations and clinical judgments. They can be used as supplements. This statement applies to the ITPA as well as to other tests.

Acknowledgment

This report is a condensed version of two addresses delivered at the forty-ninth and fiftieth Conventions of the American Speech and Hearing Association, November 5, 1974, (Las Vegas) and November 22, 1975 (Washington, DC). Requests for reprints should be directed to Samuel A. Kirk, Department of Special Education, The University of Arizona, Tucson, Arizona 85721.

References

Bartin, N. G. (1971). *The intellectual and psycholinguistic characteristics of three groups of differentiated third grade readers*. Doctoral dissertation. State University of New York at Buffalo.

Bateman, B. (1965). *The Illinois Test of Psycholinguistic Abilities in Current Research: Summaries of studies*. Urbana, IL: University of Illinois Press.

Buros, O. K. (Ed.). (1972). *The Seventh Mental Measurements Yearbook* (pp. 814–825). Highland Park, NJ: Gryphon.

Celebre, G. (1971). *Psycholinguistic abilities and oral word recognition associated with relative level of personality adjustment in primary school-age children with minimal brain dysfunction*. Doctoral dissertation. Temple University.

Cicirelli, V. G., Granger, R., Schemmel, D., Cooper, W., & Holthouse, N. (1971). Performance of disadvantaged primary-grade children on the Revised Illinois Test of Psycholinguistic Abilities. *Psychology Schools, 8*, 240–246.

Cohen, A. (1973). Smallest space analysis of the Revised Illinois Test of Psycholinguistic Abilities. *Psychology Schools, 10*, 107–110.

Cronbach, L. J., & Snow, L. S. (1969). *Final report: Individual differences in learning ability as a function of instructional variables*. Contract No. OEC. 4-6-061269-127. Stanford University: U.S. Office of Education, School of Education.

Deese, C. (1971). *A study of the discrimination by the subtests of the Revised Illinois Test of Psycholinguistic Abilities between successful and unsuccessful readers of normal intelligence*. Doctoral dissertation. Memphis State University.

Elkins, J. (1972). *Some psycholinguistic aspects of the differential diagnosis of reading disability in grades I and II*. Doctoral dissertation. University of Queensland.

Ferrier, E. E. (1962). An investigation of the ITPA performance of children with functional defects in articulation. *Exceptional Children, 9*, 32.

Foster, S. (1963). *Language skills for children with persistent articulation disorders*. Doctoral dissertation. Texas Woman's University.

Guest, K. E. (1970). *Relationships among the ITPA, receptive expressive language tasks, intelligence and achievement*. Doctoral dissertation. University of Wisconsin.

Hallom, J. J. (1964). *An exploratory study to determine psycholinguistic abilities of a group of six-year-old children with severe articulation problems*. Master's thesis. Sacramento State College.

Hammill, D. D., Parker, R., & Newcomer, P. (1975). Psycholinguistic correlates of academic achievement. *Journal of School Psychology, 13*, 18.

Hare, B. A., Hamill, D., & Bartel, N. R. (1973). Construct validity of selected subtests of the ITPA. *Exceptional Children, 40*, 13–21.

Hirshoren, A. (1969). A comparison of the predictive validity of the Revised Stanford-Binet Intelligence Scale and the Illinois Test of Psycholinguistic Abilities. *Exceptional Children, 35*, 517–522.

Hubschman, E., Polizzotto, E. A., & Kaliski, M. S. (1970). Performance of the institutionalized retardates on the PPVT and two editions of the ITPA. *American Journal of Mental Deficiency, 74*, 579–580.

Huizinga, R. J. (1971). *The relationship of the Illinois Test of Psycholinguistic Abilities to the Stanford-Binet Form L-M and Wechsler Intelligence Scale for Children*. Doctoral dissertation. University of Arizona.

Humphrey, J., & Rice, A. (1973). An evaluation of several methods of predicting Full-Scale IQ from the ITPA. *Journal of Special Education, 7*, 133–140.

Ikeda, M. (1970). *The relationships between the ITPA, reading performance, and IQ of third grade children*. Doctoral dissertation. University of New Mexico.

Jorstad, D. (1971). Psycholinguistic learning disabilities in twenty Mexican-American students. *Journal of Learning Disabilities, 4,* 143–147.

Kass, C .E. (1962). *Some psychological correlates of severe reading disability (dyslexia).* Doctoral dissertation. University of Illinois.

Kirby, E. A., Lyle, W., & Hurble, B. R. (1972). Reading and psycholinguistic processes of innate problem readers. *Journal of Learning Disabilities, 5,* 295–298.

Kirk, S. A. (1972). Ethnic differences in psycholinguistic abilities. *Exceptional Children, 39,* 112–118.

Kirk, S. A. (1975). Letters to the editor. *Journal of Learning Disabilities, 8,* 119–120.

Kirk, S. A., & Kirk, W. D. (1971). *Psycholinguistic learning disabilities: Diagnosis and remediation.* Urbana, IL: University of Illinois Press.

Kirk, S. A., & McCarthy, J. J. (1961). The Illinois Test of Psycholinguistic Abilities: An approach to differential diagnosis. *American Journal of Mental Deficiencies, 66,* 399–412.

Kirk, S. A., McCarthy, J. J., & Kirk, W. D. (1961, rev. 1968). *The Illinois Test of Psycholinguistic Abilities.* Urbana, IL: University of Illinois Press.

Kirk, W. D. (1974). *Aids and precautions in the administration of the Illinois Test of Psycholinguistic Abilities.* Urbana, IL: University of Illinois Press.

Lagerman, A. P. (1970). *Psycholinguistic characteristics of children with reading disabilities, and the effects of remediation on psycholinguistic development and reading achievement.* Doctoral dissertation. University of South Dakota.

Lombardi, T. P. (1970). Psycholinguistic abilities of Papago Indian children. *Exceptional Children, 36,* 485–494.

Macione, J. (1969). *Psycholinguistic correlates of reading disabilities as defined by the Illinois Test of Psycholinguistic Abilities.* Doctoral dissertation. University of South Dakota.

McCarthy, J. J. (1957). *Qualitative and quantitative differences in the language abilities of young cerebral palsied.* Doctoral dissertation. University of Illinois.

McCarthy, J. M. (1965). *Patterns of psycholinguistic development of mongoloid and non-mongoloid severely retarded children.* Doctoral dissertation. University of Illinois.

McLeod, J. (1965). *Some psychological and psycholinguistic aspects of severe reading disability in children.* Doctoral dissertation. University of Queensland.

Myers, P. A. (1963). *Comparison of language disabilities of young spastic and athetoid children.* Doctoral dissertation. University of Texas.

Newcomer, P., & Hammill, D. (1974). A short form of the Revised Illinois Test of Psycholinguistic Abilities. *Journal of Learning Disabilities, 7,* 570–572.

Newcomer, P., & Hammill, D. (1975). ITPA and academic achievement: A survey. *Reading Teachers, 28,* 732–741.

Osgood, C. E. (1957). Motivational dynamics of language behavior. *Symposium on Motivation.* Lincoln, NE: University of Nebraska Press.

Paraskevopoulos, J., & Kirk, S. A. (1969). *The development and psychometric characteristics of the Revised Illinois Test of Psycholinguistic Abilities.* Urbana, IL: University of Illinois Press.

Polley, D. (1971). *The relationship of the channels of communication of the ITPA and the WISC.* Doctoral dissertation. University of Northern Colorado.

Proger, B. B., Cross, L. H., & Burger, R. M. (1973). Construct validation of standardized tests in special education: A framework of reference and application to ITPA research (1967–71). In L. Mann & D. Sabatino (Eds.), *First review of special education* (165–201). Philadelphia: Buttonwood Farms.

Ragland, G. G. (1964). *The performance of educable mentally handicapped students of differing reading ability on the ITPA.* Doctoral dissertation. University of Virginia.

Ryckman, D. B. (1966). *The psychological processes of disadvantaged children*. Doctoral dissertation. University of Illinois.

Sedlack, R. A., & Weener, P. (1973). Review of research on the Illinois Test of Psycholinguistic Abilities. In I. Mann & D. Sabatino (Eds.), *First review of special education* (113–163). Philadelphia: Buttonwood Farms.

Smith, R. M., & McWilliams, B. J. (1968). Psycholinguistic abilities of children with clefts. *Cleft Palate Journal, 5,* 238–149.

von Isser, A. (1977). Psycholinguistic abilities in children with epilepsy. *Exceptional Children, 43,* 270–275.

Waugh, R. (1973). Comparison of revised and experimental editions of the Illinois Test of Psycholinguistic Abilities. *Journal of Learning Disabilities, 63,* 236–238.

Wepman, J. M., Jones, L. V., Bock, R. D., & Van Pelt, D. (1960). Studies in aphasia: Background and theoretical formulations. *Journal of Speech and Hearing Disorders, 25,* 323–332.

Westinghouse study: The impact of Head Start, Vol. 1. (1969). Columbus, OH: Westinghouse Learning Corp., Ohio University.

Wiseman, D. E. (1965). *The effects of an individualized remedial program on mentally retarded children with psycholinguistic disabilities*. Doctoral dissertation. University of Illinois.

NOTES

[1] J. Elkins, A Guttman-Lingoes nonmetric representation of the subtests of the Revised ITPA. Personal communication, University of Queensland (1973).

Chapter 19

Profiles of Children with Severe Oral Language Disorders

ANTHONY H. LUICK and SAMUEL A. KIRK
University of Arizona

ALEEN AGRANOWITZ and ROBERT BUSBY
*Speech & Language Development Center
Buena Park, California*

The major purpose of this study is to determine whether children assigned to classes for severe oral language handicaps in California by a multidisciplinary diagnostic team exhibit a characteristic ITPA performance profile or a number of distinct profiles. A factor analysis and a cluster analysis was made on the scores of 237 children.

It was found that on the factor analysis the results showed a clear auditory-vocal factor and a visual-motor factor. All five tests in the visual-motor channel were superior to the five tests in the auditory-vocal channel. Within the auditory-vocal channel the lowest scores were in auditory association and grammatic closure. Ninety-seven percent of the oral language handicapped children had the lowest scores on these two subtests. It appears from these results that the major deficit of children assigned to severe oral language classes is a deficit in the central organization process, formerly referred to as "central aphasia, or inner language."

The purpose of this report is to describe a profile analysis of ITPA scores with 237 subjects who had been assigned to classes classified as "severe oral language handicapped" in California.

Reprinted from *Journal of Speech and Hearing Disorders* 47, (February 1982), pp. 88–92.

The term "aphasia" generally refers to the loss of language after it has been acquired. In children, the lack of development of language has been referred to as "delayed language development," "developmental aphasia," or as "severe oral language disorders." The latter designation is the one currently preferred by the profession. When this study was conducted, the state of California utilized a comprehensive diagnostic procedure for identifying children who are to be assigned to special classes for children with severe oral language handicaps. In general, the California code (now noncategorical) stated that a minor may be considered to have a severe oral language handicap when:

1. The minor shows normal intellectual potential as measured by instruments that do not require oral directions or oral expression;
2. The minor's score on the auditory verbal scale of one or more standard tests or subtests of language assessment falls two standard deviations below the mean for the minor's mental age as indicated in (1) except that any minor above the two standard deviations but below one standard deviation may be designated as an aphasic and/or other severe oral language handicap if agreed upon with the unanimous decision of the admission committee;
3. The minor is nonverbal or when a spontaneous language sample of at least 50–100 utterances can be obtained and this language sample shows development judged clearly inadequate for the minor's age and in at least two of the following areas of language development—syntactic, semantic, orthologic, phonologic.
4. The diagnostic team must certify that the minor has a severe speech and/or oral language disorder not due to deafness, mental retardation, or autism. In arriving at this diagnostic decision the team utilizes systematic neurological, medical, psychological, speech, hearing, and environmental assessments conducted by licensed professionals in each of these areas.

A common test used for diagnostic purposes, before or after assignment to a class for severe oral language handicaps and to determine perceptual, memory, and language deficits in children is the Illinois Test of Psycholinguistic Abilities (ITPA). This test was developed specifically for children in the age range of three to nine years.

The major purpose of this study is to determine whether children assigned to classes for children with severe oral language handicaps by a diagnostic team exhibit a characteristic ITPA performance profile or a number of distinct profiles.

Methods

The subjects in this study consisted of children with severe oral language disorders who had been assigned to special classes in conformity with the California code. These children had been diagnosed by medical, psychological, speech and hearing specialists, and through this team declared eligible for enrollment in a public school class for children with severe oral language handicaps.

The children of this study were selected from 40 school districts and from approximately 80 different special classes. All of these children were of at least average intelligence on the WISC Performance Scale and had been assessed as having normal hearing. The characteristics of these children are listed in Table 1. The 237 subjects ranged in age from 72 to 99 months. All had been examined on the ITPA by the local psychological diagnostician or speech-language pathologist, either before or after enrollment in the special program. The ITPA was not the primary criterion for the declaration of eligibility.

TABLE 1
Population Distribution

Age (Years/Months)	N	Sex (F)	(M)
6.0 – 6.3	36	13	23
6.4 – 6.7	46	15	31
6.8 – 6.11	42	21	21
7.0 – 7.3	39	13	26
7.4 – 7.7	29	12	17
7.8 – 7.11	27	10	17
8.0 – 8.3	18	9	9
Total	237	93	144

Results

The results are presented in three sections: (1) a profile of the total group; (2) the results of factor analysis; and (3) the results of cluster analysis.

Profile of Total Group

Figure 1 presents the profile of the mean scaled scores of the ITPA for the 237 California children assigned to classes for children with severe oral language handicaps. It should be noted from this profile that the auditory tests are all

FIGURE 1
Total Scaled Score Mean Profile $N = 237$, 100% of Sample

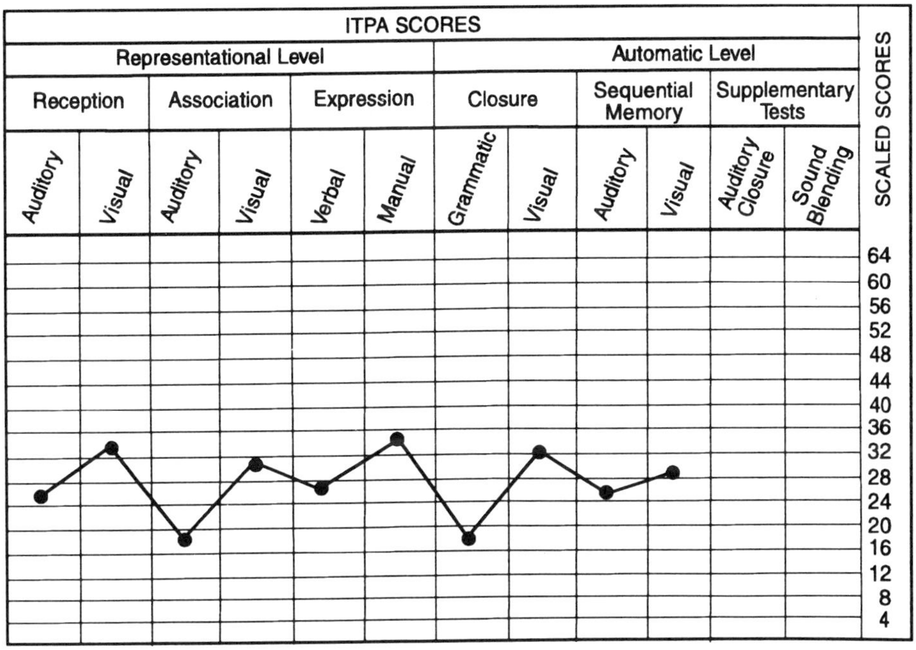

ITPA SCORES							SCALED SCORES
Representational Level			Automatic Level				
Reception	Association	Expression	Closure	Sequential Memory	Supplementary Tests	
Auditory / Visual	Auditory / Visual	Verbal / Manual	Grammatic / Visual	Auditory / Visual	Auditory Closure / Sound Blending	

lower than the visual tests, and the scaled scores for auditory association and grammatic closure are lower than the scaled scores for the other auditory-vocal tests. Actually 97% of the children had auditory and grammatic closure subtests as their lowest scores.

Results of Factor Analysis

Factor analysis studies of ITPA data have produced contradictory results. Sedlack and Weener (1973) report that one of the most common shortcomings of the factor analytic studies on the ITPA has been insufficient sample size to insure stable factors. Nunnally (1967) recommends that one-third as many factors as variables be employed (in the rotation phase of the analysis) because seldom would more factors either have substantial loading or be of scientific interest (c.f., Mann & Sabatino, 1973, p. 123). In addition, factor analysis should have 10 times as many subjects as factors (Nunnally, 1967). Failure to adhere to these basic criteria, in addition to numerous other research inconsistencies, has made questionable the factor analytic studies which have neither "proved" nor "disproved" the construct validity of the ITPA.

The present sample of 237 oral language-disordered children constitutes a unique diagnostic group. Because of the sample size it satisfies the basic criteria for factor analysis.

For the present data the Varimax rotated factor matrix after rotation with Kaiser normalization is presented in Table 2. Two major factors were extracted, with Factor 1 accounting for 80.6% of the variance and Factor 2 accounting for 19.4%, for this solution. The major loadings associated with Factor 1 are: Auditory Reception (.64), Auditory Association (.81), Verbal Expression (.56), Grammatic Closure (.67), and Auditory Sequential Memory (.33).

TABLE 2
Factor Analysis

ITPA Subtests	Factor I	Factor II
Auditory Reception	.64*	.21
Visual Reception	.31	.57*
Auditory Association	.81*	.21
Visual Association	.23	.76*
Verbal Expression	.56*	.32
Manual Expression	.17	.52*
Grammatic Closure	.67*	.21
Visual Closure	.13	.54*
Auditory Sequential Memory	.33*	.11
Visual Sequential Memory	.13	.38*

*$p < .01$

Factor 2 major loadings are: Visual Reception (.57), Visual Association (.76), Manual Expression (.52), Visual Closure (.54), and Visual Sequential Memory (.38). It is clear that the results show two major factors which are very consistent. These factors are an auditory-vocal factor, and a visual-motor factor. We can conclude that with children who have oral language disorders the ITPA reveals two factors, a visual-motor factor which is similar to nonhandicapped children and an auditory-vocal factor which is significantly depressed. The factor analysis finding in this study applies only to children with severe oral language disorders and not to a random sample of the population. This finding is not surprising since many of the children were selected on the basis of a normal performance score as compared to a lower verbal score on the Wechsler Intelligence Scale.

Results of Cluster Analysis of the ITPA Subscales

In this study we used a hierarchial clustering method based on Ward's procedure (Anderberg, 1973). The purpose was to determine if specific ITPA profile patterns with diagnostic utility could be identified in this sample of children who had been selected by a clinical evaluation team as children with severe oral language handicaps according to the California code.

Cluster analytic techniques are in their infancy as a research tool in education. It is only within the past 10 years that sufficiently sophisticated cluster analytic program techniques have been developed for use with high speed computers (Anderberg, 1973; Hartigan, 1975). Luick (1978) has utilized the procedure in identifying homogeneous subclusters of children with specific learning problem profiles.

Anderberg's (1973) program is an agglomerative method that uses a minimum variance criterion because the approach calculates the similarity between clusters, using the mean vector and sum of square vector for the comparison of clusters. In essence, clusters generated are based on the similarity of each child's scores in comparison with the scores of all the other children. Similar profiles are grouped together in a series of multicomparison stages until one group is produced containing all children. Once the clusters are statistically calculated, the researcher must determine how many profile groupings are different and internally homogeneous. This is accomplished by a second stage computer program which lists every child's subscores within each cluster and by plotting the mean profile and variance of each variable in every subcluster for comparison across groupings.

In the present study cluster analysis revealed 12 clusters which were internally homogeneous and statistically deviant enough on one or several variables to cause their assignments to a unique cluster. Upon analysis of the clusters, it was found that eight contained 98% of the subjects and tended to cluster around the group profile as a whole (see Figure 1). This paper will present only three profile clusters as they are indicative of all the other profiles which vary only in one or more of the visual areas. Such variation is not relevant to the major diagnostic conclusion which is presented below.

Figure 2 represents the profile of a cluster of 24 subjects which may be considered a typical profile of a child with a severe oral language handicap. The pattern of abilities and disabilities is similar to the profile of the total group in Figure 1 except that the discrepancies between abilities and disabilities are greater. This profile shows average visual-motor abilities. Visual reception, visual association, motor expression, visual closure, and visual memory all score at a scaled score of 36 or above, similar to the standardization population, which had a mean of 36 with a standard deviation of six. The auditory-vocal abilities are all two or more standard deviations below the standardization mean. Again we find that auditory association and grammatic

FIGURE 2
Cluster 1, $N = 24$, 10% of Sample

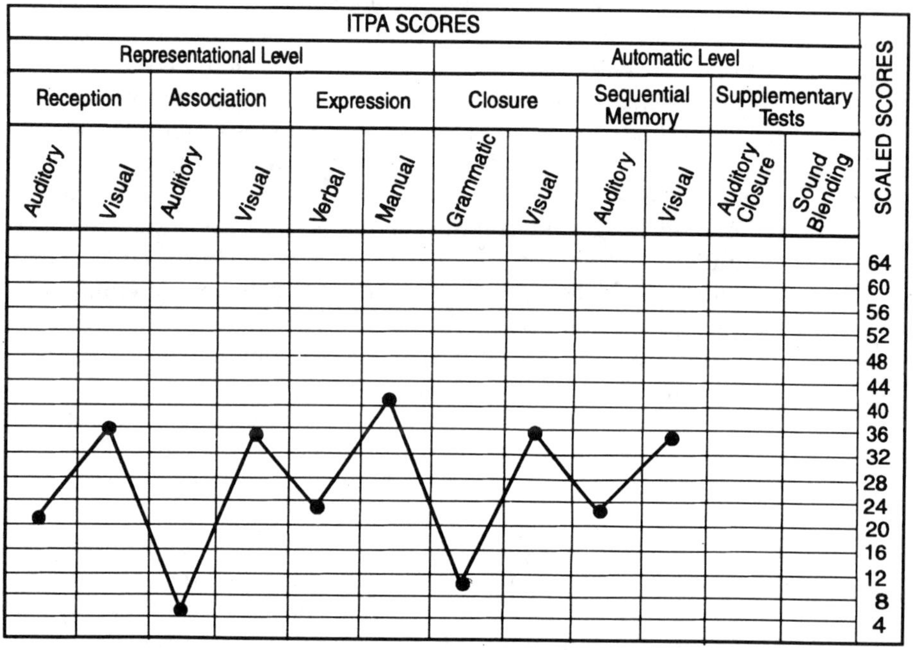

ITPA SCORES												SCALED SCORES
Representational Level						Automatic Level						
Reception		Association		Expression		Closure		Sequential Memory		Supplementary Tests		
Auditory	Visual	Auditory	Visual	Verbal	Manual	Grammatic	Visual	Auditory	Visual	Auditory Closure	Sound Blending	

closure are over three standard deviations below the mean. This profile can be interpreted as representing children with significant auditory-vocal deficit and with a notable deficit in the organizational process.

The other cluster groups may have clinical significance. Clusters A and B are plotted together in Figure 3 for comparison purposes. Cluster A presents a profile of two rare cases with very superior visual motor abilities (scaled scores of over two standard deviations above the mean of 36). Their auditory scores appear to be like those of average children with scaled scores at approximately 36. This type of profile represents a child with superior intelligence whose auditory-vocal performance is relative average but far below his visual-motor performance.

In comparison to Cluster A, Cluster B contains approximately 9.7% of the total sample. Although Cluster B demonstrates the same pattern of abilities (visual-motor channel) and disabilities (auditory-vocal channel) as the clusters in Figures 1 and 2, this profile is significantly below the mean of 36 in both channels. It should be noted that the visual-motor abilities are between $1-1\frac{1}{2}$ standard deviations (SD = 6) below the mean; but the auditory association and grammatic closure subtests are more than three standard deviations below the mean. One could expect these children to be slow learners as compared to the children in the other profiles.

FIGURE 3
Cluster A. .8% of Sample $N = 2$
Cluster B. 9.7% of Sample $N = 23$

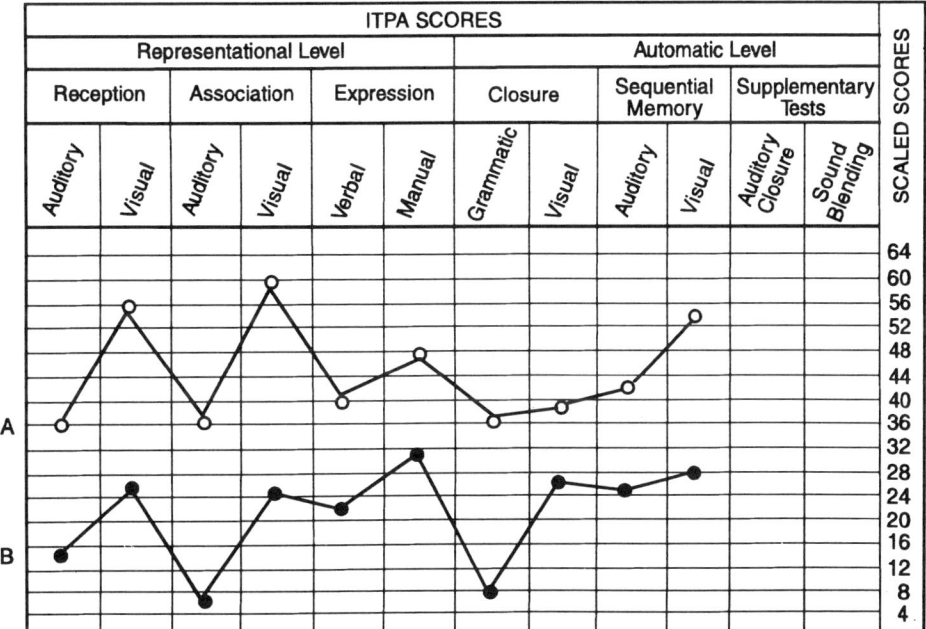

Discussion

The model of the ITPA (Kirk & Kirk, 1971) includes two channels of communication (auditory-vocal and visual-motor), and three processes (a receptive process, an organizational process, and an expressive process). These processes parallel the conventional taxonomy of aphasia that includes (1) receptive aphasia, (2) central aphasia (integrative), and (3) expressive or motor aphasia (Johnson & Myklebust, 1967).

Factor analysis of scores on the ITPA shows two very clear and consistent factors (auditory-vocal and visual-motor) for these 237 children selected by a clinical team according to the California code as having severe oral language handicaps. Cluster analysis shows a clear-cut superiority of the visual-motor channel as compared to the auditory-vocal channel.

This much may be expected from the clinical picture. What the cluster analysis uniquely shows is the discriminable deficit in the semantic and syntactic organizational process, i.e., the consistently lower scores on the Auditory Association and Grammatic Closure subtest of the ITPA.[1]

The fact that 97% of the sample showed major organizational deficits in semantic (auditory association) and syntactic (grammatic closure) areas, or in central, as opposed to receptive and expressive language areas has great significance when one considers that the sample was drawn from over 40 districts and 80 classrooms and was diagnosed by approximately 40 different teams according to the California State Code and assigned to special classes for children with severe oral language handicaps. This conclusion has been supported in a doctoral dissertation by Soroky (1979) who examined a different sample of such children in Los Angeles. Her results show that her subjects also had the lowest scores on the auditory association and grammatic closure subtests.

Considering the probability of finding such profiles in the population at large, we can state with some confidence that when a diagnostician sees a profile pattern described in Figures 1, 2, and 3, it should be considered as a possible pathonomic sign of an oral language handicap at the organizational or central level. It indicates that certain kinds of language and reasoning problems are indicative of the child with severe oral language handicaps.

In practical diagnostic application the examiner can look for an overall ITPA profile pattern similar to the mean profile presented in Figure 1. Visual channels are significantly above the auditory channels with auditory association and grammatic closure subtests showing the lowest performance in comparison to all other subtests.

The functions of auditory association and grammatic closure cover a wide range of possible functions and probably encompass much of what we refer to as "reasoning, critical thinking, and problem solving" (Kirk & Kirk, 1971) along with the ability to learn the redundancies of the language.

What probably is neglected by some language therapists and remedial teachers is remediation for the organizational or central process since most remedial procedures deal with listening exercises and verbal response exercises. The child with difficulty in organizing and utilizing verbal concepts may need to have practice in recognizing and thinking about such concepts as opposites, cause and effect, time and space relationships, number and space, part to whole, tool and user, and product, sequential order, etc.

Conclusion

The ITPA was administered to 237 California children diagnosed by a multidisciplinary team as having severe oral language handicaps. The test data were subjected to factor analysis and cluster analysis. The factor analysis showed two clear-cut factors, an auditory-vocal and a visual-motor factor. The cluster analysis revealed several clusters all of which showed:

1. That all of the [scores on the] subtests in the visual motor channel (visual reception, visual association, manual expression, visual closure, and visual sequential memory) were superior to any of the [scores on the] subtests in the auditory vocal channel (auditory reception, auditory association, verbal expression, grammatic closure and auditory sequential memory).
2. Within the auditory-vocal channel the lowest scores were on the auditory association and grammatic closure tests. Ninety-seven percent of the oral language handicapped children had the lowest scores on these two subtests.

The clinical model of the ITPA differentiates between the auditory receptive process, the auditory vocal organizational (central) process, and the verbal expressive process. From the results of this study on a large sample of children it would appear that the major handicap of oral language disordered children is in the area of the central organization process, and that the ITPA tests of auditory association and grammatic closure might serve as a screening test to identify these children operationally.

References

Anderberg, M. R. (1973). *Cluster analysis for applications.* New York: Academic Press.
Hartigan, J. A. (1975). *Cluster algorithms.* New York: John Wiley & Sons.
Johnson, D. J., & Myklebust, H. R. (1967). *Learning disabilities.* New York: Greene & Stratton.
Kirk, S. A., & Kirk, W. D. (1971). *Psycholinguistic learning disabilities, diagnosis and remediation.* Chicago: University of Illinois Press.
Kirk, S. A., McCarthy, J. J., & Kirk, W. D. (1968). *Examiners manual, Illinois Test of Psycholinguistic Abilities.* Urbana: University of Illinois Press.
Luick, A. H. (1978). *Application of cluster analysis to identify more homogeneous groups of children with learning problems.* University of Michigan. (University Microfilms No. 78-12, 925)
Mann, L., & Sabatino, D. A. (1973). *The first review of special education* (Vol. 1). Philadelphia: JSE Press.
Nunnally, J. C. (1967). *Psychometric theory.* New York: McGraw-Hill.
Paraskevopoulos, J., & Kirk, S. A. (1969). *The development and psychometric characteristics of the Revised Illinois Test of Psycholinguistic Abilities.* Urbana: University of Illinois Press.
Sedlack, R. A., & Weener, P. (1973). Review of research on the Illinois Test of Psycholinguistic Abilities. In L. Mann & D. A. Sabatino (Eds.), *The first review of special education* (Vol. 1). Philadelphia: JSE Press.
Soroky, D. L. (1979). *Comparative effectiveness of three instructional delivery systems utilized for identifying aphasic children within the Los Angeles Unified School District.* Unpublished doctoral dissertation, University of Northern Colorado.

NOTES

[1] The auditory association process was tapped by 42 orally presented analogies such as, "I cut with a saw; I pound with a _____." "A dog has hair; a fish has _____." To minimize the requirement on the receptive process the vocabulary selected for this test was two years below the chronological age. Grammatic closure was tested by 33 orally presented items accompanied by pictures which portray the content of the verbal expression, such as, "Here is a dog" (pointing to a picture of one dog); "here are two _____." or "This dog likes to bark; here he is _____." Pictures were included to avoid contaminating the test with difficulties in the receptive process (Paraskevopoulos & Kirk, 1969, p. 40).

Part VIII

Congressional and Governmental Affairs

INTRODUCTION

EDWIN W. MARTIN
National Center for Disability Services
New York

In May 1964, when Sam Kirk addressed a group of educators in Providence, RI, special education at the federal level was at a historic high-water mark. Until Public Law 88-164 was passed in 1963, there had been a very limited role for special education in what was then the U.S. Office of Education. In earlier years, the agency was primarily dedicated to developing statistical information and offering some technical assistance through publications.

After Sputnik shook the foundations of the nation's scientific and educational communities, Congress passed the National Defense Education Act (1958) to increase the supply of math and science teachers. Equally important, from a policy point of view, was that passing such legislation opened the door for a federal role in education, an area traditionally left to the states and local communities. Through that slightly open door slipped Public Law 85-926, also in 1958, a bill providing support for training leadership personnel in the area of mental retardation.

When President John F. Kennedy sponsored new programs in the areas of mental health and mental retardation, Congress added programs in teacher education and research in the area of special education (Public Law 88-164). The President created a Division of Handicapped Children and Youth in the Office of Education (OE) to administer the new programs as well as some earlier programs. For special educators and parents of children with disabilities, it was a heady time. From relatively obscure one- and two-person contingents within the Office of Education, suddenly there was to be a major administrative unit, second only to the bureaus that reported directly to the Commissioner of Education. The President asked Dr. Samuel Kirk, then at the University of Illinois, and, arguably, the nation's leading special educator, to head the new agency. Dr. Kirk agreed to serve for a period of approximately 6 months to get the new agency started on the right track. His paper to the Rhode Island group reports on the progress of this fledgling agency and communicates a sense of excitement within its descriptive and statistical content (see Chapter 20).

It is significant to note that Dr. Kirk's remarks were included in the *Congressional Record* by the late John Fogarty, Representative from Rhode Island. One of the significant powers in the House, Fogarty chaired the appropriations subcommittee that dealt with health and education matters. Students of the Congress know that while the "authorizing" committees, such as the Committee on Education and Labor, actually draft the laws and their provisions, no actual money is available to carry out their purposes unless the appropriations committee passes specific legislation providing those funds. As chairman of the relevant appropriations subcommittee, Representative Fogarty was the most powerful ally Kirk and the programs he administered could have. As a sign of their preeminence, Fogarty and some fellow Irish-Americans who headed other appropriation subcommittees were known informally within the Congress as the College of Cardinals.

The programs authorized by Public Law 88-164 and administered by the Division of Handicapped Children and Youth played a major role in strengthening special education in the United States. As the appropriations grew, more and more universities participated in the personnel training program, and a number began to develop the capacity to conduct research on the education of children with disabilities.

A key feature of the federal aid for scholarships and traineeships was that such a grant was accompanied by a matching grant to the university itself. Those grants were generally used to add faculty and otherwise strengthen the special education programs. Large universities and teacher training colleges offered courses in a number of areas: mental retardation, physical disabilities, vision problems, and so on, and their total grants amounted to hundreds of thousands of dollars. Special education programs attracted the support of university administrators and, in some cases, the envy of non–special education colleagues. As the years passed, many faculty members of university and college programs were the recipients of federal grants, and hundreds of higher education programs participated. A cadre of research specialists also developed.

The Carey Committee

By 1966, when Dr. Kirk testified before the Carey Committee (The Ad Hoc Subcommittee on the Handicapped, U.S. House of Representatives) (Chapter 21), his "honeymoon" with the federal government was over. After President Kennedy's assassination and Dr. Kirk's return to Illinois, things proceeded well for a few months, and then the Division was caught up in larger changes.

Lyndon Johnson, who deserved the title "Education President," proposed or supported a host of education bills to authorize funds for Headstart, elementary and secondary education programs, and higher education programs designed to improve access to education for children from disadvantaged backgrounds and also for a broad spectrum of American society, both minority and nonminority. Administering the Elementary and Secondary Education Act of 1965 alone was a gigantic undertaking for the Office of Education. It had not traditionally been a granting agency, and suddenly there was a $1 billion program of grants in aid to regulate and administer.

To prepare for this task, the Office of Education was reorganized, and major divisions were created, such as Elementary and Secondary, Higher and Vocational Education, and Research. The small programs of aid to special education were divided and placed in the appropriate large bureaus. While no harm was intended for special education, without the advocacy of Dr. Kirk and a special presidential priority, the specialists administering the programs began to see their area as in decline. As Dr. Kirk reported the events since his departure, the New York Democratic chairman of the ad hoc subcommittee, the irrepressible Hugh L. Carey, commented, "It was a classic case of separation of Kirk and State." (For the monolingual reader, *kirk* is the German word for church.)

Dr. Kirk was the first witness as the hearings opened in 1966. The hearings would demonstrate that only a minority of children with disabilities—an estimated one in five—were receiving special education in the nation's schools. Schools were essentially free to serve whichever children they wished and to exclude or ignore the others. It seemed clear that federal leadership was needed.

It was Dr. Kirk's purpose to try to reestablish a strong leadership base in the Office of Education and to prevent a future decline. Working closely with Chairman Carey and the staff through Bill Geer, Executive Secretary of CEC, it had been agreed that Dr. Kirk's testimony would emphasize two points: first, a new administrative unit in the Office of Education, this time a bureau, the largest administrative subdivision; and second, a commission or advisory committee of public members who would monitor the bureau's progress and report problems to the Congress.

Dr. Kirk emphasized the fundamental premise of what has been called "categorical" aid—that is, programs designed specifically to focus on a particular problem or population. He said, "It must be remembered that any minority group, unless protected, tends to become swallowed by the majority whose interest and expertise are in other areas."

At another point, he stated, "a bureau will be a Bill of Rights for the handicapped." How prescient he was. I had the privilege of moving on from the position of staff director of the Carey Committee to serve as deputy director, and then, beginning in 1969, for more than 10 years as director of the Bureau of Education for the Handicapped, which was created by the Congress as the result of the legislation Carey sponsored. Over the years, the Bureau (BEH), under its first director, Dr. James J. Gallagher, another University of Illinois Institute of Research in Exceptional Children "superstar," and then in my term, advocated for and saw the enactment of a broad spectrum of legislation assisting children and youth with disabilities. In 1975, we achieved a major public policy objective, articulated in the courts 5 years earlier: the guarantee that every child with a disability would be entitled to a "free, appropriate, public education" (Public Law 94-142).

Dr. Kirk's experience, short though it was in actual federal service, led him to understand the power that a federal agency could demonstrate, particularly one placed close to the top. The Johnson Administration, despite its sincere commitment to children from disadvantaged backgrounds, opposed creating a bureau. The administration felt that a bureau was too large a unit for a very small collection of programs, in relative terms. While the Johnson Administration had provided billions of dollars in new education aid, virtually none was targeted for children with disabilities. This constituency was still "out of sight, out of mind."

After a substantial struggle, and with Carey utilizing the power of his friend and mentor, John Fogarty, as well as of the also-powerful Chairman of the Education and Labor Committee, Adam Clayton Powell, the fight to establish BEH was won (Martin, 1968). At the same time, a new program was launched, one that provided grants to the states for the "initiation, expansion and improvement" of programs for children with disabilities. A National Advisory Committee, to be appointed by the Commissioner of Education with White House guidance, was also established. The new Act, an amendment to the Elementary and Secondary Act known as Title VI, was also given the "short title" Education of the Handicapped Act. From its small beginnings—$2.5 million in 1967—a multi-billion-dollar program has grown.

Children with Learning Disabilities

Earlier that spring, in April 1966, Dr. Kirk presented testimony to the United States Senate as its Committee on Labor and Public Welfare considered amendments to the previous year's Elementary and Secondary Education Act (Chapter 22). It was his hope that Congress would include children with learning disabilities—specific learning disabilities—in the definition of "handicapped children" that had been developed for Public Law 88-164 in 1963. While that Act supported teacher-training grants and research for children who were judged to have mental retardation, deafness, blindness, and other disabilities, it did not include a provision for children identified as having learning disabilities. As a result, applications to the Office of Education for grants to train teachers or conduct research relative to this population could not be directly supported. There was a provision of the definition that included children with "other health impairments," and that category was used occasionally to support a program involving children with neurological impairments that might include children seen as having learning disabilities. Dr. Kirk and other advocates hoped to see learning disabilities recognized as an educational and learning problem, and, while it might, in fact, have etiological roots in neurological differences, they hoped to avoid having to submit neurological evidence (often impossible to document) before a child could be identified as having learning disabilities by a school program.

It was to be a long struggle before Congressional approval. In the first Education of the Handicapped Act (1966), the definition remained unchanged. There were a variety of reasons for Congressional hesitancy. Specialists in the area did differ on the definition of "handicapped children" and the numbers of children affected. Some cited very large numbers—for example, 10% of school children. There were some Congressional staff members who feared that the new population of children with learning disabilities would dilute resources for the other, more "classically" disabled childen. Some feared the new category might include all the children then being identified as educationally disadvantaged.

Some progress was made 4 years later in 1970, when a special Act authorized grants for teacher training, research, and model demonstration programs in the area of learning disabilities. Finally, when Public Law 94-142 was passed in 1975, the definition of "handicapped children" included a subdefinition of children with learning disabilities.

Dr. Kirk played a role here, if indirectly. In 1968, as Chairman of the Advisory Committee he had earlier recommended, he worked with other committee members and BEH staff to develop a description and definition of specific learning disabilities, which was presented in a report of that committee. That definition was used in the 1970 legislation and ultimately became a part of Public Law 94-142. Even in 1975, the Congress showed some apprehension and limited the numbers of children who could be identified as having learning disabilities to a sum equal to 2% of all school-aged children until the BEH came up with more specific diagnostic guidelines. After the guidelines were approved and the "cap" removed, the percentage of children identified as having learning disabilities has gradually increased to more than 4% today, causing some concerns about overinclusion. It is interesting to speculate, however, that rather than overinclusion of nondisabled youngsters, what is occurring is a redefinition. The number of children identified as having mental retardation, for example, has been reduced proportionally.

In one final note of minor irony, when Bureau Director Gallagher nominated Kirk to serve as the first Chairman of the Advisory Committee, White House aides protested. Dr. Kirk had been writing letters to the president protesting the Vietnam War. When we persisted, they relented and approved the appointment but did not agree to hold the appointment ceremony in the White House. While we combined feelings of pleasure with disdain over that decision, later experience with other presidents showed that the Johnson White House was, in fact, permissive. Nominees of later presidents' parties were rejected for such transgressions as having supported another candidate during the primary process.

Sam Kirk will long be known as scholar, mentor, and, by those who read this text, a major influence on public policy.

Reference

Martin, E. W. (1968). Breakthrough for the handicapped. *Exceptional Children, 34*(7), 493–503.

Edwin W. Martin began his professional career working with children and adults with speech and hearing disabilities. He studied speech pathology and psychology at the University of Alabama, where he received a master's degree, and at the University of Pittsburgh, where he received his doctorate. In 1966, he was appointed staff director of the Ad-Hoc Subcommittee on the Handicapped of the U.S. House of Representatives, working to draft the first federal Education of the Handicapped Act, which provided aid to the states to support special education programs.

From 1969 to 1979, he served as director of the Bureau of Education for the Handicapped in Washington, DC, and as Associate Commissioner, then Deputy Commissioner of Education. In 1980, President Carter selected him to be the nation's first Assistant Secretary of Education for Special Education and Rehabilitative Services in the newly created Department of Education. During his Washington years, Dr. Martin was a principal architect of the national policy to extend special education to every child with a disability. Since 1981 he has been president and chief executive officer of the National Center for Disability Services in New York, an internationally known complex of education, physical medicine and rehabilitation, and career and employment research and demonstration programs. It is the nation's most comprehensive center offering services to people with disabilities.

In addition to his government and administrative duties, Dr. Martin has served on the faculties of Teachers College, Columbia University; the Harvard Graduate School of Education; and the University of Alabama and its medical school and has authored more than 50 articles and book chapters. In 1981, CEC honored him with the J. E. Wallace Wallin award.

Chapter 20

Administration of Education Programs for Handicapped Children

SAMUEL A. KIRK

Mr. Fogarty:[1] Mr. Speaker, I take pleasure in introducing for the *Record* at this point a most significant statement involving the administration of education programs for handicapped children. Last year the Congress passed Public Law 88-164, which provides federal assistance for health facilities for mentally retarded children; Title III of the Act provides for training of teachers of mentally retarded and other handicapped children. At a meeting of New England educators held on May 22 at Rhode Island College in Providence, Dr. Samuel Kirk made a progress report on the administration of the Act by the Office of Education. In view of the great significance of the Act for education and the extent to which it will help the nation's schools fill a critical gap in teachers for handicapped children, I wish to call the report to the attention of all Members of Congress. I call particular attention to the fact that the program has been extremely popular and successful with the participating institutions. In fact, requests for aid that have been submitted amount to three times the funds now authorized in the Act. I think this report signifies the need to give early attention to the Act and further extensions and improvements in it. I also wish to compliment the Commissioner of Education on his success in obtaining the temporary services of Dr. Kirk from the University of Illinois to launch this new program.

Dr. Kirk:[2] I consider it a great privilege to be a participant in what I believe to be a historic turning point in special education in the United States.

This meeting has been arranged to acquaint you with the new legislation, Title III of Public Law 88-164, which was signed by the late President Kennedy on October 31, 1963, and, also, to inform you of the program that is already underway as a result of this legislation.

From Proceedings and debates of the 88th Congress, 2nd session, *Congressional Record*, 1964, pp. 1–4.

Public Law 88-164 is cited as the Mental Retardation Facilities Construction Act of 1963. This bill contains three titles. Title I deals with an authorization for the construction of research and clinical facilities and for the construction of service facilities for the mentally retarded. Title II deals with the authorization of appropriations for the construction of community mental health facilities. Title I is being administered by the National Institutes of Health. Title II is being administered by the Bureau of State Services. Title III is entitled "Training of Teachers of the Mentally Retarded and Other Handicapped Children." It also includes support for research and demonstration. The facilitation of this title is being administered by the U.S. Office of Education. This title is an amendment to Public Law 85-926.

Major Obstacles to Progress

All of us know that during the past 15 years, efforts to educate handicapped children have often been frustrated. The American people want handicapped children educated to their highest level. They have persuaded state legislators to subsidize classes in public schools and have insisted on expanded programs. But there have been four major obstacles that have retarded development in special education and have served as a basis for many of our problems.

1. First, classroom space and diagnostic facilities have been lacking. Expanded enrollments in schools have taxed both school buildings and school budgets. Superintendents have had a difficult time finding funds and classroom space needed for special education. Titles I and II of Public Law 88-164, which provides for the construction of facilities, will indirectly help this situation slightly, even though it is not under educational auspices.

2. When space has been made available, superintendents have been unable to obtain a sufficient number of qualified teachers to conduct the classes. It has been estimated that we need 200,000 teachers to man the classes for 5 million handicapped children. We now have 50,000 to 60,000 such teachers.

3. Some colleges and universities have for some time attempted to prepare teachers, supervisors, college instructors, and research personnel. But for every one professional person prepared in the past, four were needed. The graduates from teacher training institutions have really been only a minute part of the number needed. Colleges have had increased enrollments, and funds for college staffs have been limited. Many colleges have resisted the organization of special education departments because, understandably, they have not even had sufficient funds for traditional

programs of science, engineering, law, medicine, and agriculture, [and so on]. The new programs that were established, like special education, have had a struggle to keep alive in nearly every college that initiated the program.

4. Most of the teachers in the field today have obtained training through short summer courses, extension courses, and workshops. Many teachers recruited for these classes were untrained or partially trained. So when we say we have 50,000 to 60,000 teachers of handicapped children, we will have to also say that only a portion of them have had specialized training.

Recent Steps to Remove These Obstacles

In 1958, the U.S. Congress passed Public Law 85-926, which authorized an appropriation of $1 million a year for the training of teachers and leadership personnel in mental retardation. Since that date and through 1963, 667 fellowships have been granted to 482 individuals (some receiving fellowships two or three times). Of these, the majority have become college and university instructors or state and local supervisors and directors, while some remained teachers of the mentally retarded. This legislation has been of inestimable value in the preparation of leadership personnel, and, fortunately, it will allow some college programs for the preparation of teachers of the mentally retarded to proceed at a higher level.

In September 1961, Congress passed Public Law 87-276, dealing with the preparation of teachers of the deaf. It authorized a 2-year program of grants-in-aid in institutions of higher learning for the preparation of teachers of the deaf at the senior and first-year graduate level. The law authorized the appropriation of $1.5 million a year for this purpose. During the 2-year period, 1962–63, 942 scholarships were awarded to 48 colleges and universities in 30 states and the District of Columbia. The number of students completing their preparation as teachers of the deaf was 470, more than double the number of teachers who have ever been prepared in a single year. Federal scholarship students accounted for 370 of these. This Act has been extended for 1 year. The $1,500,000 appropriated by Congress will serve to support approximately 387 additional scholarships. After this year, scholarships for teachers of the deaf will be included in Public Law 88-164.

Title III of Public Law 88-164

As indicated earlier, Title III of the Act gives the Commissioner of Education the responsibility for the administration of a program of grants-in-aid for the training of professional personnel and for research and demonstration related to the education of handicapped children. If we refer to the four obstacles to progress I mentioned earlier, you will note that this bill is a partial solution to three of these obstacles. Permit me to discuss these in some detail.

Section 301 of Title III authorizes the Commissioner to make grants to public or other nonprofit professional personnel for the education of handicapped children. This includes:

- Teachers in training at the senior level in an undergraduate program.
- Supervisors of teachers and administrators of programs, studying at the graduate level.
- College personnel to train teachers of handicapped children.
- Research personnel for research related to the education of handicapped children.

Section 301 also authorizes the Commissioner of Education to make grants to state educational agencies for the preparation of the following personnel (either directly or through contract with institutions of higher learning):

1. Teachers in all areas of the education of handicapped children, at the senior undergraduate year or at the graduate level.
2. Supervisors of such teachers.

"Handicapped children" refers to all handicapped children—the mentally retarded, the deaf, hard-of-hearing, speech impaired, visually handicapped, seriously emotionally disturbed, crippled or other "health impaired children, who by reason thereof require special education."

Forty-seven million dollars [has] been authorized for a 3-year period for this purpose. Specifically, Title III authorizes $11,500,000 for fiscal year 1964, $14,500,000 for fiscal year 1965, and $19,500,000 for fiscal year 1966. These funds will be used for stipends for students in all areas of the [education of the] handicapped and for assisting colleges, universities, and state educational agencies with the cost of instruction.

Title III also authorizes the appropriation of $6 million for a 3-year period for research and demonstration in areas related to the education of handicapped children. Under this legislation, the Commissioner is authorized to make grants to (1) institutions of higher learning; (2) state educational agencies; (3) local education agencies; and (4) other nonprofit private or public educational or research agencies and organizations for research related to all handicapped children.

Organization Within the U.S. Office of Education

To implement this new law and to continue the traditional functions of the Office of Education, a new organization has been accomplished. First, the Commissioner of Education has created a Division of Handicapped Children and Youth in the U.S. Office of Education. This gives the administration of work with handicapped children the same status as the Division of Library Services, the Division of Educational Research, the Division of Educational Statistics, and the Division of Educational Organization and Administration in the Bureau of Educational Research and Development. Last year, the work in exceptional children was under a branch within the Division of Elementary and Secondary Education, and, previous to that, it was a section under a branch. Judging from the letters received in the Office [of Education], I am sure we are all grateful to the Commissioner for giving special education the status it now holds, and we think it deserves, in the U.S. Office of Education.

Second, under the division there are four branches:

1. A branch for physical and sensory handicaps.
2. A branch for the mentally retarded and the emotionally disturbed.
3. A branch for research and demonstration.
4. A branch for captioned films for the deaf.

Third, within each branch are the specialists in that area. For example, the branch for sensory and physical handicaps contains specialists in speech and hearing [and] deaf, crippled and health-impaired, and visually handicapped [children]. The branch on the mentally retarded has specialists in the mentally retarded and in the emotionally disturbed. A third branch is charged with administering the program of research and demonstration. The branch on captioned films for the deaf has only recently been transferred to the Division of Handicapped Children and Youth.

Committees

For awarding grants to institutions of higher learning or to state and local educational agencies, the Commissioner has organized a series of committees of professional experts who will evaluate applications for training or for research and demonstration. Committees have been created with five or more members in each area as follows:

1. For the area of teacher training, six advisory committees have been selected, one for each field: visually handicapped, crippled and [children with] special health problems, emotionally disturbed, speech and hear-

ing, deaf, and mentally retarded. These committees (composed of teacher-training specialists from the field) are assigned the task of evaluating applications from institutions of higher learning and from state educational agencies for the preparation of professional personnel in all areas of the handicapped. The Commissioner relies on these committees for the approval or disapproval of applications.

2. For research and demonstration, another six committees have been appointed, one for each field, utilizing research specialists from the field. Each committee of research specialists evaluates research and demonstration applications in its field and recommends approval or disapproval. In addition to these six panels, there is an overall research committee to help with the establishment of research policies and to give final review of the applications for research and demonstration.

3. There is also appointed an advisory committee of nine distinguished scholars, most of whom are not in special education, who will advise the Commissioner on overall policies in the administration of the program.

Rules and Regulations

During November, December, and January, the staff of the Division of Handicapped Children and Youth began the formulation of rules, regulations, and procedures for the administration of the grants-in-aid program. Consultants from state and local departments of education and from universities were invited to participate and to recommend procedures. In addition, five regional conferences were held in Atlanta, Dallas, New York, Chicago, and San Francisco. Key personnel from state and local departments and institutions of higher learning were invited to attend. From these conferences, the following plan was evolved:

- Grants-in-aid for the preparation of professional personnel would be allotted to state educational agencies and to public and private institutions of higher learning for full-time traineeships (senior undergraduates) and full-time graduate fellowships, full-time summer session traineeships, and full-time, short-term institutes [with programs] of 3 or more days.
- State educational agencies were allotted a minimum of $25,000 and a maximum of $100,000, based on a population formula. Both state educational agencies and institutions of higher learning could request grants-in-aid for traineeships, fellowships, or short-term institutes.

The stipends and supporting grants established were as follows:

- Traineeships: Each traineeship recipient (senior undergraduate) shall receive a stipend of $1,600 a year.

- Fellowships: Each fellowship recipient shall receive the following stipend in addition to a dependents' allowance of $400 for each dependent (exclusive of himself)—$2,000 for the first graduate year of study; $2,400 for the second graduate year of study; $2,800 for the third graduate year of study; and $2,800 for the fourth graduate year of study.
- Short-term traineeships: Each short-term traineeship recipient shall receive a stipend of $15 a day with a maximum of $75 a week.
- Supporting grants: To partially support the institution's cost of training and study for a trainee, fellow, and short-term trainee, the participating institution or state educational agency shall receive for each traineeship, $2,000; for each fellowship, $2,500; for each short-term traineeship, full-time summer session, $75 a week; [and] special study institutes [will receive] program support. (For special institutes, the supporting grant shall be based on the cost of instruction.)

Implementation of Program

On February 10, 1964, President Johnson signed the supplementary (1964) appropriation of $12,500,000 for training of professional personnel and $1 million for research and demonstration, in addition to the previous appropriation of $1,500,000 for Public Law 87-276. By this time, the rules and regulations had been printed, and notification of the legislation had been to chief state school officers and to institutions of higher learning.

Because of the pressure of time, institutions of higher learning were requested to complete the applications by March 13, and the chief state school officers were requested to file applications by March 27. For research and demonstration, the deadline was set at March 23.

In spite of the short time involved in preparing the regulations, and only 4 or 5 weeks allotted to the field to prepare the applications, the response from the field was overwhelming. By the respective deadline dates, applications from the field had poured into the Office of Education in greater numbers than had been estimated by anyone.

From institutions of higher learning, 652 applications were received for traineeships, fellowships, summer-session traineeships, short-term study institutes, and stimulation grants. All 50 states submitted applications for grants-in-aid for training purposes. A total of 155 applications were received for research and demonstration projects.

Requests for Training Grants

Table 1 summarizes the requests received from the field for fiscal year 1964 under the Program for Handicapped Children and Youth (Public Law 88-164, Title III, sec. 301; and Public Law 87-276) for training professional personnel.

TABLE 1
Funds Requested in Applications for Teacher Training for Fiscal Year 1964 Under Program for Handicapped Children, Public Law 88-164, Title III, and Public Law 87-276

Funds requested for training programs, fiscal year 1964 .... $31,839,315
Funds appropriated by Congress, fiscal year 1964 13,000,000

Area of training	Number of institutions requesting grants	Number of applications	Funds requested
Mentally retarded	163	255	$12,830,000
Speech and hearing	138	178	6,650,715
Visually handicapped	18	30	940,000
Emotionally disturbed	55	70	3,010,000
Crippled and other health problems	40	64	2,559,000
Deaf	55	55	2,649,600
State grant requests	---	50	3,200,000
Total requests	[1]154	702	$31,839,315

[1] Total number of different participating colleges and universities is 154—139 in Public Law 88-164 and 15 in Public Law 87-276.

This table indicates that requests from institutions of higher learning and from state educational agencies far exceeded the Congressional appropriation. For the mentally retarded, for example, the largest field, the requests from institutions of higher learning were three times the funds available for that area. For speech and hearing, the requests were five times the funds allotted for that area. For the visually handicapped, the smallest area, the requests were twice the funds allotted. For the deaf, [for whom] $1.5 million had been appropriated, the requests exceeded the allotted funds by over $1 million. In no area were the allocated funds close to the requests for grants.

Table 2 presents the requests for research and demonstration for each area of the handicapped provided in the appropriation. This table shows that while $1 million was appropriated by Congress for fiscal year 1964, nearly $6 million in grants were requested in 155 applications. Since research and demonstration projects are not generally completed in 1 year, the requests for all years, including the first, amounted to nearly $15 million.

Requests for research and demonstration, fiscal year 1964, totaled $5,886,290. [The] appropriation for research and demonstration, fiscal year 1964, [was] $1 million.

TABLE 2
Requests for Research and Demonstration, Public Law 88-164, Title III, Sec. 302

Area of training	Number	Requested funds	
		Fiscal year 1964	3-year total
Mentally retarded	73	$2,633,412	$ 6,294,812
Emotionally disturbed	16	832,661	2,399,551
Speech and hearing	12	376,132	717,342
Deaf	18	685,795	1,248,879
Visually handicapped	12	356,035	673,105
Crippled and other health impaired	12	461,462	2,001,971
Others	12	540,793	1,370,512
Total requests	155	$5,886,290	$14,706,172

As indicated earlier, we had only a short period of time to develop procedures and to notify agencies that $1 million was available for research and demonstration. Actually people in the field had only about 5 weeks' time to prepare research and demonstration projects. Many phoned the office stating that they did not have sufficient time to prepare adequately a research proposal, and that they would wait until the next year. Up to a few days before the deadline date we did not know whether our people were ready for research and demonstration. To everyone's surprise, the people in the field were more than ready. Well-thought-out and well-written reports poured in. The data in Table 2 are concrete evidence of the readiness and eagerness of people to advance the education of handicapped children through research and demonstration.

Another surprise was the number of requests for research on the education of handicapped children that were submitted to cooperative research. As you know, the Cooperative Research Branch in the Office of Education has received applications and has made grants for research on handicapped children for a number of years. It would be expected that with the applications received under the new legislation (Public Law 88-164), research proposals [for] cooperative research would show a decrease. This was not the case. The Cooperative Research Branch actually received more proposals this year than ever before.

This volume of applications for training and research is difficult to interpret. My speculation is that the publicity given to our national effort by the President and Congress has given those in special education a new lease on life. Actually, I consider the present Congressional appropriation as "seed money" and that the byproducts of this legislation in services to handicapped children will far outweigh the direct benefits.

Grants-in-Aid Allocated

During the month of April and the first week in May, 13 committees met for from 1 to 4 days each to process applications. Table 3 presents the approved grants-in-aid to institutions of higher learning and points out that 41 stimulation grants were awarded to institutions of higher learning to aid them in "tooling up" for the preparation of professional personnel in one or more areas [in the education] of the handicapped. [The table also shows that] 587 traineeships were awarded to prepare teachers at the senior undergraduate level; 1,007 fellowships were awarded for master's degrees and 151 for post-master's-degree study; 672 summer-session traineeships were awarded for full-time summer-school study; and 45 short-term traineeships were awarded for special-study institutes.

Grants to State Educational Agencies

As indicated earlier, state educational agencies were allotted from $25,000 to $100,000 based on a population formula and were requested to apply for grants-in-aid for the training of professional personnel. Table 4 presents the grants made to States for full-time traineeships and fellowships, for full-time summer sessions and for short-term study institutes. Table 4 notes that all 50 states submitted applications and received grants. The emphasis by the states in their grant programs may be summarized as follows: 261 graduate fellowships; 84 undergraduate (senior) traineeships; 1,187 summer-session traineeships; and 888 participants in short-term study institutes.

As compared to the institutions of higher learning, where funds were used primarily for full-time traineeships and fellowships, the state educational agencies emphasized summer-session traineeships and short-term study institutes. For their allotment of funds, the state officials were desirous of providing summer-session training for teachers who were already employed but who were not trained or only partially trained. Actually, the institutions of higher learning utilized approximately 12% of their funds for full-term summer sessions and institutes, whereas the state educational agencies allotted approximately 43% of their funds to summer-session study and to short-term study institutes.

When we combine the grants of the state educational agencies and the colleges and universities, we find that 2,090 students will receive a full year of training through either traineeships or fellowships in 1964–65, 1,859 teachers will receive full-term summer-session instruction, 933 teachers will receive inservice instruction in new developments in their respective fields, and 41 in-

TABLE 3
Approved Grants to Institutions of Higher Learning Under
Public Law 88-164, Title III, Sec. 301, and Public Law 87-276, Fiscal Year 1964

Area of training	Number of participating—		Number of stimulation grants	Number of academic year traineeships and fellowships			Number of other traineeships	
	Institutions	States		Traineeships	Fellowships		Summer session	Short-term institutes
					Master's degree	Post-master's		
Mentally retarded	108	[1]41 +	15	347	304	84	479	0
Visually handicapped	14	11	2	29	44	4	56	20
Crippled and special health	33	20	5	54	82	12	97	25
Deaf (Public Law 87-276)	47	[2]29 +	0	135	297	0	0	0
Emotionally disturbed	28	[2]17 +	13	24	82	27	0	0
Speech and hearing	74	[2]36 +	6	0	198	24	0	0
Total	[3]154	[4]46 +	41	587	1,007	151	672	45

[1] District of Columbia and Puerto Rico.
[2] District of Columbia.
[3] Total number of different participating colleges and universities is 154; 139 in Public Law 88-164 and 15 additional in Public Law 87-276.
[4] District of Columbia and Puerto Rico. Total number of different states and other areas participating in Public Law 88-164 and 87-276 is 46 plus the District of Columbia and Puerto Rico.

TABLE 4
Approved Grants to State Educational Agencies Under
Public Law 88-164, Title III, Sec. 301, and Public Law 87-276, Fiscal Year 1964

Area of training	Number of states participating	Number of academic traineeships and fellowships		Number of other traineeships	
		Traineeships	Fellowships	Summer session	Short-term institutes
Mentally retarded	50	49	153	771	211
Speech and hearing	45	17	46	156	145
Visually handicapped	31	5	11	60	134
Emotionally disturbed	33	5	30	118	138
Crippled and special health	30	8	17	79	20
Other (supervisors, etc.)	8	0	4	3	240
Total	150	84	261	1,187	888

1 Total number of different states participating in Public Laws 88-164 and 87-276 is 50.

stitutions will initiate a training program in one or more areas under a stimulation grant.

We recognize that this number of traineeships and fellowships will not solve the extreme personnel-shortage problem, but all will agree that it will help. It is anticipated that the existing programs of teacher training will be strengthened in quality and that the numbers of students not under traineeships and fellowships will increase. The new programs in needed geographic areas will develop under the stimulation grants, and these will begin to produce needed personnel within a year or two. Under this program, we should begin to make a substantial dent in the personnel requirements of the nation in the education of handicapped children.

Research and Demonstration

It was pointed out earlier that $1 million was available in 1964 for research and demonstration and that the requests amounted to nearly $6 million. Advisory panels in each area reviewed the proposals and recommended approval or disapproval. The overall Research and Demonstration Advisory Committee reviewed the recommendations of the advisory panels and attempted to reduce the approved proposals to the amount of the appropriation. Their final recommendations for funds amounted to more than the million dollars appropriated. Currently, we have the unpleasant task of cutting budgets to conform to the Congressional appropriation.

Out of 155 proposals submitted, the committees approved 34 projects, or approximately 22%. The distribution of approved projects for research and demonstration among the different areas [is shown in Table 5].

TABLE 5
Approved Projects for Research and Demonstration

Projects	Number Approved
Mentally retarded	12
Emotionally disturbed	4
Crippled and other health-impaired	1
Visually handicapped	5
Speech-impaired and hard-of-hearing	3
Deaf	6
Multiple handicaps	3
Total	34

Summary Statement

This is the story of Title III, Public Law 88-164, and Public Law 87-276 as of May 15, 1964. In behalf of the Office of Education, the profession, and especially the children and their parents who will benefit from this legislation, I would be remiss not to mention the statesmen who have sponsored this legislation. Our gratitude must be extended to the late President Kennedy for emphasizing this legislation, to President Johnson who continues the emphasis, and to Congressman Fogarty of your state who has worked so hard and so long to obtain such legislation. I must also mention Senator Lister Hill, Congressman Oren Harris and many others who saw this legislation through the 88th Congress. Their reward will be in the benefits to handicapped children, their parents, and to our society.

NOTES

[1] Speech of Hon. John E. Fogarty of Rhode Island, in the House of Representatives, Tuesday, June 16, 1964.

[2] (Address delivered by Samuel A. Kirk entitled "Organization and Implementation of Program for Handicapped Children and Youth: Public Law 88-164, Title III, and Public Law 87-276" at the regional meeting of educators, Rhode Island College, Providence, RI, May 22, 1964.

Chapter 21

Education and Training of the Handicapped

SAMUEL A. KIRK

Mr. Carey: The Ad Hoc Subcommittee on Training and Education of the Handicapped will be in session for the further consideration of the presentations by public witnesses. It is a real pleasure and honor for me today to welcome before the subcommittee Dr. Samuel Kirk, director of the Institute for Research on Exceptional Children at the University of Illinois.

Doctor, it is sort of a reunion to have you here this morning. I well remember after the passage of the Mental Retardation Facilities Act when you went around the country in what we called "the road show" to acquaint the educators, general public, and interested persons with the provisions of this Act in the hope that we could bring about swift and effective implementation.

I know that the record will attest that one of the reasons why the Act did go into operation so effectively and successfully was the contribution you rendered during your service in the government, in the Department of Health, Education, and Welfare, and not in this field alone; but I cite this episode, because you not only were able to explain the law—which is sometimes difficult when Congress gets through—but you were able to relate it to the needs and problems of children in a most practical way. I feel that you can make a real contribution to the committee at this time by taking a hard look at what we have been able to do in the field of the handicapped, and I therefore await your statement with pleasure.

Dr. Kirk: My name is Samuel A. Kirk. I serve as professor of special education and psychology, and as director of the Institute for Research on Excep-

---

Excerpted from a statement on Wednesday, June 15, 1966, before the U.S. House of Representatives, Ad Hoc Subcommittee on the Handicapped of the Committee on Education and Labor, Washington, DC. The committee met at 9:55 a.m. pursuant to recess, in room 2257 of the Rayburn House Office Building, Hon. Hugh L. Carey (chairman of the subcommittee) presiding. Present: Representatives Carey, Scheuer, Bell, and Andrews. Also present: Dr. Edwin Martin, staff director.

tional Children at the University of Illinois. For many years, I have had the privilege of serving as a consultant to various constituent departments of [the Department of] Health, Education, and Welfare, and, particularly, to the U.S. Office of Education. In 1964, I served temporarily as Director of the newly created Division of Handicapped Children and Youth in the Office of Education.

I have been very pleased to see the recent interest and support of the federal Congress on behalf of handicapped children. Numerous acts have been passed which, for the first time in this country, paved the way for training, service, and research on behalf of handicapped children.

The enactment of federal legislation and appropriations for handicapped children has been a shot in the arm, but is not sufficient to accelerate and develop the work in this field as it should be developed. It is necessary that there be established within the office of the Secretary of Health, Education, and Welfare and its departments appropriate administrative organization [that] will vigorously stimulate accomplishments in line with the intent of Congress and the will of the people. I should like to make two recommendations for your consideration; namely, (1) that there be created a Bureau for Handicapped Children and Youth within the U.S. Office of Education, and (2) that there be created a Commission for Handicapped Children and Youth within the office of the Secretary of Health, Education, and Welfare.

Recommendation 1: Bureau for Handicapped Children and Youth, in the U.S. Office of Education

It is my opinion that Congressional acts administered by the Office of Education can be accomplished most effectively if all responsibilities of the Office of Education relating to handicapped children are organized within a bureau structure, responsible to the Commissioner of Education. Such an administrative organization is needed to advance the field throughout the country through research, training grants, service, leadership, and coordination, and dissemination of information.

This recommendation is made in the light of the history of work for handicapped children in the Office of Education and the subsequent developments.

Permit me to elucidate.

In the early [1930s], a section for exceptional children was created in the U.S. Office of Education. This section struggled with minimum personnel and minimum funds from 1931 to 1963. Responsibilities were increased when Public Law 85-926 was passed in 1958 and when it was amended under Title III of Public Law 88-164 in 1963.

On October 31, 1963, President Kennedy signed Public Law 88-164 and in his remarks announced:

> I am glad to announce at this time that we are establishing a Division in the U.S. Office of Education to administer the teaching and research program under the act. This will be called the Division of Handicapped Children and Youth.

This Division of Handicapped Children and Youth was organized in the U.S. Office of Education with four branches, and within a short period of time was so successful in administering Title III of Public Law 88-164 as well as giving leadership to the field throughout the nation that it was awarded a Presidential citation by President Johnson, on February 8, 1965:

> ... in special recognition of an outstanding contribution to greater economy and improvement in Government operations during the 10th anniversary of the Federal incentive awards program.

The present organization of the U.S. Office of Education, in my opinion, does not now permit the development of work for handicapped children at the federal level that was intended for the Division of Handicapped Children; namely, the unification and coordination of research and development, service, training, leadership, and coordination, and dissemination of information. To accomplish these, it is essential that all elements dealing with handicapped children be grouped under a bureau structure responsible to the Commissioner of Education.

I have proposed that a Bureau for Handicapped Children and Youth be organized within the U.S. Office of Education, because I see no way that the task can be accomplished under the existing structure. Programs for handicapped children are minority operations. To accomplish the task needed in the United States, this work must at present be institutionalized with a name, a workable organization, and with definite operational goals. It cannot be dispersed among different bureaus and be placed at the bottom of the totem pole and then be expected to accomplish the needed task of development of adequate programs of education for handicapped children within the educational establishment.

It must be remembered that any minority group, unless protected, tends to become swallowed by the majority whose interest and expertise are in other areas. The Bill of Rights was established to protect the minority from the tyranny of the majority. The establishment of a Bureau of Handicapped Children and Youth in the Office of Education will give handicapped children their bill of rights.

The generalization here is obvious. At this stage of our development, when the work for the handicapped is dispersed under general categories, the handicapped, a minority group, is neglected in each category. When a program and a purpose are institutionalized under a name, the program moves forward; that is the reason I am recommending the creation of a Bureau of Handicapped Children and Youth in the U.S. Office of Education. I repeat: a bureau will be a Bill of Rights for the handicapped.

Recommendation 2: A Commission for Handicapped Children and Youth in the Office of the Secretary of Health, Education, and Welfare

I am recommending that a Commission for Handicapped Children and Youth be organized in the Office of the Secretary of Health, Education, and Welfare. This commission should consist of a permanent staff in the office and 12 nonsalaried members from the profession, from universities and state departments of education, appointed for a 3-year period on a rotating basis for a period of 6 years. The duties of this commission would be to periodically survey the various programs under HEW and to recommend to the departments of HEW programs and procedures that will advance the field of the handicapped nationally. Such a commission will be, in a sense, a liaison body between the universities and state departments, and the federal agencies. It would also be a coordinating agency among the various departments and bureaus of Health, Education, and Welfare now administering research, training, and service programs for handicapped children and youth.

Such a commission will serve as an advisory body for developmental programs to all HEW departments. Its responsibility, if accomplished effectively, would prevent a split between people in the field and those in the federal agencies; it would balance the responsibilities of each. There is a danger of people in the field going in one direction and the federal agencies in another. They should be partners in a common endeavor. To continue this partnership from year to year requires a continuing commission whose major responsibility is coordination of departments in Health, Education, and Welfare, and liaison with operating units in the field.

Chapter 22

Elementary and Secondary Education Act of 1966

SAMUEL A. KIRK

Senator Prouty: The subcommittee will come to order. The first witness will be Dr. Samuel A. Kirk and two colleagues.

We are indeed happy to hear from this panel, which will outline for the subcommittee learning problems of children. These represent a rapidly developing area in the field of special education.

Dr. Kirk, I understand that you were recently honored at Toronto by your colleagues through the award of the 1966 Wallin Award, and for the record I should like to read the citation [that] accompanied it. It will serve to demonstrate your undoubted competence as an authority in this very important area.

> In recognition of outstanding professional leadership, The Council for Exceptional Children presents the 1966 Wallin Award to Samuel A. Kirk, Professor of Education and Psychology and Director of the Institute for Research on Exceptional Children, University of Illinois. He has made an immeasurable contribution to special education through his scholarly publications, the preparation of teachers and research personnel, and his extensive research efforts, particularly in the areas of mental retardation and learning disabilities. His role in the development of the Division of Handicapped Children and Youth, United States Office of Education, merits particular commendation.
>
> An internationally recognized authority in his field, Dr. Kirk has contributed of his time and talents to lay and professional organizations. He is past president of the Council, and his continuous service is reflected in CEC's publication, research, convention, and legislative activities.
>
> Conferred upon him, by his professional associates in appreciation of his scholarship, leadership, service, and dedication is CEC's highest honor.
>
> Under date of April 21, 1966.

From *Report [of] the Committee on Labor and Public Welfare, United States Senate, Eighty-Ninth Congress, Second Session.* Washington, DC: U.S. Government Printing Office, 1966. Present: Senators Kennedy of New York, Prouty (presiding pro tempore), Javits, Williams of New Jersey, and Kennedy of Massachusetts, members of the full committee.

Dr. Kirk, I am delighted to read this into the record and congratulate you most sincerely on this singular honor.

Now, you may proceed in any manner, and I wish you would introduce your colleagues first.

Dr. Kirk: Thank you, Senator Prouty. I certainly appreciate the opportunity to appear before this subcommittee and to discuss with you problems of children with learning disorders.

I have brought with me two experts that I would like to call on a little later to present their points of view: Dr. Richmond S. Paine, who is a neurologist at the Childrens Hospital of the District of Columbia and professor of pediatrics and neurology at George Washington University School of Medicine. Dr. Paine is also chairman of a national task force organized by the Public Health Service on neurological diseases of blindness, the Office of Education, and the National Society for Crippled Children and Adults.

I also have with me Dr. Jeanne McCarthy, who is director of special services in the Schaumburg School System in Illinois, who represents an ongoing program in one representative school system.

Children with Learning Difficulties

Children with learning disabilities have only recently begun to receive the attention that they deserve from parents' groups and public schools. The reason for the neglect of this group is the complexity of the problem and the diverse disabilities [that] come within this category. Societies, in general, usually begin their provisions for handicapped children by supporting the handicaps that are obvious to them. Blindness, for example, is readily recognized by both lay and professional personnel. For that reason, schools for the blind were organized in Boston and New York as far back as 1832. Since that date, we have organized state schools for the deaf and the blind and for the crippled and the mentally retarded, and other handicapped children.

The groups of children who are not so readily diagnosed and identified by either lay or professional personnel naturally tend to be neglected and enter the arena requesting help at a later date. One of these groups we have entitled "learning disabilities."

Children with learning disabilities, as defined educationally, are those who have a retardation, a disorder, or a developmental defect in one or more of the processes of speech, language, reading, spelling, writing, arithmetic, or other school subjects, who do not appear to profit or develop under ordinary instructional procedures, and who require special remedial instruction—special education for the amelioration of their disability. The Association for Learning Disabilities, a national organization concerned with this problem, defines this group as children or youth with normal or potentially normal intelligence who have learning disabilities of a perceptual, conceptual, or coordinative nature or related problems.

These children are in our schools and are in general failing, particularly in some aspect of behavior or communication. They do not fit into the traditional categories of the blind, the crippled, the deaf, the gifted, the mentally retarded, or special health problems. Actually, this group of children cuts across various disability groupings. Thus, learning disabilities are found among children who are otherwise average in intelligence as well as among children who are below average or superior in intelligence. It is not uncommon to find a child with an IQ of 130 who has attended school for several years and who has, for example, not begun to learn to read. Many such children fail in school, become discouraged, and join the ranks of the school dropouts. We also find children who are diagnosed as mentally retarded, but who are better classified as [having] learning disabilities since they have normal abilities in some areas and markedly limited abilities in other areas, giving the appearance of mental retardation. Remediation programs for some of these children, when successful, remove them from the classification of mental retardation.

The child with learning disabilities has now become recognized as a special problem in education. He certainly does not fit into any one of the traditional categories of handicapped children. When a teacher finds a child in class who is not performing normally, she may refer him for an eye examination. The specialist finds that the child can see, so he does not fit into the class for the visually handicapped. When his hearing is checked, it is found that he hears, so he does not fit into the class for the acoustically handicapped. His intelligence is normal or near normal, so he cannot be placed in a class for the mentally retarded. Furthermore, he is not crippled and does not have a health problem that requires attention. He needs help—he needs special education—but not in the class for other handicapping conditions.

Many Facets to Learning Disabilities

If these children all presented the same picture, their identification and remediation would be made easier. But there are many facets to learning and the same cause may affect differing facets in different children. Consider the following three children, each of whom has a learning disability.

    a. One child was examined by three different ophthalmologists who each declared the boy's vision to be normal. Yet he could not recognize different objects. He could not even recognize his classmates until they spoke to him. He is a child who requires intensive remediation in visual perception and visual recognition. Without training in this area, he could not succeed in school.

b. Another child could hear tones normally. Repeated ear examinations resulted in the diagnosis of normal hearing acuity, yet he could not understand the spoken word. He acted as if he were deaf, but he was not deaf. He also needs intensive instruction in auditory understanding.

c. There are many children who are normal in intelligence but [who] are unable to learn to read by the ordinary methods. Yet under special remedial instruction these children are capable of learning to read and to spell. This severe reading disability, sometimes called dyslexia, is the most common form of learning disability.

During the last decade such children [have] attracted the attention of research workers in education, psychology, and medicine. Specialized examinations have been developed, and remedial procedures have been and are being organized. Personnel are being trained in small numbers, and parents' groups have organized a national association entitled "The Association for Children With Learning Disabilities."

I notice that Mrs. Louise Mesirow, who is the president of the National Association for Children With Learning Disabilities, is here today, and she is available to answer questions relating to the national organization that has evolved only in the last 2 or 3 years.

Because many children with learning disabilities have been diagnosed as brain-damaged, and because many brain-damaged children have learning disabilities, these terms are sometimes thought of as synonymous. It should be pointed out, however, that a dysfunction of the brain may have widely different effects in different people. Some are crippled physically [such as in] cerebral palsy, but may have brilliant minds. Some are extremely retarded mentally. Some have difficulties of attention and concentration or difficulty inhibiting physical activity. Still others may perform normally in most situations but have special areas of difficulty, such as in understanding numbers and quantitative concepts or in getting meaning from the printed page. Some can understand concepts but have difficulty in communication. Some are blocked, or have deficiencies in visual or auditory perception.

Similarly, there are many children for whom no definitive diagnosis of brain damage is possible but who have abnormal learning problems. Sometimes the child seems normal in every other respect—physically, intellectually, emotionally—but has great difficulty learning by routine methods. Children with severe reading disabilities—dyslexic children—are a case in point. Every school has them, and many schools provide special help for them. They cannot learn in the classroom by the usual group methods. Careful diagnosis can usually pinpoint behavioral characteristics [that] explain the difficulty and point the way to remediation.

Special Category—Learning Disabilities

I would like at this point to show several slides just to point out that these children differ from the normal child, and also differ from mentally retarded children because of the discrepancies in growth.

We now have methods of examining children to delineate the different abilities and disabilities [that] these children show in their psychological makeup.

[The] child [profiled in Figure 1] is 8 years old. You notice that on some of the points in the profile this child is normal in some respects, but [she] is very defective in visual perception and what we call here "motor encoding" and in some of the other visual areas. This child, according to the profile, is at the 4-year level in some areas and at the 8-year level in other areas. . . .

[Figure 2 shows] a profile of a test and a retest on the same child after 7 months of remediation. This is just to indicate that these disabilities are remediable even though this child was diagnosed by a very eminent neurologist as having . . . diffused brain damage. In spite of this diagnosis, we were able to improve some of the disabilities through remediation, as shown on the test and retest in the profile when she was 8 and 9 years old.

[Figure 3] is a profile of a child who, at the age of 4, was not uttering a sound. She was diagnosed at several clinics as very mentally retarded and recommended to a state institution but never got there because of the waiting list.

On intelligence tests, she was below 2 years of age at the age of 4. We put her under intensive training as an experiment to determine whether this severely mentally retarded child—who had some normal abilities at the 4-year level with some very severe disabilities—could be trained. Children who possess some normal abilities, in spite of severe disabilities, can thusly be differentiated from a mentally retarded child. According to this philosophy, if the child has certain abilities that are normal and some that are very abnormal or deficient, then this child may be classified as a case of [a child with a] learning disability rather than as a case of [a child with] mental retardation. A mentally retarded child would be relatively low on all points in such a profile.

This child was put under intensive instruction for several years. You will notice that the top profile is approximately 4 years above the first highest profile each. Incidentally, all of the tests show similar acceleration. According to our calculations, this child developed 1 year in all of these functions for every year of training. During a 4-year period, she wound up in the third grade at the age of 8. She was placed in the regular grades, since at the age of 6 she was too high to be placed in a class for the mentally retarded.

I present this case to show that some children classified as mentally retarded are better classified as [children with a] learning disability rather than as mentally retarded, and that remedial instruction with these children can in some cases remove them from the category of mental retardation.

FIGURE 1
Results of Remediation

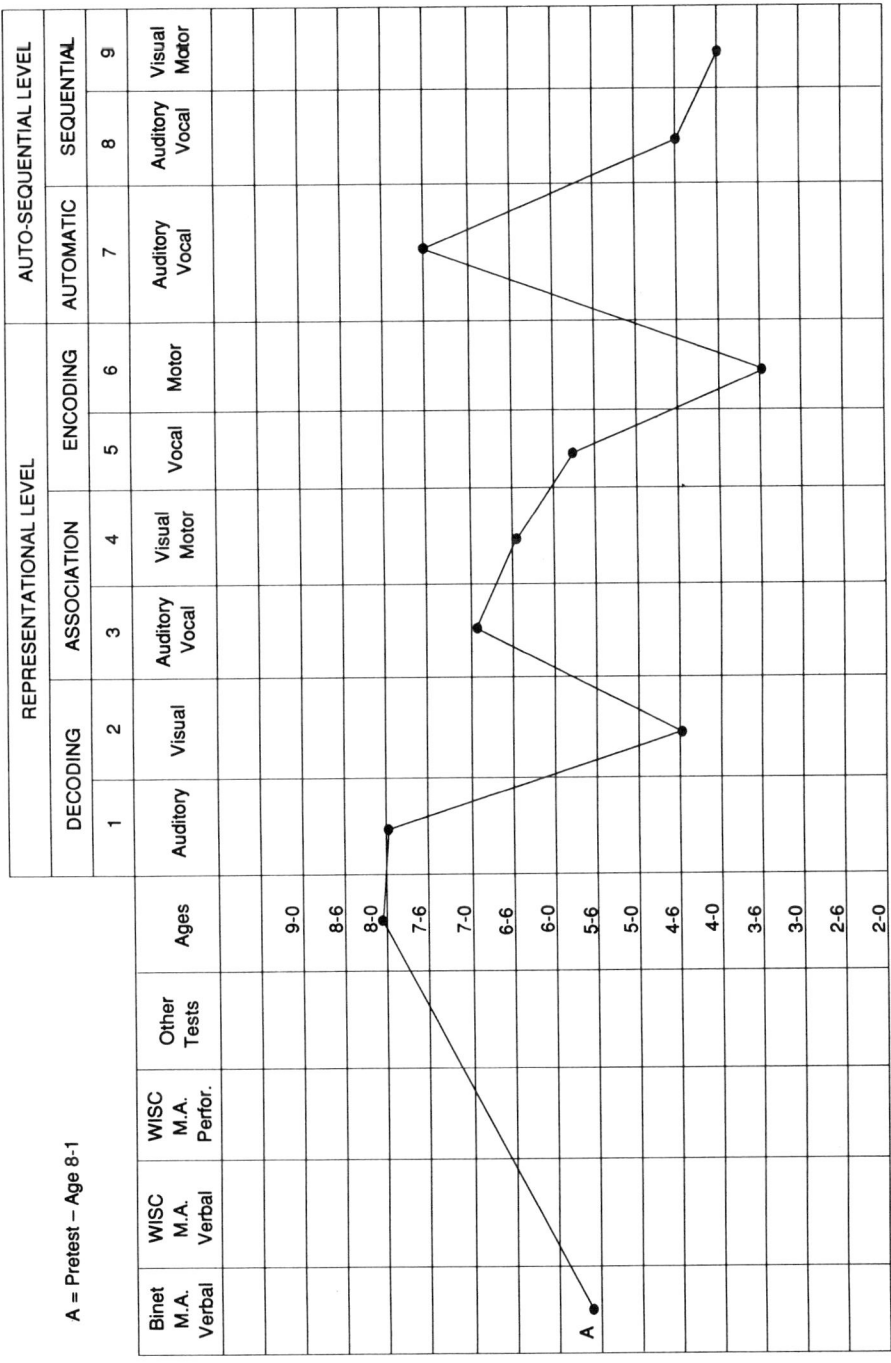

FIGURE 2
Results of Remediation

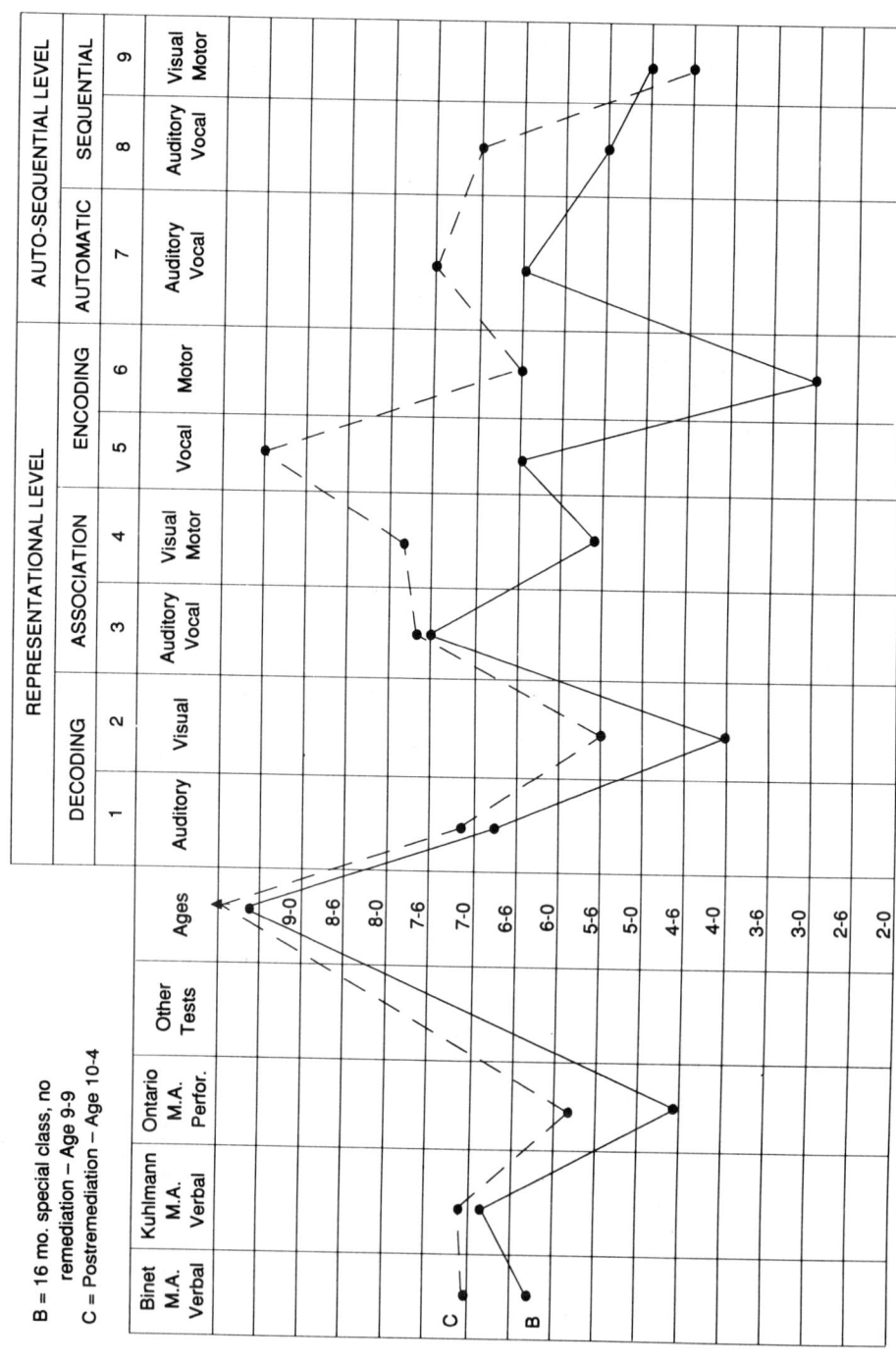

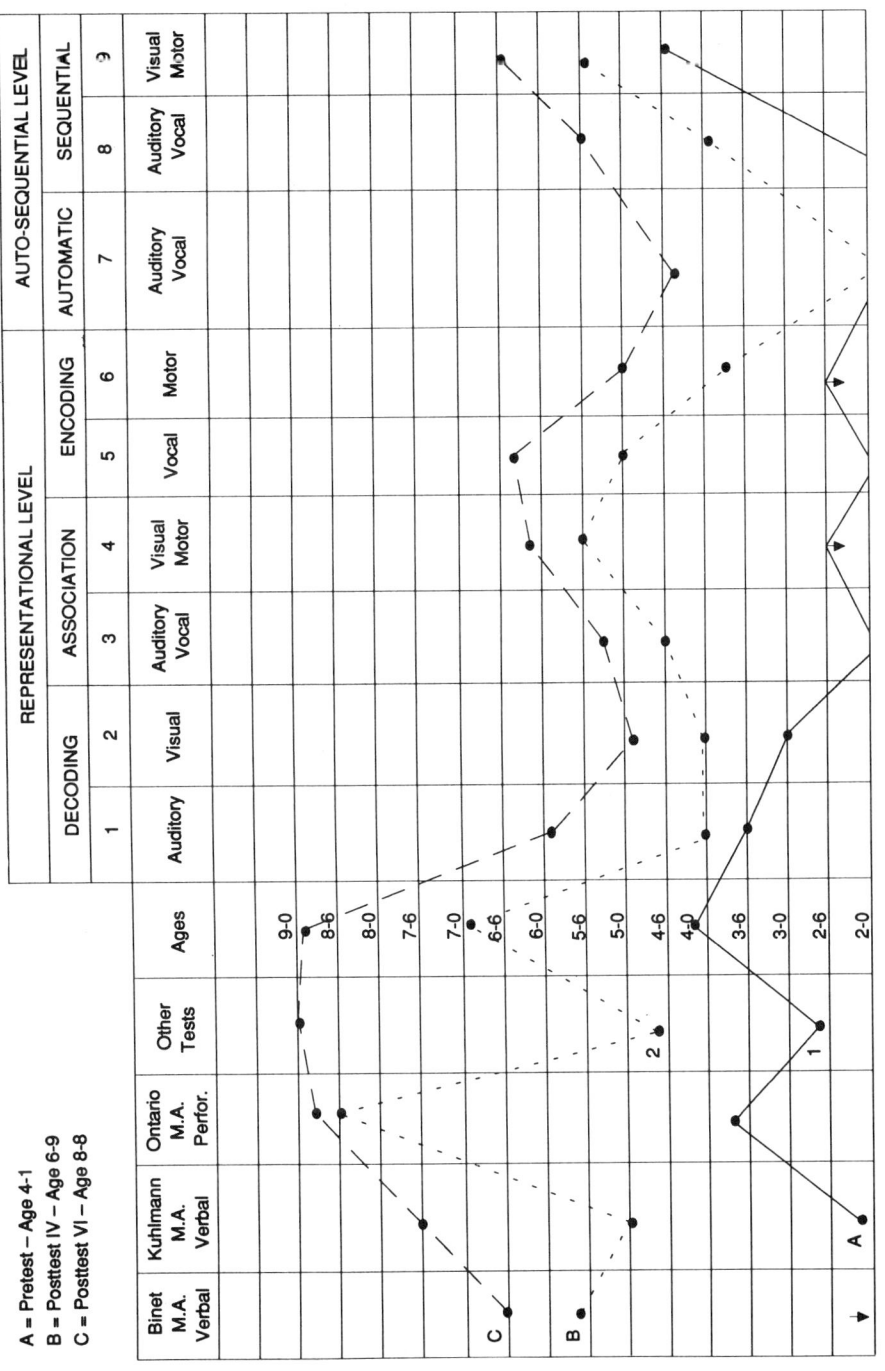

Remedial Training

Senator Prouty: Doctor, could you explain the nature of this intensive training?

Dr. Kirk: You will notice from the profile [in Figure 3], in the last column (9), that this child tested normal in a test of the ability to remember things seen in sequence. We call it *visual sequencing*. At the age of 4, this child was a little bit above normal in sequencing ability. She could see things and sequence things and discriminate them visually. She could also understand what she heard (test 1). She is not a visual-perceptually handicapped child, but she has other disabilities as shown in the lower points in the lowest profile.

What we did was to try to train her to speak spontaneously. We found that, and because of her ability to understand language (test 1, auditory decoding), and because she could sequence (test 9) we were able to train her to read before the age of 6. This achievement a severely mentally retarded child cannot do. We then taught her to speak through reading. For example, we would say, "How old are you?"

Her answer was, "6."

We then wrote on a card: "I am 6 years old," and by saying to her: "How old are you," and presenting her with a card, which says, "I am 6 years old," she could read the sentence: "I am 6 years old." Then we would take the card away and ask her again: "How old are you," and from memory she would say, "I am 6 years old." In other words, we used her abilities to train her disabilities. That is why it is necessary to analyze abilities as well as disabilities. This is only one phase of the methods used with her.

Actually, at the age of 4, we sent a teacher to the home to tutor her in an attempt to ameliorate her disabilities. At the age of 6 1/2, she was admitted to the first grade rather than to a class for the mentally retarded, since at this time she tested above the classification of mental retardation. We continued tutoring for a while in the first grade and then dropped her. She continued to progress. She is now at the third-grade level at the age of 8 1/2 and reading and writing at that grade level. She is not considered completely normal, but she certainly is not mentally retarded.

[Figure 4] represents the profile of a boy who was normal or above normal in intelligence. The reason I present this case is to demonstrate that learning disabilities constitute different kinds of defects in children—that is, one child may have great difficulty in hearing and understanding, but he can see quite well and interpret what he sees; another child may be just the opposite, without any defect in hearing or in vision.

[The] boy [profiled in Figure 4] had been in school [up] to the age of 9. He was known as "the boy who does not speak." He could repeat what you said to him. He did not have a speech defect. But he did not speak spontane-

FIGURE 4
Results of Remediation of an Expressive Disability

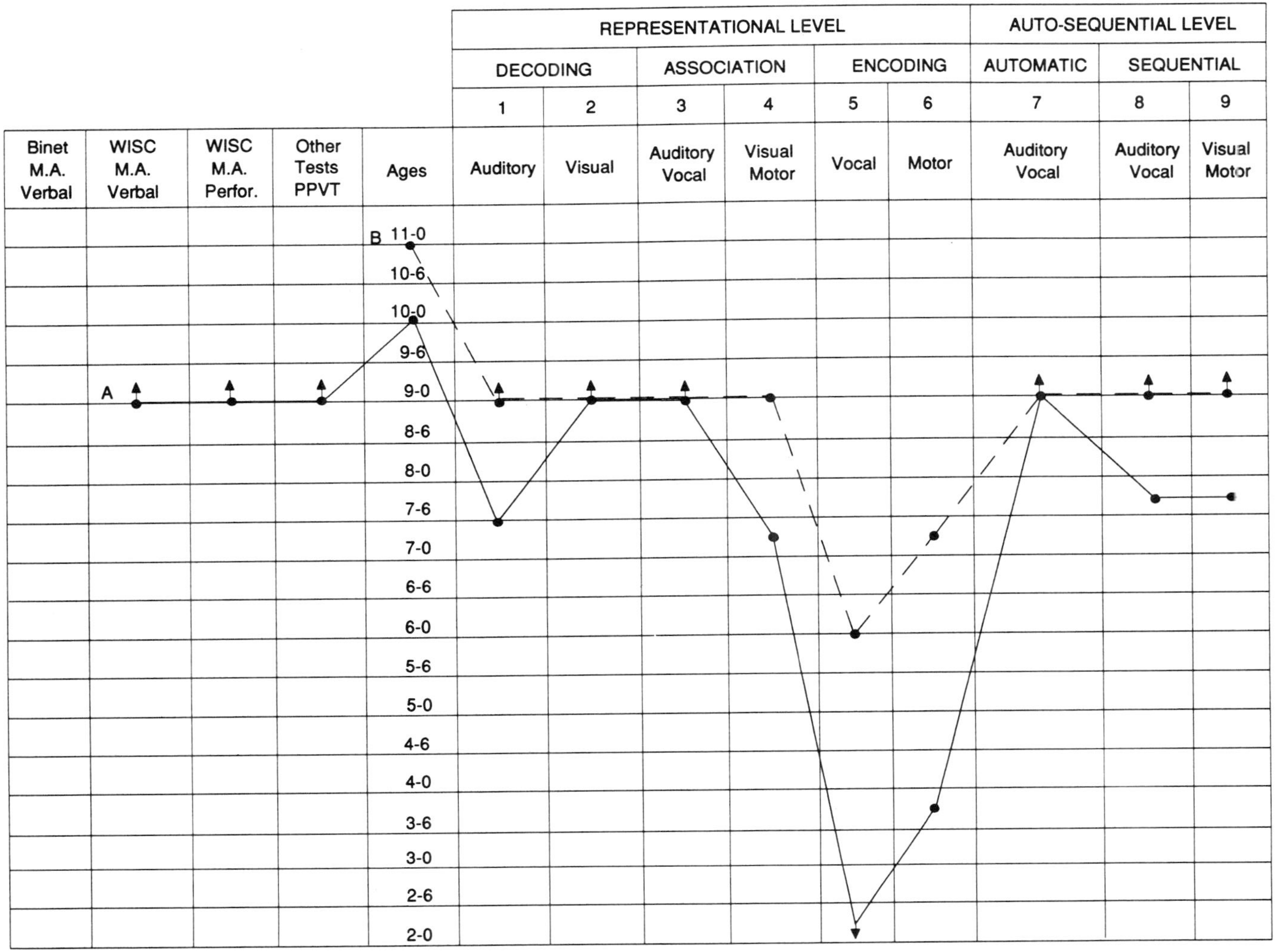

ously or converse. For example, when the teacher asked a question in class he would raise his hand, but when the teacher called on him he stood up but nothing came out. He could not express his ideas.

That is a disability in expressive ability, both in motor expression, the ability to express himself by gestures or in writing, and in the ability to express himself in words spontaneously.

The profile shows the test-retest results after 7 months of training. He had been in school up to the age of 9 with little progress in expressive ability. You will notice from the profile that he improved from an expressive disability of 2 and 3 years of age to 6 or 7 years, an improvement of over 3 years in 7 months. He has been progressing very well in class without further tutoring.

This is a case which some people would call expressive aphasia. He understands, but he cannot spontaneously express himself. He learned to read, but he could not learn to express himself in writing. Without special help for his disability, he could become a dropout [from] school, but he is now progressing quite normally.

The method of teaching him was technical and complicated. Briefly, we used a typewriter and a tape recorder. Lessons were programmed through computers using a sequence of statements that he could read, listen to what he read, and type these missing parts. For example, he would be presented with the sentence, "The ball is round." He would read that sentence, then press a button to activate the tape recorder and hear what he read. The next sentence presented was: "The ball is r-o-u-n—." He had to fill in with the typewriter the "d." For the next presentation, he had to fill "n-d," and, later, fill in the words in the sentence, "The ——— is ———." In other words, we taught him spontaneous speech on a typewriter and a tape recorder. He made marked progress, as shown in the test, with this particular method. This case has resulted in further research on the programming of materials for this particular type of disability.

Diagnosis of Learning Disabilities

The point I wish to make with these cases . . . is that a learning disability is a discrepancy in growth within the child in speech, language, reading, writing, arithmetic, and other areas. When we are able to examine the psychological processes of these children and determine wherein they have abilities and disabilities, we can then organize remedial programs to ameliorate the deficiencies that exist.

Because different professions are concerned with different aspects of the problem, numerous names and labels have evolved. The medical profession tends to label in terms of etiology—brain-injured, cerebral dysfunction, minimal brain damage, and so forth. Those whose prime concentration is on "what it is and what to do about it" tend to use behavioral terms such as "perceptual disorders," "reading disability," "conceptual disorders," "learning disorders," and so forth. To most educators, the term "learning disability" is the most appropriate since it is necessary to organize learning materials to teach the child.

Federal Programs

Several years ago, I had the privilege of administering the newly created Division of Handicapped Children and Youth in the U.S. Office of Education. The congressional Act, Title III, of Public Law 88-164, allowed for the training of teachers of the mentally retarded and other handicapped children. This Act authorized the training of professional personnel for the mentally retarded, the deaf, speech-impaired, and so forth, and added "crippled or other health-impaired children who by reason thereof require special education." Parents and school personnel interested in children with learning disabilities were disappointed that the [condition] called "learning disabilities" per se was not included in this list of handicapping conditions. We were, however, able to interpret how the U.S. Office of Education could include this group and notified colleges that applications for work in this area would be considered. Only four colleges proposed programs for [training teachers of children with] learning disabilities in 1964. Two years later, in 1966, approximately 10 such programs are being partially supported under this federal legislation.

Proposals

It is my opinion that it would be appropriate for Congress to consider giving this type of child an identity in legislation for handicapped children. This could be done by inserting the term "and/or learning problems" in existing legislation. Wherever the phrase "crippled or other health problems" appears, it could be expanded to read "crippled or other health and/or learning problems."

The term "or other health problems" used in section 301, Title III of Public Law 88-164 was used to include children with epilepsy, cardiac disorders, and so forth, without naming all health problems. The term "learning problems" would then also include a series of learning disorders in children without naming each one, [such] as aphasia, agraphia, and many names that have been given.

Giving Congressional recognition to an existing problem in the schools today could lead to (a) improving diagnostic procedures; (b) developing more fully effective remedial procedures; (c) organizing programs in schools for such children; and (d) training a [corps] of remedial specialists to cope with this problem....

Personnel Needs

Senator Prouty: Dr. Kirk, in your judgment, how many trained personnel do we need to really take care of this problem at the national level?

Dr. Kirk: Up to this point, Senator Prouty, we have not had accurate surveys of the prevalence of this kind of child with learning disabilities in the public schools. So it is rather difficult to estimate the number of teachers needed for this program. My offhand guess at the moment would be that this group constitutes between 2 and 5 percent of the school population. If we can have the figures for the school population and divide it by a certain figure, such as 1 teacher to 8 or 10 such children, we could arrive at some sort of a figure with respect to the numbers of professional personnel needed to cope with this problem.

We have at the present time very few highly trained people in this field because of the lack of training centers and because of the late recognition of this problem in the public schools.

Senator Prouty: Well, you certainly believe that a survey should be made so that we will have some idea of the magnitude of the problem?

Dr. Kirk: Yes, sir.

Senator Prouty: I think you have all contributed a great deal to our understanding of this problem.

I understand we are due to have a roll call vote in a few minutes in the Senate so probably we will have to take a recess until that has been completed.

I do feel that you have made a real contribution and certainly I am sure we are going to call on you all again for guidance in this very important matter. . . .

Part IX

Social Issues

INTRODUCTION

JAMES J. GALLAGHER
Director
Institute for Carolina Child and Family Policy
Frank Porter Graham Child Development Center
University of North Carolina at Chapel Hill

The speeches and articles in Part IX reveal the social policy issues of special concern to Sam Kirk. They were written during a period of over 30 years but remain consistent in philosophy—each paper featuring a concern for the policies of our country and the values they reflect. The two earlier chapters focus on the role of education in strengthening the country. Dr. Kirk points out with great clarity in Chapter 23 that it was the public school system that provided the base from which the armed services in World War II provided trained manpower to defeat the Axis countries. He continues in Chapter 24 to address the idea of the power of education as a part of the total strength of the nation and how it would be unwise for us to not invest major resources in that activity as one goal of maintaining a strong country.

The last two chapters show a different side to Sam Kirk, revealing him to be not just an advocate of public policy but a determined player in that sphere. Perhaps no one in special education has played a larger role than Sam in the development of the legitimacy of the field in the public policy arena. He mentions that in the 1960s the status of special education in the U.S. Office of Education was raised two levels, from a section to a division. What he doesn't say was that it was raised largely because of his own credibility and in anticipation that he would provide the leadership that would justify that change. As those in special education well know, the Bureau of Education for the Handicapped—now the Office of Special Education Programs—has played a leading and significant role in American education for the past quarter-century. One of Sam Kirk's legacies is the laying of a solid groundwork of professional legitimacy at the federal level to make that possible. His ideas and his goals are well represented in the federal legislation during that very productive period. His speech on gerontology probably reveals as much about Sam's orientation toward life and society as any other. He supported youth over gerontology even though he could have been a distinguished member of the gerontology group. But it was youth that was crying out for reform and a better society, and that was always the side that Sam found himself on.

This multidimensional man made contributions of momentous proportions in research, personnel preparation, and research administration, but a good case could be made that his longest-lasting contribution lay in the area of social policy, where his talents were recognized by those within and outside the field of special education.

James J. Gallagher received his doctorate in child and clinical psychology from Pennsylvania State University and worked in a child guidance clinic and a university psychological clinic before joining the staff of the Institute for Research on Exceptional Children at the University of Illinois. He spent 13 years with Samuel A. Kirk there and left to assume the directorship of the newly created Bureau of Education for the Handicapped in the U.S. Office of Education. After 3 years in Washington, he directed the Frank Porter Graham Child Development Center at the University of North Carolina for 17 years. He currently is Kenan Professor of Education and director of the Carolina Institute for Child and Family Policy at Chapel Hill, North Carolina.

Chapter 23

Education as National Defense

SAMUEL A. KIRK

In this era of uncertainty most Americans are entreated in evolving an adequate method of national security and national defense. Most Americans want peace. Most Americans want the extension of democracy. Most Americans want adequate national defense in case of war. But Americans do not agree on the best method of national defense. Many have proposed the same methods and procedures which have been proposed for centuries, even though these methods and procedures which have been proposed for centuries, even though these methods are antiquated and have not protected people in the past.

The Support for Military Training

This year finds the American public discussing one such method—that of military conscription in time of peace. The President of the United States has asked Congress to conscript eighteen and nineteen year old youths for military training. This year also Congress is considering such bills more seriously than ever before. Many groups, including a few veterans' organizations, are devoting much of their time to propaganda for the establishment of military conscription.

All of these individuals or groups that are proposing military conscription are thinking—as they have always thought—they are presenting the same arguments they have always presented. In effect they say, we want to conscript youth for a period of a year for two major reasons. One is to scare other nations from attacking us and thus achieving peace; the other is that these youths with one year of military training will defend us in case of war. They continually use these arguments in the face of the fact that Germany, Japan, and Italy instituted military conscription for precisely the same reasons and as a result attacked other nations and lost the war.

Reprinted from *Progressive Education* (1968), 25(7), 119–120 and 144.

Education Prepared the Armed Forces

The use of military conscription in this atomic age does not seem to be the answer to the problem of national defense. Let us then consider other methods, such as the extension of education at all levels, which may in the long run come closer to the answer than any other approach. The extension of education may give us a better chance for the permanent peace, for the extension of democracy, and for national defense than any other proposal including universal military training.

This statement is of little value unless it is supported by evidence. No one should be expected to believe it unless it has some merit. The purpose of this paper is to submit the proposition that the extension of education is the most adequate procedure for national defense, for peace, and for the extension of democracy.

In 1941 the United States entered the war, supposedly unprepared. Japan, Germany, and Italy had had military conscription for many years. They had trained many men. They had prepared for war. Yet within a short period of time the United States built the most powerful Navy, the most powerful Air Force, and the most powerful Army the world had ever seen. We not only prepared in a short time but we won the war. And during the war our men showed superior military skill over the enemies even though they had a much shorter period of military training and were not under a system of military conscription.

How could we take a civilian army and navy and excel with only a short period of training? Some, of course, say that we won because we had great natural resources. But that is not the answer. Russia, China, and India had more natural resources than we have. They had more manpower. The real answer to the question is that we had the best educated and trained army and navy in the world, because of our universal public education. The answer is that we had men and women who were trained to do many things in civilian life, and who were able to utilize these civilian skills for military purposes.

When the war started, the Army and Navy took civilians who, because of their education and experience, were already trained for modern war. When a man entered a reception center in the Army his education and experiences were recorded and he was assigned to the military job where his training and ability could be best utilized. Training was accelerated because most of the men were educated in our schools and universities.

For a long time after the onset of the war the Navy did not draft men. They were interested in recruiting specialists for Navy jobs. The naval officers were commissioned directly from civilian life. Practically all of the officers in the Navy were college graduates or had equivalent technical training in some field. It can rightly be said that the schools of America trained the Navy. The training in the Navy consisted of short courses for those who were already trained in some specialty in civilian life.

Who trained the engineers in the Army? Who trained the doctors and nurses? Who trained all of the other specialists? These men and women were trained in civilian schools, and when given a short adaptation course [they] applied their skills to a military situation.

Some will say, "But who trained the bombardiers, the navigators, the pilots? Certainly they were not trained in civilian schools." Let us analyze this a moment. During the beginning of the war the Air Force recruited Air Force personnel who were high school graduates. We had no pilots, bombardiers, or navigators who were illiterate. The Air Force wanted educated men because if these men had been educated they could be trained in six to nine months. In other words it was the basic knowledge acquired during eight years of grade school and four years of high school that made it possible for the Army and Navy to train men to be pilots, navigators, or bombardiers in a short period of six to nine months.

And who trained the radar specialists, the weather men, and practically all the technicians used by the military forces? I happened to be an education officer during the war and was sent to a military school for four weeks. Certainly no one can say that this four week period was sufficient to train an education officer. After the public schools had trained me for eight years, the high schools for four, and the universities for seven, I was able to perform in my capacity with a minimum of four weeks of training. This is cited as an example to indicate that the schools of America were responsible for the training of the men and for the rapid manner in which we trained a military force and won the war. The schools of America are our best national defense, because through them we may train the statesmen and leaders that will keep us at peace, or educate our men for defense in case of war.

Education Made Industrial Production Possible

Many claim that because of our industrial developments we were able to win the war. But who trained those who managed the industries? Who trained the technicians, the engineers and the various skilled laborers that manned the industries? We must remember that industries are manned by men. Planes are designed and built by men. And the efficiency of industry is due to the genius of men—men who have had the opportunity through a free school system to develop their genius.

And again, who trained the atomic scientists? These men were not only trained in civilian institutions but they continued to be in a civilian capacity as they developed the atomic bomb. Universal military training will not develop atomic scientists, but education will.

In addition to ascribing to the schools the credit for training the Army and Navy, we also have some evidence that the more educated the soldier, the more valuable he becomes in war situation.

Need for More and Better Education

Many studies were made during the war by the Morale Services Division. They found on numerous instances that there was a direct relationship between greater morale and fighting efficiency. And that there was greater efficiency among those who were educated. For example in all units it was found that the higher the education of the man the less likely that he would go AWOL. A study of those who went AWOL indicated very clearly that the AWOL rate was predominantly higher among those with lesser education. The venereal disease rate was also greater among those that were less educated. Promotions among enlisted men were more common for the educated than the uneducated. This and other evidence indicates that even in the fighting fronts among the infantry, education of enlisted men contributed to a more efficient army.

During the war the German Army recognized the youth movements, mass meetings, and decrease in educational standards would eventually affect the efficiency of the German Army. Shortly after the outbreak of the war the supreme command of the Armed Forces issued a proclamation to elementary schools as follows: "further lowering of education standards would no longer be tolerated, education imparted in schools must be better than at the beginning of the war." Hitler, who was not interested in education, recognized that education is an all important factor in training an army. In other words Hitler recognized too late that education was very important for a military machine.

Our military force, strengthened by its background of education, could have been still stronger had our education system been better and more inclusive. We learned during the war that our educational system need expansion. The evidence for this statement may be stated as follows:

First, during the war we inducted one quarter million men who were illiterate. These were of little value to the Army because they could not adjust without an education. The army was forced during war time to set up special training units to train adult men to read and write. Because our educational system was not good enough we spent millions to train men to read and write during war time. We thereby prolonged the war, and consequently increased the casualties.

Secondly, after our troops entered North Africa it was discovered that many of our men did not know what war was about. Shooting a gun was one thing. The "will to shoot" was another. And in order to produce this "will to shoot," the Army organized a vast orientation and education program to inform the men about democracy, our allies, our enemies, and why we fight. This situation indicates to us that our educational system was defective also in the area of the social sciences.

And a third factor which indicated that our education was not good enough was the establishment of the ASTP and the V5 and V7 programs. The Army and Navy did not have enough college trained men. They had to send soldiers and sailors back to college under Army and Navy auspices because we were short of college trained men. This expenditure of time and money during war should be a warning to us that we must extend education in time of peace for the purpose of national defense.

In conclusion, it can be said that military conscription has not proven to be either an instrument of peace, or a technique of defense. Evidence has been produced to support the proposition that an extension of our educational system at all levels gives us the best chance for peace, democracy, and national defense. To extend education we need better schools for all children. We need better teachers. We need federal aid to education so as to equalize educational facilities throughout the country and to eradicate illiteracy. We need a bill of rights for superior civilian students comparable to that of veterans so that in case of a crisis, we will have sufficient college and professionally trained men. Compulsory military training of eighteen and nineteen year old youths will not give us national security. An extension of education at all levels has a better chance of accomplishing our objectives.

Chapter 24

Education and the National Welfare

SAMUEL A. KIRK

Our forefathers established free public education and compulsory education in order that *all* children might receive this education and thereby provide an intelligent basis for making the decisions required of the electorate. This concept has gradually expanded to include, at least lip-service, all the children of all the people, regardless of race, religion, economic status or level of IQ. No child, white or black, rich or poor, smart or dull, is supposed to be excluded from the American ideal of educating all the children of all people.

So much for our philosophy. How about our practice? How are we faring in these matters, and where are we headed? Do we have equal opportunities in education for all children at all levels?

In the first place, I think it is a myth that we have equal educational opportunities for all children. I do not mean to imply that all children should get the *same* education—but appropriate education to the limit of their ability. Geographical, social, racial, and economic factors create wide divergence in educational opportunities. Unfortunately, the good schools and highly trained teachers are usually found in the affluent communities and affluent states. In the slums and the inner cities and in the poor states, we are apt to find poor schools, old buildings, and less well-trained teachers.

In the second place, colleges are not free. Tuitions are increasing even in state universities. State legislators often seem to be more interested in protecting special interests than in expanding higher education and making education available to a wide segment of the population, thus keeping up with the changing times.

In the third place, very little is being done in the line of technical training, adult education, and inservice training.

We have become complacent and self-satisfied, but in the mid-1950s, we were jarred from our complacency. We had been told that the Soviet Union was inefficient, ignorant, and backward. But who was it that launched Sput-

---

Speech given to the Young Democratic Club, Tucson, Arizona, March 25, 1968.

nik—on their way to the conquest of space? We were shocked and surprised that another country was ahead of us in certain aspects of science.

All of a sudden we wanted to know what was to blame for our becoming a second-rate power in space. In the study that followed we made some interesting discoveries.

First, we really did not have the educated manpower and professional personnel to move ahead. We were very short of scientists, engineers, mathematicians, teachers, and doctors.

Second, we found our universities, even the state universities, were not free for all the people who had the ability to attend, but were basically for those who had the money to attend a university. With rising tuition costs and rising costs of living, a poor boy, no matter how bright, had little chance of attending a university.

In desperation, even under a conservative administration (1952–1960), Congress passed two bills to alleviate the situation in education. One bill was the *National Defense Education Act*, known as NDEA. This bill offered fellowships to students in physics, chemistry, mathematics, and related areas and gave funds to universities to hire faculty for these students. It was a start, but actually this bill supported only a few students. The second bill established the *National Science Foundation* to conduct research and to subsidize programs for training in science and mathematics and related areas.

After Sputnik, we began to look into the educational system of the Soviet Union to find out how they educated their professional personnel and scientists. We found in general that the Soviets had taken seriously our ideal of education, educating all the children of all the people, and they actually implemented it in practice.

I am not an authority on Soviet education, but I did have the opportunity, with five other scientists, to be sent to Russia in 1962 to investigate their program of education and rehabilitation for handicapped children. In brief we found several facts:

1. The Russians are fanatic about the education of their children and youth.
2. They have established extensive provisions for education from the nursery school through university and graduate school or through technical institutes.
3. Education is not only free to everyone, but at higher levels if the young people must live away from home scholarships are given for board and room in addition to free tuition. In other words, their scientists, doctors, teachers were all paid to go to the university. Incidentally, I found later that England, in the midst of its austerity, gives free tuition and maintenance to all students attending their public colleges and universities. The United States is becoming unique among the major world powers in charging people to go to the university.

We read very little in the local press about the educational developments in the Soviet Union. What we hear about Russia in our news media is primarily its military power and its domination of other countries. We hear very little about the support they give to their educational institutions and to the capable students who attend the universities.

I am concerned about the meager support that education receives in this country in contrast to the great support of education in the Soviet Union. To support education and individual students in this country at the rate the Soviet Union supports education would require more financial support than we have been willing to provide.

I believe that a program of social and industrial development in any country is dependent upon a literate and knowledgeable population with sufficient highly trained personnel to advance science, industry, government, the humanities, and the arts. History provides evidence that revolutions occur primarily in countries where the people are uneducated. No country in recent history has attained world leadership without a high degree of education.

In the 16th century, King Sulieman developed schools, recruited bright young men from Greece, the Roman Empire, and other countries, gave them a superior education so that they might help in developing the Ottoman empire, which flourished and dominated the world for some time in science, military, art and other areas.

The aim of the Soviet Union is, as I see it, to educate all of [its] people to the highest level to which they are capable, and through their accomplishments in science, art, music, et cetera, gain world leadership through demonstrating their way of life to the world. They will be unable to overcome the United States militarily, but if we continue with our present course and they with theirs, it is possible that they can achieve their aims through nonmilitary means.

The late President Kennedy recognized these problems. He knew that education in this country must receive greater support.

He knew that a substantial number of our youth and adult population were illiterate.

He knew that public assistance of the illiterate and jobless were increasing from year to year.

He knew that the increasing shortage of professional personnel would have a detrimental effect on the nation.

He knew that poverty in the richest nation on earth was a scourge on the democratic way of life.

He knew that we were developing a caste system—of haves and have-nots. And, he knew that if we continue our course, we would wind up with one half or two thirds of our population supporting the other half or one third.

He knew that our course is a reversal of our original purpose of recognizing the independence of our citizens and the dignity of man.

He knew that America must reverse this trend, so that everyone will be an independent citizen with the dignity to which he is entitled by his birthright as an American.

It was under Kennedy's leadership that the Congress was apprised of the situation, and the 88th Congress in 1963 and 1964 become known as the Education Congress. [It] passed a great number of bills in 1963 and 1964, and, later, under President Johnson, launched a plan to reverse the course of this country through increased federal aid to education. The 88th Congress passed:

1. The Higher Education Facilities Act, to help build classrooms in universities.
2. ... The [expanded] National Defense Education Act, to give more scholarships to students, and to support universities with funds for faculty.
3. ... The Mental Retardation Facilities Act.
4. ... The Vocational Education Act.
5. ... The Manpower Development Act, to train adult illiterates to read and write and for job preparation.
6. ... The Economic Opportunities Act, largely educational, called the "War on Poverty."
7. And, in 1965, ... the Elementary and Secondary Education Act.
8. ... The Health Profession Education Act ... to prepare more personnel and facilities for health.

These bills were passed because we had been going backward. In the health professions, the situation was becoming alarming. For example, in 1950, we had one physician for every 1,300 people. In 1960, there was one physician for every 1,700 people. And, worse still, one out of every five physicians licensed in the United States trained in a foreign medical school.

After Kennedy's death, President Johnson was determined to continue the support of education. He tried to reduce the military budget (believe it or not) by about $2 billion and use this money for federal aid to education and for the "War on Poverty."

We were on the road to bringing this country to what it can achieve as a dynamic democratic society. But through poor advice, miscalculation, or otherwise, the president made a grave mistake. He supported the Vietnam War. We were told that we needed a few hundred thousand men to put out a few brushfires and to contain communism in Asia. Then we needed 300,000 men. Then 400,000. Then 500,000. All of you know the story of what has happened in Asia, and, worse still, what has happened and what is happening at home.

The great beginning that was made in education and in the War on Poverty in 1963–64 was now blocked from extensive development. The promise to move rapidly ahead in education at all levels, to fill the gap created from neglect, and in keeping with an increasing population, have not been fulfilled. Instead, $33 billion dollars a year of our resources are being spent annually in Vietnam.

The War on Poverty has also been blocked from really being a war on poverty. The first appropriation was for a billion and a quarter dollars. Many expected that by 1968 the budget would be 10 billion, if we are to remove poverty and public assistance from our midst. This year, however, the budget was less than 2 billion. And most of us know that we either remove the slums and win the war on poverty . . . or suffer the consequences. The longer we wait, the more difficult it will be for us.

Rioting in the inner cities has become a small revolution. Our first reaction emotionally is to send tanks, guns, bombs, and quell all riots by force. These are the tactics we have tried to use in Vietnam, without success. The *Civil Rights Commission Report* outlines this ominous situation and calls for renewed efforts without the use of guns.

With riots in the inner cities, student demonstrations on campuses across the country, marches on Washington, refugee Americans in foreign countries, and an increase in crime and delinquency, we are in a situation we have never had to face before.

My personal solutions to many of our problems would include:

1. Stop the war in Vietnam. Work immediately for a negotiated settlement to protect the farmer and peasant, and leave the rest of the settlement to the Vietnamese. I have no faith that communism will last. The Vietnamese, like the Russians and the Chinese, will work their way out of communism, just as Czechoslovakia now stands a chance of doing.
2. Triple the education budget. Remove illiteracy. Train a sufficient number of technicians and skilled workers, as well as the increased number of professional personnel needed by our society.
3. Spend whatever is needed to eliminate slums, unemployment, and the need for social welfare. This may represent $10 to $20 billion for each of the next 5 years.

By educating and developing all of our people, the rest of the programs for developing science, industry, agriculture, arts, humanities, education—and yes, even effective politics—will follow.

I think the recent efforts to expand education of the handicapped and eliminate discrimination against racial, sexual, and economic deterrents to education for all the children are moving in the right direction.

Chapter 25

Youth Challenges Gerontocracy

SAMUEL A. KIRK

Many people today are concerned about what we call the generation gap or the conflict of generations. There are unquestionably marked differences of opinion between the young and the old, and between the concerned young/old and the unconcerned old/young. We do not have to limit the differences in values, differences in attitudes, and differences in methods of producing change. It is commonplace to state that youth are more idealistic and probably more humanistic, than those who have seen more of life and have become more involved in making a living. This, of course, is not new, since Aristotle stated that youth love honor more than they do money.

I have entitled this sermon "Youth Challenges Gerontocracy." The term *gerontocracy* was coined by Sir James Fraser, an anthropologist, in describing the government of the Australian aborigines. The political organization of the tribe was that of an oligarchy of old and influential men who made all the decisions and rules for the tribe without the consent, participation, or discussion with the younger men.

The anthropologist Feuer, in a recent book entitled *The Conflict of Generations*, states that student movements tend to arise in societies that are gerontocratic—societies in which religion, ideology, and the family are especially designed to strengthen the rule of the old. It is in such a society, he states, that an uprising of the young will be most apt to occur. The aim, unfortunately, of most uprising of the young is primarily to de-authorize the old. Seldom do the young evolve a blueprint for solutions, but they feel that the older generation has discredited itself and has lost its moral and ethical standards.

I should state at the outset that we should not stereotype all youth as protesters or rebels. It is possible that the recent student movements throughout the world may involve a minority, rather than a majority of youth. But let us not be deceived by the minority nature of movements. Most changes in our

---

Paper presented at the Unitarian Universalist Church of Tucson, Arizona, on January 11, 1970.

society have started out as minority ideas and movements by minority groups and later become majority ideas. No major change in history has come about by majority action at the outset. All have started as minority ideas.

A Gallup poll, last summer, demonstrated quite clearly the generation gap and the uniformity of opinion of the majority of college students as opposed to the general public. This poll shows that, although only 28% of college students have participated in demonstrations, 81% of those who did not participate in demonstrations shared the opinion that students should be represented on policy-forming boards in society and in universities. In contrast, only 25% of the general public believed that students should be given this responsibility. They feel that students are in college to be educated and that if they desire this privilege, they must abide by the decisions of their elders or get out.

What does this mean? It means that 75% of the general public wants to retain a gerontocracy in the management of societies' affairs, while the overwhelming majority of students want to determine the policies of society and universities by what they call participatory democracy in which students have a voice in decisions that govern their lives. In France, after the student strike at the University of Paris, the students requested representation on the policy-forming board of the University of Paris. The faculty did not grant equal representation, whereupon deGaulle ordered that one-half of the board consist of student representatives.

If Feuer is correct that student movements tend to arise in societies that are gerontocratic, it may be wise for us to look into our own society for gerontocratic aspects that may stimulate student movements and youth rebellion.

The best current example of gerontocracy is the South Vietnam war. This is an instance in which older statesmen—the president, the State Department, the military authorities—made the decision to wage a war. No consultation was made with the young men who were going to be drafted to fight this war. The results of this gerontocratic act are obvious. It has alienated a substantial portion of our youth; it has triggered many of them into becoming activists; it has caused them to demand participation in decision making in government and in universities; it has caused them to ask the questions, "What right has a group of old men to start a war thousands of miles away and force us to kill people who have not done anything to the United States and are not even capable of attacking us?"

Although the student unrest cannot be ascribed entirely to the Vietnam War or to racial problems, it certainly has aroused the youth of this country to look at what is happening and to examine the power a few people have on their lives. These issues, which seemed to them legitimate issues to oppose, served as a wedge for noting other gerontocratic acts in our society. Many young people are congregated in colleges, and as they looked at their immediate environments they saw conditions to which they objected. So, they protested the recruitment efforts of the Dow Chemical Company because of the napalm they made for burning human beings in the war. They protested university facilities and faculty being used for biological and chemical warfare research. They protested the dehumanization of universities due to large enrollments, and the loss of their own identity in an "IBM" number.

Gerontocracy alone cannot explain the student movement and student unrest. Related to this possible cause is the advent of a highly developed technology. The rapid rate of change in civilization, the knowledge explosion, and the developments of modern science are making many people—often older people—become obsolete faster. This is a possible reason why younger people lose respect for what their parents are doing. A farmer's son not too long ago watched his father plow so that he could learn to plow the fields. Today the young man disregards what his father is doing—because the son knows that he himself will not be plowing fields but possibly running a computer, something his father does not and will not understand.

Because of the rapid changes in our society, because of phenomenal technological growth, it has become necessary for the younger generation to strike off on new paths, often in directions that their elders know nothing about. This manifests itself in dress, appearance, demonstrations, and in opposing what the older generation has felt is orthodox in our society in the management of government and universities, and in the canons of religion, law, morals, sex, and other areas.

In addition to gerontocracy and the more rapid advancement of this technological age, the conflict of youth between humanism and materialism is another major factor in producing the generation gap. Although this existed to some extent in other generations, it was not as acute. Somehow, by the time previous generations grew up to discover that these ideals are more wishful thinking than reality, they were themselves involved in the status quo; they became a part of the establishment.

But one may ask, "Why is youth more humanistic or idealistic? Where did they get those ideas?" The answer is, of course, from our history as a nation. This nation was built on idealistic philosophies such as "all men are created equal," all are entitled to "life, liberty, and the pursuit of happiness," and the Bill of Rights and other pronouncements of the founding fathers of this nation. But they also obtain their idealism from their parents and teachers, who taught them as children about justice, equality of men, peace as a major aim of our society, the brotherhood of man, the ideal of service to mankind, and so forth.

The difficulty between generations began when the children grew up and took our verbalized ideals seriously. Imbued with the idealism of our forefathers and the moralisms of their parents and teachers, they looked around and found that the ideals were not practiced.

- They found that we do not have equal opportunities for all the people regardless of race, sex, or religion, and that unwitting racism existed in our country.
- They found that some children do not have enough to eat in the richest and greatest country in the world.
- They found that we have had four wars in this century, contradicting our verbalized ideals about peace.
- They found that the military establishment is not a "servant of the people" as they were told, but that this servant of the people is now becoming, as Eisenhower said, "a military-industrial complex" that is dominating the federal budget and, consequently, our society. While President Johnson was praying for peace on Sunday, he was sending bombs and napalm over Asia the rest of the week.
- They found that political parties have become corroded, boss-controlled, and neither accessible nor responsive to the youth group.

They concluded, rightly or wrongly, that to preserve our democratic society, it is necessary to make the massive changes necessary for social reconstruction. Fortunately, the overwhelming majority of youth are opposed to violent measures for the achievement of these goals, but they want society to move faster into these changes. They are showing impatience with the continuation of what they consider to be an immoral war and an increasingly mechanized and computerized and polluted materialistic society. The militants have also warned us of the impending crises. As Eldridge Cleaver has said, "When the sane people don't do it, when all the good middle-class people don't do it, then the madmen have to do it." Many of the same middle-class youth want to do it and do not want the madmen to do it. My question is, "Will the general public move to help the sane people do it, or will they legislate repressive measures that will make some middle-class youth madmen?"

Immediately after World War II (from 1945 to 1955), a large segment of the student body of universities was made up of veterans returning to school under the G.I. Bill. These veterans were older, more mature, and more serious about their studies than were the other students. They had learned to obey authority in the military and had no overt objections to the rules and regulations of society or the university. They addressed their professors by the habitual "Yes, Sir!" and "No, Sir!" Many were married or became married during their college period. They were interested in completing college as soon as possible and joining the established order.

The young people of this era are sometimes referred to as the Silent Generation. This was also the McCarthy Era when it was dangerous to hold any belief contrary to the established view of things. These young men, in their efforts to get ahead in the world and make up for the years denied them by the war, were not interested in politics or in reform, and if they did have some misgivings about the way society was being run, they were not about to upset the apple cart by expressing any dissent. Campuses were quiet then except for a few "panty raids" or "water fights" conducted by the undergraduates of the usual college age.

But in the late 1950s, there arose in our society a new generation of students who were not veterans and who had been raised in an atmosphere [that] encouraged personal autonomy and individuality. This minority group of students [was] skeptical of the intrinsic value of money-making and status, and also skeptical about the claims of established authority.

By 1960, a large group of young people, born to the educated and affluent class, were to some degree in conflict with the prevailing values. Unlike other generations, they were not faced with a scarcity of jobs—but rather with an array of careers. But these many opportunities in a capitalist society were opposed to their fundamental humanist aspirations. In a sense, they became estranged from capitalistic culture and what they considered superficial values of a materialistic, dehumanizing society.

These students, congregated in colleges, were seeking major issues. It was at this time, in 1960, that the civil rights movement began. This movement led these young intelligentsia to see the relevance of political opposition. The movement, especially among white students, grew out of their humanistic values. It began to occur to them that to do nothing meant that they were a part of the oppressive apparatus of society. Participation in the civil rights movement was a way out of their dilemma. This movement opened their eyes to other political issues, and the values of the gerontocrats—the war, the militarization of society, space explorations, and the priorities given to property rights over human rights.

By 1962, the movement had grown and developed in many universities. [Members of this new movement] met at Port Huron in 1962 and organized the Students for a Democratic Society [SDS].[1] It is interesting to note that the SDS statement of policies known as the Port Huron Statement was not revolutionary. It stated clearly that they reject the Marxism in the Soviet bloc [that] has become official dogma used to justify crimes against humanity. [It] also stated that Western social democracy was largely a tool for the stabilization of capitalism. [The SDS members] construed their tasks as a political reform movement rather than a revolutionary movement. They were optimistic about the possibilities of change through political action within the context of American politics. They hoped that the labor movement, the religious community, the liberal organizations, and the intellectual community would unite to produce reform. They wanted to break through the atmosphere of apathy and educate students about political issues.

But this did not happen. The student activists soon found that most liberals and labor movements were interested in retaining the status quo. They found that it was impossible to change politics from within since they were forced to play politics according to the rules that would maintain the power of the same political groups.

After several years of work, and the tragedy of Vietnam, they rejected the legitimacy of the American political system—although some tried again under Eugene McCarthy.

At this point, SDS changed [its] tactics to militancy. They concluded that only extreme action of a disruptive nature will work. Working through the system, they felt, was a trap. Confrontation, disruption, direct action became their motto. They knew that their actions would produce the use of force by the state, and that the presence of the police would alienate the middle group of nonactivists. They took advantage of the disillusioning experience of the generation of Americans with the draft and the Vietnam War. Their tactics have tended to educate the rest of the student population to the gerontocratic nature of our society. A good example is found at Harvard when 200 students took over a building. The president [of the university] called the police. The police action on the campus at Harvard removed the 200 students from the building, but it resulted in 10,000 students going on strike in sympathy with the 200 students and against the presence of police on the Harvard campus. In a way, the students followed what Mr. Lincoln said last Sunday, in his review of Erikson's book on Mahatma Ghandi, "that rebellion is superior to obedience, when rebellion is necessary to maintain identity."

Among the issues that students raise are racism, the military-industrial complex, poverty and hunger in the midst of plenty, imperialism, economic oppression of minorities, misplaced priorities of the nation, the draft, the Vietnam War, materialism, dehumanization of society, and outmoded values and cliches. They state that they reject the notion "my country right or wrong." They prefer "my country right, and if it's wrong we will change it and make it right." To the insulting slogan "Love America or leave it," their answer is "Because we love America we will change it."

The riots at the Chicago Democratic Convention were an example of the thrust of the activists of the younger generation. They stated that the convention was a farce, that the delegates were the Establishment and that there was no point in voting. The were tired of voting against someone and for the so-called lesser evil. Their aim was to expose the moral character of current authority, to lay it bare, to show the world what established authority will do in a confrontation. Those of you who watched television saw what happened. And those of you who have read the Walker Report, entitled *The Chicago Police Riots*, can judge whether established authority met the challenge.

What may result from this youth revolt against the values of their elders? One can predict various possibilities—some pessimistic and some optimistic. For example:

Some feel that the conflict in our society between the young and the old, the "haves" and "have-nots," minority groups and the majority, is going to increase. This increase in conflict may lead to revolution on the one hand or to control of society by decree under some form of a police state. These people urge the militants to "cool it off" before suppression occurs and to effect change gradually under the present political system.

A second group feels there is no possibility of reform under the present system, that the present system and its set of values is so deeply ingrained that change is very difficult. Problems of pollution, which are becoming acute and frightening, are a good example. Everybody is against pollution but no one seems to do anything about it, since doing something about it means making major changes in our way of life. If we close the copper mines, for example, we discriminate against the labor force as well as the owners and the stockholders. If the government takes over the mines and pays the labor force and the stockholders until technology can control pollution, there will be many shouts of "socialism." And so it is with most of our problems. We await a severe crisis before we do anything about it. This is too slow for the new generation who feel that we do not have time to await natural crises but must recognize the crisis which is upon us.

Still others feel that we have always had problems and that we always will; that the present youth will grow up and join the Establishment; that the poor will join the ranks of the middle-class; and that current conflicts and confrontations will decrease.

Then there are others who feel that the conflicts will increase, that the present activist generation will provide the political leaders of the future, and that they will be replaced in college by a more militant group of our present secondary school students who are already politically and socially more sophisticated.

As an optimist, I look for hopeful signs [that] may indicate that we are moving toward more rapid constructive changes. I mentioned earlier that we have old/young and young/old. We do not have a clear-cut generation gap. It is just that it has taken the college students and the black militants to shake us up a bit, coalesce our attitudes. There are many among the rich, the intellectuals, [and] the liberals who are seeking reform and who also oppose racism, hypocrisy, poverty in the midst of plenty, imperialism, and superficial values. It is more than just youth who want a return to the idealism of our forefathers and the basic tenets of participatory democracy. These others, as well as our activist youth, want to change our national priorities from the emphasis on militarism and manipulation by the power of money to the more humanistic and equitable goals of society. Even among those whom we think of as rigid adherents of the status quo there are some who are beginning to question our present values and to recognize that the students have a just cause. I was surprised to read that Stuart Alsop—who is not exactly a radical—stated in *Newsweek* last summer that if the movie "The Graduate" reflects the reality of middle-class life, then "if ever there was an older generation that deserved to be de-authorized it is the current one."

The year 1969 saw more confrontations, more demonstrations on college campuses, then ever before. The first reaction of the public to student disruption was to call the police, dismiss the students (or jail them) and pass laws against dissent and disruption. But fortunately there were cooler heads in Congress, such as the Brock Committee.[2]

Representative Brock, a Republican from Tennessee, led 22 of his colleagues in Congress in visiting 50 college and university campuses throughout the country. They interviewed a variety of students, faculty, presidents, and administrators. After careful study, they recommended no repressive legislation by Congress. To quote their report, "Any action by the Congress or others would, for example, penalize innocent and guilty alike . . . and would only serve to confirm the cry of the revolutionaries and compound the problem. . . . The fundamental responsibility for order and conduct on the campus lies with the university community." In addition, the Committee made such statements as: "There is on the campus today a new awareness of potential student power and the emergence of a large group, probably the vast majority of student leaders and a substantial number of intelligent, concerned and perplexed young people, which has genuine concern over what it feels is the difference *between the promise and the performance of America.*"

It is encouraging that a Congressional Committee (made up of members of the party generally considered the more conservative) would face the issue in this manner and make recommendations to the President for reform such as [the following]:

1. No repressive legislation.
2. Lowering the voting age to 18.
3. Reforming the draft procedures.
4. Providing more open communication between students and administration and between students and community.
5. Encouraging youth to participate in politics and run for political office.

I realize that these recommendations of a Congressional committee are made partly for the record. Also, they may be attacking the superficial aspects and the end results of deeper problems. As Thoreau has said, "There are a thousand hacking at the branches of evil to one who is striking at the root." Perhaps today's society will make more rapid progress if more will strike at the root.

Another encouraging sign is the slight inklings in Congress of the necessity to change priorities. This year Congress attempted to increase the budget for *people*—that is, for health, education, and welfare—by $1 billion over the budget recommendations of either [President] Johnson or [President] Nixon. They also made attempts to decrease the military budget, although success this year has not been noteworthy. Hopefully we may anticipate substantial results in the next few years. Sentiment is growing in this direction.

It is obvious that we have reached a stage where there is no question but that change in our national priorities and values must come. The question is when and how.

To repeat—if the sane people don't do it, if the good middle-class don't do it, the madmen have to do it.

NOTES

[1] From a mimeographed paper, "The Revolt of the Young Intelligentsia," by Richard Falk, Associate Professor, University of California, Santa Barbara, CA.

[2] "Congress Looks at the Campus," *Congressional Record*, 91st Congress, 1st session, U.S. Government Printing Office, Tuesday, June 24, 1969.

Chapter 26

The Federal Role in Special Education: Historical Perspectives

SAMUEL A. KIRK

Some years ago when I was visiting the Navajo reservation, I was impressed by the fact that, until recently, the Navajos had had no written language and consequently no written history. To obtain their history (other than that of governmental records), it was necessary to visit with 80- and 90-year-old Navajos and listen to their accounts of the tribe's experiences. I suspect that the editors of this publication decided to use the same anthropologic procedures and have asked me to write this historical review as I saw it, since I have been around in special education much longer than most people. Therefore, some of the anecdotes and historical stories that I shall present are not necessarily taken from authentic written records, but from personal experience. These may or may not have had something to do with the course of events in special education.

Federal Support of Special Education

Organized federal support for special education was initiated subsequent to President Hoover's White House Conference on Children and Youth in 1929. In conjunction with this conference, the officials appointed a number of committees dealing with various fields of the gifted and the handicapped. The proceedings of this conference were published in three volumes. The first volume, published in 1931, defined exceptional children as including the handicapped and gifted and recommended that the U.S. Office of Education establish a section on Exceptional Children and Youth. The second volume (1932) dealt with the administration of programs at the national, state, and local levels. The third volume (1933) dealt specifically with problems of the different types of handicapping conditions and their educational provisions.

Reprinted from *UCLA Educator*, 20(2), Spring–Summer, 1978.

Following the White House Conference, and upon the recommendation of that conference, the United States Office of Education established a Section on Exceptional Children and Youth. It employed Elise Martens, as senior specialist, to head this section.

Elise Martens created considerable leadership in the United States, operating primarily alone with one secretary and little other help. At that time there was no federal financial support. There were no research funds; there were no training funds; there were small travel funds. The best the federal government could do was to allow Martens to publish some bulletins of national interest and to correspond with state departments and universities that had teacher training centers.

After World War II, Martens was able to obtain the services of Romain Mackie. After Martens retired in 1952, the section was headed by Arthur Hill and later by Mackie. It should be mentioned that a "section" is the bottom of the totem pole in the hierarchy of government offices (Section, Branch, Division, Bureau). The status of this section was never elevated above this level from 1931 until 1963, a period of 32 years.

Two Catalysts for Change

Following the second World War, two major events occurred that stimulated programs for exceptional children. First, a number of states that previously had not supported programs of special education in the public schools passed laws to subsidize such programs. Illinois and California seemed to lead the way both in appropriations and in organizing new rules and regulations for their operation.

The second major impetus was the parent movement. Parents of mentally retarded children found themselves without service. The state residential schools were overcrowded and there were no provisions in public schools, especially for the trainable mentally retarded child. The tax-paying parents found themselves rejected by two state agencies. The public schools would not accept trainable mentally retarded children, and the state institutions were overcrowded and had a two- to three-year waiting list. The parents became frustrated and angry by this situation, paying school taxes [and] for institutions, but obtaining no services from either.

Consequently local and national parent groups joined together to form the National Association for Retarded Children. This group became a lobby in Congress during the early 1950s, informing state legislators and Congress that facilities throughout the country were inadequate, professional personnel were at a premium, and research in the education of the mentally retarded was sporadic. I understand at that time that some prominent people had seen President Eisenhower and informed him of the undesirable emergency situation for their handicapped children. President Eisenhower requested the Secretary of Health, Education, and Welfare to make proposals for federal programs to accelerate services to handicapped children.

Federal Planning

In 1953, I was invited to Washington by the Commissioner of Education to assist the Office of Education in the formulation of a national program for mentally retarded children. The Commissioner, recognizing that the Office of Education was not attacking the problem with sufficient vigor, requested that I meet with representatives of the Institute of Mental Health. These representatives were directed to formulate federal plans for the different departments of HEW. They were unfamiliar with the needs of special education and requested that I bear the burden of recommending a federal program for the Office of Education.

At that time the assignment was not an unfamiliar one for me. Two years previously I had been working with Ray Graham, the astute Head of Special Education in Illinois, on similar needs in that state. We found two major obstacles to the advancement of programs for exceptional children, namely (1) our ignorance of what should be done with these children, and (2) the paucity of highly trained professional personnel. We recommended to the state officials that we establish a research institute to answer some of our pressing problems, and that we provide a number of training centers for the preparation of professional personnel. The state responded to our recommendation by organizing at the University of Illinois an Institute for Research on Exceptional Children, in cooperation with the Department of Public Instruction and Mental Health. The state colleges and universities were encouraged to prepare professional personnel.

With this background I recommended two major directions for the federal Office of Education.

1. The first recommendation was for educational research funds. It was pointed out that at that time little research in the education of the mentally retarded was being conducted. The little research that was being accomplished came from private funds. The Institute of Mental Health was supporting several projects in mental retardation, including a grant to me to study the effects of preschool education on the mental and social development of young mentally retarded children.

2. The second recommendation was for federal funds to support the preparation of professional personnel. It was pointed out that (a) only a few colleges prepared teachers of the mentally retarded, (b) many classes throughout the country were being manned by relatively untrained or partially trained personnel, (c) colleges and universities were unable to support departments of special education, and (d) the richer states with

heavy state subsidies for classes for the mentally retarded were "stealing" trained personnel from the poorer states.

The recommendation for the preparation of professional personnel was not immediately accepted and was not presented to Congress. At that time, in spite of the fact that the federal government was subsidizing the training of occupational therapists, physical therapists and other personnel outside of education, there appeared to be a prejudice against the federal support of teacher preparation through the Office of Education. This prejudice probably stemmed from the fear that if the federal government were to support education financially, it would then control the process of education. Since education in this country is the responsibility of state and local policy makers, many believed that such support was not appropriate at the federal level.

Cooperative Research

The recommendation for research was more readily accepted and bills were introduced for research in education. The Cooperative Research Bill, Public Law 83-531, passed Congress and became law in 1954. At that time the Commissioner of Education was interested in obtaining research funds for education and believed that the prevailing interest of Congress in the mentally handicapped would help support research for education in general. The 1955–56 appropriation included $1,000,000 for educational research, but to the dismay of the Commissioner and many educators, the bill included an amendment by Representative Fogarty allotting $675,000 of the total appropriation for educational research in the education of the mentally retarded.

The earmarking of funds for research in mental retardation was not readily accepted by the general educators who found they had little money left for research in general education. Also, educators in other areas of special education felt that the mentally retarded had scooped the legislation for themselves. Immediately amendments to the bill were introduced, and within two years the earmarking of funds for the mentally retarded was removed.

The following graph shows what happens when funds are not earmarked for a particular situation. It will be noted from Figure 1 that, during the first year of operation, 61 percent of the million dollars was awarded to research on the mentally retarded. As soon as the earmarking was removed in 1959, award funds for the mentally retarded began to decrease, and by 1963, only five percent of the available funds appropriated for research was awarded for the mentally retarded. These funds were all used for continuations of projects previously begun, and no new grants for research in mental retardation were available. These data were presented to Congress as an example of what happens to minority groups when funds were not earmarked for a particular purpose.

FIGURE 1
Proportion of Appropriations Under PL-531 for Research on the Mentally Retarded

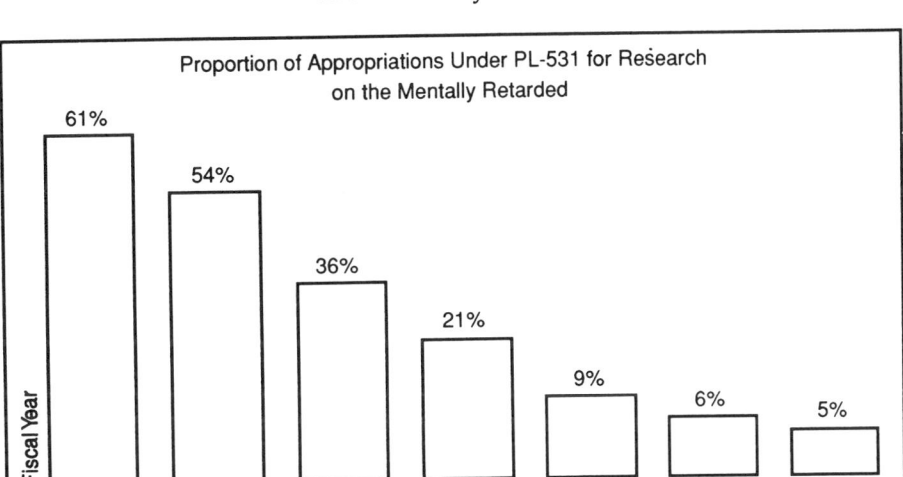

SOURCE: Congressional Record. Education and Training of the Handicapped. Hearings before the ad hoc Committee on the Handicapped, 89th Congress. 2nd Session. Part 1. June 6, 1966, p. 378.

Teacher Preparation

Four years after the Cooperative Research Bill was passed, the need for personnel throughout the country continued. In 1958, Public Law 85-926 was passed by Congress with an appropriation of $1,000,000. This bill provided grants to institutions of higher learning and to state education agencies to encourage teacher training for the mentally retarded.

Our committee, which was appointed by the Office of Education to help establish the policies for this bill, decided that the most effective disbursement of limited funds would be to subsidize colleges and universities that would train leadership personnel in the field of the mentally retarded. Students seeking advanced degrees received a subsidy of $2,500 each, and an additional $2,500 per student was granted to the university to defray the expenses of instruction. This particular bill initiated programs in many universities throughout the country, even though until then only four or five universities had been training leadership personnel in the field of special education.

In 1961, Congress passed Public Law 87-276, which provided funds to train teachers of the hearing-impaired. A million and a half dollars were appropriated for this function, because at that time there was an acute shortage of teachers of the deaf to man the many programs that were being organized in public and residential schools.

The Kennedy Era

Shortly after the election of President Kennedy, a President's Committee on Mental Retardation was appointed by the President to study their problems and related disabilities in children. Task forces were organized to survey programs for handicapped children in other countries. Task forces visited England, the Scandinavian countries, and the Soviet Union in 1962. In 1963, Lloyd Dunn and I published an article citing our experiences as part of the 6-man team that visited the Soviet Union for three weeks. It is my understanding that, when the Chairman of the Committee relayed our report about the Soviet Union, President Kennedy showed some concern and said to the Chairman, "Do you mean to tell me that the greatest and richest country in the world is not doing as good a job as the Soviet Union?" The chairman confirmed the comment of the Committee. The following January, President Kennedy presented Congress with a request for legislation for research and training for handicapped children.

Congress's response to the President's request was Public Law 88-164, the Mental Retardation Facilities and Community Mental Health Centers Construction Act of 1963. This amended the legislation of 1958 and 1961 and included research and training for all handicapped children.

In signing this bill on October 21, 1963, President Kennedy stated, "I am glad to announce at this time that we are establishing a new division in the U.S. Office of Education to administer the teaching and research programs under the Act. This will be called the Division of Handicapped Children and Youth, and will be headed by Samuel A. Kirk, who is now professor of education and psychology and director of the Institute of Research on Exceptional Children at the University of Illinois." By a stroke of the President's pen, the 32-year-old Section on Exceptional Children and Youth obtained a double promotion (bypassing the status of "branch") to a Division, with three branches, each having several sections.

As a personal note, prior to the signing of the bill, I had naively accepted an invitation to become a consultant to the program. Upon my arrival in Washington, the Commissioner of Education said: "I have called your university to obtain your salary. We are unable to match your salary by 5,000 dollars, but in the public interest I am asking you to accept the Directorship of the new Division to help us launch this historic bill." To my dismay, and not wanting to go to Washington, I told him that I was not trained in either administration or in the federal bureaucracy. I had students and research responsibilities and would find it difficult to leave the university. The Commissioner continued, "We have a car waiting outside to take you to the White House for lunch with some of the President's advisors." At the White House I tried all over again to explain the difficulties of leaving a university, but I was solemnly told that citizens do not lightly turn down requests from the President of the United States. I returned home with the earlier words of President Kennedy ringing in my ears: "Ask not what your country can do for you, but ask what you can do for your country." I had to accept. Three weeks after President Kennedy had signed Public Law 88-164, the world was wounded by his assassination.

The Division for Handicapped Children and Youth

In February of 1964, the Division for Handicapped Children and Youth was granted an appropriation from Congress of $14,000,000 under which it was necessary to (1) develop rules and regulations for the administration of the act; (2) distribute the rules and regulations with applications for grants to all interested universities and state departments of education; (3) appoint seventeen committees of professionals to evaluate the forthcoming applications for research and/or training grants; and (4) have all the funds committed by the following June. On June 16, Congressman Fogarty introduced into the *Congressional Record* a report from the U.S. Office of Education entitled, "Organization and Implementation of Program for Handicapped Children and Youth, Public Law 88-164, Title III." Congressman Fogarty stated on June 16, 1964:

> Mr. Speaker, I take pleasure in introducing for the *Record* at this point a most significant statement involving the administration of education programs for handicapped children. Last year the Congress passed Public Law 88-164, which provides federal assistance for health facilities for mentally retarded children; Title III of the act provides for training of teachers of mentally retarded and other handicapped children. At a meeting of New England educators, held on May 22 at Rhode Island College in Providence, Samuel Kirk made a progress report on the administration of the act by the Office of Education. In view of the great significance of the Act for education, and the extent to which it will help the nation's schools fill a critical gap in teachers for handicapped children, I wish to call the report to the attention of all Members of Congress. I call particular attention to the fact that the program has been extremely popular and successful with the participating institutions. In fact, requests for aid that have been submitted amount to three times the funds now authorized in the Act. I think this report signifies the need to give early attention to the act and further extensions and improvements to it.

As a result of Congressman Fogarty's efforts, Congress doubled the appropriation the following year.

Every ten years the President of the United States awards a Presidential Merit Award to the most efficient department of the U.S. Government. That year, shortly after Morrey Wirtz took over as Director of the Division, the Division of Handicapped Children and Youth was presented with the Presidential Merit Award by President Johnson. "For efficiency in government, this award is granted."

It is ironic to note that, in the fact of the Presidential Merit Award and other accolades, the Division was abolished 18 months after its creation when the Office of Education was reorganized by the White House into four Bureaus in 1965. In the shuffle, the functions of the Division were distributed among the Bureau of Research, Elementary and Secondary Education, and other Bureaus. Personnel who had been acquired to administer specialized programs for the handicapped were dispersed and placed in other departments.

Congress, however, was interested in advancing the work with handicapped children in spite of the White House reorganization. Between 1965 and 1967, Congress passed an array of bills including:

> Public Law 89-313, Title I of the Elementary and Secondary Act (ESEA), which provided funds to support the education of handicapped children in state-operated schools and hospitals, 1966.
>
> Public Law 89-258, extending the legislation for captioned films for the deaf and equipment to other media, 1966.
>
> Public Law 89-105, providing more funds and more traineeships for research and demonstration centers under the Community Mental Health Centers Act of 1965.
>
> Public Law 89-36, establishing the National Technical Institute for the Deaf, 1967.

The Bureau of Education for the Handicapped

Congress was also interested in the administration of these bills by the U.S. Office of Education. Because of the dispersion of programs for handicapped children and adults among a number of departments within HEW, and the dispersion of the programs within the Office of Education in 1965, the House of Representatives appointed a Congressional committee to study the administration of programs for the handicapped. The committee was chaired by Congressman Hugh Carey, now the governor of New York. This committee held hearings and obtained recommendations on a number of problems. Among these was my testimony before the Carey Committee (1966), which stated:

> When the work for the handicapped is dispersed under general categories, the handicapped, a minority group, is neglected in each category. When a program and a purpose are institutionalized under a name, the program moves forward. That is the reason I am recommending the creation of a Bureau for Handicapped Children and Youth in the U.S. Office of Education (p. 3811).

Alarmed by the disintegration and abolition of the Division of Handicapped Children and Youth, the Council for Exceptional Children and twelve other organizations gave support to the idea of a Bureau for Education of the Handicapped or a similar organization within the Office of Education.

These recommendations struck a receptive chord with the Carey Committee. Whereupon the committee introduced, within the Elementary and Secondary Education bill, the creation of a Bureau for Handicapped Children, and a National Advisory Committee to the Bureau (Public Law 89-759, Title VI, of ESEA).

Such a recommendation coming from the legislative branch of government was at variance with the usual governmental procedure, since the Office of Education, a branch of HEW, is part of the executive branch of government under the direction of the White House. Congress did, however, pass such a bill over the objection of the White House. In January 1968, the Bureau for the Education of the Handicapped was organized. James Gallagher was appointed deputy director with Edwin Martin as assistant director and later director of the Bureau.

In addition to the establishment of the Bureau, Congress established a National Advisory Committee for the Handicapped, which was designed to do two things: (1) to protect the Bureau against the onslaughts of pressure groups and especially from more powerful Bureaus in the Office of Education, and (2) to protect the Bureau from itself. It was to be a liaison between the field and the federal government. It forwarded recommendations to Congress through the Commissioner of Education.

The National Advisory Committee for the Handicapped, during the course of the first two years of its existence in 1968 and 1969, made a number of recommendations including two that were supported by Congress in the form of (1) the 1969 Learning Disability Act, and (2) the Early Education Assistance Act. These two programs have flourished since Congress recognized these areas.

The Bureau for the Education of the Handicapped began by organizing (1) a Division for Research, (2) a Division for Training, and (3) a Division for Service. Highly professional personnel were recruited to man the divisions, branches and sections. The prediction that a Bureau would integrate the various functions into a workable program on behalf of exceptional children was fulfilled. In addition, the Bureau has exerted a major leadership function throughout the nation and has helped states and universities advance their responsibilities.

The culmination of the work of the Bureau over a period of eight years resulted in Public Law 94-142, The Education of All Handicapped Children (1975). This bill is current and its success or failure will be told at the beginning of the next century.

This history says:

We hope these truths to be self-evident, that all children, handicapped and nonhandicapped, are created equal and that they are endowed by their creator with certain inalienable rights, among them the right to equal education to the maximum of each child's ability. To secure these rights, Public Law 94-142 was established. We, the people of the United States, solemnly declare that all handicapped children shall be educated at public expense, and that their education will be in the least restrictive environment.

References

Dunn, L. M., & Kirk, S. A. (1963). Impressions of Soviet psycho-educational services and research in mental retardation. *Exceptional Children, 29*, 299–303, 305–311.

Education and Training of the Handicapped. Statement of S. A. Kirk before the Ad Hoc Subcommittee on the Handicapped, 89th Congress 2nd Session, Part I, June 6, 1966, Washington, DC: U.S. Government Printing Office.

Fogarty, J. (1964). Organization and implementation of programs for handicapped children and youth, Public Law 88-164, Title III. Proceedings and debates of the 88th Congress, 2nd Session. *Congressional Record*, Washington, DC: U.S. Government Printing Office.

White House Conference on Child Health and Protection. (1931). *Special education: The handicapped and the gifted*. New York: The Century Company.

White House Conference on Child Health and Protection. (1932). *Organization for the care of handicapped children: National, state and local*. New York: The Century Company.

White House Conference on Child Health and Protection. (1933). *The handicapped child*. New York: Appleton-Century Company.

Bibliography

1932

Kirk, S. A., Hegge, T. G., & Sears, R. (1932, May). Reading cases in an institution for mentally retarded problem children. In *Proceedings of the 56th Annual Session of the American Association for the Study of the Feeble-Minded* (pp. 249–312). Philadelphia.

1933

Kirk, S. A. (1933). The influence of manual tracing on the learning of simple words in the case of subnormal boys. *Journal of Educational Psychology, 24,* 525–535.

1934

Kirk, S. A. (1934). The effects of remedial reading on the educational progress and personality adjustment of high-grade mentally deficient problem children: Ten case studies. *Journal of Juvenile Research, 18,* 192–205.

Kirk, S. A. (1934, May 19). Right-handed rats made "southpaws" by brain lesions. *Science News Letter.*

Kirk, S. A. (1934). A study of the relation of ocular and manual preference to mirror reading. *The Pedagogical Seminary and Journal of Genetic Psychology, 44,* 192–205.

1935

Kirk, S. A. (1935). Attitudes toward behavior problems in an institution for high-grade mentally deficient problem children. *American Association on Mental Deficiency, 40,* 368–385.

Kirk, S. A. (1935). Hemispheric cerebral dominance and hemispheric equipotentiality. *Comparative Psychology Monographs* (Vol. 11, No. 5, Serial No. 55). Baltimore: Johns Hopkins Press.

Kirk, S. A. (1935). Reading disabilities in relation to maladjustment. *The Compass Needle, 1*(7), 13–17.

Kirk, S. A., & Kirk, W. D. (1935). The influence of the teacher's handedness on children's reversal tendencies in writing. *Journal of Genetic Psychology, 47,* 473–477.

1936

Hegge, T. G., Kirk, S. A., & Kirk, W. D. (1936). *Remedial reading drills.* Ann Arbor, MI: George Wahr.

Kirk, S. A. (1936). Extra-striate functions in the discrimination of complex visual patterns. *Journal of Comparative Psychology, 21*(2), 145–159.

Kirk, S. A. (1936). Teachers as mental hygienists. *Mental Hygiene News, 2*(9), 1–3.

1938

Kirk, S. A. (1938). Behavior problem tendencies in deaf and hard of hearing children. *American Annals of the Deaf, 83,* 131–137.

Kirk, S. A. (1938). Integrating personality. *Childhood Education, 14*(8), 356–358.

Kirk, S. A., Biddle, W. W., Still, B., Ward, L. B., & Wilner, O. L. (1938, May). Suggested directions for faculty counselors. *Educational Administration and Supervision,* pp. 321–337.

Kirk, S. A., & Streng, A. (1938). The social competence of deaf and hard of hearing children in a public day school. *American Annals of the Deaf, 83,* 244–254.

1939

Kirk, S. A. (1939). Reading aptitudes of mentally retarded children. *American Association on Mental Deficiency, 44*(2), 158–162.

1940

Kirk, S. A. (1940). *Teaching reading to slow-learning children.* Boston: Houghton Mifflin.

1941

Kirk, S. A. (1941). The slow or mentally retarded learner. In W. S. Gray (Ed.), Adjusting reading programs to individuals. *Supplementary Education Monograph,* pp. 272–278. Chicago: University of Chicago Press.

1942

Kirk, S. A., & Ward, L. B. (1942). Studies in the selection of students for a teachers college. *Journal of Educational Research, 35*(9), 665–672.

1943

Kirk, S. A. (1943). *Teaching devices for special training units* (War Department Pamphlet

No. 20-22). Washington, DC: U.S. Government Printing Office.

Kirk, S. A., & Stevens, I. (1943). A pre-academic curriculum for slow learning children. *American Journal of Mental Deficiency, 47*(4), 396–406.

1946

Kirk, S. A. (1946). Educational reconditioning in Army general hospitals. *Journal of Exceptional Children, 12*(7), 194–198.

Kirk, S. A. (1946). The mentally handicapped: A social potentiality. In *Proceedings of the Third Governors Conference on Exceptional Children* (pp. 21–28). Chicago: Commission for Handicapped Children.

1947

Kirk, S. A. (1947). Tutoring as therapy, by Grace Arthur [Book review]. *Mental Health Bulletin, 25*(4), 7–8.

1948

Kirk, S. A. (1948). Education and health of the partially seeing child, by Winifred Hathaway (Book review). *Educational Administration and Supervision, 34*(7), 445–447.

Kirk, S. A. (1948). Education as national defense. *Progressive Education, 25*(7), 119–120, 144.

Kirk, S. A. (1948). An evaluation of the study of Bernardine Schmidt. *Journal of Exceptional Children, 15*(2), 34–40, 54.

Kirk, S. A. (1948). An evaluation of the study of Bernardine G. Schmidt entitled: "Changes in personal, social, and intellectual behavior of children originally classified as feeble-minded." *Psychological Bulletin, 45*(4), 321–333.

Kirk, S. A. (1948, January). The school's responsibility for handicapped children. *Epsilon Bulletin* (State University of Iowa, College of Education), pp. 10–12.

Kirk, S. A. (1948). What parents should know about reading. *University of Chicago Round Table, 527,* 3–6.

Kirk, S. A., & Erdman, R. L. (1948). Education of mentally handicapped children (Selected annotated bibliography). *University of Illinois Bulletin*. Urbana: Bureau of Research and Service, University of Illinois.

Kirk, S. A., & Perry, J. (1948). A comparative study of the Ontario and Nebraska tests for the deaf. *American Annals of the Deaf, 93,* 315–323.

1949

Kirk, S. A. (1949). Characteristics of slow learners and needed adjustments in reading. *Supplemetary Education Monographs* (No. 69). Chicago: University of Chicago Press.

1950

Johnson, G. O., & Kirk, S. A. (1950). Are mentally handicapped children segregated in the regular grades? *Journal of Exceptional Children, 17*(3), 65–68.

Kirk, S. A. (1950). Exceptional children. *Illinois Parent-Teacher, 33*(9), 16–17.

Kirk, S. A. (1950). Introduction. In *The education of exceptional children* (49th yearbook of the National Society for the Study of Education, Part I, pp. 1–2). Chicago: University of Chicago Press.

Kirk, S. A. (1950). Needed projects and research in special education. In S. A. Kirk, H. J. Baker, W. W. Charters, E. H. Martens, & E. H. Stullken, *The education of exceptional children* (49th yearbook of the National Society for the Study of Education, Part II, pp. 320–334). Chicago: University of Chicago Press.

Kirk, S. A. (1950). Presentation of the 1949 yearbook of the National Society for the Study of Education. *Journal of Exceptional Children, 16*(8), 233–236, 239.

Kirk, S. A. (1950). A project for pre-school mentally handicapped children. *American Journal of Mental Deficiency, 54*(3), 305–310.

Kirk, S. A., Baker, H. J., Charters, W. W., Martens, E. H., & Stullken, E. H. (1950). *The education of exceptional children* (49th yearbook of the National Society for the Study of Education, Part II). Chicago: University of Chicago Press.

Kirk, S. A., & Committee. (1950). Basic facts and principles underlying special education. In S. A. Kirk, H. J. Baker, W. W. Charters, E. H. Martens, & E. H. Stullken, *The education of exceptional children* (49th yearbook of the National Society for the Study of Education, Part II, pp. 3–17). Chicago: University of Chicago Press.

Kirk, S. A., & Lord, F. E. (1950). The education of teachers of special classes. In S. A. Kirk, H. J. Baker, W. W. Charters, E. H. Martens, & E. H. Stullken, *The education of exceptional children* (49th yearbook of the National Society for the Study of Education, Part II, p. 320–334). Chicago: University of Chicago Press.

1951

Kirk, S. A. (1951). The development of reasoning in children with normal and defective hearing, by Mildred C. Templin (Book review). *The Elementary School Journal, 51*(9), 533–534.

Kirk, S. A., Black, M. E., Duffin, R. M., Garrison, I. K., & Johnson, G. O. (1951). Educating the mentally handicapped in the secondary schools. *Illinois Secondary School Curriculum Program Bulletin 12* (Circular Series A, No. 51). Springfield: Office of the Superintendent of Public Instruction.

Kirk, S. A., & Johnson, G. O. (1951). *Educating the retarded child*. Boston: Houghton Mifflin.

Kirk, S. A., & Johnson, G. O. (1951). Educating the retarded child (Book review). *Psychological Book Previews, 1*(4), 56–60.

1952

Kirk, S. A. (1952). Cultural factors in mental retardation. In *Problems in the differential diagnosis of the etiology of mental deficiency* (pp. 63–71). Springfield, IL: Issued by Vernon Nickell, Superindendent of Public Instruction.

Kirk, S. A. (1952). Experiments in the early training of the mentally retarded. *American Journal of Mental Deficiency, 56*(4), 692–700.

Kirk, S. A. (1952). New hope for the mentally retarded. In *Rehabilitation of the mentally retarded and emotionally disturbed, Part II* (pp. 1–6). (Report of proceedings of the Fifth Annual Workshop on Guidance, Training and Placement, Federal Security Agency). Washington, DC: U.S. Office of Vocational Rehabilitation.

1953

Kirk, S. A. (1953). The mentally retarded: Counseling for psychological acceptance of disability. In *Rehabilitation service series* (No. 200, pp. 32–37). Washington, DC: U.S. Office of Vocational Rehabilitation.

Kirk, S. A. (1953). What is special about special education? The child who is mentally handicapped. *Journal of Exceptional Children, 19*(4), 138–142.

Kirk, S. A., Cain, L. F., DiCarlo, L. M., Myerson, L., & Newland, T. E. (Eds.). (1953). The education of exceptional children. *Review of Educational Research, 23*(5).

Kirk, S. A., & Kolstoe, O. P. (1953). The mentally retarded. *Review of Educational Research, 23*(5), 400–416.

Kirk, S. A., & Kolstoe, O. P. (1953). Research in exceptional children. *Pi Lambda Theta Journal, 31*(3), 151–154.

Kirk, S. A., & Spalding, W. B. (1953). The Institute for Research on Exceptional Children at the University of Illinois. *The Educational Forum, 17*(4), 413–422.

1954

Kirk, S. A. (1954). How fare the handicapped and the gifted in today's crowded schools? *Educational Leadership, 12*(1), 15–17.

Kirk, S. A. (1954). Research on the mentally retarded. In *Proceedings of the Institute on Mental Deficiency* (pp. 42–53). Nashville: Tennessee Department of Mental Health.

1955

Kirk, S. A. (1955). The emotionally disturbed child: Signs, symptoms, and causative factors—Educator's point of view. In *Proceedings of the Fourth Annual Conference on Crippled Children*. Richmond: Virginia Council on Health and Medical Care.

Kirk, S. A. (1955). Research on the education of the mentally retarded. *The Slow Learning Child, the Australian Journal for Teachers of Backward and Subnormal Children, 1*(3), 96–102.

Kirk, S. A. (1955). The retarded child in home and school. In *Proceedings of the Fourth Annual Conference on Crippled Children* (pp. 41–50). Richmond: Virginia Council on Health and Medical Care.

Kirk, S. A. (1955). Review of Leavell Language Development Service. *Journal of Exceptional*

Children, 22(3), 120–121.

Kirk, S. A., Karnes, M. B., & Kirk, W. D. (1955). *You and your retarded child: A manual for parents of retarded children*. New York: Macmillan.

1956

Kirk, S. A. (1956). How Johnny learns to read. *Exceptional Children*, 22(4), 158–160.

1957

Kirk, S. A. (1957). A doctor's degree program in special education. *Exceptional Children*, 24(2), 50–52, 55.

Kirk, S. A. (1957). *Public school provisions for severely retarded children: A survey of practices in the United States*. Albany: New York State Interdepartmental Health Resources Board.

Kirk, S. A. (1957). Vocational rehabilitation: An educator's critique on past, present, and future programs. In *Vocational training and rehabilitation of exceptional children* (pp. 27–35). (Proceedings of the 1957 Spring Conference of the Woods School). Langhorne, PA: The Woods School.

1958

Kirk, S. A. (1958). *Early education of the mentally retarded: An experimental study*. Urbana: University of Illinois Press.

Kirk, S. A. (1958). Education in diagnosis. In *Conference on Diagnosis in Mental Retardation* (pp. 197–207). Vineland, NJ: The Training School.

Kirk, S. A. (1958). Educational research. In *The First Conference on Mental Retardation* (pp. 55–59). Montreal: Canadian Association for Retarded Children.

Kirk, S. A. (1958). The effects of early education. In V. Glennon (Ed.), *Frontiers of elementary education* (pp. 66–70). Syracuse, NY: Syracuse University Press.

Kirk, S. A. (1958, December). The mentally retarded child: Development, education, and guidance, by M. L. Hutt and R. G. Gibby (Book review). *Contemporary Psychology*, pp. 370, 372.

Kirk, S. A., Smiley, B., Dawson, F. L., Saperstein, E., Bull, J., Cline, E. C., Couch, W. L., Graham, R. Kunce, P. H., Levy, J., & Talso, P. J. (1958). *Report of the Commission on Mental Retardation*. Springfield: Illinois Department of Public Welfare.

1959

Kirk, S. A. (1959). Remedial work in the elementary school. *National Education Association Journal*, 48(7), 24–25.

Kirk, S. A. (1959). Research and service emphasis with the mentally retarded. *The Slow Learning Child*, 6(2), 66–67.

Kirk, S. A. (1959). The subnormal child and home, by Schonell, F. J. Richardson, J. A. & McConnel, Thelma S. (Book review). *The Slow Learning Child*, 6(1), 55–56.

Kirk, S. A., & Weiner, B. B. (1959). The Onondaga census: Fact or artifact? *Exceptional Children*, 25(5), 230–231.

1960

Kirk, S. A. (1960). Are special classes beneficial? *The Slow Learning Child*, 7(1), 11–14.

Kirk, S. A. (1960). Foreword. In J. J. Gallagher, *The tutoring of brain injured mentally retarded children* (p. v–viii). Springfield, IL: Charles C Thomas.

Kirk, S. A. (1960). Some factors in the diagnosis of mental retardation: State aided community mental health clinics in Illinois. In *Fifth meeting of clinic administrators* (pp. 64–68). Springfield: Illinois Department of Public Welfare.

1961

Kirk, S. A. (1961). Research in educating retarded children. *The Bulletin of the Canadian Association for Retarded Children*, 2(2), 23–26.

Kirk, S. A. (1961, February). Social, psychological, and educational aspects of mental retardation, rehabilitation and research in retardation. In *Proceedings of the Conference on Vocational Rehabilitation of the Mentally Retarded* (pp. 37–43). (Held in Dallas, Texas, and sponsored by the National Association of Retarded Citizens and the Office of Vocational Rehabilitation.) Washington, DC: U.S. Office of Vocational Rehabilitation.

Kirk, S. A., & McCarthy, J. J. (1961). The Illinois Test of Psycholinguistic Abilities: An approach to differential diagnosis. *American Journal of Mental Deficiency*, 66(3), 399–412.

McCarthy, J. J., & Kirk, S. A. (1961). *The Illinois Test of Psycholinguistic Abilities*. Urbana: University of Illinois Press.

1962

Kirk, S. A. (1962). *Educating exceptional children*. Boston: Houghton Mifflin.

Kirk, S. A. (1962). The effects of educational procedures on the development of retarded children. In *Proceedings of the London Conference on the Scientific Study of Mental Deficiency* (pp. 419–428). Dagenham, England: May and Baker.

Kirk, S. A. (1962). Effects of educational treatment. In R. L. Masland, R. E. Cooke, & L. C. Kolb (Eds.), *Mental retardation* (pp. 289–294). Baltimore: Williams and Wilkins.

Kirk, S. A. (1962). Reading problems of slow learners. In H. A. Robinson (Ed.), The underachiever in reading. *Supplementary Educational Monographs, 24*(92), 62–69. Chicago: University of Chicago Press.

Kirk, S. A. (1962). The research approach. In *The development of research in vocational rehabilitation* (pp. 28–41). (Proceedings of a conference on research in state program development.) Gainesville: University of Florida, College of Health Related Services.

Kirk, S. A., & Bateman, B. D. (1962). Diagnosis and remediation of learning disabilities. *Exceptional Children, 29*(2) 73–78.

Kirk, S. A., & Bateman, B. D. (1962). Diagnosis and remediation of learning disabilities. In *Selected convention papers, 40th Annual CEC Convention* (pp. 99–102). Washington, DC: The Council for Exceptional Children.

Kirk, S. A., Kety, S. S., Dunn, L. M., Lourie, R. S., Lowry, O. H., & Waisman, H. A. (1962). The President's Panel on Mental Retardation. *Report of the Mission to the USSR*. Washington, DC: U.S. Government Printing Office.

1963

Dunn, L. M., & Kirk, S. A. (1963). Impressions of Soviet psycho-educational service and research in mental retardation. *Exceptional Children, 29*(7), 299–303, 305–311.

Kirk, S. A. (1963). American and Russian systems of special education. In *26th Biennial Conference report, Association for Special Education* (pp. 89–92). London: Premier Press.

Kirk, S. A. (1963). Behavioral diagnosis and remediation of learning disabilities. In *Proceedings of the Conference on Exploration into the Problems of the Perceptually Handicapped Child* (pp. 1–7). Chicago: Perceptually Handicapped Children.

Kirk, S. A. (1963). Diagnosis and remediation of learning disabilities. In *26th Biennial Conference report, Association for Special Education* (pp. 54–61). London: Premier Press.

Kirk, S. A. (1963). Rearranging our prejudices. In *Selected convention papers, 41st Annual CEC Convention* (pp. 121–125). Washington, DC: The Council for Exceptional Children.

Kirk, S. A., & Becker, W. (Eds.). (1963). *Conference on Children with Minimal Brain Impairment*. (Proceedings of conference sponsored by Easter Seal Research Foundation, National Society for Crippled Children & Adults, Inc., Chicago, Illinois.) Urbana: University of Illinois Press.

Kirk, S. A., & McCarthy, J. J. (1963). *The construction, standardization and statistical characteristics of the Illinois Test of Psycholinguistic Abilities*. Madison, WI: Photo Press.

Kirk, S. A., & Weiner, B. B. (Eds.). (1963). *Behavioral research on exceptional children*. Washington, DC: The Council for Exceptional Children.

1964

Kirk, S. A. (1964). A model of a communication process. In *Report of the proceedings of the International Congress on Education of the Deaf, Gallaudet College* (pp. 450–457). Washington, DC: U.S. Government Printing Office.

Kirk, S. A. (1964). Organization and implementation of programs for handicapped children and youth, Public Law 88-164, Title III, and Public Law 87-276. In Administration of education programs for handicapped children, Proceedings and debates of the 88th Congress, Second Session, *Congressional Record*. Washington, DC: U.S. Government Printing Office.

Kirk, S. A. (1964). Presentation of research on pre-school education. In *Proceedings of Conference on Mental Retardation for Chairmen of Pediatric Departments* (pp. 28–33). New

York: American Academy of Pediatrics.
Kirk, S. A. (1964). Research in education. In G. D. Stevens & R. Heber (Eds.), *Mental retardation* (pp. 57–99). Chicago: University of Chicago Press.
Kirk, S. A., & Bateman, B. D. (1964). *Ten years of research at the Institute for Research on Exceptional Children*. Urbana: University of Illinois Press.
Kirk, S. A., & Sava, S. G. (1964). *The organization and implementation of programs for handicapped children and youth, 1964*. Washington, DC: U.S. Government Printing Office.

1965

Kirk, S. A. (1965). Diagnostic, cultural, and remedial factors in mental retardation. In S. F. Osler & R. E. Cooke (Eds.), *The biosocial basis of mental retardation* (pp. 129–145). Baltimore: Johns Hopkins Press.
Kirk, S. A. (1965, July). Educating the handicapped. In *Consultant's papers, The White House Conference on Education*, July 20–21, 1965, II (pp. 89–96). Washington, DC: U.S. Government Printing Office.
Kirk, S. A. (1965, November). Educational aspects of mental retardation. In International Congress of Pediatrics, *Group panel discussions, XI Kokusai Shonikagaku Kaigi* (p. 310). Tokyo.
Kirk, S. A. (1965). Language, intelligence, and the educability of the disadvantaged. In *Language programs for the disadvantaged* (pp. 250–267). (Report of the NCTE Task Force on Teaching English to the Disadvantaged). Washington, DC: National Council of Teachers of English.
Kirk, S. A. (1965). Oligophrinia: Mental deficiency in children, by M. S. Peusner (Book review). *Children's Press Limited*.
Kirk, S. A. (1965). The role of the school in community mental health. In *Proceedings of the Council of Universities of the Mental Health Planning Board*. Allerton Park, IL: Allerton House.
Kirk, S. A. (1965). Statement before Senate Subcommittee (89th Congress) on Senate Bill S. 1400 (a bill to extend and expand Title III of the Mental Retardation Facilities and Community Mental Health Centers Construction Act of 1963) (pp. 50–54). Washington, DC: U.S. Government Printing Office.

1966

Kirk, S. A. (1966, March). Appendix A: The federal program for training teachers of the deaf. In S. P. Quigley (Ed.), *Preparation of teachers of the deaf*. (A report of a national conference, Virginia Beach, Virginia.) Washington, DC: U.S. Department of Health, Education, and Welfare.
Kirk, S. A. (1966). The challenge of individual differences. In M. M. Tumin & M. Bressler (Eds.), *Proceedings of a Conference on Quality and Equality in Education, Princeton University, December 1964*. Washington, DC: Office of Education, U.S. Department of Health, Education and Welfare.
Kirk, S. A. (1966). *The diagnosis and remediation of psycholinguistic disabilities*. Urbana, IL: Institute for Research on Exceptional Children.
Kirk, S. A. (1966). Editor's introduction. In W. Otto & R. A. McMeney, *Corrective and remedial teaching* (pp. vii–ix). Boston: Houghton Mifflin.
Kirk, S. A. (1966). Foreword. In J. L. Frost & G. R. Hawkes (Eds.), *The disadvantaged child: Issues and innovations* (pp. xi–xiii). Boston: Houghton Mifflin.
Kirk, S. A. (1966). *Lectures on handicapped children*. Tokyo: NHK Japanese Broadcasting Co. (Note: This book is published in Japanese only.)
Kirk, S. A. (1966). The new emphasis in school psychology. In *Focus on the education of handicapped children* (pp. 24–35). (Proceedings of the 17th Annual Conference of the California Association of School Psychologists and Psychometrists.)
Kirk, S. A. (1966). Retarded children. In *Encyclopaedia Britannica* (pp. 238–240). Chicago: Encyclopaedia Britannica.
Kirk, S. A. (1966). Statement before the Ad Hoc Subcommittee on Training and Education of the Handicapped of the Committee on Education and Labor, House of Representatives (89th Congress) on investigation of the adequacy of federal and other resources for education and training of the handicapped, Part I (pp. 377–392). Wash-

ington, DC: U.S. Government Printing Office.

1967

Kirk, S. A. (1967). Amelioration of mental disabilities through psychodiagnostic and remedial procedures. In G. A. Jervis (Ed.), *Mental retardation* (pp. 186–219). Springfield, IL: Charles C Thomas.

Kirk, S. A. (1967). Foreword. In W. Otto & D. Ford, *Teaching adults to read* (pp. vii–viii). Boston: Houghton Mifflin.

Kirk, S. A. (1967). Handicapped children. In *Notes and working papers on administration and programs authorized under Title III of Public Law 89-10: The Elementary and Secondary Education Act of 1965, as amended by Public Law 89-750 for the Subcommittee on Education of the Committee on Labor and Public Welfare, United States Senate (90th Congress)* (pp. 231–245). Washington, DC: U.S. Government Printing Office.

1968

Kirk, S. A. (1968). Editor's foreword. In B. Farber, *Mental retardation: Its social context and social consequences* (pp. v–vi). Boston: Houghton Mifflin.

Kirk, S. A. (1968). Editor's introduction. In Rees, *Deprivation and compensatory education* (p. ix). Boston: Houghton Mifflin.

Kirk, S. A. (1968). Editor's introduction. In *Operant procedures in remedial speech and language training* (pp. v–vi). Boston: Houghton Mifflin.

Kirk, S. A. (1968). The Illinois Test of Psycholinguistic Abilities: Its origin and implications. In J. Helmuth (Ed.), *Learning disorders* (Vol 3., pp. 395–428). Seattle: Special Child Publications.

Kirk, S. A. (1968). The National Advisory Committee on Handicapped Children. *Exceptional Children, 34*(7), 481–484.

Kirk, S. A. (1968). A new vista for exceptional children. *Selected convention papers, 46th Annual CEC Convention* (pp. 320–325). Washington, DC: The Council for Exceptional Children.

Kirk, S. A. (1968). Statement before the Select Subcommittee on Education of the Committee on Education and Labor, House of Representatives (90th Congress) on H.R. 17829, a bill to authorize preschool and early education programs for handicapped children (pp. 31–37). Washington, DC: U.S. Government Printing Office.

Kirk, S. A., Bernhard, D. L., Irwin, J. V., Jones, M. J., Kelly, W. A., Levin, S. M., Melcher, J. W., Rose, O. V., Schunhoff, H. F., Strother, C. R., Trevino, V. M., & Wilderson, F. B. (1968). *First annual report of the National Advisory Committee on Handicapped Children, January 31, 1968: Special education for handicapped children.* Washington, DC: U.S. Department of Health, Education, and Welfare, Office of Education.

Kirk, S. A., Karnes, M. B., & Kirk, W. D. (1968). *You and your retarded child* (2nd ed.). Palo Alto, CA: Pacific Books.

Kirk, S. A., McCarthy, J. J., & Kirk, W. D. (1968). *The Illinois Test of Psycholinguistic Abilities* (rev. ed.). Urbana: University of Illinois Press.

1969

Kirk, S. A. (1969). Introduction. In W. Otto & K. Koenke, *Remedial teaching: Research and comment* (pp. vii–viii). Boston: Houghton Mifflin.

Kirk, S. A. (1969). *Educating exceptional children.* (Translation of original English language edition, 1962). Tokyo: Kaigaihyoronsha.

Kirk, S. A. (1969). The effects of early education with disadvantaged infants. In M. Karnes (Ed.), *Research and development program on preschool disadvantaged children* (pp. 233–248). Washington, DC: U.S. Department of Health, Education, and Welfare, Office of Education, Bureau of Research.

Kirk, S. A. (1969). Statement before the General Subcommittee on Education, 91st Congress, First Session, on H.R. 8660 and H.R. 9065, Children with Learning Disabilities Act of 1969, July 8, 9, and 10, 1969 (pp. 155–157). Washington, DC: U.S. Government Printing Office.

Kirk, S. A., Celebrezze, A. M., Irwin, J. V., Jones, M. J., Kelly, W. A., Levin, S. M., Melcher, J. W., Schunhoff, H. F., Strother, C. R., Trevino, V. M., & Wilderson, F. B. (1969). *Better education for handicapped chil-*

dren (Second annual report of the National Advisory Committee on Handicapped Children, June 30, 1969). Washington, DC: U.S. Department of Health, Education, and Welfare, Office of Education.

Kirk, S. A., Irwin, J. V., Jones, M. J., Kelly, W. A., Levin, S. M., Melcher, J. W., Schunhoff, H. F., Strother, C. R., Trevino, V. M., & Wilderson, F. B. (1969). *Interim emergency report of the National Advisory Committee on Handicapped Children, May 6, 1969*. Washington, DC: U.S. Department of Health, Education, and Welfare, Office of Education.

Paraskevopoulos, J., & Kirk, S. A. (1969). *The development and psychometric characteristics of the revised Illinois Test of Psycholinguistic Abilities*. Urbana: University of Illinois Press.

1970

Kirk, S. A. (1970). The educability of intelligence. In *Focus on the pre-school child* (pp. 21–34). (Proceedings of the Annual Conference of Educational Psychologists). London: Hamilton House.

Kirk, S. A. (1970). The effects of early intervention. In H. R. Haywood (Ed.), *Social-cultural aspects of mental retardation* (p. 495). New York: Appleton-Century-Crofts.

Kirk, S. A. (1970). Lecture. In *Final report, U.S.O.E. Advanced Institute for Leadership Personnel in Learning Disabilities*. Department of Special Education, University of Arizona, Unit on Learning Disabilities, Division of Training Programs, Bureau of Education for the Handicapped, U.S. Office of Education.

Kirk, S. A. (1970). Reflections on learning disabilities. In *Seventh Annual International Conference of the Association of Children with Learning Disabilities* (pp. 209–215). Pittsburgh: ACLD.

1971

Kirk, S. A. (1971). Classification and placement of the mentally retarded. In *Proceedings: Conference on the Education of Mentally Retarded Persons* (pp. 95–103). St. Louis.

Kirk, S. A. (1971). Editor's introduction. In J. W. Lerner, *Children with learning disabilities: Theories, diagnosis, and teaching strategies* (p. iv). Boston: Houghton Mifflin.

Kirk, S. A., & Kirk, W. D. (1971). *Psycholinguistic learning disabilities: Diagnosis and remediation*. Urbana: University of Illinois Press.

Kirk, S. A., & McCarthy, J. J. (1971). Learning disabilities. In L. C. Deighton (Ed.), *The encyclopedia of education* (Vol. 5, pp. 441–446). New York: Macmillan and Free Press.

1972

Kirk, S. A. (1972). *Educating exceptional children* (2nd ed.). Boston: Houghton Mifflin.

Kirk, S. A. (1972). Ethnic differences in psycholinguistic abilities. *Journal of Exceptional Children, 39*(2), 112–118.

1973

Kirk, S. A. (1973). The education of intelligence. *The Slow Learning Child, the Australian Journal for Teachers of Backward and Subnormal Children, 20*(2), 66–83.

Kirk, S. A. (1973). Learning disabilities in perspective. In *West Virginia School Health Conference on Learning Disabilities preview series: Leadership Training Institute in Learning Disabilities*. Tucson: University of Arizona.

Kirk, S. A. (1973, February). *Where are we in learning disabilities?* Paper presented to the Second Western Regional Conference, sponsored by the Association for Children with Learning Disabilities and the California Association for Neurologically Handicapped Children.

1974

Kirk, S. A. (1974). Education of the exceptional. In H. H. Benton (Ed.), *Encyclopaedia Britannica* (15th ed., pp. 431–434). Chicago: Encyclopaedia Britannica.

Kirk, S. A. (1974). Learning disabilities: The past and the future. In H. F. Eichenwald & A. Talbot (Eds.), *The L-D child* (pp. 14–22). Dallas: The University of Texas Health Center.

Kirk, S. A. (1974). *Suggestions for the organization and implementation of the National Center for Special Education—CENESP* (Monograph). Brazilia: Report to USAID for the National Center for Special Education, Ministry of Education and Culture.

Kirk, S. A., & Lord, F. (1974). *Exceptional children: Educational resources and perspectives.* Boston: Houghton Mifflin.

1975

Kirk, S. A. (1975). Labeling, categorizing and mainstreaming in the United States. In *Proceedings of the International Conference of Special Education* (pp. 40–55). Canterbury, England: University of Kent.

Kirk, S. A. (1975). LD leaders strike back at distorted reporting: Reply. *Journal of Learning Disabilities, 8,* 318–319.

Kirk, S. A., & Elkins, J. (1975). Characteristics of children enrolled in the Child Service Demonstration Centers. *Journal of Learning Disabilities, 8,* 630–637.

Kirk, S. A., & Elkins, J. (1975). Identifying developmental discrepancies at the preschool level. *Journal of Learning Disabilities, 8,* 417–419.

Kirk, S. A., & Elkins, J. (1975). *Summaries of research on the revised Illinois Test of Psycholinguistic Abilities.* Tucson: Leadership Training Institute in Learning Disabilities, Department of Special Education, University of Arizona.

Kirk, S. A., & McCarthy, J. (Eds.). (1975). *Learning disabilities: Selected ACLD papers.* Boston: Houghton Mifflin.

1976

Kirk, S. A. (1976). General and historical rationale for early education of the handicapped. In N. E. Ellis & L. Cross (Eds.), *Planning programs for early education of the handicapped.* Chapel Hill: Technical Assistance Development System, University of North Carolina.

Kirk, S. A. (1976). Personal perspective. In J. M. Kauffman & D. Hallahan (Eds.), *Teaching children with learning disabilities* (pp. 238–269). Columbus, OH: Charles E. Merrill.

1977

Kirk, S. A. (1977, August). Special education yesterday, today and tomorrow: An interview with Frances Connor, Samuel Kirk and Burton Blatt, Part I. *The Exceptional Parent,* pp. 9–14.

Kirk, S. A. (1977, October). Special education yesterday, today and tomorrow: An interview with Frances Connor, Samuel Kirk and Burton Blatt, Part II. *The Exceptional Parent,* pp. 16–21.

Kirk, S. A. (1977). Specific learning disabilities. *Journal of Clinical Child Psychology, 6,* 23–26.

Kirk, S. A., & von Isser, A. (1977). The effects of Head Start on psycholinguistic functions. *Journal of Clinical Child Psychology, 6,* 93.

Kirk, S. A., von Isser, A., & Elkins, J. (1977). Ethnic differences in Head Start children. *Journal of Clinical Child Psychology, 6,* 91–92.

1978

Kirk, S. A. (1978). An interview with Samuel Kirk. *Academic Therapy, 13,* 617–620.

Kirk, S. A., & Kirk, W. D. (1978). The uses and abuses of the ITPA. *American Journal of Speech and Hearing Disorders, 43,* 58–75.

Kirk, S. A., Kliebhan, J. M., & Lerner, J. (1978). *Teaching reading to slow and disabled learners.* Boston: Houghton Mifflin.

1979

Kirk, S. A. (1979). Current trends affecting staff training. In *Proceedings: Fourth Asian Conference on Mental Retardation, Integration of the Mentally Retarded in Our Community* (pp. 107–118). Kuala Lumpur, Malaysia.

Kirk, S. A., & Gallagher, J. J. (1979). *Educating exceptional children* (3rd ed.). Boston: Houghton Mifflin.

1980

Kirk, S. A., & Berry, P. (1980). Issues in specific learning disabilities: Towards a data base for decision making. *The Exceptional Child, 27*(2), 115–125.

1981

Kirk, S. A. (1981, April). Changes in the field of mental retardation: A conversation with Samuel A. Kirk. *Education and Training of the Mentally Retarded,* pp. 119–124.

Kirk, S. A. (1981). Comment on the term dyslexia. *The Reading Instruction Journal, 24*(3).

Kirk, S. A. (1981). Learning disabilities: A historical note. *Academic Therapy, 17*(1), 5–11.

Kirk, S. A., Senf, G. M., & Larsen, R. P. (1981).

Current issues in learning disabilities. In W. M. Cruickshank & A. A. Silver (Eds.), *Bridges to tomorrow. Vol. 2. The Best of ACLD*. Syracuse, NY: Syracuse University Press.

1982

Kirk, S. A. (1982). Current concepts and controversies in learning disabilities. In *Proceedings of Queensland Special Education Association State Conference*. Australia.

Kirk, S. A. (1982). The educability of intelligence. *The Directive Teacher, 4*(2), 6.

Kirk, S. A. (1982). Evolution and present status of early education of the handicapped. *The Exceptional Child, 29*(2), 71–78.

Luick, A., Kirk, S. A., Agranowitz, A., & Busby, R. (1982). Profiles of children with severe oral language disorders. *Journal of Speech and Hearing Disorders, 47*, 88–92.

1983

Kirk, S. A. (1983). Exceptional Children begins its 50th anniversary year. *Exceptional Children, 50*, 6–8.

Kirk, S. A., & Gallagher, J. J. (1983). *Educating exceptional children* (4th ed.). Boston: Houghton Mifflin.

Kirk, S. A., & Kirk, W. D. (1983). On defining learning disabilities. *Journal of Learning Disabilities, 16*(1).

1984

Kirk, S. A., Blatt, B. B., & Morris, R. J. (1984). Introspection and prophecy. In *Perspectives in special education: Personal orientations* (Chapter 2). Glenview IL: Scott Foresman.

Kirk, S. A., & Chalfant, J. C. (1984). *Academic and developmental learning disabilities*. Denver: Love.

1985

Kirk, S. A., Kirk, W. D., & Minskoff, E. (1985). *Phonic remedial reading lessons*. Novato, CA: Academic Therapy.

1986

Kirk, S. A. (1986). Redesigning delivery systems for learning disabled students. *Learning Disabilities Focus, 2*(1), 4–6.

Kirk, S. A., & Gallagher, J. J. (1986). *Educating exceptional children* (5th ed.). Boston: Houghton Mifflin.

1987

Kirk, S. A. (1987, Winter). The learning disabled preschool child. *TEACHING Exceptional Children, 19*(2), 78–80.

1989

Kirk, S. A., & Gallagher, J. J. (1989). *Educating exceptional children* (6th ed.). Boston: Houghton Mifflin.

1993

Kirk, S. A., Gallagher, J. J., & Anastasiow, N. J. (1993). *Educating exceptional children* (7th ed.). Boston: Houghton Mifflin.